THE SUN NEVER SETS

NYU SERIES IN SOCIAL AND CULTURAL ANALYSIS
General Editor: Andrew Ross

Nice Work If You Can Get It: Life and Labor in Precarious Times
Andrew Ross

City Folk: English Country Dance and the Politics of the Folk in Modern America
Daniel J. Walkowitz

Toilet: Public Restrooms and the Politics of Sharing
Edited by Harvey Molotch and Laura Norén

Unhitched: Love, Marriage, and Family Values from West Hollywood to Western China
Judith Stacey

The Sun Never Sets: South Asian Migrants in an Age of U.S. Power
Edited by Vivek Bald, Miabi Chatterji, Sujani Reddy, and Manu Vimalassery

The Sun Never Sets

South Asian Migrants in an Age of U.S. Power

Edited by Vivek Bald, Miabi Chatterji, Sujani Reddy, and Manu Vimalassery

Afterword by Vijay Prashad

NEW YORK UNIVERSITY PRESS

New York and London

NEW YORK UNIVERSITY PRESS
New York and London
www.nyupress.org

References to Internet Websites (URLs) were accurate at the time of writing.
Neither the author nor New York University Press is responsible for URLs that
may have expired or changed since the manuscript was prepared.

LIBRARY OF CONGRESS CATALOGING-IN-PUBLICATION DATA
The sun never sets : South Asian migrants in an age of U.S. power / edited by Vivek Bald,
Miabi Chatterji, Sujani Reddy, and Manu Vimalassery ; afterword by Vijay Prashad.
pages cm.
Includes bibliographical references and index.
ISBN 978-0-8147-8643-7 (hardback)
ISBN 978-0-8147-8644-4 (pb)
1. South Asians—United States—History. 2. South Asia—Emigration and immigration—
History. 3. United States—Emigration and immigration—History. 4. Immigrants—United
States—History. I. Bald, Vivek, editor of compilation.
E184.S69.S86 2013
304.8'73—dc23
2013004767

Portions of chapter 3 have appeared previously in Vivek Bald, *Bengali Harlem and the Lost
Histories of South Asian America* (Cambridge: Harvard University Press, 2013) and in Vivek
Bald, "'Lost' in the City: Spaces and Stories of South Asian New York, 1917–1965," *South
Asian Popular Culture* 5.1 (2007): 59–76, and are used by permission.

New York University Press books are printed on acid-free paper,
and their binding materials are chosen for strength and durability.
We strive to use environmentally responsible suppliers and materials
to the greatest extent possible in publishing our books.

Manufactured in the United States of America
10 9 8 7 6 5 4 3 2 1

Contents

Acknowledgments

This book has its roots within the American Studies Program in the Department of Social and Cultural Analysis at New York University. The editors would like to thank the community of students, scholars, and activists there, as well as the many other people who have nourished and guided the project. They include Rich Blint, André Carrington, Andrew Cornell, Aniruddha Das, Sohail Daulatzai, Arlene Dávila, Lisa Duggan, Alyosha Goldstein, Gayatri Gopinath, Miles Grier, Christina Hanhardt, Madala Hilaire, Peter Hudson, Walter Johnson, Ronak Kapadia, Kerwin Kaye, Robin D. G. Kelley, Aleyamma Mathew, Biju Mathew, Raza Mir, Naeem Mohaiemen, Ananya Mukherjea, Gary Okihiro, Rupal Oza, Jan Padios, Michael Palm, Dawn Peterson, Khary Polk, Vijay Prashad, Junaid Rana, Ashwini Rao & CSFH, Anandaroop Roy, Zach Schwartz-Weinstein, Julie Sze, Jack Tchen, Emily Thuma, Saadia Toor, and Adam Waterman. We are especially grateful to Andrew Ross, who has advised and encouraged us on this project from the book's inception to its completion.

This has been a collaborative effort not only among the editors but also among our contributors, who have pushed and refined our collective arguments with their essays, have waited patiently, and worked furiously to meet deadlines. Their contributions have brought the book to life. Different configurations of the work in this volume were presented in earlier form at the conferences of the American Studies Association, the Association of Asian American Studies, and the Marxist Literary Group, and we thank those who engaged with us in those contexts. We are also thankful for the time and great care that Sharmila Rudrappa, Sukhdev Sandhu, and two anonymous reviewers took to read and comment on the book in its manuscript form—the critical feedback provided at this stage was invaluable. Our editor at New York University Press, Eric Zinner, championed this book from the time it was little more than an idea, and patiently guided us through the process of making it a reality. We are deeply grateful to him and to his editorial team at the Press, Ciara McLaughlin, Alicia Nadkarni, and production editor Alexia Traganas.

Vivek Bald additionally thanks the following friends and colleagues whose engagement sustained and pushed forward his work in and on this volume: Hishaam Aidi, Jigna Desai, Brent Hayes Edwards, Kale Fajardo, Juan Flores, Madala Hilaire, John Hutnyk, Khyati Joshi, Amitava Kumar, Scott Kurashige, Vinay Lal, George Lipsitz, Gita Rajan, Miriam Jiménez Román, Nayan Shah, Nikhil Pal Singh, Lok Siu, Seema Sohi, Gayatri Chakravorty Spivak, Laura Tabili, Jack Tchen, Habib Ullah Jr., and Alaudin Ullah. I am also thankful for the support and encouragement of my colleagues at MIT: Chris Capozzola, Ian Condry, Sasha Costanza-Chock, Junot Diaz, Fox Harrell, Sally Haslanger, Helen Elaine Lee, Tom Levenson, Ken Manning, Nick Montfort, Jim Paradis, Bruno Perreau, Abha Sur, Emma Teng, William Uricchio, and Jing Wang. I am especially grateful for the friendship and sustained intellectual engagement of the other members of the editorial collective—Miabi Chatterji, Sujani Reddy, and Manu Vimalassery—and of Kym Ragusa and Rachel Rosenbloom.

Miabi Chatterji would like to thank her family: Debajyoti and Smee Chatterji; Ananya Chatterji and Steve Droste; Kooheli Chatterji and Christian Loeffler; and Serena Chatterji Droste. Many thanks to all the colleagues and associates who helped with this book, listed previously, and a heartfelt thanks to my coeditors for putting their focus, energy, and insight into this volume. And for all kinds of help and love through the past several years: Sarah Bernstein, Robin Carton, Arvind Grover, Becca Howes-Mischel, José Itzigsohn, Nathan Levitt, Soniya Munshi, Lorraine Ramirez, and Ragini Shah, you are all deeply appreciated. The folks on the board at the RESIST Foundation, at the Restaurant Opportunities Center New York 2005–2008, at Allegheny College 2008–2009, and involved with Youth Solidarity Summer 2002–2007 all cradled this project and provided me with much-needed networks of support.

Sujani Reddy would like to thank, first and foremost, my fellow editors, Manu, Miabi, and Vivek. It has been many years and many moments since we began the conversation that has coalesced in this book. May it be many more years and many more moments that we continue to collaborate. You all enrich my life enormously. My own contribution to the conception and execution of this book would not have been possible without the insight and inspiration of the many New York City leftist and/or progressive organizations that I have worked with over the years, including South Asian Magazine for Action and Reflection (SAMAR), Coalition Against Anti-Asian Violence (CAAAV), Youth Solidarity Summer (YSS), and the Asia Pacific Forum radio collective. At the Rockefeller Archive Center, Mary Ann Quinn's help was invaluable. The last stages of this book were completed with the intellectual and institutional support of the American Studies Department at Amherst College and the Five College Asian/Pacific/American Studies Certificate Program.   For their support and encouragement I also want to acknowledge Andrew Hsiao, Leyla Mei, Tomio Geron, Chandana Mathur, Annanya Bhattacharjee, Manu Goswami, Gaiutra Bahadur, Shanna Lorenz, Marcelo Montes Penha, Natalie Sullivan Bimel, Jennifer Guglielmo, Elisabeth Armstrong, Kara Lynch, Chris Tinson, and Amina Steinfels. Last but not least, I want to thank my family: Narashima Reddy, Nirmala Reddy, Sumathi Reddy, Jonathan Rockoff, and Nikhil Reddy Rockoff.

Manu Vimalassery would like to thank and acknowledge the Vimalassery and Kocherry diasporas, the World Forum of Fisher Peoples, the Native American and Indigenous Studies Association, and the Julius Ford/Harriet Tubman Healthy Living Community. In addition to my fellow editors, Saad Abi-Hamad, Antoinette Burton, Jodi Byrd, Dantae Davies, Mike Funk, Karlos Hill, Fred Hoxie, David Jimenez, Moon-Kie Jung, Hye-Kyung Kang, Thomas Kocherry, Mo Lotif, Raza Mir, Dave Roediger, Pat Romney, Mérida Rúa, Josh Rubin, Dean Saranillio, Rani Varghese, Robert Warrior, Paul Wiley, and Diana Yoon (among others) have helped make these years of intellectual and political growth. Thomas, Tessy, Priya, Anand, Amir, Diana, Maya: thank you for reminding me where I am, who I am, what I am about.

Introduction

VIVEK BALD, MIABI CHATTERJI, SUJANI REDDY,
AND MANU VIMALASSERY

In her painting *Vanwyck Blvd* (2005), visual artist Asma Ahmed Shi-koh subtly reworks the New York Metropolitan Transit Authority's iconic subway map. From afar, viewers might recognize the muted blue, gray, and yellow representation of the city, with boldly colored subway lines coursing like arteries through Manhattan and connecting it to the Bronx, Queens, Brooklyn, and Staten Island. Stepping closer, they will find that every piece of text across the five boroughs, including place-names, subway stops, and the map's key, has been rendered into Urdu, connecting this image as much to Pakistan and Northern India as to New York. New York City has been claimed as part of a larger geogra-phy—of people, of language, of lives—that stretches outward from the South Asian subcontinent, across decades and across oceans. We begin with this painting because it enacts the kind of intervention that this collection sets out to make, as a countermapping, as a tool with which to read and navigate the scholarship, politics, and subjectivities that have come to constitute the South Asian diaspora in an age of U.S. power.

Maps have played a central role in the imperial expansions that have displaced hundreds of thousands of South Asians over the past two centuries and set them in motion across the globe. For centuries, maps fed the imagining of imperial power as it spread out from con-tinental Europe, the United Kingdom, and the United States, and they continue to function as tools of imperial perception and control.[1] In military strategy sessions, corporate boardrooms, and broadcast news studios, maps mark out the spaces of U.S. geographic knowledge and power, tracing the trajectories of military "surges," outlining proposed paths for natural gas pipelines, or introducing "new" sites of crisis and concern to the U.S. population, such as Kandahar, Bagram, Kabul, or Guantánamo. Like the navigational charts of explorers and slave-ship captains in centuries past, these maps do more than plot spaces. They inscribe geographies of capitalist expansion: locations of raw materials, sites of production, networks of distribution, and hot spots of resistance. They also outline racial and imperial boundaries, as walls are erected to secure national borders, and the divisions between green and red zones enable military occupations overseas.[2]

Colonized and racialized people have long created their own maps to navigate landscapes of imperial power, even if these take different forms from those we expect of conventional cartography. Their maps emerge through everyday experience and are conveyed by word of mouth; they are used to move through and survive in unfamiliar, often contentious terrain. Diasporas produce maps of this kind; they are cartographic processes in their own right, respectively unspooling and connecting people over space. As they move, settle, congregate, and spread, global migrants and their descendants transform abstract and unwelcoming spaces into the embodied places of daily life. They make material, tangible, and rooted their experiences and struggles, their personal and collective gains and losses.

Shikoh's rendering of the MTA map operates in these ways. The work was created amid the large-scale incarceration and popular demonization of Muslim immigrants, when any "Muslim-looking" person in a public place with a camera or a map was seen as a potential terrorist and risked arrest. In this moment of immobilization and alienation, the painting reinscribes New York City as a space of South Asian Muslim mobility and place-making. Against the enforced monolingualism of U.S. culture, the Urdu that Shikoh spreads across New York's five boroughs evokes alternate and multiple poetic and religious traditions, histories of migration, formations of neighborhoods and communities, and experiences of racialized subjectivity. Her map suggests places of work and residence linked across boroughs by train lines, locations of mosques and community centers, sites of pleasure and enjoyment, and cultural institutions. It orients passengers who move through networks of surveillance and incarceration, memories and premonitions of traumatic violence, and grounds of protest and resistance. It charts the process of a migrant community making a life for itself—claiming and transforming the city.

Vanwyck Blvd brings up many of the shared concerns of our editorial collective. We came together in the opening years of the twenty-first century in New York City. As Ashutosh Gowariker's *Lagaan* filled movie theaters around the country and Andrew Lloyd Webber's *Bombay Dreams* hit Broadway, the U.S. public seemed entranced with selective, and primarily Indian, elements of South Asian culture. Magazines like *Newsweek* and *Time Out New York* ran feature stories trumpeting the arrival of South Asians on the U.S. political, economic, and popular cultural landscape, pointing to chai at Starbucks, yoga studios on every corner, and bhangra on *The Sopranos*. They trumpeted a $60,000 "median income of Indian American families" and presented profiles of South Asian success stories in the arts, entertainment, business, and technology.[3] At the same time, the public largely turned away from the experiences of working-class and Muslim South Asians, and from the severe hardships many faced in a post-9/11 environment of increased surveillance, detention, and deportation. These groups became perpetual suspects as the image of the menacing terrorist became ubiquitous on movie and television screens, in national and local media, and in the political rhetoric used to justify the curtailment of civil rights and the prosecution of wars. Each of us engaged this particular moment in multiple ways: as cultural producers, media makers, organizers, activists, community members, and graduate students. Over the ensuing years, what began as a series of casual conversations developed into a shared desire to connect what we saw occurring in the public culture with the intellectual work that was also emerging at this time.

The division that characterized the post-9/11 political climate—between one group of South Asians that was celebrated for its entrepreneurship and "culture" and another that was demonized as a threat to the nation—was stark but not new. This division has existed in one form or another throughout a more than century-long history of South Asian migration to and through the United States. Three signal moments have dominated scholarly descriptions of this history: 1917–1924, 1965, and September 11, 2001. These are each moments of state action: the first marks the era during which a series of U.S. laws and court decisions resulted in the barring of South Asians from entry to the United States and defined them as racially ineligible for citizenship; the second marks the moment that the United States "reopened" its doors for the immigration and naturalization of a large but select sector of highly educated and highly skilled South Asian migrants; and the last marks the beginning of the contemporary "War on Terror" in which South Asian and Muslim immigrants were singled out for surveillance, incarceration, and deportation. In all three of these instances, South Asia or South Asians became visible in dominant U.S. culture because the state sought to delimit and shape the United States through legal boundaries to entry and settlement (immigration law), and/or through the targeting and deportation of the nation's others and "enemies." The implicit subject of a history centered on these moments, in other words, is the U.S. nation-state itself; its imperatives remain the grounds upon which South Asian American stories have been largely told, analyzed, and understood.

The essays in this collection tell a different story; they reframe the study of South Asians in the United States. This volume places immigration laws within a larger context, tracking the global migration of South Asians using frameworks of empire and global power. For our contributors, the South Asian diaspora has been shaped not just by the openings and closures of specific immigration policies but by capitalist expansion, war, militarism, partition, displacement, religious mobilization, globalization, neoliberalism, and political movements. Our goal here is to bring together scholarship that addresses the phenomena that are occurring around us, documents how people are shaping and responding to these phenomena, and illuminates how the current social, cultural, and political moment is connected to the past. *The Sun Never Sets* thus presents a group of writings that challenge the dominant assumptions structuring the field while providing tools with which to understand the contemporary political and economic conjuncture and the places of South Asian migration within it.

The Developing Field

Through the 1970s and 1980s, most scholarly writing on South Asians in the United States took the 1965 Hart-Cellar Immigration and Nationality Act as central—both conceptually and empirically. These works focused on the generation of immigrants who arrived in the wake of the act, and documented that group's purported economic and assimilationist success.[4] By doing so, they helped to solidify an association between South Asian immigrants with professional and entrepreneurial backgrounds and the figure of the "model minority," an association that persists in popular cultural representations of South Asian Americans and continues to be embraced and celebrated by many South Asian Americans.

The work of South Asian and South Asian American feminist scholars marked a critical turn in the scholarship in the 1990s. Building upon the insights of black and Third World feminist activism and critique in the 1970s and 1980s, and participating in the emergence of postcolonial studies and transnational feminism, these scholars—such as Annanya Bhattacharjee, Inderpal Grewal, Sucheta Mazumdar, Chandra Talpade Mohanty, Gayatri Chakravorty Spivak, and Kamala Visweswaran— simultaneously addressed the global and local relations of power that structured what was only then coming to be named the "South Asian diaspora." Their work placed discussions of "diaspora" and "transnationalism" within the context of shifting regimes of capital accumulation, drawing out a historical continuum moving from territorially based empire to neocolonialism. They revealed the ways that model minority South Asianness in the diaspora was built upon confining women to the role of maintaining an ossified, mythic, nationalist "culture" in the realm of the home, family, and community. They explored the hegemonic and counterhegemonic potential of South Asian diasporic literary and cultural texts and pointed toward the possibilities and practices of transnational political alliances, shadowing and working in opposition to the spread of global capital. Their work was groundbreaking in its insistence on interdisciplinary methodologies, its analyses of the intersections of different forms of power—along lines of gender, sexuality, race, class, nation, and empire—and in the connections it drew between multiple frames of experience and struggle.[5]

During and since the 1990s, several groups of academics, activists, and artists also collectively published anthologies that gave voice to the model minority's "others": lesbian, gay, bisexual, queer, and transgendered peoples; survivors of religious, sexual, intimate, and state violence; leftist activists; religious minorities; feminists; workers in "nontraditional fields"; and working-class immigrants and their families.[6] These collections opened the terrain of what could be spoken about, much less published, on South Asian Americans. They aimed for a wider audience than many scholarly works, and they provide a model for combining creative expressions and political polemics with more traditional scholarly writing. At the same time, much of the work in the edited volumes of the 1980s and 1990s still focused on elite Indian Americans and the racism, sexism, and homophobia they experienced. As Kamala Visweswaran put it in her critical 1997 article "Diaspora by Design," "The globalization of the bourgeoisie [was] being understood" in the literature "in cultural, racial, or ethnic, rather than class terms."[7] We thus take up the legacy of these edited collections even as we expand upon the forms of "otherness" they addressed, in order to account more fully for the differences in class, region, and religion that mark contemporary South Asian communities.

At the turn of the millennium, Vijay Prashad offered another strident critique of the model minority myth, expanding upon the earlier work of Visweswaran, Mazumdar, and Bhattacharjee.[8] In his book *The Karma of Brown Folk*, Prashad argued that South Asian Americanists and the media had not accounted for the structural engineering behind the idea of the "model minority" and its antiblack, anti-Latina/o, and antipoor agenda. He outlined the ways in which the Hart-Cellar Act contained overlapping provisions that privileged skilled, professional-managerial immigration from Asia in general. These combined with the Nehruvian state's prioritized training of scientific and medical labor to produce the Indian American bourgeoisie. In piloting this collection, we took our lead from Prashad's intervention and the work that has followed in its wake.

The past decade has been a critical period for the study of South Asians in the United States not only because of the political and cultural climate but also because enough scholarship has amassed that we can speak of an emerging scholarly field. Scholars have shifted analytical focus, and their work has spoken richly across fields and disciplines. Some standout works have established avenues for the further development of South Asian American studies, and its engagement with other fields. For example, Gayatri Gopinath framed queer diasporic desire and resistance in her contribution to cultural studies and queer of color critique. Jasbir Puar traced the intersecting logics of homonationalism, race, imperialism, and neoliberalism through her interventions in queer, cultural, and political theory. Sharmila Rudrappa's feminist and community-based ethnographies analyzed ways that state multiculturalism offers routes to American-ness through the performance of narrowly defined ethnic authenticity. Vijay Prashad excavated South Asian histories of polyculturalism and cross-racial encounter in the Americas, enriching the fields of comparative and relational ethnic studies. Biju Mathew described the lives, work, and cross-community organizing of South Asian taxi drivers, providing a model of urban and labor studies with relevance to the current moment. Monisha Das Gupta compared the organizing dynamics of South Asian women's, queer, and labor activism in 1990s New York City, demonstrating new avenues for social movement analysis. Sunaina Maira explored the effects of the post-9/11 national security state on Muslim American youth, contributing to the rich literature on the interactions of marginalized young people with state structures and institutions.[9]

The Sun Never Sets builds upon the momentum of this latest turn in the scholarship. The works collected here continue to loosen the hold that changes in immigration law have had on the emerging field. We instead examine South Asian migration through larger histories of imperialism and neoliberalism—and come to a fuller understanding of imperialism and neoliberalism through the histories and experiences of migrants. We conceive of the historical periods organizing the field less around changes in national law than around transitions in global capitalism and imperialism. Critical to such a reframing is a reexamination of "diaspora" as an analytic framework. As we take up diaspora within a context of imperialism, we pay close attention to both the utility and the limitations of its use as it configures certain conceptions of movement, settlement, and the attendant negotiations with power. In what follows we elaborate on how the essays in this volume speak to these interventions and their interrelation.

Shifting Imperialisms and Neoliberal Globalization

The phrase "the sun never sets on the British Empire" was a statement of pride and celebration in nineteenth-century and early twentieth-century Britain. Here, we have dropped the second half of the phrase in order to mark the questions this collection raises about historical continuities and contemporary relations of global power. While the "empire" most commonly and readily associated with South Asia is that of the British, the United States has pursued its own major economic and geopolitical ambitions in the region for more than a century and has ultimately achieved significant political and economic power on the subcontinent. Indeed, over the course of the twentieth century, the contours of imperialism changed and shifted; the territorial empire of the British gave way to the spread of U.S.-led globalization. We argue that the increasing flows of people, money, goods, culture, and ideas between South Asia and the United States over the past several decades cannot be considered apart from this shift; they cannot be disentangled from the United States' long-standing and ongoing military, geopolitical, and economic pursuits in the region.

Our decision to open the collection with a focus on South Asian migration and expatriate radicalism in the early years of the twentieth century is informed by this understanding. We see Britain and the United States in this period as two imperial powers developing in an evolving dynamic of cooperation and competition.[10] From this standpoint, the contributions by Nayan Shah, Seema Sohi, and Vivek Bald significantly expand upon earlier literature on Ghadar radicalism in the United States during the 1904–1924 period. Most of this scholarship, dating from the 1970s and 1980s, viewed the politics of Indians in the early twentieth-century United States narrowly through the lens of Indian nationalism. The U.S. and Canadian West Coast was seen as an overseas outpost for the unfolding of subcontinental politics, and the Indians who became involved in the Ghadar movement there were understood to be primarily engaged in a struggle, from afar, against the British colonial state. Shah, Sohi, and Bald present a different picture of this period. Collectively, their work demonstrates that South Asian migrants were constantly crossing in and out of—and coming up against—both British and U.S. spheres of power as they made their way across the globe to the United States. They had to navigate the surveillance and border regimes that both empires were constructing in parallel and in concert with one another—in Calcutta, Singapore, Suez, the Philippines, Hawaii, Panama, and Belize; at the frontier between the United States and Mexico; in the engine rooms of British steamships; and at the porous docklands of the U.S. Atlantic coast. Once on U.S. soil, these migrants continued to face the power, policies, and pursuits of both Britain and the United States; here, they were simultaneously challenging their colonization as British subjects and their racialization and criminalization by an anti-immigrant, anti-Asian, antiradical U.S. state.

Sujani Reddy's chapter on the roots of Indian nurse immigration to the United States approaches this "early" period of South Asian migration from a different angle, that of the movement of U.S.-based institutions onto the subcontinent under the aegis of British colonization. Reddy foregrounds the critical role played by the Rockefeller Foundation in first remaking the global map of colonial medicine, and then promoting India's first generation of Indian nursing leaders through their access to U.S.-centered models of professionalization. Reddy thus redraws our framework for understanding the arrival of this all-too-often neglected segment of post-1965 professional managerial immigrants, moving us away from explanations that continue to center the machinations of U.S. immigration law (Hart-Cellar), toward one that uncovers the shifting terrain of Anglo-American imperialism in the decades leading up to the Cold War and the onset of American ascendancy.

The United States' geopolitical involvements in South Asia during this later period, from the 1950s through the 1980s, form the often unacknowledged background to the military, surveillance, criminalizing, and carceral regime that South Asian migrants now face in the post-9/11 world. In the years that we have been working on this project, Afghanistan and Pakistan have been on the front line of U.S. imperial policy. They have been the focus of an intense U.S.-led military campaign to "root out" groups like the Taliban and Al Qaeda, which themselves came into being as a result of earlier covert U.S. military involvements in the region during the Cold War—namely, the provision of U.S. money and arms to proxies fighting the Soviet Union and Afghan socialists and communists during the 1980s. The United States has been deeply involved in the Afghan-Pakistan region since that time, its foreign policy directed by a desire for the stability of, and/or control over, a territory that is crucial for the transshipment of oil and natural gas from Central Asia to Western markets. Years of U.S. support for military and antipopular governments in Pakistan, added to economic policies pushed by U.S. foreign aid and the International Monetary Fund (IMF)—from structural adjustment to the mechanization of agriculture—have also spurred the migration of increasing numbers of Pakistanis to the United States since the 1980s. These imperial dynamics have led us to focus particularly on the Af-Pak region and its migrants in the United States.

In his essay, Junaid Rana discusses how working-class Pakistani migrants in New York found themselves at the center of the domestic flank of the "War on Terror." While earlier Pakistani immigrants were largely professionals who had benefited from the 1965 Hart-Cellar Act, Rana focuses on a more recent migration stream, made up largely of young, lower-middle-class men who entered the economies of U.S. cities in the 1980s and 1990s as a labor pool for the service sector. As their communities grew in areas like Midwood in Brooklyn, some of these migrants were eventually able to bring family members to the United States, but many more, separated from their biological families on the subcontinent, forged new bonds and affiliations, both among themselves and with other immigrants and workers, across lines of nationality, language, and ethnicity.[11]

In the immediate aftermath of the World Trade Center attacks, as the U.S. state targeted South Asian, Arab, and Muslim men as terror suspects, its actions directly and immediately affected these families, networks of kin, friends, intimates, and neighborhoods. South Asians, particularly Muslims and the working class, saw their lives disrupted by a range of state actions: immigration "sweeps" that disappeared thousands of South Asian, Arab, and Muslim men; the passage of the USA PATRIOT Act and the creation of the National Security Entry-Exit Registration System (NSEERS); federal and local police initiatives to entrap community members in prefabricated terrorist plots; and the continuing detention and deportation of migrants netted through all these programs. The artistic interventions of the Visible Collective, discussed here by Naeem Mohaiemen, foreground the experiences of Muslim and South Asian immigrants who have had to navigate the policing and hypersurveillance of U.S. public spaces in this moment. Their work, alongside Rana's, helps us understand that the country's post-9/11 policies have racial and gendered dimensions whose impacts are not captured in official statistics about detainees and deportees. Rana specifically points us to the thousands of "voluntary" return migrants, who left the United States after experiencing the escalation of both everyday racism and racial violence at the hands of law enforcement. Experiences of imprisonment, deportation, and exile live on far beyond U.S. borders and shape returnees' understandings of their own global prospects, whether in Pakistan or as migrant laborers in the Persian Gulf and other parts of the world.

Rana's and other contributions to *The Sun Never Sets* call into question the notion that the war on immigrants following the attacks of September 11, 2001 constituted a historical break with the past or that the policies that the United States pursued in its wake were exceptional. The system of detention and deportation used and expanded following September 11 is not new, nor is the targeting of South Asian, Arab, and Muslim migrants. Many of the United States' institutions and practices of inspection, detention, and deportation were pioneered during the turn-of-the-century period of Asian exclusion and antiradicalism. Rather than seeing 9/11 as ushering in an era of disciplining immigrants of color, we instead see it as one moment in a more than century-long history of using incarceration and deportation as ways to police and contain communities of color. This time line includes the federal government's War on Drugs of the 1980s and the draconian 1996 Illegal Immigration Reform and Immigrant Responsibility Act (IIRIRA) that vastly increased the number of deportable offenses and reduced potential deportees' legal rights. Soniya Munshi elaborates in this volume on the ways that IIRIRA and the Violence Against Women Act demanded that immigrants fit into specific, preassigned, and one-dimensional subject categories in order to receive benefits from the state: victim, abuser, illegal, or dependent, for example. These demands on immigrants disproportionately affected those most vulnerable to state sanction and coerced immigrants trying to avail themselves of the legal system into working with the criminal justice system.

By the time that Af-Pak became the front line of the U.S.-led "War on Terror"—at home and abroad—neoliberal globalization had altered the political and economic landscape bridging South Asia and the United States. The roots of this phenomenon also go back several decades. The era of Third World decolonization and nonalignment in the 1940s, 1950s, and 1960s presaged a political-economic backlash from the First World.[12] This pushback culminated in the resurgence of neoclassical economic orthodoxy in the West, implemented in large part through the structural adjustment programs promoted by the World Bank, the IMF, and architects of the Washington Consensus.[13] A key tenet of these policies has been the assertion that large corporations must be able to seek new markets, sites of production, and workforces over time, in order to maintain or increase their rate of profit. Nations that attempt to shield their economies from foreign competition with protectionist policies, state-run and nationalized industries, or import-substitution industrialization (strategies that Pakistan, Bangladesh, and India all tried in the postindependence period) are considered major obstacles to corporate expansion. Neoliberals argue that such protectionist policies impede the free market and should be dismantled. They also assert that newly emerging markets in former Third World countries, now known as the Global South, provide the greatest opportunities for corporate profit making—in ways that resonate with the earlier imperial mining of labor and resources. International institutions, especially those that lend to southern countries, should therefore work to ensure that these emerging markets open up to foreign investment. This last argument has manifested, since the 1980s, in the IMF's policies of structural adjustment, austerity programs, and overall liberalization in the South. International lenders, with cooperation from South Asian ruling coalitions, implemented structural adjustment in South Asia in the 1980s and 1990s.

India has figured as a major focus of U.S. capital expansion over the past two decades of neoliberal globalization. It is one of the fastest-growing global markets for U.S. goods, as well as a source of cheap "outsourced" labor for U.S. technology, communications, and legal firms—while simultaneously looming as a potential future economic competitor. Although economic liberalization pursued by the Indian state under international pressure in the 1990s inaugurated this period, U.S. corporate and entrepreneurial capital has been central in this process. The entry of U.S. capital into India has in turn been aided by an Indian American professional class that continued to grow in size and wealth over the course of the 1980s and 1990s. As the U.S.-based Campaign to Stop Funding Hate (CSFH) has revealed, the growing power, influence, self-confidence, and presence of this group of nonresident Indians (NRIs) have not only been evident in a plethora of U.S. media reports celebrating Indian American entrepreneurs and CEOs, heralding India as the next economic superpower, and celebrating the arrival of Bollywood within U.S. popular culture but also manifest in the quiet flow of hundreds of thousands of NRI dollars to support the violently reactionary Hindu nationalist Sangh Parivar in India.

The rise of an Indian American bourgeoisie has been paralleled by a vast expansion in the number of workers in India itself who have been incorporated into U.S. economic circuits as factory laborers for U.S.-based and multinational corporations or semiskilled workers in technology and outsourcing enclaves in cities such as Hyderabad, Bangalore, and Gurgaon. In his contribution to this volume, Immanuel Ness focuses on Hyderabad as a case study for complicating depictions of the emergence of a globally connected Indian middle class tied to the proliferation of outsourcing. Rather than an uncritical celebration of "India Shining,"[14] Ness's analysis of shifting labor markets emphasizes that the advantages of neoliberal globalization have gone to India's capitalist classes. In contrast, neoliberal economic policies have put enormous pressure on the poor and working classes to fend for themselves with little state support in the most basic services, even as they often become the service providers for the new IT elite. Their dislocation and impoverishment have also provided the grounds for many South Asians to risk international migration, increasingly under the terms of short-term, temporary guest worker programs in the Persian Gulf, Europe, and the United States.

While neoliberal policies are affecting subcontinental communities in critical ways, the United States has also been fundamentally restructured. Neoliberal globalization debilitated the manufacturing sector and catalyzed the enormous growth of the service sector over the course of the 1970s and 1980s. Immanuel Ness provides the political-economic context for us to see how South Asian migrants are being called upon to work in insecure and unstable portions of this economy, from trucking to construction. Miabi Chatterji's essay shows us the ways that South Asian immigrants to the United States have, in the past thirty years, joined the ranks of working-class recent immigrants of color who are asked to perform affective labor for the urban elite. Chatterji focuses specifically on the ways that those immigrant workers in New York's service sector with more cultural capital can use the instability and lack of regulation of the service industry to their own benefit, against the co-ethnic employees that they manage. These work sites bring migrant workers from the Global South together, at times producing the conditions for affinities and alliances and at other times for workplace division and conflict. Ness's and Chatterji's work reveals how economic displacement and divestment from social welfare caused by neoliberal policy continue to pit low-status, racialized workers against one another in the richest metropolitan centers of the global economy.

Together, these scholars present the decline of territorially based colonization and the rise of neoliberalism not as two separate and unrelated events but as continuous with one another. They help elaborate the contours of U.S. imperialism—over time as well as in its current phase—and examine how U.S. empire has set particular forms of migration in motion and structured the allocation of labor across multiple sectors, geographic locations, and time periods.

Places and Spaces of Diaspora

As we have elaborated earlier, we treat the growth of the modern South Asian diaspora as part of a long-term process of Western capitalist expansion. Following the British abolition of slavery, indentured migration from China and British India constituted the two largest streams of state-sanctioned labor migration in the world, inaugurating histories of dispersal and settlement that continue today. We understand the South Asian diaspora not as something singular and fixed but as a formation that has been and continues to be in constant flux, and therefore—like its parallel term "nation"—diaspora is also an arena in which meanings and identities are continually articulated and rearticulated, asserted and contested. Our work here is self-consciously part of this contestation. It is an effort to expand who and what constitutes the South Asian diaspora as it has come to exist in the United States—whose lives and experiences, what structures of power and inequality, what dynamics of movement, settlement, struggle, and change we must account for as a starting point toward a more critical and less singularly celebratory representation of "South Asian America."

In his essay, Nayan Shah describes how South Asian migrants, in the first decades of the twentieth century, evaded structures imposed by the both the U.S. and British empires across the Pacific and Central America and strictures against the immigration of women from their communities. They developed new routes of migration, new means of avoiding state attempts to prevent their entry, and new forms of intimacy, responsibility, and family, even while they were never entirely able to escape state interventions that required their demonstration of legitimate forms of sociality, domesticity, and livelihood. Shah emphasizes ways that individual South Asian men were able to build and sustain diasporic lives through strategies of elusion and diversion, strategies that Seema Sohi and Vivek Bald also draw out in their essays on South Asian migrations in this period. These essays show that South Asian migrants, in Bald's words, have "treated laws not as a fixed structure of permissions and prohibitions to be followed but as a shifting field of obstacles and openings to be navigated." Read alongside the more contemporary analyses of Soniya Munshi and Linta Varghese, these essays describe how some of the most adverse effects of U.S. immigration policies are those hidden from view, in the daily lives of the undocumented, dependent, and newly arrived.

Part of what is useful about diaspora as an analytical tool is its ability to engage the dynamics of migration and settlement, displacement and place-making, at multiple scales of analysis. Here, Gayatri Gopinath's analysis of "region" in the work of recent queer South Asian diasporic artists provides a rich counterpart to the historical and ethnographic work elsewhere in the collection, providing space to meditate on and critique the affective and aesthetic dimensions of diasporic life, and the ways they reproduce or rub against dislocations of space and power. Raza Mir and Farah Hasan analyze the affective dimensions of religious spaces, which strengthen what they refer to as "coping ability," crucial for surviving everyday and crisis forms of indignity and brutality that South Asian Shias in New Jersey routinely face. Their arguments provide a point of resonance with Gopinath's analysis, moving into the realm of community institutions and the adaptation of rituals to new social and political needs. Junaid Rana, in his essay, explores both the affective and disciplinary dimensions of the post-9/11 deportation and imprisonment regime, as experienced by Pakistanis in the United States, as an integral part of current manifestations of Islamophobic racism that fuel the "War on Terror."

The essays collected here examine not just nations and transnational movement but a range of spaces—homes, workplaces, religious institutions, neighborhoods, and regions—that are crucial to understanding experiences of migration, dispersal, connection, and rootedness, as they shape the formation of new identities and collectivities. Such "small spaces," to invoke Linta Varghese's term, make visible the social asymmetries that structure diasporas—that mark their geographic and subjective maps, their lines of power, inclusion, and exclusion.[15] Collectively, these essays, and others in this collection focus on multiple geographies and scales of diaspora, to bring otherwise unexamined spaces and relationships under scrutiny, revealing, among other things, histories of intimacy, affinity, and affiliation across racialized and diasporic communities.

It is here—at the point where, in Brent Edwards's and Earl Lewis's words, "any study of diaspora is also a study of 'overlapping diasporas'"—that the usefulness of "diaspora" as an analytic framework can also begin to break down.[16] First, because "diaspora" is organized around a linear "homeland-diaspora" model, it privileges those with a direct connection to this "place of origin." In so doing, it obscures communities with multiple migration histories, for example, or the significance of those members of other racialized/ethnic groups with whom South Asian migrants have partnered in the United States, and whose productive and reproductive labor has been central to the constitution of new affiliations, families, and communities "in diaspora." Attention to their presence allows our contributors to describe not only histories of migration outward from a shared origin but also the dynamics of circulation—of people, ideas, goods, cultural forms—between multiple points across the globe, and the consequences of encounter, interaction, and intermixing across multiple lines of difference in the varied places in which migrants settle and make new lives.

Because it invariably privileges those who are mobile, "diaspora" also shifts our attention away from "those who cannot move"—the rural and urban poor who are nevertheless directly affected by the same circuits of capitalist imperialism that create international migration. Amanda Ciafone's essay makes clear that, in this framing of diaspora, we lose sight of groups of people who have raised their voices against the forces of their own marginalization and that of others who are similarly positioned across the globe. Ciafone focuses on the transnational struggle against environmental degradations caused by water extraction in Coca-Cola bottling plants across India, where local communities have risen up to demand a closure of the plants and a restoration of their water rights. A transnational network of anti–corporate globalization and environmental justice activists have helped raise the profile of these local struggles and begun to fight the multinational on its "home turf" in the United States and across the Global North. Ciafone's contribution helps us connect the entry of multinational corporations such as Coca-Cola into a liberalizing Indian economy with global struggles of resistance, rather than focusing only on immigration. Her chapter, along with those of Ness and Reddy, historicizes different moments in the movement of multinational and U.S.-based capital onto the subcontinent in ways that are related but not reducible to the movement of labor onto the international market. Their work thus raises questions about how we think and frame "diaspora" as a category of analysis and a lived reality over a century of political and economic shifts across the globe.

Finally, as Manu Vimalassery establishes in his essay, the concept of "diaspora" and the politics stemming from it too often assume terra nullius, that collective delusion of empty land emanating from an inability to see indigenous peoples, a lingering trace of the modern Western imperial project. His essay reminds us that the limits of the nation-state are not to be found solely in immigration law but that the politics of detention and deportation need to be read as part of the longer and continuous history of invasion and military occupation through which the United States has asserted its sovereignty in North America, and in the world at large. The degree to which diaspora analyses and politics lose sight of this is the degree to which they follow the nation's or, more accurately, the empire-state's vision of itself.[17] In tendencies to foreground mobility and cosmopolitanism, diaspora analysis can too easily avert attention from prior and ongoing histories of colonialism, and resistance that proceeds from indigenous communities, especially in North and South American, Caribbean, African, and Pacific contexts, all primary sites of the South Asian diaspora. Invocations of "diaspora" that fail to engage indigenous critique can thereby facilitate ongoing imperial projects that efface claims and enactments of indigenous sovereignty and autonomy. In an analysis of South Asians in U.S. global power, we do well to remember that South Asians are a relatively recent group to have been rendered "Indian" over the long history of imperialism in the Americas.[18]

In this vein we would do well to note that *Vanwyck Blvd* is now the property of the U.S. State Department and is on display at the U.S. embassy in Karachi. There, it performs a very different form of mapping than the one that began this introduction: placing Karachi as an imperial periphery of Manhattan and enacting global power through a knowing engagement with and appropriation of local cultures. This serves as a reminder and caution, present throughout the essays in this collection, that diaspora can serve the interests of imperial power and is not, in itself, a mode of resistance.

Structure

The collection is divided into three parts. Each presents a set of essays organized around a common theme, and each group of essays is meant to speak to the two others that constitute the book. The first part, "Overlapping Empires," consists of three chapters that explore one of the least emphasized periods in South Asian American studies. Extending from the late nineteenth century to the mid-twentieth century, they include decades that are all too often overlooked because of the wide scope and supposed strength of immigrant exclusion. In the second part, "From Imperialism to Free-Market Fundamentalism: Changing Forms of Migration and Work," the contributors examine the workings of the U.S.-led economic order that developed over the latter half of the twentieth century and into the present, focusing on the ways neo-liberal globalization has affected, disciplined, and created new circuits of migration for both capital and labor, and the effects of these circuits across social space. The final part, "Geographies of Migration, Settlement, and Self," reassesses some of the key spatial categories, relationships, and locations that inform studies of South Asian migration and circuits of U.S. power: from region, nation, and diaspora to borders and prisons. Along with the preceding essays, these visions of migration, settlement, and self might help us draw a new map, which not only presents a fuller picture of South Asians in the United States but also helps us to build a politics that is more fully alive to the needs and possibilities of justice in this moment.

NOTES

1. Paul Carter, *The Road to Botany Bay: An Exploration of Landscape and History*, Minneapolis: University of Minnesota Press, 2010. James R. Akerman, ed., *The Imperial Map: Cartography and the Mastery of Empire*, Chicago: University of Chicago Press, 2009. Glenn Hooper, ed., *Landscape and Empire, 1770-2000*, Aldershot: Ashgate, 2005. Simon Gikandi, *Maps of Englishness: Writing Identity in the Culture of Colonialism*, New York: Columbia University Press, 1996. Ricardo Padrón, *The Spacious Word: Cartography, Literature, and Empire in Early Modern Spain*, Chicago: University of Chicago Press, 2004. Graham Huggan, *Territorial Disputes: Maps and Mapping Strategies in Contemporary Canadian and Australian Fiction*, Toronto: University of Toronto Press, 1994.

2. Rajiv Chandrasekaran, *Imperial Life in the Emerald City: Inside Iraq's Green Zone*, New York: Knopf, 2006. Dahr Jamail, *Beyond the Green Zone: Dispatches from an Unembedded Journalist in Occupied Iraq*, Chicago: Haymarket Books, 2007. Nir Rosen, *In the Belly of the Green Bird: The Triumph of the Martyrs in Iraq*, New York: Free Press, 2006. Wendy Brown, *Walled States, Waning Sovereignty*, New York: Zone, 2010.

3. "South Asian New York Issue," *Time Out New York* 334, March 25–April 1, 2004, 12–30. Barbara Kantrowitz and Julie Scelfo, "American Masala," *Newsweek*, March 22, 2004, 50.

4. Leona B. Bagai, *The East Indians and Pakistanis in America*, Minneapolis: Lerner, 1972. Maxine P. Fisher, *The Indians of New York City: A Study of Immigrants from India*, New Delhi: Heritage, 1980. Roger Daniels, *History of Indian Immigration to the United States: An Interpretive Essay*, New York: Asia Society, 1989. Arthur W. Helweg and Usha Helweg, *An Immigrant Success Story: East Indians in America*, Philadelphia: University of Pennsylvania Press, 1990. Edwin Eames and Parmatma Saran, *The New Ethnics: Asian Indians in the United States*, New York: Praeger, 1980.

5. Anannya Bhattacharjee, "The Habit of Ex-nomination: Nation, Woman, and the Indian Immigrant Bourgeoisie," *Public Culture* 5, no. 1 (1992): 19–44. Inderpal Grewal, "The Postcolonial, Ethnic Studies, and the Diaspora: The Contexts of Ethnic Immigrant/Migrant Cultural Studies in the U.S.," *Socialist Review* 24, no. 4 (1994): 45–74. Inderpal Grewal, "On the New Global Feminism and the Family of Nations: Dilemmas of Transnational Feminist Practice," in Ella Shohat, ed., *Talking Visions: Multicultural Feminism in a Transnational Age*, Cambridge: MIT Press, 1998. Sucheta Mazumdar, "Colonial Impact and Punjabi Emigration to the United States," in Lucie Cheng and Edna Bonacich, eds., *Labor Immigration under Capitalism*, Berkeley: University of California Press 1984, pp. 316–336. Sucheta Mazumdar, "What Happened to the Women? Chinese and Indian Male Migration to the United States in Global Perspective," in Shirley Hune and Gail Nomura, eds., *Asian/Pacific Islander American Women: A Historical Anthology*, New York: NYU Press, 2003, pp. 54–78. Chandra Talpade Mohanty, "Crafting Feminist Genealogies: On the Geography and Politics of Home, Nation, and

Community," in Ella Shohat, ed., *Talking Visions: Multicultural Feminism in a Transnational Age*, Cambridge: MIT Press, 1998. Chandra Talpade Mohanty, *Feminism without Borders: Decolonizing Theory, Practicing Solidarity*, Durham, NC: Duke University Press, 2003. Gayatri Chakravorty Spivak, "Diasporas Old and New: Women in the Transnational World," *Textual Practice* 10, no. 2 (1996): 245–269. Kamala Visweswaran, "Diaspora by Design: Flexible Citizenship and South Asians in U.S. Racial Formations," *Diaspora* 6, no. 1 (1997): 5–29.

6. Deepika Bahri and Mary Vasudeva, eds., *Between the Lines: South Asians and Postcoloniality*, Philadelphia: Temple University Press, 1996. Sunaina Maira and Rajini Srikanth, eds., *Contours of the Heart: South Asians Map North America*, New York: Asian American Writers' Workshop; distributed by Rutgers University Press, 1996. Rakesh Ratti, ed., *A Lotus of Another Color: An Unfolding of the South Asian Gay and Lesbian Experience*, Boston: Alyson Publications, 1993. Lavina Dhingra Shankar and Rajini Srikanth, eds., *A Part, Yet Apart: South Asians in America*, Philadelphia: Temple University Press, 1998. Women of the South Asian Descent Collective, ed., *Our Feet Walk the Sky*, San Francisco: Aunt Lute Books, 1993. Shamita Das Dasgupta, ed., *A Patchwork Shawl: Chronicles of South Asian Women in America*, New Brunswick, NJ: Rutgers University Press, 1998. *South Asian Magazine for Action and Reflection* (*SAMAR*) has also been a deep resource for activists and academics thinking about South Asian migration; the pieces *SAMAR* has published over the years have pushed our conceptualization of the politics and culture of the South Asian diaspora.

7. Visweswaran, 11.

8. Vijay Prashad, *The Karma of Brown Folk*, Minneapolis: University of Minnesota Press, 2000.

9. Gayatri Gopinath, *Impossible Desires: Queer Diasporas and South Asian Public Cultures*, Durham, NC: Duke University Press, 2005. Jasbir Puar, *Terrorist Assemblages: Homonationalism in Queer Times*, Durham, NC: Duke University Press, 2007. Sharmila Rudrappa, *Ethnic Routes to Becoming American: Indian Immigrants and the Cultures of Citizenship*, New Brunswick, NJ: Rutgers University Press, 2004. Vijay Prashad, *Everybody Was Kung Fu Fighting: Afro-Asian Connections and the Myth of Cultural Purity*, Boston: Beacon Press, 2001. Biju Mathew, *Taxi! Cabs and Capitalism in New York City*, New York: New Press, 2005. Monisha Das Gupta, *Unruly Immigrants: Rights, Activism and Transnational South Asian Politics in the United States*, Durham, NC: Duke University Press, 2006. Sunaina Maira, *Missing: Youth, Citizenship and Empire after 9/11*, Durham, NC: Duke University Press, 2009.

10. This section builds on insights found in the groundbreaking collection *Labor Migration under Capitalism* (1984), in which editors Lucie Cheng and Edna Bonacich set forth an analysis that challenges the regional compartmentalization of "push-pull" theories of migration, which treated factors in "sending" and "receiving" countries as separate and coincidental. Historian Sucheta Mazumdar's contribution to the collection presented South Asian labor migration,

specifically, Punjabi immigration to North America, and Western capital expansion—in this case British colonization—as phenomena that should be considered in the same frame of analysis.

11. Mathew, 143–176.

12. Vijay Prashad, *The Darker Nations: A People's History of the Third World*, New York: New Press, 2007

13. The literature on this turn is vast. For examples of writings that influence our understanding, please see Lisa Duggan, *The Twilight of Equality? Neoliberalism, Cultural Politics and the Attack on Democracy*, Boston: Beacon Press, 2003. David Harvey, *A Brief History of Neoliberalism*, New York: Oxford University Press, 2005. Aihwa Ong, *Neoliberalism as Exception: Mutations in Citizenship and Sovereignty*, Durham, NC: Duke University Press, 2006.

14. "India Shining" was a slogan popularized by the incumbent Bharatiya Janata Party (BJP) during the 2004 Indian general elections. Its circulation thus encapsulated the party's embrace of neoliberal economic policies alongside Hindu fundamentalism.

15. Farah Jasmine Griffin, *"Who set you flowin'?": The African-American Migration Narrative*, New York: Oxford University Press, 1995. Laurence J. C. Ma and Carolyn Cartier, eds., *The Chinese Diaspora: Space, Place, Mobility, and Identity*, Lanham, MD: Rowman and Littlefield, 2003. Katherine McKittrick and Clyde Woods, eds., *Black Geographies and the Politics of Place*, Cambridge, MA: South End Press, 2007. Julia Brauch, Anna Lipphardt, and Alexandra Nocke, eds., *Jewish Topographies: Visions of Space, Traditions of Place*, Burlington, VT: Ashgate, 2008.

16. Brent Hayes Edwards, "Diaspora," in Bruce Burgett and Glenn Hendler, eds., *Keywords for American Cultural Studies*, New York: NYU Press, 2007, 83; Earl Lewis, "To Turn as on a Pivot: Writing African Americans into a History of Overlapping Diasporas," *American Historical Review* 100 (1995): 765–87.

17. Left Quarter Collective, "White Supremacist Constitution of the U.S. Empire-State: A Short Conceptual Look at the Long First Century," *Political Power and Social Theory* 20 (2009): 167–200.

18. Jodi A. Byrd, *Transit of Empire: Indigenous Critiques of Colonialism*, Minneapolis: University of Minnesota Press, 2011.

PART I

Overlapping Empires

1

Intimate Dependency, Race, and Trans-Imperial Migration

NAYAN SHAH

In 1907, seventeen-year-old Jawala Singh left his bride to the care of his father and uncle's joint household and traveled by rail with his cousin Punu Singh from his village in Punjab to Calcutta.[1] In Calcutta, Jawala and Punu booked passage and set sail for Hong Kong, sidestepping U.S. consular agents, who discouraged Punjabi laborers from journeying to the United States, and British colonial officials, who regulated the emigration of indentured laborers. After living at the Hong Kong gurudwara for several weeks and working at the docks and warehouses, they bought tickets for a ship bound for Honolulu and San Francisco. However, Hong Kong–based "quarantine authorities," directed by U.S. public health officers and hired by the steamship company, separated the two cousins and removed Jawala Singh with a diagnosis of trachoma. Relying on local remedies, Jawala Singh treated his eyes, and they cleared up. However, his medical record now dashed his chances for purchasing direct passage on North American–bound ships.[2]

In the late nineteenth and early twentieth centuries, the U.S. and British governments coordinated and consolidated such systems to control and police the mobility of workers and travelers. They created globally extensive infrastructures of exit and entry regulations, documentation requirements, and inspection sites and practices, and they regulated private passenger steamship companies to monitor and manage human mobility. Racial suspicion was at the heart of their regulatory scrutiny and guided both the policing of smuggling operations and the judgments of health inspectors and shipping agents. Like many South Asian and Asian migrants in the early twentieth century who migrated to find work outside their homes and send remittances to their families, Jawala Singh confronted, navigated, and resisted these racialized imperial and nation-state obstacles. Singh journeyed on a circuitous route through Manila, Panama, and Mexico and eventually lived, prospered, and died in New Mexico. Every step of the way, Singh and other migrants encountered a global system set up and maintained by both American and British imperial powers that sought to constrain and redirect their mobility and their access to work.

This chapter examines how South Asian migrants confronted and evaded obstacles that the U.S. and British empire-states set up across multiple jurisdictions in the Pacific and Central America. South Asian migrants mobilized flexible forms of citizenship and identity to navigate state barriers and harnessed social, kinship, and institutional networks and forms of intimate dependency to enable their mobility and survival. Both Canada and the United States instituted policies toward Asian immigrants to deter permanence and stability, including laws and procedures that excluded women. This process intensified Asian migrants' kinship ties and made their networks more globally extensive. At the same time, the exclusion and absence of women among South Asian immigrants reinforced the precariousness of male solo migrants.

As representatives of a society that promoted individualism, bureaucrats expressed wariness of communal alliances; immigration officers scrutinized and sought to disrupt the very interdependent ties of kinship, the social and institutional networks, that enabled migrant men to survive in British and American imperial locations along the Pacific Rim and in Mexico and the United States. However, the political economy of migration, race, and gender in this case created an environment along the Mexican-American borderlands that fostered new forms of alliance—specifically, interracial marriages, business partnerships, and family networks. While the policies of the British and U.S. empires nationalized and racialized immigrant outcomes, they also defined and circumscribed legitimate forms of kinship and alliance by denigrating and criminalizing those social ties that did not fit into a model of monogamous marriage and the nuclear family. However, mixed-racial and mixed-status families confounded and complicated the U.S. federal government's attempts to restrict South Asians' claim to legitimate residence in the United States and buffeted remigration and deportation cases in the middle of the twentieth century.

Migration Geography and Regulations

The journeys that Jawala Singh and other Punjabi migrants took out of Calcutta both followed and departed from those of the more than 30 million migrants who left colonial India from 1834 to 1930. More than 90 percent of South Asian migrants traveled across the Bay of Bengal to work in plantations in British imperial possessions, including 4 million who went to Malay and the Straights Settlements, 8 million to Sri Lanka, and 15 million to Burma. Most of these migrants were Tamil, Bengali, and Bihari male laborers and families whose passage and recruitment were "assisted" by debts and obligations to regional merchants who coordinated their placement with British plantation owners. Another 2 million migrated in similar fashion to British possessions in the Caribbean, Pacific, and Indian Oceans. Punjabi migrants composed a part of the approximately 2 million merchants, travelers, and soldiers who journeyed throughout Southeast Asia and the Indian Ocean, following opportunities and networks in Hong Kong, Macao, Shanghai, Singapore, and Manila. A much smaller number, approximately 80,000, of these ambitious Punjabi, Sindhi, and Afghani merchants, former soldiers, and laborers filtered beyond the coastal Southeast Asia orbit to migrate for opportunities in Canada, Australia, Hawaii, the United States, Mexico, Panama, and Argentina. It was the migration of these "free" emigrants that ignited immigration controversies in Canada, Australia, South Africa, and the United States.[3]

The British imperial concerns for nefarious schemes to dupe South Asians into indentureship contracts and transport them to the Caribbean plantations resulted in the 1883 Emigration Act, which required government oversight over labor contracts beyond "Ceylon and the Straights Settlements." Since the overwhelming majority of "assisted" emigrants journeyed within that orbit, the regulations also exempted merchants, travelers, soldiers, and military personnel recruited for service in China and Africa and thereby facilitated the migration of "free" service workers, laborers, and merchants.[4] British imperial efforts for the managed containment of indentured workers were matched by the United States' 1885 Alien Contract Labor Law, which expressly forbade any company or individual from bringing foreigners into the United States under contract to perform labor, except for domestic servants, artists, and lecturers. The specter of contract laborers haunted U.S. concerns about the dangers of racialized labor from India and China, as well as unskilled laborers from Eastern and Southern Europe.[5]

When confronted with several thousand South Asian male laborers migrating to West Coast ports in the period of 1905 to 1912, the U.S. and Canadian governments responded by marshaling health inspections to identify and deport those suffering from a "loathsome contagious disease" and summarily exclude and deport anyone else who inspectors predicted was liable to become destitute. Medical and public charge exclusions were established in 1891 and strengthened in subsequent years. In the first decade of the twentieth century, the United States expanded its exclusion regime beyond its own borders, imposing public health inspection routines in ports across the globe and punishing shipping companies that allowed suspect passengers to travel to North America. With the intensification of medical exclusion procedures in sending ports like Hong Kong and Shanghai and receiving ports like Seattle and San Francisco, South Asian migrants diverted their travels to U.S. imperial locations such as Manila and the Panama Canal Zone, where after six months residence, they could make their way to the mainland United States with less scrutiny. In 1913, when this remigration loophole from U.S. territories was closed, migrants increasingly used clandestine passageways through the Panama Canal Zone, Central America, and Mexico to enter the United States.[6]

The racial scrutiny of migration took a more formal turn in 1917, when the United States restricted the immigration of all laborers from Asia by creating a geographic "barred zone" that converted restrictions on Chinese and Japanese laborers to the broader region. Two years earlier, in 1915, the British government in India had imposed a similarly restrictive regulation under the Defence of India Passport Act that made it a criminal offense to embark on a journey from any port in British India without a passport.

Under mounting pressure from white settler populations across the British Empire, the British government in India had closely followed the attempts made by the Chinese government in 1888 and the Japanese government in 1895 to mandate passports as a defense against the discriminatory and humiliating exclusions on their emigrants to North America.[7] As race became increasingly central in the development of British immigration and residency regulations in the white settler dominions of Australia, Canada, and South Africa, British regulations administered in Britain's colonial ports of Calcutta, Shanghai, Hong Kong, and Singapore combined with U.S. regulations administered in its colonial territories of Hawaii and the Philippines to constrain the mobility of South Asian and Chinese laborers and create the framework for their policing and exclusion.

Government officials in the United States, Canada, and Britain communicated frequently, sharing information, suspicions, and bureaucratic policies and strategies on how to interpret the value or danger of Asian migrants. They traded their assessments of migrant capabilities, theories about geographic and racial predispositions to disease and disability, the likelihood of becoming destitute, and the dangers of migrants' political and cultural habits to Anglo-American civilization and democracy. The "intimate encounter" filtered a specific assessment of both racial groups and individuals.[8] Immigration inspectors and politicians in Canada and the United States feared that an Asian migrant would become a vagrant and public charge and so focused their scrutiny on the "private" network of support that would buoy the individual's needs so that he would not drain resources from the public. The bureaucratic procedures of immigrant entry had contradictory effects.

They demanded to see immigrants as "autonomous" and "independent" individuals, but they also assumed that an immigrants' web of dependence through a network of kin, friends, co-villagers, coreligionists, and compatriots would be necessary to sustain the migrants in a hostile environment.

State power and sovereignty came into being over the regulation of human mobility. States simultaneously regulated individual identity through passports, permits, and visas, and channeled human mobility through defined gateways, transportation systems, and territorial boundaries. Through extraterritorial surveillance, travel and identity documentation, and investigation systems, states consolidated their authority and reinforced the necessity of reciprocal if uneven relationships between clearly bounded nation-states. As historian Adam McKeown has argued, the world of passports, visas, and permits does not record a "preexisting reality" but creates "stable, documentable identities for individuals and divide[s] those individuals across an international system of nation states."[9] U.S. immigration historians have explained how a nationalizing agenda proliferated exclusionary racialization and divided people into either citizens or aliens. They have also charted how individuals labeled as "aliens" caught within the system are stripped of constitutional protections by the plenary powers of the nation-state.[10] By subjecting individuals to standardized inspection practices that measured the physical body—including the face, fingerprints, and bodily fluids and wastes—immigration inspectors had a new field of data with which to interpret and predict the bodily fitness and capacity of immigrants, as well as a racial topography upon which to map individual capacity and destiny.

Manila Transit

When denied passage to the United States from Hong Kong, Jawala Singh worked as a night watchman for several months and then embarked to Manila to work as a peddler and laborer.[11] Labor demands grew in the Philippines as the United States vanquished Philippine rebels and imposed rule over the archipelago and as U.S. and British capital investment invigorated sugar plantations and global trade. Former South Asian police officers and soldiers stationed in Shanghai and Hong

Kong and merchants and laborers in Singapore and Penang migrated to Manila at the end of the first decade of the twentieth century. Drawn by reports of higher pay rates and opportunity, some men worked for short periods as night watchmen or peddled clothing and goods on the streets of Manila. U.S. Customs officials administered entry and residency permits. Parsee, Bengali, and Sikh merchants established thriving businesses supplying clothing, tools, and plumbing supplies. The growing Sikh population supported a gurudwara in Manila following the establishment of similar temples in Hong Kong, Shanghai, Singapore, and Penang. Many South Asian watchmen and guards complained of oppressive heat, lack of reliable work, and limited business opportunities. At the same time, steamship companies, eager to bolster eastbound passenger traffic, launched recruitment campaigns promising lucrative, high-wage employment a short distance from the gateway ports of Honolulu, Seattle, and San Francisco. South Asian merchants helped prospective passengers such as Jawala Singh secure the loans necessary to pay their passage.[12]

After a six-month stay in the Philippines, South Asian migrants could obtain a certificate of residence status in the Philippines and could thereby bypass vigorous physical examinations in Seattle and San Francisco. The United States had to balance the goals of fostering the Philippines trade and increasing commerce with Asia against U.S. political pressure for regulating Asian immigration.[13] In 1912, U.S. immigration commissioner Ellis De Bruler sounded the alarm of "invasion" of South Asians from the Philippines. He warned that "this back-door entrance" would become a pipeline for "a horde of these East Indians" to invade "our shores, creating disturbances" and widespread unrest among white "laboring classes." In Manila, U.S. Customs officers estimated that 6,000 to 7,000 indigent "Hindus" "gambled, peddled," and performed at "fairs giving conjuring exhibitions while awaiting an opportunity to embark for Pacific Coast ports."[14]

In June 1913, the U.S. Congress closed the loophole that had allowed South Asian, Chinese, and Japanese migrants who claimed residency in Puerto Rico, the Philippines, and Hawaii to remigrate to the continental United States.[15] With the expansion of U.S. empire, the scope of potential Asian migrants had widened as Chinese, Japanese, and South Asians labored in plantations across the Pacific and in the Caribbean.

Yet even as these migrants were hindered from entry to the continental United States, the U.S. government encouraged and facilitated the migration of "indigenous" Puerto Ricans and Filipinos throughout the 1910s and 1920s to work in the United States as farm laborers, in service industries, and in light manufacturing. The U.S. government continued to finesse and reassess racial taxonomies to facilitate and bar mobility.[16]

The political controversy over the "backdoor" raised the specter of "contract laborers" arriving in the form of South Asian workers from the Philippines. South Asian migrants were singled out by their race and their transit through Manila. Although immigrants arriving from Europe were asked for documentation of financial resources, paternal and fraternal support, and family histories of land and business ownership as proof of fitness for entry to the United States, when South Asian migrants offered these same conventional proofs of financial support, they were interpreted as signs of "assisted" contract immigration—not as insurance against indigence. Although such promises of jobs and family assistance hardly qualified as abusive corporative contracts, immigration officers insisted that these offers were evidence of "assisted" migration for potential "coolies," unilaterally excluding racially suspect immigrants and branding them as "likely to become public charges." The conflict between the migrants and inspectors over the meaning of "assistance" hampered men who were cast as common laborers. This was the case, for example, with Natha Khan, who arrived in San Francisco from Manila, where he had worked for six months as a night watchman after a decade of working as a police officer in Hong Kong. Angel Island immigration authorities refused entry for Natha Khan, despite proof of his substantial savings and income-producing property in India, and a statement from his already-established cousin Ahmad Khan, pledging that he would support Natha and find him work in the United States and adding, "What belongs to one member of my family belongs to all."[17] Ahmad pledged his own savings and stated that he would even mortgage investment property in Vancouver and take out loans from other North America–based relatives to furnish a bond for Natha Khan. Immigration authorities ignored Khan's work history as a policeman, his family history of owning a farm, and his local networks of support and judged that he would join the thousands of unemployed and indigent laborers at the height of the 1913 economic depression and add to the hostile climate toward "Hindus" and other Asians who were the target of white worker resentment. Savvy to the economic and political climate, Ahmad vowed that he would take his cousin to find work in the "lumbering business and in sawmills in Washington and Oregon," where opportunities were more plentiful. Despite all these proofs of financial and family support, immigration commissioner Edsell branded Khan—along with scores of other South Asian men traveling from Manila—as "ordinary laboring class" and thus as a future burden to charity and state resources.[18]

Throughout the early twentieth century, Asian migrants depended on networks of fraternal relations that were developed through family lineages, shared local or regional origins, or common faith and circumstances. These systems of group affiliation enabled their survival in British and American colonies in East Asia and in Canada and the United States. Canadian and U.S. immigration inspectors scrutinized fraternal intimacies, examining the financial support between fathers and sons, as well as between lateral kin, adult brothers, uncles, cousins, and nephews. In these male-sutured networks of intimate dependence, assistance to other men was viewed in terms of investment and financial backing. South Asian male migrants also eased their mobility by banding together, sharing meals, housekeeping duties, and material support in boardinghouses, hotels, bunkhouses, and ranches in Hong Kong, Shanghai, Manila, Panama, northern Mexico, and the United States. For migrant men, the measure of their duty and honor among each other was their ability to support their parents, siblings, wives, and children in India. In their home villages, their trans-imperial migration reinforced patriarchal umbrellas combining the resources of several generations of male relatives, reinvesting remittances and shouldering responsibility for multigenerational households of elders, married and widowed women, unmarried youth, and children. Although the need to find work may have motivated migration decisions, immigrants such as Natha and Ahmad Khan had to claim status and resources that exceeded those of "common laborers," by documenting skill, education, and capital. Immigration inspectors and policy makers required documentation for arriving immigrants to demonstrate persuasively their capacity to both possess and organize capital. Immigration officials judged the resources and liabilities of intimate dependents in their overall assessment of an individual's suitability for entry. As much as the ideology of the self-sufficient individual held sway, official judgment of an individual migrant's potential for success in the United States depended heavily on an evaluation of the migrant's social web of dependency. The existence of intimate dependents—spouses, children, parents, siblings, and cousins—could be either a source of concern about the migrant becoming a state burden or a reassurance of the migrant's capacity for self-sufficiency.

Legal entry into the United States for South Asians was increasingly restricted to students, merchants, skilled tradesmen, religious instructors, and priests, but it hinged upon documentation and substantiation through interrogation. Prem Singh, who arrived at Angel Island in October 1913, experienced the advantages of being treated as a student by immigration officers. Even though his high school and college diplomas were stolen on board the ship, his comportment and fluency in English convinced immigration inspectors to believe his statement that he came to study to be an irrigation engineer.[19] Inspector F. H. Ainsworth assessed Prem's capabilities and was impressed with his "general manner in testifying, also from his general appearance, clean cut features and gentlemanly attitude." He did not have specific enrollment plans but had the confidence of Ainsworth, who believed that Singh was "of the class who come to the United States not knowing exactly what college or what institution they may enter, but who are taken in hand by their countrymen who belong to a club or an association and live near the college at Berkeley, California." Ainsworth anticipated that with the guidance of other students, Singh would begin to take classes in English and other subjects and would matriculate at a local university. Inspector Robinson dissented and argued that Singh's claims were fraudulent and that he was "a member of the laboring classes and a person likely to be a public charge" because of the "limited money in his possession." After Prem Singh was in detention for a month, the Hindustan Association in Berkeley "unanimously elect[ed] Prem Singh as [an] active member of [the] association" and facilitated his release and entry to the United States.[20] The assistance from both relatives and strangers that Prem Singh mustered was not much greater than that of laboring immigrants such as Natha Khan. Yet his appearance, his manners, family history, and ability to read, write, and speak in English marked him as a member of the student class, and he demonstrated the necessary social capital to be released from detention and allowed to enter.

Panamanian and Mexican Gateways

By 1914, South Asian migrants attempting to travel via the large commercial passenger lines that sailed across the Pacific from the major ports of Hong Kong, Shanghai, Yokohama, and Manila to the North American West Coast faced intensified scrutiny over medical disability and calculations of likely destitution and "assisted migration." These severe obstacles to mobility at official ports diverted the itineraries of South Asian migrants farther south to Panama and Mexico.

Several years before this intensification, Jawala Singh had raised funds for travel to the Panama Canal Zone, rather than face possible deportation at Angel Island, as he was justifiably leery of courting another health exclusion.[21] High demands for manual labor and dockworkers and opportunities for merchants drew migrants from Europe, the Caribbean, North and South America, and Asia to the Panama Canal Zone. South Asians converged from among Gujarati, Sindhi, and Parsi merchants, Sikh watchmen and guards stationed in British ports in East Asia, former indentured laborers from Trinidad, Jamaica, and Guyana, and Bengali sailors on British ships and numbered 10,000 people of South Asian origin by the 1920s. Hindus, Muslims, and Sikhs maintained temples and mosques in Panama City and Colón.

When Panamanian authorities restricted immigration, they scrutinized the employment practices of non-European merchants. In the 1920s and 1930s, Panama imposed immigration restrictions on West Indian immigrants as well as Chinese, Syrian, and South Asian merchants and their families, and demanded that 75 percent of mercantile and retail jobs be filled by Panamanians.[22] The cultural networks of diasporic merchant communities facilitated migration and were mercantile inversions of the logic of imperial rule. In the Panama Canal Zone, the U.S. government encouraged merchants to provide the staff necessary to consolidate class, status, and the circulation of capital that made imperial commerce possible. Gujarati, Sindhi, and Parsee shopkeepers and import-export trading firms aspired to wealth but not political power, and they remained outsiders. As anthropologists John Kelley and Martha Kaplan suggest, they were Weber's pariah capitalists, sustained by their own diasporic cultural institutions and the strategies of self-determination that facilitated transnational trade and opportunities.[23]

Sindhi merchants also helped Indian revolutionaries travel from Japan via Panama into North America, connecting them to North Indian students, Punjabi laborers, and Bengali sailors.[24] After working for a time at the docks or in Parsi and Sindhi retail establishments and warehouses in Panama, these political radicals traveled up the Pacific coast through Guatemala and Mexico to the U.S.-Mexico border, where they joined migrants from Southern Europe, the Middle East, and Asia who had been diagnosed with eye infections and other disabilities that disqualified their entry through U.S. ports in New York or San Francisco. Since the 1890s, prospective U.S.-bound immigrants had traveled to Mexico and used overland gateways. The numbers of Syrians, Japanese, and Chinese using these routes rose in the first decade of the twentieth century. By 1907, the U.S. Immigration Service was so alarmed by how frequently immigrants bypassed the more stringent inspections at Ellis Island and other Atlantic ports that it dispatched an inspector, Marcus Braun, to investigate migration patterns and regulations in Mexico. Braun examined human smuggling operations that passed from Havana, Cuba, to Vera Cruz, Mexico, and then onward by railway lines to El Paso, Texas. At ports in Beirut, Naples, Marseilles, and Le Havre, transportation agents and private immigration hustlers redirected Syrians from traveling to Boston and New York to the Caribbean and Mexico. Braun characterized Syrians not as contract workers "like Japanese and Chinese" but as "peddlers" who were trying to reach their compatriots in small cities such as New London, Connecticut, and Fort Wayne, Indiana, that were central points for Syrian merchant networks. In addition to Syrian peddlers, Braun suspected Japanese and Korean contract laborers, Japanese "Geisha girls," and Sephardic Jews of utilizing legal gateways on the U.S.-Mexico border to dodge more stringent regulations in U.S. ports on both the Atlantic and Pacific coasts.[25]

Chinese, Japanese, and South Asian migrants took trains and hitched rides on stagecoaches to the northern Mexico border towns of Mexicali, Hermosillo, and Juarez, working in construction or as farm laborers along the way. South Asian workers would also travel by ship or overland through Guatemala and take short boat trips up the Pacific coast of Mexico to Guaymas and then to the mouth of the Colorado River, where they traveled by stagecoach to one of the ranches managed by South Asians near Mexicali and Tijuana.[26] There, they would draw on personal and commercial connections to ease the crossing of the border and to facilitate labor contracting and the smuggling of goods and people. Like the Chinese and Syrian publications of this era that provided coaching and information for potential migrants, the *Hindustan Ghadar* published maps of Mexico and detailed routes of accessible and reliable entry into the United States.[27] Along with Mexican and Mexican American men, South Asian men on both sides of the U.S-Mexico border like Hardit Singh Dhillon of Mexicali, Mexico, and Bhulla Singh of Brawley, California, smuggled South Asian laborers across the border and eventually to jobs in orchards and ranches in Stockton, Fresno, and Marysville.[28]

This movement of South Asian migrants through the Panama Canal Zone, Guatemala, and Mexico to the U.S. border persisted into the 1920s. In 1928, the *San Francisco Examiner* reported a large and thriving human smuggling trade across the Mexican border, with large labor camps of several hundred South Asian workers in Tijuana and Mexicali. These camps supplied laborers for the northern Mexico farm and ranching economy and persisted into the 1940s. The camps also were lucrative grounds for Mexican, Mexican American, and South Asian coyotes, who smuggled South Asian, Chinese, and Japanese workers, charging them $200 per person to be ferried across the border to California.[29] Coyotes and migrants themselves developed elaborate strategies to cross the border and evade U.S. Border Patrol. South Asians would disguise themselves by cutting their hair, relinquishing turbans, shaving their beards, and grooming small "Mexican" mustaches. They would then purchase a "good suit of clothes" and would be indistinguishable from Mexicans when they crossed the border at the main highways. As historian Erika Lee and other scholars have documented, Chinese, South Asian, and Syrian migrants passed as "Mexican" by changing the way they dressed and by learning small amounts of Spanish, which enabled them to legally cross the U.S.-Mexican border.[30] The increasing suspicion of U.S. border patrols and U.S. and Mexican customs and immigration officials, however, drove many prospective immigrants to cross through the desert rather than at official border gateways.[31]

In order to manipulate and subvert the state's sovereign powers of credentialing identity, prospective border crossers destined for the United States accessed the thriving trade in producing documentation for the journey. Smuggling networks contracted with small printing businesses to create counterfeit Mexican passports and advised clients on how to manipulate the British embassy's registration lists. Mexican entrepreneurs and South Asian labor contractors and agents obtained new passports on behalf of South Asian men whose fictive identities matched the names of older registration lists and men who had already successfully crossed the border to the United States. Using fictitious names, they would apply for replacement passports from the British, claiming their documents had been stolen and listing new forwarding addresses in Mexicali. Armed with new British passports and identities, the men legitimately entered the United States at border checkpoints such as Calexico and Nogales.[32] By 1926, British consular authorities clamped down on issuing replacement passports and pressured the Mexican government to create new head taxes and regulative obstacles for Asian and Middle Eastern immigrants to travel through Mexico.[33]

Borderlands Identities

When Jawala Singh crossed the U.S. border at Agua Prieta into Douglas, Arizona, in May 1909, he had no need to disguise his identity. However, his subsequent life over two decades in the Mexican-American borderlands demonstrated how successfully and flexibly he made use of Mexican identity to make himself socially legible and viable in the political economy of the borderlands. After traveling to California to join his cousin Punu Singh and friends working on ranches and orchards in the Sacramento and San Joaquin Valleys, Jawala traveled east to El Paso, Texas, and followed work leads to the irrigated farmland across the New Mexico state border in Mesilla.[34] When Jawala Singh arrived in the Mesilla Valley in 1910, much of the Southwest was on the verge of commercial agriculture transformation through the construction of extensive federally sponsored dams and irrigation systems. Construction of the Elephant Butte Dam and the development of the Elephant Butte Irrigation District began in 1911 and were completed in 1916. The new irrigation system made it possible for farmers in the Mesilla Valley to grow water-intensive crops such as alfalfa, lettuce, cotton, cantaloupes, corn, hay, hot peppers, and pecans. However, the capital demands for fertilizer and tax payments dislodged long-settled Hispanic farmers from the valley. Within twenty years, the majority of Hispanic farmers who owned small farms lost hold of the best land. Much of this land went to Anglo merchants but also to intrepid tenant farmers like Jawala Singh, who leased and eventually purchased land in the district.[35]

Jawala Singh's success as a tenant farmer dovetailed with his eagerness to establish permanent political and social ties in Mesilla. When he came to New Mexico, he lived among the Mexican ranchers and laborers there, but he worked for Anglo farmers and businessmen. Jawala Singh gradually undertook a process of "Hispanicizing" his name and origins in his official registrations at the county courthouse in Las Cruces. In the 1910s, he adapted his first name of "Jawala" to "Julius" and "Julio." He dropped Singh as his last name and made a version of his first name, "Jubala," into his new surname.[36] In 1915, his petition for naturalization claimed his origin as "los Indios," which allowed him to capitalize on the ambiguity of Mexican mestizo heritage as well as to Hispanicize his origins in India. Although he did not pursue naturalized citizenship, Julio Jubala's change of name and identity leveraged into great financial success as he amassed savings and gained loans to purchase forty acres of property in Mesilla. Eighteen months later, on December 8, 1917, at the age of twenty-seven, he married Maria Fierro, who was twenty-eight years old.[37] Despite the fact that he had already married in India, Julio Jubala managed to expand his property holdings in the United States through his marriage with and divorce from Maria Fierro and subsequent remarriage to the daughter of his principal Mexican American labor supervisor. All along, he maintained his marriage in Punjab and kept news of his personal life secret from his two families.[38]

Julio's familiarity with local officials and use of community property law enabled him to continue to acquire land even after New Mexico passed a constitutional amendment in 1921 that made it impossible for immigrants racially excluded from naturalized citizenship to own land. Even after 1923, when the Supreme Court ruled that South Asians were racially ineligible for naturalization along with Chinese and Japanese immigrants, Julio Jubala's attorneys were able to manipulate his 1929 divorce settlement such that he was able to retain ownership of 125 acres. In exchange for keeping all the farmland and farm equipment, he ceded all his personal property, made a cash settlement, and promised to build his ex-wife an adobe home to satisfy her need for domestic security in the aftermath of the divorce. Julio's friendship and business relationship with the county clerk allowed him to dodge the impact of the Alien Land Law and corner the capital-producing property for his own future economic viability.[39]

Julio Jubala's two marriages fit a pattern of interethnic partnership in the Southwest United States where federally sponsored irrigation systems and transportation infrastructure attracted a diverse population of labor migrants to work the farms and ranches in West Texas, southern New Mexico, central Arizona, and Imperial County, California. The channels of migration to this region were carved out by the Southern Pacific passenger railway routes, which brought Punjabi and Japanese men from across Mexico and California in contact with Mexican men and women, and with white and African American rural migrants from Oklahoma, Texas, Arkansas, and Missouri.[40]

In the Mexican-U.S. borderlands, stretching from Texas to California, the labor market and marriage networks followed similar patterns in the 1910s, connecting South Asian male migrants and Mexican women and children. The Alvarezes were one such family. Doña Petra Alvarez and her three daughters and son arrived by train in El Paso, Texas, in 1916 after fleeing the turmoil of the Mexican Revolution. They learned of opportunities in California and quickly made their way by train to Imperial County, California, where the family lived and picked cotton on the Edwards ranch in Holtville for two South Asian tenant farmers, Sher Singh and Gopal Singh. Within months, twenty-one-year-old Antonia Alvarez had married thirty-six-year-old Sher Singh, and eighteen-year-old Anna Anita Alvarez had married thirty-seven-year-old Gopal Singh. Such social and kinship ties often brought South Asian men and Mexican American women together in rapid serial marriages that were "reinforced and expanded" by strong ties among Mexican women, tenancy partnerships between Punjabi men, and Catholic godparent ties.[41]

In the southwestern United States and in northern Mexico, intermarriage and lineage surfaced in the everyday language of social identities and revealed a persistence of racial taxonomies. For instance, in

Sonora and Chihuahua, Mexico, there is continued resilience, to this day, of terms like "Arabes," "Chino," and "Hindu" to designate families with non-European male ancestors who intermarried with mestizos.[42] Conversely, in the United States, in official documents, the salience of the category "Mexican" usurped the complexity of family lineages. Curiously, in Imperial County, California, the designation of "Hindu"— irrespective of Muslim, Sikh, or Hindu spiritual identity—persisted throughout the twentieth century in reference to families who had a South Asian ancestor in the early decades of the twentieth century, as distinct from those whose origin was in post-1960s Indian or Pakistani immigration.[43] In the first decades of the twentieth century, U.S. federal census and immigration documentation persistently used "Hindu" as a catchall category for persons from British colonial India; later, in the mid-twentieth century, however, the term was eclipsed by "East Indian" and, eventually, the Cold War area studies term "South Asian." On the U.S.-Mexico borderlands, the persistence of "Hindu" identity reproduced a conspicuous racialization that continued to set various "Asiatic races" apart from those with the Spanish/European ancestry that constituted the authentic lineage of Mexico.

Regulating Mixed-Status Families

Multiracial families posed a problem for how the U.S. government interpreted immigration regulations and distributed citizenship. When such families traveled outside the United States, many Mexican American, Puerto Rican, and African American women who had married South Asian men discovered that they had been stripped of U.S. citizenship because of their husband's racial "ineligibility for naturalized citizenship." In 1929, Felicita Soto Dhillon, born in Austin, Texas, left the United States and traveled with her husband of more than ten years, Harnam Singh Dhillon, and their children to his family's home in Punjab. Two years later, when they returned to the United States, immigration officials at Angel Island detained, separated, and threatened to deport members of the family based on a motley array of medical and immigration exclusions.

Harnam and Felicita Dhillon had taken precautions to ensure that the family would be allowed to return. They had made sure they had proper documentation, birth certificates for the children, proof of his merchant status and business interests, and had proper reentry permits. However, when the family returned to San Francisco on May 5, 1931, the three American-born children, Besanta, Than, and Ramon, were admitted "as natives of the United States," but their parents' and infant brother's statuses were suspect. Their mother and their Hong Kong–born brother, Jak, were diagnosed with hookworm. In a formulaic and rote response by the medical inspector, Jak, as a twenty-two-month-old toddler, was recommended for exclusion because his "affliction" would "affect his ability to earn a living." The disease diagnosis and exclusionary procedures served to wrest him from his siblings and split apart his family. In those tense two weeks, Jak's parents agonized over how their varying citizenship status would fracture their family. Despite his legal arrival in the United States in the early 1910s, Harnam Singh was relegated by the 1917 immigration law to the status of "native of barred zone," and immigration officers viewed him as a "common laborer" despite documentation showing that he was a member of a restaurant partnership in the United States. Bhola Singh, the priest of the Stockton Sikh temple, intervened to pay a bond for hookworm treatment on Angel Island for Felicita and her son Jak. After legal pressure, Harnam Singh was released on June 4 to rejoin his older children. Although Felicita Soto was a U.S. citizen born in Austin, Texas, her marriage to Harnam retroactively annulled her U.S. citizenship status. After three days of treatment, Felicita and Jak were cleared of hookworm and able to rejoin their family.[44] The state continued to underscore male prerogatives of independent movement by judging male capability and making women's citizenship dependent on husbands' status. The children's citizenship status was distributed according to the accidents of their birthplace.[45]

In the case of European immigrants, U.S. authorities had begun to use statutory and administrative measures in the 1930s to avert deportation and keep families unified, but the same policy was denied to Asians because they were ineligible for naturalization. Advocates and attorneys for the protection of immigrant rights decried the injustice that European, Canadian, and Mexican immigrants could seek administrative relief to suspend deportation proceedings and legalize the entry of immigrants in hardship cases, particularly in instances where deportation would disrupt families and households with children.[46]

In the United States, even prior to the formal rescinding of immigration restrictions and naturalization barriers for South Asians in 1946, claims to national citizenship became increasingly subordinated to the priority of sustaining and unifying married couples and their children. However, official determinations of who was deserving or undeserving of such relief recalibrated the place of race in a system that affirmed family reunification but recognized only some family forms, mobility practices, and livelihoods as "permanent settlement" and others as "transience."

The circulatory migration of Jawala Singh was echoed two decades later in the journey of Sher Singh, who left Punjab in November 1920 and worked in local police departments in Macao and Hong Kong for several years, periodically returning to his home village. In the mid-1930s, Sher Singh ventured farther afield, looking for better work opportunities. He traveled via Manila to Panama, where he worked for two years; in 1937, when Panamanian officials cracked down on work and residency permits for Asian workers, Singh journeyed to Mexico, where he worked on the ranches and farms of Mexicali for the next seven years. Then, on March 24, 1944, he crossed the U.S. border at Calexico. Months after his crossing, U.S. immigration authorities arrested him, but the Mexican government refused to accept his deportation despite evidence of his seven-year residency in Mexico, and World War II made it impossible to deport Singh to India.[47]

After the war, and with India's and Pakistan's independence from Britain in 1947, the U.S. Justice Department redoubled efforts to deport undocumented workers back to their natal homes. Many of the men who were most readily deported lived in the United States but had left wives and children behind in India. However, there were a number of South Asian men who had married Mexican American, white, Puerto Rican, and African American women and claimed that the hardship of deportation would destroy their ties with their American-born wives and children. The values of family cohesion frequently trumped overstayed visas and undocumented entry. Sher Singh had hoped to take advantage of the dispensation when he married a widow, Adela Martinez, a Puerto Rican woman with seven children who had moved to Arizona in the late 1920s, as part of a large-scale recruitment of Puerto Rican workers by Arizona cotton growers.[48] She was widowed twice, first when her first husband died in Glendale in 1930 and then when her second husband died in 1940. In 1947 at the age of fifty-six, Adela met and married Sher Singh. Antimiscegenation laws in Arizona curtailed her ability as a provisionally "white" woman to marry a "Hindu" man, so Sher Singh married Adela Martinez on October 27, 1947, in Lordsburg, New Mexico. They then traveled to Mendota, an agricultural and ranching town west of Fresno, California. Less than a month later, Sher Singh petitioned the U.S. federal court for a stay of his deportation because of his marriage to Adela Martinez, "a resident citizen of Phoenix," drawing on other cases that stayed deportation to keep a family with mixed citizenship status out of "serious hardship." By the time the courts heard the case, they had been married for two years, and the federal judge ordered Sher Singh to remain in the United States.[49]

Normalizing the Future

British and U.S. imperial regulatory strategies for policing and diverting migration were based upon a globalized inspection and identity system that both generated and depended upon "knowledge" of racialized bodies to affect state administrative control. U.S. inspectors, administrators, and judges placed the racial category "Hindu" within a hierarchy of personhood through which South Asian migrants were denied full membership and liberty of movement. Despite Britain's pretensions to universal and egalitarian membership within its empire, colonial subjecthood was similarly a subordinated and disenfranchised status when it came to both movement within the Empire and migration to other nation-states such as the United States. Over time, the U.S. federal and state governments understood "Hindu" persons as part of the "Asiatic" or "Oriental" race, relegating them to a vulnerable noncitizen status and organizing a system through which they were dispossessed of land rights, suffrage, and naturalization, and their female spouses divested of national citizenship.

However, migrants eluded barriers to mobility and opportunity by diverting their itineraries, by engaging in strategies of racial passing and cultural adaptation, and by reorganizing intimate, kinship, and marriage ties. Their social, institutional, and intimate networks sustained other South Asian migrants and enabled survival through local and global networks of intimate interdependency in hostile and bewildering environments. Migrants' community ties and the composition of inter-racial and flexible identities in the Mexican-American borderlands con-founded and confused state-determined national and racial taxonomies. The forms of belonging that they created were often uneasy and unsta-ble and always existed under the stress of state surveillance, capitalist dislocation, and the vagaries of racial exclusion in marriage, property, and citizenship. However, no matter how belonging was expressed by noncitizens and provisional citizens in their variety of mutable interests, needs, and desires, the U.S. nation-state required that they live in ways that could be contained and tethered to legitimate forms of sociality, domesticity, and livelihood. Even when South Asian migrants engaged strategies of settlement, marriage, and family formation, their ties con-tinued to be vulnerable to state intervention and repudiation. Little by little, after the 1940s, the explicit racial infrastructure that denied marriage, property ownership, immigration, and naturalization was chipped away. However, the price of incorporation into the broader U.S. nation was a normalization that would convert some foreign migrants into citizens if they could contain their national allegiance and demon-strate monogamous marriage and middle-class family life.[50]

NOTES

1. This essay excerpts revised text from Nayan Shah, *Stranger Intimacy: Making the Legal Borderlands of North America* (Berkeley: University of California Press, 2011). I am grateful for the engagement and editorial suggestions of members of the editorial collective, particularly Sujani Reddy and Vivek Bald. This essay benefited from discussion with faculty and students at the Heidelberg Univer-sity, University of Manitoba, and University of Texas at El Paso.

2. "In the Matter of the Estate of Julio Jubala," Supreme Court of New Mexico, No. 4137, pp. 201–203.

3. Adam McKeown, *Melancholy Order: Asian Migration and the Globalization of Borders* (New York: Columbia University Press, 2008). Sunil Amrith, "Tamil Diasporas across the Bay of Bengal," *American Historical Review* 114 (2009): 547–572. Hugh Tinker, *A System of Slavery: Export of Indian Labor Overseas* (London: Oxford University Press, 1974).

4. Radhika V. Mongia, "Historicizing State Sovereignty: Inequality and the Form of Equivalence," *Comparative Studies in Society and History* 49 (2007): 384–411. Sunil Amrith, *Migration and Diaspora in Modern Asia* (Cambridge: Cambridge University Press, 2011). Marilyn Lake and Henry Reynolds, *Drawing the Global*

Colour Line: White Man's Countries and the International Challenge of Racial Equality (Cambridge: Cambridge University Press, 2008). China (in 1888) and Japan (in 1896) introduced passports for selected travelers in order to regain control over the demeaning U.S. legislation denying entry to Chinese and Japanese travelers and immigrants.

5. Moon Ho Jung, *Coolies and Cane* (Baltimore: Johns Hopkins University Press, 2005). Gunther Peck, "Reinventing Free Labor: Immigrant Padrones and Contract Laborers in North America," *Journal of American History* 83 (1996): 848–871.

6. Erika Lee, *At America's Gates: Chinese Immigration during the Exclusion Era 1882–1943* (Chapel Hill: University of North Carolina Press, 2007). Amy L. Fairchild, *Science at the Borders: Immigrant Medical Inspection and the Shaping of the Modern Industrial Labor Force* (Baltimore: Johns Hopkins University Press, 2003). Nayan Shah, *Contagious Divides: Epidemics and Race in San Francisco's Chinatown* (Berkeley: University of California Press, 2001). McKeown, *Melancholy Order*.

7. "Compulsory Passport Regulation," *Proceedings A*, June 1917, nos. 8–22. Mongia, "Historicizing State Sovereignty." Lake and Reynolds, *Drawing the Global Colour Line*.

8. Martha Gardner, *The Qualities of a Citizen, Women, Immigration and Citizenship, 1870–1965* (Princeton: Princeton University Press, 2005), p. 2.

9. McKeown, *Melancholy Order*, pp. 1–4. John Torpey, *The Invention of the Passport: Surveillance, Citizenship and the State* (Cambridge: Cambridge University Press, 2000).

10. Mae Ngai, *Impossible Subjects: Illegal Aliens and the Making of Modern America* (Princeton: Princeton University Press, 2004). Lee, *At America's Gates*. Kelly Lyttle Hernandez, *MIGRA! A History of the U.S. Border Patrol* (Berkeley: University of California Press, 2010).

11. "In the Matter of the Estate of Julio Jubala," pp. 201–203.

12. Karam Singh National Archives San Bruno (hereafter NASB), RG 85 Arriving Investigations, Box 731, File 12924/4-9. Inder Singh, RG 85, Box 731, File 12924/4-6. Inder Singh, RG 85, Box 736, File 12973/14-1. Julian Go and Anne L. Foster, eds., *The American Colonial State in the Philippines: Global Perspectives* (Durham, NC: Duke University Press, 2003). Paul Kramer, *The Blood of Government: Race, Empire and the United States and the Philippines* (Chapel Hill: University of North Carolina Press, 2006).

13. W. C. Hopkinson to Zurbrick, Officer of Inspector in Charge, Vancouver, February 24, 1912, National Archives II, College Park, Maryland (hereafter NARA II), RG 85, File 52903/110A. Daniel J. Keefe to Warner A. Parker, Washington DC, January 26, 1914, NARA II, RG 85, File 52903/110D.

14. Letter from Ellis Bruler, Immigration Commissioner, Seattle to Immigration Service, Washington, DC, March 29, 1913 NARA II, RG 85, File 53173/40.

15. "Sound Port to Be Strict with Hindus," *Tacoma Ledger*, June 26, 1913. In re Rhagat Singh et al. No. 15,479; In re Sundar Singh et al., No. 15,480, District Court Northern District California, First Division, 209 F. 700.

16. Dorothy Fujita Rony, *American Workers, Colonial Power: Philippine Seattle and the Transpacific West 1919-1941* (Berkeley: University of California Press, 2002). Carmen Teresa Whalen and Victor Vazquez-Hernandez, eds., *The Puerto Rican Diaspora: Historical Perspectives* (Philadelphia: Temple University Press, 2005).

17. Natha Khan, NASB, RG 85, Box 764, File 13145/5-5.

18. Ibid.

19. Prem Singh, NASB, RG 85, Box 735, File 12973/8-1.

20. Ibid.

21. "In the Matter of the Estate of Julio Jubala," pp. 201–203.

22. British Library India Office Records, L P &J/8/278, Collection 108/28/A, pp. 11–15, 22–33, 328–335, 469–472, 546–548, 559–563, 625–644, 748–749, 767–769, 776–777; L P&J/8/280, pp. 8–10.

23. John D. Kelley and Martha Kaplan, "Legal Fictions after Empire," in *The State of Sovereignty: Territories, Laws, Populations*, ed. Douglas Howland and Luise White (Bloomington: Indiana University Press, 2009), pp. 169–195. Claude Markovits, *The Global World of Indian Merchants, 1750–1947: Traders of Sind from Bukhara to Panama* (Cambridge: Cambridge University Press, 2000).

24. Padmavati Chandra interview transcript, November 18, 1922, pp. 1–6, 27–71, Box 4, Folder 4:1, University of California Bancroft Library, 2002/78 South Asians in North America Collection.

25. NARA II, RG 85, Files 52320/1 and 52320/1A.

26. L P&J/12/211, File 943/1924, pp. 45–48.

27. *Hindustan Ghadar*, vol. 1, pt. 2 April 4, 1914, Box 7, Folder 21, UC Bancroft Library, 2002/78 South Asians in North America Collection.

28. Correspondence between Godrey Fisher, British Consulate (LA), to Gerald Campbell, SF Consulate, July 30, 1924, L P&J/12/211, File 943/1924, pp. 10–13, 16–18, British Library, India Office Collection (hereafter BL IOC).

29. *San Francisco Examiner*, August 2, 1928.

30. Lee, *At America's Gates*; Kitty Calavita, "The Paradoxes of Race, Class, Identity and 'Passing': Enforcing the Chinese Exclusion Acts, 1882–1910," *Law and Social Inquiry* 25 (2000): 1–40. Julian Lim, "Chinos and Paisanos: Chinese Mexican Relations in the Borderlands," *Pacific Historical Review* 79 (February 2010): 50–85. Theresa Alfaro Velcamp, *So Far from Allah, So Close to Mexico: Middle Eastern Immigrants in Modern Mexico* (Austin: University of Texas Press, 2007).

31. Letter from Consulate, SF to Chilton, Charge D'Affaires, British Embassy, June 25, 1928, L P &J/12/202, pp. 90–93, BL IOC.

32. Letter from G. E. Ferard to undersecretary of Foreign Office, March 2, 1917, L P&J/12/211 File 943/1924, pp. 33–35, BL IOC.

33. Weekly Report Intelligence Bureau, Government of India, December 23, 1926; letter from the British Legation in Mexico to Vasquez Vela, Immigration Department, Ministry of the Interior, May 23, 1927; letter from Reed Paige Clark, American Consular Service to J. B. Browne, British Consul, Mexico City, May 16, 1927; memo from J. B. Browne, Consulate General, Mexico City, May 11, 1927L P&J/12/211 File 943/1924, pp. 41–42, 44, BL IOC.

34. "Findings of Fact and Conclusions of Law of Soledad G. Jubala and J. F. Nevares" (February 15, 1935), pp. 35–36. In the Matter of the Estate of Julio Jubala." U.S. Bureau of Immigration and Naturalization, Declaration of Intention, of Julius Jubala, December 11, 1915, p. 243.

35. Joan Jensen, "Farm Families Organize Their Work, 1900–1940," in *Essays in Twentieth Century New Mexico History*, ed. Judith Boyce De Mark (Albuquerque: University of New Mexico Press, 1994), pp. 13–28. Ira G. Clark, "The Elephant Butte Controversy: A Chapter in the Emergence of Federal Water Law," *Journal of American History* 61 (1975): 1006–1033. Paul A. Lester, "History of the Elephant Butte Irrigation District" (master's thesis, New Mexico State University, 1977).

36. U.S. Bureau of Immigration and Naturalization, Declaration of Intention of Julius Jubala, December 11, 1915, p. 243, Dona Ana County Court House, Las Cruces, New Mexico.

37. Record of Marriage between Julio Jubala and Maria Fierro on 19th November 19, 1917, recorded in the Dona Ana County, New Mexico, Marriage Record Book Number 4, p. 520. According to these records, Julio Jublio was born in "Las Indias" on July 22, 1890.

38. For further elaboration on the marriages, family, and property disputes of Julio Jubala/Jawala Singh, see Nayan Shah, "Adjudicating Intimacies in U.S. Frontiers," in *Haunted by Empire: Race and Colonial Intimacies in North American History*, ed. Ann Laura Stoler (Durham, NC: Duke University Press, 2006).

39. "In the Matter of the Estate of Julio Jubala," pp. 82–84.

40. Karen Leonard, *Making Ethnic Choices: California's Punjabi-Mexican Families* (Philadelphia: Temple University Press, 1994), 63. Eric V. Meeks, *Border Citizens: The Making of Indians, Mexicans and Anglos in Arizona* (Austin: University of Texas Press, 2007).

41. Leonard, *Making Ethnic Choices*, p. 95.

42. Gerardo Renique, "Race, Region, and Nation: Sonora's Anti-Chinese Racism and Mexico's Postrevolutionary Nationalism, 1920s–1930s," in *Race and Nation in Modern Latin America*, ed. Nancy P. Appelbaum, Anne S. Macpherson, and Karin Alejandra Rosemblatt (Chapel Hill: University of North Carolina Press, 2033), pp. 211–236. Erika Lee, "Orientalisms in the Americas: A Hemispheric Approach to Asian American History," *Journal of Asian American Studies* 8 (2005): 235–256. Velcamp, *So Far from Allah, So Close to Mexico*.

43. Leonard, *Making Ethnic Choices*.

44. File of "Dhillon, Felicita Soto," NASB, RG 85, File 30348/3-2, Box 2989. Dhillon, Tanh (John), NASB, RG 85, File 30348/3-5, Box 2989. Dhillon, Besanta Sigh, NASB, RG 85, File 30348/3-4, Box 2989. Dhillon, Ramon, NASB, RG 85, File 20248/3-6, Box 2989.

45. Western Union Telegram in file dated March 13, 1950, INS Dhillon, Jak Singh NASB, RG 85, File 30348/3-3, Box 2989.

46. Ngai, *Impossible Subjects*. Gardner, *Qualities of a Citizen*.

47. Singh, Sher, Folders 53 and 54 Carton 1, Wayne Collins Papers, Bancroft Library BANC MSS 78/177.

48. Meeks, *Border Citizens*, 113–114, 272.

49. Writ of Habeas Corpus, Sher Singh v. Irving F. Nixon, Southern Division of the U.S. District Court for the Northern District of California (1947); marriage certificates and correspondence in Singh, Sher, Folders 53 and 54, Carton 1, Wayne Collins Papers, Bancroft Library BANC MSS 78/177.

50. This striking effect has been astutely analyzed in immigration law and bureaucratic practice in the United States by Margot Canaday, *The Straight State: Sexuality and Citizenship in Twentieth Century America* (Princeton: Princeton University Press, 2009). Siobhan B. Somerville "Sexual Aliens and the Racialized State: A Queer Reading of the 1952 U.S. Immigration and Nationality Act," in *Queer Migrations: Sexuality, U.S. Citizenship, and Border Crossings*, ed. Eithne Luibhéid and Lionel Cantú (Minneapolis: University of Minnesota Press, 2005). Chandan Reddy, "Asian Diasporas, Neoliberalism, and Family: Reviewing the Case for Homosexual Asylum in the Context of Family Rights," *Social Text* 84–85, vol. 23, nos. 3–4 (2005): 101–119.

2

Repressing the "Hindu Menace"

Race, Anarchy, and Indian Anticolonialism

SEEMA SOHI

We are not anarchists, but republicans. That is why the British Government is in such fear of our purely ethical and educational work. Had we been "anarchists" we would have openly said so....We aim at nothing less than the establishment in India of a republic, a government of the people, by the people, for the people in India.[1]
—Ram Chandra

When immigration inspectors in San Francisco arrested the prominent Indian radical Har Dayal on March 25, 1914, as an "undesirable alien" whose alleged adherence to anarchist doctrines meant that he was in the United States in violation of immigration laws, Dayal promptly stated that his arrest was not an "immigration case" but a "political question." Dayal believed that he was being targeted by U.S. officials, whom he accused of complying with the requests of British imperial authorities, because of his role "as one of the most active and determined leaders of the revolutionary movement in northern India."[2] Dayal was an active figure in radical politics in the San Francisco Bay Area and the broader Pacific Coast—where he regularly delivered lectures about an India free of British rule and expressed his vision of working-class solidarity before audiences including the Industrial Workers of the World

(IWW). He was one of the leaders of the Ghadar Party, a revolutionary anticolonial group founded in 1913 that called for the overthrow of British rule through armed revolution.

While Dayal's arrest certainly appeased British officials, the Bureau of Immigration had its own reasons for going after him. At the same time that Indians were exploiting American political ideals and the United States' reputation as a hospitable place for those seeking freedom and democracy, the United States was on its way to becoming Britain's successor as the global hegemonic power. During the first two decades of the twentieth century, in addition to formulating exclusionary practices through racially discriminatory immigration laws, the U.S. state also targeted "foreign agitators" who were, in the words of Representative John Raker of California, making the country a "hotbed of revolution" by using it as a base to organize radical political movements both domestically and abroad.[3] In the years leading up to the First World War, antiradicalism and calls for Indian exclusion were deeply intertwined. Bureau of Immigration files, surveillance reports, and congressional hearings attest to the activism of Indian anticolonialists and the vigilance and scrutiny of the states that monitored them. Together, U.S. and British officials appealed to regional, national, and transnational practices and policies of anti-Asian racism and ideological antiradicalism and cast Indian anticolonialists as a "Hindu menace"—a distinctly antiradical racial formation that linked "aliens" and "radicals" and, in the eyes of U.S. officials, necessitated Indian exclusion and deportation.[4]

These interimperial exchanges between U.S. and British officials spurred a series of critical writings by Indian radicals in North America and across the world, who articulated radical critiques revealing the contradictions between the United States' exceptionalist claims as the global defender of liberty and equality and the "special relationship" it maintained with Britain as manifested in its cooperative surveillance efforts and repression of Indian anticolonialism.[5] By arguing that "the yearnings of the oppressed for a measure of political freedom always appear 'anarchistic' to the oppressor," Indian radicals challenged the ways in which British and U.S. officials invoked anarchy both to target political radicals domestically and to deny nationalist aspirations and democratic hopes to colonized peoples by suppressing independence struggles across the world through military intervention and colonial subjugation.[6] The racialization and criminalization of the "Hindu" enabled the U.S. and British states to defend their imperial presence in Asia while advocating for the implementation of more far-reaching U.S. antiradical and exclusionary immigration laws, which were framed as critical to protecting the country from dangerous and subversive "foreign agitators" and maintaining white supremacy across the globe.

Interimperial Exchanges and "Special Relationships": Surveillance and Repression in North America

The British surveillance apparatus that emerged in India beginning in 1906 followed Indian anticolonialists as they traversed the globe, settling intermittently in cities including London, Paris, and Tokyo, in search of safe havens to organize beyond Britain's imperial reach. After being watched by the British secret service in these cities, many Indians went to the United States, where they mistakenly believed they would find a more congenial space to continue their anticolonial organizing.[7] However, with the cooperation of U.S. and Canadian immigration officials, the British government's surveillance apparatus extended its reach to North America, and British authorities began searching for ways to deport Indian anticolonialists to India, where they would be subject to imperial sedition laws.

In 1908, British officials began circulating reports that "the seditious movement in India [was] being directed from the Pacific Coast" and that British Columbia was a center of "revolutionary agitation."[8] The passage of a racially discriminatory law in Canada during the spring of 1908—known as the "continuous journey" provision—politicized Indian migrants in British Columbia, who began linking racial discrimination in North America to their status as colonized subjects. The law declared it illegal for any immigrant to enter Canada who did not arrive by continuous journey from his country of birth or citizenship. Because there were no steamship lines sailing directly from ports in India to the western Canadian provinces, the law made it, in the words of one British official, "practically impossible for the ordinary Indian labourer to enter Canada."[9] In January 1909, the Canadian government, prompted by British concerns that Indian agitators were making "strenuous efforts" to turn the resentment of Indian migrants "against the Canadian immigration laws into active hostility to the British Government," hired William C. Hopkinson to begin monitoring Indians in British Columbia.[10]

Hopkinson began his surveillance work in Vancouver, where he soon heard reports from U.S. immigration officials in the city that Indians from British Columbia were manufacturing "bombs and other explosives to be used by their countrymen against the British Government" and applying for "admission to the United States for the purpose of promoting rebellion against the British Empire."[11] This led Hopkinson to begin watching Indians in British Columbia as well as in the Pacific Coast states. Hopkinson had strong allies in U.S. immigration offices for whom he offered his translating services in exchange for free entry into the United States for himself and Indian informants.[12] Believing that the U.S. antianarchy law would be the most effective way to rid the country of "Hindu agitators," U.S. and British officials built deportation cases for prominent Indian radicals initially by casting them as anarchists.

According to the 1903 Immigration Act, "anarchists, or persons who believe in, or advocate, the overthrow by force or violence the government of the United States, or of all government" were to be excluded from the United States. National hysteria about anarchism began after the assassination of President William McKinley on September 6, 1901, by the anarchist Leon Czolgosz. Although Czolgosz was an American citizen, U.S. officials used his Polish descent to add anarchists to the list of excludable immigrants, effectively fusing images of the "alien" and the "radical" in the American consciousness.[13] The specter of bomb-throwing radicals assassinating officials across Europe and the United States caught the attention of the U.S. Congress. For twenty-five years, beginning with the assassination of Czar Alexander II in 1891, officials and public figures in France, Italy, Austria, Portugal, Spain, the United States, Greece, Serbia, Russia, and Britain had been targeted by anarchists and, later, nationalists, who saw themselves performing on a global stage and challenging the foundations of the imperial-capitalist world.[14] Congress's response to McKinley's assassination was to create an immigration law that legitimized the "exclusion, deportation, and non-naturalization of all immigrant anarchists" and that treated foreigners as the potential bearers of anarchist and revolutionary ideologies, a legacy that would have devastating consequences for radicals for years to come.[15] The 1903 act provided a crucial foundation for the antiradical and exclusionary immigration laws that would follow over the next two decades by giving federal officials the authority to punish individuals based solely on political beliefs and associations.

The first U.S.-based Indian anticolonialist that Hopkinson attempted to deport under the antianarchy law was Taraknath Das. As a university student in Bengal, Das had been immersed in the antipartition movement until 1905, when the British Indian government put out a warrant for his arrest.[16] After briefly trying to organize Indian students at the University of Tokyo, Das arrived in Seattle on July 16, 1906, at the age of twenty-two. He was the first Indian migrant to claim asylum in the United States as a political refugee escaping tyrannical British rule in India. Having little money, he worked as an unskilled laborer before making his way to Berkeley, where he established the Indian Independence League and started a free evening school where migrants could learn English and American history in order to pass naturalization tests. By 1907, the league had fallen apart, and Das began working as an interpreter for the U.S. Immigration Service in Vancouver. Closely observing immigration inspections, Das coached arriving migrants on how to answer questions during the examination, protested the discriminatory conduct of immigration officials, and helped Indians file habeas corpus petitions.[17]

In early 1908, Das published the first issue of *Free Hindusthan*, a bimonthly journal that encouraged Indians to resist exclusion in Canada and warned the British government that continued injustice against Indians would lead to "an upheaval which will rend the Empire into pieces."[18] Canadian official Thomas McInnes forwarded copies of *Free Hindusthan* from Vancouver to Ottawa and London, warning that the intention of Das's publication was to "make the government hesitate in any policy of exclusion or even restriction by threat of revolt in India."[19] The anti-British rhetoric of the *Free Hindusthan* alarmed British officials, who immediately pressed for its suppression, prompting Canadian authorities to begin monitoring Das and intercepting his mail.[20] In the late spring of 1908, sensing that the political environment in Canada was becoming too repressive and realizing "the difficulty of working freely in a British Dominion," Das moved his operation to Seattle, where he continued printing *Free Hindusthan* on the presses of the

Seattle Socialists. He then began delivering lectures calling for the end of British rule to Indian workers in labor camps and lumber mills along the Pacific Coast.[21]

Within a few months, Das enrolled in Norwich University, a military college in Northfield, Vermont, where he continued to denounce the oppressive policies of the British Empire. Canadian and British surveillance followed Das across the country as officials became convinced that his intention was to study military engineering in order to make bombs that would aid his cause to overthrow British rule in India. British ambassador James Bryce in Washington, DC, grew so concerned that Das would attract more Indians to Norwich that he put pressure on the university to prohibit "Hindu agitators" from enrolling. Insisting that British officials could rely upon the United States to protect imperial interests, British military attaché Lieutenant Colonel B. R. James assured the India Office that U.S. authorities would "always be in sympathy with us in matters of this kind, as they have an idea that the education which they are now giving to the Filipinos may tend to breed the same class of agitator there." Within less than a year, the university expelled Das for his anti-British speeches.[22] Appealing to a shared fear of and mutual opposition to the threat that anticolonial movements in Asia and the Pacific posed to their overseas interests, British and U.S. officials cast Das and the Indians he might attract to Norwich as "Hindu agitators" bent on military training.

After his expulsion from Norwich, Das went to New York, where George Freeman, the Irish leader of the anti-British movement in the United States and editor of the *Gaelic American*, offered his press to Das to continue printing *Free Hindusthan*. Within a couple of years, Das would cease publication due to lack of funds, but not before the distribution of 2,000 copies of his journal worldwide.[23] The appearance of *Free Hindusthan* in India in the summer of 1910 caught the attention of American diplomats there who expressed sympathy with British anxieties over Indian anticolonial agitation and warned the State Department of Indian political activities in the United States. In June 1910, for example, W. H. Michael, the American consul general in Calcutta, wrote to the assistant secretary of state to discuss his correspondence with C. R. Cleveland, the inspector general of the Criminal Investigation Department of India. Cleveland had forwarded to Michael copies of what he described as Taraknath Das's "revolutionary and anarchical paper" and asked Michael if it would be possible to have such radical publications, which were beyond British reach, "suppressed by the friendly Governments which have been made places of refuge for such men as those publishing the 'Hindusthan.'"[24]

Though Michael's inquiry did not lead to the suppression of *Free Hindusthan*—there was no law to prevent Das and other Indian radicals from printing their revolutionary papers in the United States—American diplomats in India continued to keep the State Department informed about the activities of Indian anticolonialists in the United States. Less than two months later, Michael again wrote to the secretary of state's office reporting that when Indians applied to his office with a view of going to the United States, he questioned them "to determine whether they were in sympathy with sedition in India or not."[25] Since 1908, immigration officials had questioned Indian migrants seeking entry to the United States about their stand on "organized government" and whether they had "heard of the plots in India to upset the present government."[26] Thus, examinations of incoming Indians before they even left for the United States became an important tool to advance antiradicalism.

In the late spring of 1914, Henry D. Baker of the American consulate in Bombay wrote to the political secretary of the government of India to express his concerns about reports that a "flood of literature from California" published by Indian revolutionaries was regularly arriving in Bombay and that the Ghadar Party was "training" Indian revolutionaries "to wage war against the English and dream of mutiny."[27] In June 1914, Baker received a letter from the Bombay police commissioner, who wrote that he "would be conferring a great benefit upon the Criminal Intelligence Department" if he would convince officials in Washington "to look closely into this matter, which forms a source of continual anxiety to the Government of India." In addition, Cleveland, who was then the director of the Criminal Intelligence Department in Simla, wrote to Baker to stress that the British imperial government had "been put to a good deal of inconvenience by the transmission through the post of a great quantity of anarchistic literature emanating from San Francisco, where it is manufactured by a group of seditious Indians, who seem to [have] become intoxicated by the freedom of restraint which they are allowed to enjoy in the United States."[28]

By the late summer of 1914, Baker assured British officials in India that, as the consul at Bombay, he had "an important duty" to promptly report to the U.S. government "any individuals who may leave this port for the United States, and are known to be anarchists." Baker stressed that U.S. immigration laws should exclude "any anarchists or persons who believe in or advocate the overthrow by force or violence of the Government of the United States, or of all government." He went on to argue that "by the term 'all government' is apparently meant, the government not merely of the United States, but *of any country in the world*," thus framing Indian opposition to British rule as potentially both anti-American and anarchistic. Baker requested that the British Secret Service Department send him "due notice of any persons who may be leaving here for the United States at any time, and who may be suspected or known to be anarchists."[29] Baker would then transmit this information to the government of the United States with the hope that it would "enforce its immigration laws accordingly."[30] Michael and Baker's correspondence with State Department officials and British officials in India illustrates that American diplomats were aiding British efforts to repress Indian anticolonialism abroad by seeking to forbid any Indian with anti-British leanings from leaving India and then encouraging immigration officials to use the antianarchy law to prevent the landing of those who made it to U.S. immigration stations.

Building the Case against Dayal and Indian Anticolonialism

Ultimately, Hopkinson was unable to prove that Taraknath Das was an anarchist. Nonetheless, he continued to believe that the antianarchy law would be the most effective way to deport Indian anticolonialists in the United States. Hopkinson first traveled to San Francisco in the fall of 1911 to meet with immigration officials at Angel Island about Das and returned the following year, alarmed by reports of a "Nation Day" celebration organized by Indian students at the University of California, Berkeley, during which students and their supporters delivered speeches demanding Indian independence. Dayal, who had been the target of British surveillance in England, India, and France, first came to Hopkinson's attention at this time; since arriving in the United States, he was undetected by officials.

Raised in an intellectual environment among a family of lawyers, Dayal had been a brilliant student in India. The government of India awarded him a scholarship in 1905 to attend Oxford University in England, and like many Indians who traveled to Britain for higher education, he was expected to return to India and enter government service upon completion of his studies. Though he attended Oxford for more than two years, he resigned his scholarship before finishing his program in protest against British rule in India.[31] He then briefly returned to India to speak "against the despotic and predatory" British government but left after only six months due to "repressive laws and spies [that] were making further work impossible within the country."[32] Dayal returned to London in August 1908 but soon went to Paris, where he joined other Indian nationalists and met up with Egyptian nationalists and Russian revolutionaries. After a couple of years he left for Martinique, and after a few weeks there went on to Puerto Rico before finally arriving in New York on February 9, 1911.

Dayal studied Buddhism at Harvard and soon met Teja Singh, who called his attention to the Indian laborers on the Pacific Coast struggling for racial and economic equality.[33] Singh had previously taught at Khalsa College in Amritsar, Punjab, and had enrolled in the Teachers College at Columbia University in July 1908. In April 1911, Dayal left for California, believing he could lead Indian workers in the cause for Indian independence. He worked briefly as a lecturer for Stanford University while also meeting with other radicals in the San Francisco Bay Area, where he became secretary of the Socialist Radical Club, an organization that regularly held meetings to discuss socialism, feminism, and social change.[34] In January 1912, Har Dayal and Jawala Singh, a prosperous farmer from the San Joaquin Valley of California also known as the "Potato King," established the Guru Gobind Singh Scholarship to fund students from India to attend the University of California in Berkeley, in the hopes that they would return to India and use both their practical training and their exposure to democratic governments abroad to contribute to the growing movement for political and economic independence.[35] A group of mill workers in Oregon who had been organizing weekly gatherings to discuss their own experiences with economic exploitation and racial discrimination in the lumber mills of the Pacific Northwest since 1912 called on Har Dayal to join them in the spring of 1913. Out of these meetings emerged the Ghadar Party, the most revolutionary group of Indian migrants to organize outside of India during the early twentieth century.[36] Theorizing economic exploitation and racial exclusion—in the United States and white settler territories across the British Empire—and colonial subjugation as inextricably linked, the Ghadar Party's meetings in Oregon that summer were the catalyst for the emergence of a radical anticolonial politics in North America, one that was rooted in calls for the overthrow of British imperial rule through armed struggle.

Dayal's involvement with various radical labor and political groups on the Pacific Coast—particularly the IWW, whose radical labor organizing had made it the target of U.S. surveillance and repression since the group's emergence in 1905—and his role as one of the leaders of the Ghadar Party made him an easy target for British and U.S. officials. An anti-Indian exclusionary movement along the Pacific Coast was already well under way. A series of congressional hearings around the issue of Asian exclusion during the early decades of the twentieth century referred repeatedly to the successful passage of exclusionary legislation in Canada, Natal, and Australia, as legislators and immigration authorities insisted the United States pass similar legislation to confront the impending "emergency" of the "Hindu invasion." Frustrated by the lack of legislation to exclude Asians, U.S. immigration officials at both local and federal levels took it upon themselves to restrict Indian migration. Immigration inspectors relied on a clause of the immigration law that allowed them to exclude any migrant they deemed "likely to become a public charge" to prohibit the entry of large numbers of Indians beginning in 1908. By 1909, immigration officials were excluding 50 percent of Indians seeking entry to the United States not through exclusionary legislation but through executive restriction.[37] Within a few years, authorities were pointing to Dayal and the Ghadar Party's radical anticolonial politics to further justify calls for Indian exclusion.

By January 1913, Hopkinson was regularly traveling to San Francisco and meeting with British consul general Andrew Carnegie Ross, who warned him about the growing "sedition" movement among Indian students at UC Berkeley. Hopkinson then met with U.S. Department of Justice special agent Don S. Rathbun, who arranged to monitor all mail to and from India that was moving through the Berkeley and San

Francisco post offices. Finally, Hopkinson met with U.S. immigration officials in San Francisco, who assured him they would be happy to deport "Hindu agitators" if sufficient evidence was produced that they had violated the nation's immigration laws.[38] Hopkinson began regularly attending Dayal's public addresses, which he described as full of ideas espousing "socialism, anarchism, and all matters pertaining to political agitation," and spent the next year gathering materials so that U.S. officials could deport Dayal as an anarchist.[39]

In June 1913, Hopkinson asked John Clark to send U.S. immigration officers to a series of lectures that Dayal—whom he now regularly referred to as a "notorious Hindu revolutionist and anarchist"—planned to deliver in the Pacific Northwest that summer to gather intelligence that would build a deportation case against Dayal.[40] At Hopkinson's request, immigration inspectors in Seattle, Portland, and San Francisco attended Dayal's lectures that summer and fall and reported back to the commissioner general of immigration, Anthony Caminetti, that Dayal had spoken about revolutionaries in France and Russia as well as the IWW in the United States. To Hopkinson and U.S. immigration inspectors, Dayal's statements and the venues in which he delivered them were proof of his anarchist beliefs.[41]

Pacific Coast immigration inspectors exploited Dayal's and Oregon-based mill workers' minor affiliations with the IWW to push exclusionary, antiradical agendas. Astoria immigration inspector Charles H. Reily insisted that "*most* of the members of the Hindu nationalist party were also I.W.W.'s," which to him "was evidence of their proficiency in the art of blowing people up."[42] Public fears and hysteria about the dangers of the IWW were easily transferred to "Hindu agitators," who were now coming to play an important role in the federal government's antiradical imagination. According to Reily, Indian migrants were extremely critical of cooperation between British officials and U.S. immigration authorities and were particularly hostile toward Hopkinson, who was often vilified at Indian political meetings and whose close relationships with U.S. immigration and Justice Department officials highlighted the interactions between the two states and their manipulations of U.S. immigration and antiradical laws to repress Indian anticolonialism.

By the summer of 1913, U.S. officials were paying close attention to Indian anticolonialists, who had now begun challenging U.S. imperialist aspirations as well. In December 1910, Indians who gained legal entry to the Philippines began sailing into Seattle and San Francisco insisting that, because they were simply "traveling from one part of the United States to another," they had a right to be landed on the U.S. mainland.[43] While U.S. immigration inspectors immediately issued deportation orders to the migrants, they would discover that deporting them was not so simple, for these men arrived not from a foreign port but from a U.S. territory. The political mobilization of Indians around these cases prompted U.S. officials to warn that Indian migration was taking on a dangerous political dimension in which Indians were challenging and exploiting immigration policies for their own radical agendas.[44] In June 1913, the secretary of labor amended immigration policy with regard to migration from U.S. imperial territories without congressional approval, making it nearly impossible for Indians to gain entry to the U.S. mainland from the Philippines. The antiradical imperatives of the federal government and the Bureau of Immigration's efforts to restrict "undesirable" immigration were reflected and reinforced through the Philippines cases and would be extended even further over the next decade, culminating in the passage of a series of exclusionary and politically repressive immigration laws between 1917 and 1924.

In August 1913, Hopkinson reported that he had received information from an Indian informant, Henry Edward Pandion, about anarchist activity among Indian migrants on the Pacific Coast. Pandion, a Guru Gobind scholarship winner–turned–informant who British consul general Andrew Carnegie Ross had introduced to Hopkinson in San Francisco, reported that Bhikaiji Rustomji Cama, more commonly known as Madame Cama, "in company with several anarchists is coming to the United States, in a short time . . . to join a Hindu anarchist named Har Dayal."[45] Madame Cama was a leader of Indian nationalists in Europe and editor of the Paris-based revolutionary newspaper *Bande Mataram*. Edited by Har Dayal from 1909 to 1911, *Bande Mataram* was a critical voice for Indian revolution read by Indian anticolonialists across the globe.[46] Hopkinson had been monitoring the connection between Cama and Indians in North America since the summer of 1911, when he began intercepting "seditious literature from France addressed to many of the Hindus" in Vancouver.[47] While Cama's paper was unapologetically anticolonial, Hopkinson's allegations that Cama was an "anarchist" illustrate that officials were using the term to refer to the dangers Indian anticolonialists posed to the stability of imperial governments, rather than to government as such.

By January 1914, San Francisco immigration inspector Samuel Backus, who had been meeting regularly with Hopkinson over the past year, began insisting that Dayal and his "highly revolutionary" and "inflammatory" paper *Ghadar* were connected to the anarchist movement in the United States, and warned that Dayal was "making periodical addresses at various points on the Pacific Coast under the same auspices wherefrom such agitators as Emma Goldman secure their support."[48] In his regular correspondence with Commissioner General Caminetti during the winter of 1914, Backus complained that Indians were giving the San Francisco immigration office "more and more concern as circumstances disclose to us the possible purposes for which at least a large number of them are in the United States," namely, "to foment and foster a revolutionary movement in India."[49] Backus had been criminalizing Indians since assuming his post as immigration commissioner at Angel Island. According to Backus, having "been for a long while subjected to a very careful supervision and rigid Government" under British rule, those "Hindus" that were able to gain entry to the United States were "apt to mistake liberty for license" and become "undesirable if not positively criminal."[50]

Backus sent Caminetti a list of the names and locations of 112 Indian anticolonialists in the United States, suggesting that after setting a precedent with Dayal's case, officials would enact deportation proceedings against other Indians. Additionally, Backus sent Caminetti a transcript of Dayal's famous October 31, 1913, speech at Jefferson Square Hall in San Francisco—which would be the Bureau of Immigration's central piece of evidence against him after his arrest—warning that "Har Dayal has been connected with alleged revolutionary movements in this vicinity for some time and, as will be seen from the speech referred to, he may be considered as anarchistic."[51] Backus included a photograph of a group of Indian students at UC Berkeley who were "supporters" of Ghadar and were "actively engaged in rifle and revolver practice in the hills of Berkeley." In an effort to combat Indian anticolonialism, Backus wrote that the San Francisco immigration office would "scrutinize with the greatest care all Hindu applications for admission in order that we may bring the fullest strength of the immigration laws against those who may be coming to join in the movement referred to."[52] In February 1914, Backus submitted an application for a warrant to arrest Har Dayal as an anarchist.[53]

While U.S., British, and Canadian officials kept their cooperative efforts to repress Indian anticolonialism confidential, Indians in North America began to declare with increasing vehemence that U.S. officials were repressing Indian anticolonialists at the insistence of the British government. Although U.S. immigration authorities insisted that there was no connection between Dayal's role in anti-British organizing and his arrest as an anarchist, the evidence reveals that British officials were deeply involved in Dayal's case.[54] Yet, it was not simply Anglo-American relations that motivated U.S. officials to go after Dayal but the anti-Asian and antiradical imperatives of immigration authorities, who had looked for ways to exclude "Hindus" for years.

"Licking the Boots of England": Indian Critiques of U.S. Imperial Relations

In the days following Dayal's arrest, San Francisco newspapers reported that his case was the outcome of a "nation-wide investigation into the actions of Hindoos" who "preach sedition" against the British government. Rumors quickly spread that Dayal's arrest would be the precedent upon which immigration officials would go after all "Hindoos" in the United States.[55] While Dayal had connections with anarchist and socialist networks across Europe and the United States, he repeatedly insisted that the Ghadar Party had "no connection with any school of anarchism." Many of the Punjabi workers and Sikh veterans who filled the ranks of the Ghadar Party had little involvement in the radical political circles that Dayal moved in. Regardless, the Ghadar Party emerged at an apex of political radicalism in the United States and thus captured the attention of U.S. officials.

Dayal's ruminations on the American labor movement, his praise of Russian revolutionaries and of Japan's victory in the Russo-Japanese War, and his attacks on British rule were the basis of immigration inspector Frank Ainsworth's interrogation of the radical anticolonial leader. Dayal was extremely critical of the American Federation of Labor's (AFL) commitment to the existing economic order and believed workers who sought any kind of substantive change in economic and social conditions were better off joining the ranks of the IWW. Between 1911 and 1914, Dayal spoke frequently before the IWW in the San Francisco Bay Area, where he theorized the condition of the Indian colonial subject through a critique of capitalist development and connected the struggles of Indians to the exploitation of workers around the globe. In contrast to the AFL's inability to locate race and labor relations within an international economic and colonial structure, Dayal and other Indian anticolonialists highlighted the international dimensions of economic exploitation.[56] Linking capital and imperial expansion, Dayal argued for the global solidarity of workers across national and racial lines and encouraged workers to employ "revolutionary tactics" to fight "against the capitalist class."[57] Dayal's anticolonial and anticapitalist articulations coincided with and helped fuel the assumptions of the Justice Department and Bureau of Immigration that the influence of radical labor organizing would be weakened with the deportation of "alien" agitators. Convinced that the ranks of the IWW and other radical groups were filled with foreign agitators, U.S. officials believed that their deportation would restore harmonious labor relations.[58]

Dayal's consistent praise of Russian revolutionaries—from whom he claimed to have derived "inspiration" and whose political writings he was translating for distribution in India—was also of concern to U.S. officials. Years before the Bolshevik revolution of 1917, Indian anticolonialists looked to the struggles of Russian revolutionaries for guidance and inspiration. While comparing Russia to India by emphasizing the corrupt and despotic rule of government officials, the exploitation of peasants, and the ruthless power of the zamindars (landlords), Dayal emphasized in a December 1913 issue of *Ghadar* that the "people of Russia have given birth to new principles, new manners, new ideas, new aspirations, and new enterprises for mankind."[59] Dayal's criticism of the AFL and his exhortation to the American working class to look to Russia rather than the conservative labor movement in North America for guidance and reform, were also cited as proof of his dangerous radical politics by immigration authorities.[60]

Ainsworth also highlighted Dayal's praise of Japan's victory in the Russo-Japanese War in his October 31, 1913, speech in San Francisco, during which Dayal claimed that Japan's victory signaled that the "color barrier is being thrown down everywhere" and thus "opened a new era for the Asiatic races by giving them self-confidence and respect."[61] Hopkinson also expressed concern that fellow Ghadar Party leader Bhagwan Singh had warned the British Empire, as well as its white settler colonies, to "take notice" of the "Japanese victory against Russia."[62] Ghadar Party writings often invoked Japan's victory in the Russo-Japanese War to argue that "the future of humanity depends on the great masses" of Asia and to warn that "the sooner the white people realize that the better."[63] The Immigration Bureau's file on Dayal highlighted *Ghadar* articles that U.S. officials interpreted as a threat to white supremacy, including one issue that discussed the recent comments of a British official who had publicly declared, "I do not like black and yellow men." Whereas Indian newspapers were appalled at the statement, Dayal suggested that such words served as a clear example that British imperialism was rooted in theories of racial superiority. Rather than seeking to have British officials mask such sentiments, Dayal believed that such statements should be highlighted as constitutive of British imperialism and liberalism. Thus, Dayal addressed the British official in the next issue of *Ghadar*, writing, "Our thought with regards to you is the same. You do not like us and we do not like you; therefore, it would be proper for you to go to a distance from before our eyes. Take your white carcass to your cold and barren country, and leave our land for us."[64] Such claims of racial self-determination were certainly alarming to U.S. officials, who interpreted Indian anticolonial critiques as a threat not just to the British Empire but to white supremacy itself.

In the days following his arrest, Dayal articulated a scathing critique of the U.S. Immigration Bureau's complicity with British officials. He blamed his arrest on "British secret service operatives" who had spied on him for months and were "acting through the Democratic administration" in their attempts to "stamp out all revolutionary movements to overthrow the British government" in India. He insisted that his arrest called "public attention to the despicable pro-British subservience of the U.S. Government," which he accused of "licking the boots of England."[65] Finally, Dayal argued that the "sole aim" of *Ghadar* was to highlight the injustices of British rule *in* India, and that it was "simply ridiculous" that he was "being prosecuted in the United States and in the twentieth century because of my ideas. I have broken no laws, and I have not

advocated [the] breaking of any laws. The only overt act I have committed is advocating the overthrow of the British in India by an armed
revolt."[66] However, with the passage of the Immigration Act of 1903,
Congress gave immigration officials the authority to exclude and deport
immigrants precisely because of their political beliefs and associations.

After Dayal's interrogation, Ainsworth released him on $1,000 bail,
and within a month Dayal had fled the United States for Switzerland.[67]
In May 1914, Commissioner General Caminetti acknowledged that
the government had been without jurisdiction to arrest Dayal, as the
three-year statute of limitations expired before the issuance of the warrant. Dayal arrived in New York on February 9, 1911, and the warrant of
arrest was not issued until February 10, 1914. In the eyes of U.S. officials,
Dayal's case was proof that the existing time limits needed to be revised
in order to effectively go after "alien" radicals.[68]

Dayal's critiques of U.S. subservience to England were at once per-
ceptive and limited. In insisting that U.S. officials had arrested him at
the request of the British government, Dayal and other Indian anticolonialists pointed to political repression, immigrant exclusion, and U.S.
cooperation with British imperial interests as evidence of the nonex-
ceptionalism of the United States. After Dayal's arrest, many Indian
migrants began to question America's claim to being the sole repository of justice and liberty, and argued that if Indian migrants could
not engage in anticolonial organizing and publish their "literature of
freedom" in the United States, they would go to "to some other country" where their compatriots were publishing journals without fear of
deportation.[69] At the same time, however, Dayal's critiques of U.S. and
British relations also ignored the racially exclusive antiradical practices
of the U.S. state. The congressional hearings on the issue of "Hindu"
migration that would convene while Dayal's case was pending revealed
that, for immigration and congressional officials, antiradical political
repression and calls for Indian exclusion went hand in hand.

Constructing and Eliminating the "Hindu Menace"

In February 1914, the House Committee on Immigration and Naturalization convened to discuss two pending bills introduced by Representatives John Raker and Denver S. Church of California, both of which

sought to impose severe restrictions on "Hindu laborers." While they initially centered on the question of economic competition and labor, calls for Indian exclusion during the hearings soon became indistinguishable from the committee's concerns over Indian anticolonialism. Insisting that, in the words of committee chairman John Burnett of Alabama, "a great many" of the Indians seeking entry to the United States were "anarchists teaching the principle of the overthrow of government," Representatives Burnett, Raker, and Church of California, and Albert Johnson of Washington, portrayed Indian migrants as fertile ground for the spread of political radicalism and linked their calls for Indian exclusion to the need for greater measures to restrict political radicalism.[70]

Immigration authorities also used the hearings to emphasize the need for an increase in the statute of limitations within which "aliens" could be deported. Special immigration inspector Roger O'Donnell used his testimony to insist that the existing three-year time limit was hindering the ability of U.S. officials to go after undesirable aliens and pushed for more funding, employees, and power for the Bureau of Immigration—the justification for which was, in part, the insidious threat of the "Hindu menace." As the hearings went on, the "menace" that "Hindus" allegedly posed was seamlessly transferred from threats to public health, labor, and the American standard of living to the dangerous and subversive nature of Indian migrants' political activism.

During the final days of the hearings, the congressional committee aggressively questioned Tishi Bhutia Kyawgh Hla, secretary of the Hindustan Association of the United States, about the activities of Dayal as well as the Indian anticolonial movement more broadly. Commissioner General Caminetti had provided Chairman Burnett with details about Dayal's arrest and his radical affiliations, along with copies of Dayal's October 31, 1913, speech, excerpts of which were read during the hearings. Representative Johnson accused Bhutia of belonging to "one of the many organizations in various parts of the world which are interested in fomenting a movement for the overthrow of the British authority in India" and interrogated him about his organization's links to Dayal. Representative Church warned that "the Hindus down in my country, in the interior of California, are . . . acquiring all the knowledge they can so as to be in a position in the future to rebel against the form of government under which they are at the time living." Meanwhile,

Representative Raker claimed that he had a "whole bundle of papers" containing "inflammatory articles and statements that the Hindus in this country and other countries are working for the purpose of gathering all the strength they can with the hope eventually of overthrowing the English Government in India."[71]

Bhutia argued that Indian revolutionary desires to overthrow the British government in India did not translate into a desire to overthrow the American government. Additionally, Bhutia insisted that he, like many other Indians organizing against British rule from the United States, were "Democrats" who were seeking to overthrow the British government and replace it with a democratic form of governance, what Ram Chandra—Dayal's successor as the leader of the Ghadar Party— often called the "United States of India."[72] Although Bhutia advocated passive resistance to achieve his political goals, when pushed by Raker, who insisted that Indians would seek to bring about independence through violence if necessary, Bhutia's pointed response, "You did it in this country," employed a strategy frequently used by the Ghadar Party, which often likened itself to American revolutionaries.[73] Seeking to draw parallels between the Indian struggle for freedom and the American Revolution in his writings, Ram Chandra had also asked the American people to recall "that the founders of this great republic, who accomplished exactly what we hope today for India," were also "stigmatized by the British as 'plotters and seditionists.'" Chandra emphasized the British government's long history of characterizing independence movements as anarchistic, writing that "when the American colonists dumped the British tea overboard in Boston harbor rather than pay an unjust tax thereon, King George III wrathfully exclaimed that such anarchy in America must be suppressed."[74] Yet, as the hearings and the bureau's targeting of Indian anticolonialists made clear, in the eyes of the U.S. state there were few, if any, commonalities between "Hindus" and American revolutionaries. In labeling Indian anticolonialists as a "Hindu menace," U.S. officials refused to acknowledge Indian social, political, and economic subjugation under British colonial rule or to legitimate their calls for the establishment of a democratic government in India. Rather, U.S. and British officials framed Indian revolutionary aspirations not as a legitimate struggle for freedom but as anarchistic rebellion in need of imperial discipline.[75]

Both the 1914 hearings and the Bureau of Immigration's arrest and interrogation of Dayal in the spring of 1914 were important moments in Indian racialization.[76] During the hearings, anti-Asian racism and antiradicalism were inseparable. With little or no effort made to distinguish differences in ideology, Indian anticolonialists were interchangeably described as "anarchists," "agitators," and "IWWs." Although immigration officials were unsuccessful in deporting Dayal and thereby establishing a precedent for the deportation of Indian anticolonialists as anarchists, the significance of Dayal's arrest lies not in disputing whether the anticolonial movement he led had anarchist beliefs or associations but in how immigration and congressional officials cast *all* Indians who challenged the legitimacy of the British imperial government as anarchists who should be monitored, excluded, and expelled.

While U.S. and British attempts to exploit the nation's antianarchy law to repress Indian anticolonialism were ineffective, the specter of the "Hindu menace" continued to haunt legislators, the Immigration Bureau, and Justice and State Department officials. In June 1916, the U.S. attorney general wrote to the secretary of state to express his frustration that while Indian anticolonialists had been under "investigation for a considerable period by this Department," as of yet, "no evidence sufficient to warrant conviction of any violation of the Federal criminal laws has been established."[77] The following year, however, immediately following U.S. entry into the First World War, the Justice Department arrested dozens of Indian anticolonialists. The U.S. state's prosecution of fourteen of those arrested during the sensational and highly publicized "Hindu Conspiracy" trail that convened in San Francisco in November 1917 can be traced back to early 1914 with the arrest of Dayal. Both of these highly politicized and contested moments relied upon the racialization of "Hindus" as a "menace" engaged in a worldwide "conspiracy" of revolt and anarchy. Linked with anarchism and subversive radical political movements, the specter of the "Hindu menace" also contributed to the passage of the 1917 Immigration Act—a piece of legislation that at once increased the statute of limitations for deportation to five years and excluded Indians from the United States through its "barred zone" provision.

Western imperial expansion was intertwined with discourses of anarchy in a dialectical relationship that both legitimated imperial projects and repressed freedom movements that sought to overthrow them.

Antianarchy politics were inextricable from U.S. and British imperial fears of revolutionary anticolonial struggles abroad and domestic fears about anticapitalist struggles. U.S. and British officials cast colonized Asia as both a potential breeding ground for the spread of anarchism and a space in which the threat of anarchism needed to be contained through imperial domination and control. In a U.S. context, the moral panic around anarchism, linked and articulated in part through the alleged threat of the "Hindu," justified demands for the exclusion of racially and politically "undesirable" migrants. Thus, anarchy was indispensable for U.S. and British officials, who used it to justify their own imperial and exclusionary aims. Indeed, just as the specter of anarchy was deployed by U.S. and British officials to justify increasing imperial expansion abroad, the specter of the anarchist, the "Hindu," the "alien agitator," or those deemed otherwise "un-American," justified the expansion of federal intelligence and repression during the first two decades of the twentieth century. By 1914, the racialized figure of the "Hindu agitator" was a vivid symbol of the presence of "alien radicals" whose political organizing was cast as a threat to the very nation itself.

NOTES

1. Ram Chandra, *India against Britain: A Reply to Austin Chamberlain, Lord Harding, Lord Islington, and Others* (San Francisco: Hindustan Ghadar Party, 1916), 23, Box 1, Folder 32. South Asians in North America Collection, Bancroft Library Archives, University of California, Berkeley (hereafter BL).

2. "Har Dayal States His Position: Undergoes Three-Hour Examination before Immigration Authorities," *San Francisco Bulletin* (March 27, 1914), File 53572/92-92A, Records of the U.S. Immigration and Naturalization Service, RG 85, National Archives, Washington, DC (hereafter NA).

3. Representative John Raker of California quoted in "Hearings on the Restriction of Hindu Laborers," Committee on Immigration and Naturalization, House of Representatives, 63rd Cong., 2nd sess. (Washington, DC: Government Printing Office, 1914), 190.

4. For more on the connections between antiradical and exclusionist immigration policy, see William Preston's *Aliens and Dissenters: Federal Suppression of Radicals, 1903–1933* (Urbana: University of Illinois Press, 1963).

5. The idea for tracing these "inter-imperial" dynamics and connections comes from Paul Kramer's "Empires, Exceptions, and Anglo-Saxons: Race and Rule between the British and U.S. Empires, 1880–1910," *Journal of American History* 88, no. 4 (2002): 1315–1353.

6. Ram Chandra, *India against Britain*, 25. For more on the relationship between imperial expansion and anarchism, see Amy Kaplan, *The Anarchy of Empire in the Making of U.S. Culture* (Cambridge: Harvard University Press, 2002).

7. Joan Jensen, *Passage from India: Asian Indian Immigrants in North America* (New Haven: Yale University Press, 1988), 163.

8. "Indian Seditious Movement Directed from the Pacific Coast," *Liverpool Courier* (May 21, 1908). Also see T. R. E. McInnes to Frank Oliver, Minister of the Interior, Ottawa, March 23, 1908, Immigration Central Registry File Series, 1873–1968, RG 76, Volume 384, 536999, Public Archives of Canada (hereafter PAC).

9. Report from the Government of India, Department of Commerce and Industry, March 11, 1909, Calcutta, RG 76, Volume 384, 536999, PAC.

10. Jensen, 163. Also see "Note on the Hindu Revolutionary Movement in Canada" (1919), and "Indian Seditious Movement Directed from the Pacific Coast," *Liverpool Courier* (May 21, 1908), RG 76, Volume 384, 536999, PAC.

11. Everett Wallace, Vancouver, to Commissioner of Immigration, Montreal, January 6, 1909, File 51388/5, RG 85, NA. Also see "Indian Seditious Movement Directed from the Pacific Coast." Also see T. R. E. McInnes, Vancouver, to Frank Oliver, Minister of the Interior, Ottawa, March 23, 1908, RG 76, Volume 384, 536999, PAC.

12. Jensen, 164.

13. Preston, 4.

14. Benedict Andersen, *Under Three Flags: Anarchism and the Anti-colonial Imagination* (London: Verso, 2005), 3.

15. Preston, 30.

16. The partition of Bengal in October 1905 resulted in a national anti-British movement that involved nonviolent and violent protests and boycotts. To deal with growing political agitation, the British Indian government passed a series of politically repressive acts that authorized officials to prohibit political meetings, close newspaper offices that printed seditious articles against the British Indian government, and imprison anyone who delivered speeches on political subjects deemed threatening to British imperial interests. Many of those radicals who arrived in North America during the first decade of the twentieth century fled India after the partition for fear of being arrested under the newly enacted repressive laws.

17. Tapan Mukherjee, *Taraknath Das: Life and letters of a Revolutionary in Exile* (Bengal: National Council of Education, 1997), 9–12.

18. Das quoted in Mukherkee, 15. See also "Note on the Hindu Revolutionary Movement in Canada" (1919), RG 76, Volume 384, 536999, PAC.

19. T. R. E. McInnes to Frank Oliver, March 23, 1908, RG 76, Volume 384, 536999, PAC.

20. Norman Buchignani, Doreen M. Indra, and Ram Srivastava, *Continuous Journey: A Social History of Indians in Canada* (Toronto: McClelland and Steward, 1985), 25.

21. Letter Das wrote to the *Vancouver News-Advertiser*, June 12, 1908, quoted in Mukherjee, 16–17. Also see Jensen, 167.

22. B. R. James quoted in Jensen, 167.

23. Mukherjee, 15. Arun Coomer Bose, "Indian Nationalist Agitation in the United States of America and Canada till the Arrival of Har Dayal in 1911," *Journal of Indian History* 43 (1965): 235.

24. W. H. Michael, American Consulate-General, Calcutta, to the Assistant Secretary of State, Washington, DC, June 23, 1910, Records of the State Department, RG 59, File 845, MG 335, Roll 2, NA.

25. W. H. Michael to the Assistant Secretary of State, August 11, 1910, File 52903/110, RG 85, NA.

26. Board of Special Inquiry Proceedings in the Case of Rajoor Singh, U.S. Immigration Service, Vancouver, B.C., November 30, 1908, File 52269/21, RG 85, NA.

27. American Consulate, Bombay, to Secretary of State, Washington, DC, May 27, 1914, File 845, MG 335, Roll 2, RG 59, NA.

28. Commissioner of Police, Bombay, and Cleveland quoted in Baker to the Secretary of State, August 21, 1914, File 845, MG 335, Roll 2, RG 59, NA.

29. Baker to L. Robertson, Political Secretary to Government, May 27, 1914, File 53572/92-92A, RG 85, NA.

30. American Consulate, Bombay (Baker), to Secretary of State, Washington, DC, May 27, 1914, File 845, MG 335, Roll 2, RG 59, NA.

31. U.S. Department of Labor, Immigration Service, Hearing in the Case of Har Dayal, March 26, 1914, File 53572/92-92A, RG 85, NA.

32. Dayal quoted in "Har Dayal States His Position," *San Francisco Bulletin* (March 27, 1914), File 53572/92-92A, RG 85, NA.

33. Emily C. Brown, *Har Dayal: Hindu Revolutionary and Rationalist* (Tucson: University of Arizona Press, 1975), 85.

34. Jensen, 124, 176.

35. Sirdar Jawala Singh, "The Guru Gobind Singh Sahib Educational Scholarships," Moorland, CA (January 1, 1912), Box 5, Folder 5, BL.

36. Kalyan Kumar Banerjee, *Indian Freedom Movement: Revolutionaries in America* (Calcutta: Jijnasa, 1969), 18. Not every Indian radical in Canada and the United States joined the Ghadar Party—including important figures like Taraknath Das and Saint Nihal Sing—yet U.S., British, and Canadian surveillance structures referred to most radical activities, writings, speeches, and "conspiracies," particularly between 1914 and 1917, as part of the Ghadar movement.

37. U.S. Department of Labor, "Hindu Migration to the U.S.," January 23, 1914, File 52903/110C, RG 85, NA.

38. Hopkinson quoted in W. W. Cory to Sir Joseph Pope, Under-Secretary of State for External Affairs, Ottawa, March 4, 1914, RG 25, Volume 1139, Folder 40, Part 2, PAC. Also see Brown, 131. See also Jensen, 178.

39. Hopkinson quoted in Brown, 132.

40. Hopkinson quoted in John Clark, Office of the Commissioner, Montreal, to Commissioner-General of Immigration, Washington, DC, June 10, 1913, File 53572/92, RG 85, NA.

41. Commissioner-General Anthony Caminetti to Immigration Service, Seattle, June 12, 1913, File 53572/92, RG 85, NA.

42. Charles H. Reily, Immigrant Inspector, Astoria, Oregon, to Acting Inspector in Charge, Portland, Oregon, January 14, 1914, File 53572/92-92A, RG 85, NA, my emphasis.

43. Henry Marshall, brief for all seven aliens, presented to Department of Labor, December 30, 1913, File 53627/89, RG 85, NA.

44. "Hindus Leaving in Hostile Frame of Mind: Some Declare They Are Disgusted with Canada and Will Soon Leave," *Vancouver Province* (December 6, 1913), File 52903/110C, RG 85, NA. Also see Memorandum from Assistant Superintendent of Immigration, Ottawa, January 5, 1914, RG 25, Volume 1138, 1139 Folder 40, PAC.

45. Brown, 131; Hopkinson to undisclosed recipient, August 2, 1913, File 53572/92, RG 85, NA.

46. Maia Ramnath, "Two Revolutions: The Ghadar Movement and India's Radical Diaspora, 1913–1918," *Radical History Review* 92 (2005): 11.

47. Hopkinson to W. W. Cory, August 4, 1911, RG 76, Volume 384, 536999, PAC.

48. Samuel Backus to Commissioner-General Caminetti, January 23, 1914, File 52903/110D, RG 85, NA.

49. Backus to Commissioner-General Caminetti, February 3, 1914, File 53627/67, RG 85, NA.

50. Backus to Secretary of Commerce and Labor, March 12, 1912, File 53396/10, RG 85, NA.

51. Samuel Backus to Commissioner-General Caminetti, January 23, 1914, File 52903/110D, RG 85, NA; Samuel Backus to Commissioner-General Caminetti, January 30, 1914, File 53572/92-92A, RG 85, NA.

52. Backus to Commissioner-General Caminetti, January 23, 1914, File 52903/110D, RG 85, NA.

53. Backus to Immigration Bureau, Washington, DC, February 3, 1914, File 53572/92-92A, RG 85, NA.

54. Memorandum prepared by Commissioner-General Anthony Caminetti, April 4, 1914, File 53572/92-92A, RG 85, NA; Caminetti to Paul Kennedy, Secretary, Friends of Russian Freedom, New York, April 14, 1914, File 53572/92-92A, RG 85, NA.

55. "Hindoo Suspect Is Taken by U.S. Agents," *San Francisco Chronicle* (March 26, 1914), and "Why Har Dayal Is Undesirable," *Daily News*, Santa Barbara, California (March 30, 1914), File 53572/92-92A, RG 85, NA.

56. Maia Ramnath, "Two Revolutions: The Ghadar Movement and India's Radical Diaspora, 1913–1918," *Radical History Review* 92 (Spring 2005): 26.

57. "Extract from a Report Dated January 31, 1913" (author unknown), File 53572/92, RG 85, NA.

58. Preston, 99.

59. "Preparations for the Revolution in Russia," *Ghadar* (December 9, 1913), File 53572/92-92A, RG 85, NA.

60. Extract from a speech delivered by Har Dayal, Jefferson Square Hall, San Francisco, October 31, 1913, File 53572/92-92A, RG 85, NA.

61. Ibid.

62. Hopkinson to unknown recipient, October 20, 1913, RG 76, Volume 384, 536999, PAC.

63. Extract from a speech delivered by Har Dayal in Jefferson Square Hall, File 53572/92-92A, RG 85, NA.

64. *Ghadar*, title and date unknown, File 53572/92-92A, RG 85, NA.

65. "Hindoo Savant Drags Bryan into the Case," *San Francisco Chronicle* (March 29, 1914), File 53572/92-92A, RG 85, NA.

66. "Dayal Denies Adherence to Anarchy," *San Francisco Examiner* (March 28, 1914), File 53572/92-92A, RG 85, NA.

67. "Har Dayal States His Position," *San Francisco Bulletin* (March 27, 1914), File 53572/92-92A, RG 85, NA. Also see Acting Commissioner, Ellis Island, to Commissioner-General of Immigration, May 8, 1914, File 53572/92-92A, RG 85, NA.

68. Department of Labor to Mr. Larned, May 26, 1914. Also see Certificate of Admission of Alien, U.S. Department of Labor, Immigration Service, Ellis Island, April 3, 1914, File 53572/92-92A, RG 85, NA.

69. Har Dayal, *Shabash* (San Francisco: Hindustan Ghadar Party, 1913), 14, Box 2, Folder 2, BL. Also see "Har Dayal States His Position," *San Francisco Bulletin* (March 27, 1914), File 53572/92-92A, RG 85, NA.

70. "Hearings on the Restriction of Hindu Laborers," Committee on Immigration and Naturalization, House of Representatives, 63rd Cong., 2nd sess. (Washington, DC: Government Printing Office, 1914), 164–167.

71. Church quoted in Hearings 82 and 84, Raker on 164–167.

72. Ram Chandra, *India against Britain*, Box 1, Folder, 32, BL

73. "Hearings on the Restriction of Hindu Laborers," Committee on Immigration and Naturalization, House of Representatives, 63rd Cong., 2nd sess. (Washington, DC: Government Printing Office, 1914), 164–167, 172.

74. Ram Chandra, *India against Britain*, Box 1, Folder 32, BL.

75. Kaplan, 117.

76. While the 1923 *United States v. Thind* case is often cited as a critical moment of Indian racialization in that it revealed the fluidity and uncertainty of racial categories, particularly in determining where "Hindus" fit in existing racial categories because of their scientific classification as "Caucasian," I would argue that 1914 was also a critical moment of Indian racialization.

77. U.S. Attorney General to Secretary of State, June 3, 1916, File 845, MG 335, Roll 2, RG 59, NA.

3

Desertion and Sedition

Indian Seamen, Onshore Labor, and Expatriate
Radicalism in New York and Detroit, 1914–1930

VIVEK BALD

The Detroit branch of the United India League of America held a meeting recently when it was announced that the name had been changed to "Independence League of India."...The majority of the [Indian] students at the Michigan University...as well as the lascars, belong to this society. It is stated that the seamen are more enthusiastic than the students "because they don't have to go back to India."
—Confidential dispatch from British consulate, Detroit, to the British embassy, Washington, DC, September 25, 1929

Over the summer months of 1927, the New York–based magazine *Asia* published a three-part autobiographical essay by the expatriate Indian nationalist Sailendranath Ghose. Ghose was well known to many American readers by this time. A decade earlier, his name had been splashed across U.S. newspapers when he and dozens of other Indians were rounded up in New York, Chicago, and San Francisco and charged as part of the "Hindu-German Conspiracy"—a case in which he and his codefendants were accused of working with enemy German agents to smuggle arms through the United States to India to support an armed insurrection against the British.[1] Now, long after the dust had settled, *Asia* magazine had invited Ghose to tell the story of his youth and to describe his entry into nationalist politics. It was an odd venue for such a story. The magazine's pages were normally devoted to articles by amateur Orientalists, describing their journeys through the lands of the mysterious East, and even in this case, Ghose's account of his radicalization as a college student and his narrow escape from British authorities shared space with glossy photographs of temples, pagodas, and art objects and advertisements for tours of Egypt and Morocco. The account itself, however, is perhaps most interesting for its final paragraphs, in which Ghose almost casually revealed a connection between Indian revolutionaries and the world of merchant sailors.[2]

In 1914, Ghose wrote, he had been on the run from the British in his native state of Bengal. After months of keeping one step ahead of the law, moving from village to village on the outskirts of Calcutta, he sought assistance from one of his college professors in the city, and the professor, recognizing that Ghose had to get out of the country, sent him to "a certain stevedore" in an area close to Calcutta's docks. At this point, Ghose recalled, "I changed to Mahommedan dress, began to grow a beard, and went to live in the quarter where the people from the ships pass their time on shore." After several days, he continued, "I was becoming familiar with the atmosphere of ships [and] I was put in touch with a man who supplied outgoing ships with such men as they needed." Soon Ghose had his chance to set out to sea. A ship was leaving for Philadelphia, and Ghose's middleman put into motion what was by then a common ruse used to get men on board ships with no questions asked. The Philadelphia-bound ship had engaged a full Indian crew and was set to leave Calcutta at midnight, when "it was found that two of the men engaged for the stoke-hole were missing." The last-minute defection of these men had been prearranged by Ghose's contact, who now took Ghose and another man to the crew manager and presented them as seamen who were immediately ready to fill the place of the missing engine-room workers. "So I signed on," wrote Ghose, "I do not remember in what name, and before midnight I was aboard the ship…[bound for] America, where perhaps I should have a better chance than there seemed to be for me in India just then."[3] With this, the maritime trade became Ghose's conduit to a new political life in exile—in New York, he would author pamphlets, make public speeches, coordinate shipments of guns back to the subcontinent, make common cause with other expatriate radicals, and drum up support for Indian independence from American liberal writers and politicians.[4]

However, Ghose's story—in which he temporarily transformed himself from an upper-class Hindu physics student into a working-class Muslim sailor in order to escape from Calcutta to the United States—reveals only one side of the nexus between Indian revolutionaries and seamen. The other side consisted of the seamen themselves. By the time of Ghose's journey, tens of thousands of Indian men—predominantly Muslims from rural areas of East Bengal, West Punjab, and the North-West Frontier—were moving around the globe as maritime workers. These men faced British power in its barest form in their everyday work on steamships, and both in port and on ship, they came in contact with other colonial workers—Irish, Arab, African—engaged in struggle against the British.[5] In the 1910s and early 1920s, thousands of Indian seamen were moving on and off the waterfronts of Manhattan, Brooklyn, Staten Island, and New Jersey in their capacity as firemen, stokers, coal passers, and stewards on British vessels. For Sailendranath Ghose and other elite revolutionaries, these men constituted a population into which they could "disappear" in order to resist British attempts at capture. But in New York and other U.S. ports, these seamen were engaged in their own acts of disappearance and resistance—in some cases, deserting their ships in order to escape intolerable labor conditions and find better work onshore, and in other cases, joining the independence struggle and, at great risk, using their mobility as seamen to smuggle pistols and revolutionary pamphlets across the globe.

Asian Americanist scholars have documented in detail the history of Punjabi farmers, mill hands, and revolutionaries on the U.S. and Canadian West Coast. However, little is yet known about this other population of early twentieth-century (im)migrant workers from the subcontinent, nor of the ways their lives became entwined with Indian expatriate nationalism. In the pages that follow, I will begin to address this gap in South Asian American historiography. First, I will examine U.S. archival records to provide a sense of the numbers of Indian seamen who were moving through the port of New York in the 1910s and 1920s, how many were deserting their ships, and where these men were finding work onshore. Next, I will examine the role of a key middleman on the New York City waterfront, the Egyptian boardinghouse keeper Mohammed Abdou, in assisting the desertion of Indian seamen and facilitating their reshipping as clandestine operatives of the Indian nationalist cause. Finally, I will explore the trajectory and transformations of one particular Indian seaman, Amir Haider Khan, who jumped ship in New York in 1918, joined ranks with Ghose's Friends of Freedom for India, and became an emissary of the Ghadar Party. Through his story, I will trace the trajectory of scores of other seamen who lived, worked, and struggled in the United States during his day.

My purpose is not merely to fill in a missing chapter in South Asian American history. I believe that the inclusion of this population of migrants, immigrants, and sojourners challenges a number of previous assumptions about the South Asian presence in the United States in the early decades of the twentieth century. First, their stories demonstrate that South Asian labor migration to the United States was neither limited to the West Coast nor brought to a halt by the 1917 Immigration Act. In the 1910s and 1920s, Indian Muslim seamen were a significant, ongoing presence in East Coast port cities, from Baltimore to Philadelphia, New York, and Boston, and Indian maritime deserters were a smaller but equally constant presence in New York City and in U.S. factory towns stretching from the Eastern Seaboard across the Midwest. The fact that few of these men settled permanently in the United States—that they were primarily sojourners rather than immigrants—does not diminish their importance within the larger narrative of "South Asian America."[6] In fact, they were significant enough as a presence to draw the attention of news writers, British consular officials, U.S. immigration officers and members of Congress, and anti-Asian union leaders.[7]

Indian seamen also constituted an independent and as yet underexamined arena of nationalist activity—one that was connected to the world of Indian expatriate elites but was animated by its own dynamics, in which sailors came to an understanding of the need for Indian freedom through their own experiences of colonial power, inequality and injustice; in which they communicated the need for action to other workers in and on their own terms; and in which they engaged in anti-British activities—particularly the smuggling of various items and materials—that capitalized on their unique mobility as a workforce. As such, their movement through East Coast cities and maritime networks led Indian seamen along potentially different trajectories of politicization, in which they came in contact not only with expatriate elites but also with other colonial and immigrant workers, and other workers of color onshore in the United States, and could thus come to an understanding of the struggle for Indian independence in relation to the struggles of other oppressed and racialized workers.

From Ships' Holds to Factory Floors

The Immigration Act of 1917 is best known within Asian American studies as the legislation that instituted the "Asiatic Barred Zone"—expanding the restrictions of the 1882 Chinese Exclusion Act so that migrants from a geographic swath that took in almost the entire continent of Asia were barred from immigrating to the United States. The 1917 act included another, lesser-known, provision—Section 36—that required shipping companies to report to the authorities at U.S. ports not only all the passengers they were bringing into the country on incoming ships, but all the "alien seamen" they employed on these vessels. This provision made visible, on one ship manifest after the next, a population of Indian workers who had in fact been a regular presence in New York's docklands since at least the turn of the century and who would continue to arrive and depart from the city's waterfront even under Asian exclusion. The numbers are striking. In the years immediately prior to the passage of the 1917 act, Ellis Island passenger manifests only recorded between 50 and 100 Indians arriving at the port of New York each year—mostly students, traders, and other temporary visitors. The following year, after seamen were included in the count, this number jumped into the thousands. In 1917, for example, U.S. authorities recorded roughly 2,100 Indian arrivals in New York; this rose to more than 7,500 in 1918, then continued at around 2,000 per year from 1919 to 1924. The vast majority of these arrivals were the Indian Muslim crew members of incoming steamships. Archival records suggest that in the decade from 1914 to 1924, between 20,000 and 25,000 of these Indian workers moved in and out of New York's dock areas.[8]

For the most part, this was a transient population. The majority of maritime laborers were in port in New York for only a few days, or at most a few weeks, as their ships docked, unloaded, reloaded, and then set back out to sea. Still, the size of the Indian population is significant. The presence of Indian seamen in U.S. ports had long been a source of contention between Britain's Board of Trade, labor unions, and shipping lines, not to mention U.S. immigration officials. Due in large part to the efforts of white British labor unions, a clause had been added to the 1894 British Merchant Shipping Act that forbade British shipping lines from using Indian "lascar" seamen on voyages to any Atlantic port above 38° north latitude during the six "winter" months between October and March.[9] Because Indian maritime workers were paid so much less than their white European counterparts, however, British shipowners had strong economic incentives to use Indian seamen for these routes year-round. In 1902, a group of shipping companies successfully pushed back against the "lascar line" provision of the Merchant Shipping Act, gaining a partial repeal that would allow them to use Indian crews below deck in engine rooms and kitchens.[10] While it left other restrictions in place, ship manifests suggest that this change had substantial consequences for the number of Indian seamen arriving in the banned winter months. Over the course of January 1919, for example, eight British steamships sailed into New York manned by crews from the subcontinent, bringing 450 Indian seamen into port in the dead of winter. The vast majority were Muslim men from Bengal.[11]

Indian seamen, in turn, had their own incentives to leave their ships in New York and seek out better, or higher-paying, work onshore. The opportunities to do this increased during the First World War. In these years, not only were there larger numbers of Indian seamen in circulation on British steamships globally, but when their ships docked in U.S. ports, British lines now found themselves competing with American wartime industries for the labor of Indian and other colonial/immigrant men. Rozina Visram has described a common wartime practice in Britain in which factory owners sent their representatives to the docks in order to poach Indian workers from the ships.[12] The same practice appears to have existed in New York, and perhaps in ports farther south, such as Philadelphia and Baltimore, where immigrant workers were in high demand throughout the war in the steel, munitions, and shipbuilding industries.[13] Hundreds of Indian seamen successfully made this move from maritime to factory work. Over the late 1910s and 1920s, these men built up networks to facilitate undocumented labor migration—networks that became the conduits for continuing chain migration, even in the face of a tightening anti-Asian legal regime.

By 1930, groups of Indian Muslim ex-seamen were working as laborers in factories across the whole of the United States' industrial belt: in
the Manville asbestos factory in Hamilton, New Jersey; in steel mills in
Bethlehem, Pennsylvania, and Youngstown, Ohio; in the Sun Shipbuilding Company's shipyard in Chester, Pennsylvania; and in Ford auto factories in Detroit and Dearborn, Michigan.[14] The largest numbers were
in Detroit and in Lackawanna, New York, just outside Buffalo on the
banks of Lake Erie. The latter was the site of what was then the largest
steel plant in the world, run initially by the Lackawanna Steel Company,
and after 1922, by Bethlehem Steel. This plant, which came to occupy
more than 1,000 acres of land, had, according to one description, "its
own ship canal, locks, bridges," and railway lines, and produced steel
"bars, sheets, rail, tie plates" and fabricated parts for construction and
other industries.[15] Census records show that by 1920, there was already
a well-established infrastructure for escaped Indian seamen to live and
work in Lackawanna. Here, two men who had arrived in the United
States in the early 1910s—one an Indian named Meah, and the other
listed as "East Indian" but whose name, Abdul Djebara, suggests he may
have been Arab—were running boardinghouses on Fifth Avenue and
Ridge Road, just outside the entrance to the steel plant. Between them,
their addresses were home to forty Indian Muslim men, ranging in age
from eighteen to thirty-five. Most had arrived over the course of the
war, between 1914 and 1919.[16]

Draft registration records confirm these numbers, showing close to
fifty men who fit the profile of Indian seamen working in the Lackawanna plant in 1917 and 1918. All had Muslim surnames, about half
were recorded as being specifically from the port city of Calcutta (the
rest were listed simply as "East Indian"), and most were nonliterate.[17]
Tellingly, one of these men was known by the surname "Serang"—the
occupational name for the headman of an Indian steamship crew—
and on census records, the majority were recorded as "firemen" in the
town's steel plant.[18] The evidence suggests, in other words, that these
were men who had successfully transferred skills they had built up
firing furnaces in the boiler rooms of British ships to equivalent, and
probably better-paid, labor onshore in the United States. Such skills,
indeed, would have made steamship engine-room workers especially
attractive to U.S. factory owners.

In Detroit, the population of Indian ex-seamen working in Ford auto factories grew in the immediate postwar period and continued through the 1920s.[19] Here, these men joined multiple streams of labor migration. By 1930, census records show that Detroit's Ford plants—and the city's working-class neighborhoods and rooming houses—were full of workers from all over the country and all over the world: African Americans from the U.S. South who had come to the city as part of the Great Migration, as well as Afghans, Arabs, Syrians, Turks, Greeks, Maltese, Poles, and other immigrants from Europe, the Middle East, and the Americas. Although Indian men usually roomed together, they lived in buildings and areas that they shared with these other groups. By the late 1920s, for example, there were several Indian group households and even a small Indian restaurant in the middle of the working-class African American neighborhood of "Black Bottom" on the east side of downtown Detroit. As in Lackawanna, this Indian presence was built upon a network of ex-maritime workers, boardinghouse keepers, and other middlemen, who guided escaped seamen from New York to Detroit and set them up with lodging and factory jobs.[20] In Detroit, Indian workers became part of a new industrial paradigm, deskilled and spread out across countless individualized tasks. On 1930 census sheets, their jobs read like an enumeration of every position on the Fordist assembly line: "fireman," "molder," "drill press," "punch press," "machine operator," "motor assembly," "body builder," "oiler," "sander," "polisher."[21]

The growing population of Indian men in U.S. factories did not go unnoticed. In 1920 and 1921, the federal government engaged in a series of factory sweeps aimed at capturing and deporting undocumented Asian workers under the provisions of the 1917 Immigration Act. These raids netted small groups of Indian and Chinese workers, who were sent to Ellis Island and eventually dispatched from the country.[22] In 1922, Indian seamen came to wider public attention after they emerged as targets of violence in the midst of a railroad shop workers strike in Jersey City, New Jersey. This strike revealed the structure of racialized labor into which Indian seamen had been thrust. When white rail workers called the strike, the Erie and Lackawanna Railroads immediately sought out low-wage, nonunionized Indian, Chinese, and African American workers to sidestep their organizing efforts. A series of local "employment agents" supplied the railroad owners' needs by canvassing the docks of New York and New Jersey and facilitating the desertion of Indian and Chinese seamen to take up strikers' jobs in the railroad's steam power shops. At the end of the first week of the strike, in July 1922, most of the violence that had arisen was thus not between workers and employers but between the striking white workers and their Asian and black nonunion replacements.[23]

It is unclear whether these seamen knew when they took the rail yard jobs that they were being thrown into the middle of a labor dispute. According to a Jersey City police captain, "A Bowery employment agency had promised [Indian and Chinese seamen] $3 a day and lodging and meals." After they were brought across the water from Manhattan, these men were housed in buildings within the rail yard compound, where "close guard was being maintained over the imported men" by an armed security force that the Erie Railroad had hired. The seamen, however, were put upon by all sides. The Indian workers, according to the police captain's report, had to be "rescue[d] . . . from a mob which was threatening them with clubs and stones." Significantly, the Jersey City police neither arrested the Asian seamen nor did much to prevent them from coming back. Nor did federal immigration officials cite the Erie Railroad for hiring "alien" workers in violation of the existing labor laws or go after the "Bowery employment agents" for their role in this violation.[24] When an industrial concern as large as the Erie Railroad needed to use Asian seamen to beat the strike and ensure the continuation of rail services, local and federal officials were willing to look the other way. They let the railroad's agents and hired guns circumvent immigration and labor laws as they saw fit and concentrated their own energies on simply keeping things from boiling over into violence. Asian seamen, for their part, were largely left to fend for themselves in the middle of the dispute.

What is important to note here is that the hundreds of Indian seamen who were jumping ship in New York in search of industrial jobs in the late 1910s and early 1920s were not alone in their approach to the law. All the actors here—from British shipping companies to American industrial concerns to local government officials, port-side middlemen and the seamen themselves—treated laws not as a fixed structure of permissions and prohibitions to be followed but as a shifting field of obstacles and openings to be navigated in order to achieve specific goals, or,

in the case of the more powerful actors, as a set of regulatory mechanisms to be wielded, ignored, manipulated, or reformulated as social,
economic, and political conditions (and their own needs) changed.
British shipping companies were pushing back against the "lascar line"
provision of the 1894 Merchant Shipping Act in order to use low-wage
colonial workers and maintain their dominance in the field of global
transport and trade; American firms from the Ford Motor Company
to Bethlehem Steel to the Erie Railroad were hiring undocumented
immigrant laborers to meet the demands of wartime production, maxi-
mize profits, and break the hold of U.S. unions; local and federal officials were enforcing or easing off on immigration laws according to the
pressures of nativist politics and the needs of industry; and small-time
"Bowery employment agents" were facilitating the illegal desertion and
hiring of Asian seamen to supply industrialists' needs and generate
their own profits. It was in this broader context of the manipulation and
circumvention of laws that Indian seamen were deserting in New York
City—escaping indenture-like conditions on British ships and taking
their chances on finding better work onshore.

Sailors, Radicals, and Radical Sailors

While New York was the point of entry for scores of Indian maritime
workers who moved on to factory jobs elsewhere, by the 1920s and
1930s, the city had also developed its own semipermanent population
of Indian seamen and ex-seamen. These settlements resembled those,
described by Tabili, Visram, Balachandran, Ahuja, and others, that
had grown during the same period in British port cities like London,
Glasgow, Liverpool, Southampton, and Hull.[25] In New York, Indian
seamen were part of a large mixed population of maritime workers
who were moving in and out of boardinghouses near the West Side
waterfront, while Indian ex-seamen were making their way farther
into the city and settling in some of Manhattan's most heterogeneous
immigrant neighborhoods—on the Lower East Side and in Harlem.
As was the case in Britain, there were key individuals onshore who
worked to facilitate these movements. Their knowledge and manipulation of the maritime industry and immigration laws and their ability
to find accommodations and work for escaped seamen put them at the

center of a growing, if undocumented, Indian Muslim community in New York City.

Mohammed Abdou was one of the first of these men. Abdou was an Egyptian boardinghouse keeper, restaurant owner, and maritime employment agent who operated from a row of four-story tenements at 19–22 West Street, near the southern tip of Manhattan, in the late 1910s and 1920s. There were other boardinghouses and restaurants in New York frequented by escaped Indian sailors, but the reason we know of Abdou's is because he was connected not just to the Indian maritime population but to the groups of exiles and expatriates from across the British Empire who had found a haven for their anticolonial activities in interwar New York City. Abdou's story, teased out from British surveillance records, reveals much about both the structure of Indian maritime desertion in the 1920s and the ties between the ex-maritime population and Indian expatriate nationalism.

Archival records show that Mohammed Abdou arrived in New York City in 1916 and set up shop almost immediately on West Street, across from Piers 2 and 3, in an area crowded with seamen, longshoremen, traders, and travelers. By the early 1920s, Abdou was running a building at 22 West Street with almost fifty boarders from Egypt, Algeria, Greece, India, and Syria, as well as an employment agency at 19 West Street, named Abdou & Daud. It was around this time that Abdou began to garner the interest of British authorities. On February 12, 1921, Captain R. W. Crome, the master of the S.S. *Kandahar*, owned by the British shipping company Ellerman & Bucknall, composed an urgent letter to his superiors in London. "Please . . . advise our ships masters," he wrote, "that however they may be inconvenienced for lack of a crew, to have no direct dealing with one [Mr.] Abdoo, a boarding house keeper of West Street, New York, also if possible to prevent the same individual [from] having access to any steamers, dock, wharf, or pier over which they exercise control." The reason for Captain Crome's warning was that he had discovered that members of his Indian crew had hidden a crate full of "seditious literature" in the hold of his Calcutta-bound ship. Crome had hired all these men in New York City; all were supplied by Mohammed Abdou's employment agency after another group of Indian seamen had deserted the *Kandahar*. The "seditious literature" included pamphlets written by U.S.-based Indian radicals—members of the Ghadar Party in California and the Friends of Freedom for India in New York—as well as personal correspondence from some of the leaders of these groups to their comrades in Bengal. "I have now very good reasons to believe," wrote Crome in his letter, "that Abdoo is a dangerous character, and that his influence with natives of India at New York is of the same [dangerous] nature." A month later, Crome wrote again to add that he had "every good reason to believe that certain societies in America will endeavour to ship in our steamers one revolutionary per month . . .[t]hese men to be provided with the necessary propaganda." Before Captain Crome's discovery, Mohammed Abdou had been in Ellerman & Bucknall's good favor. Just weeks earlier, another Ellerman employee, D. Isbister, had written to the London office praising Abdou for his assistance in relation to the *Kandahar*. Isbister had been struggling to deal with a spate of desertions and complained that Indian desertion in New York was exceedingly difficult to control, in part because when Indian sailors deserted, "the men usually go to Buffalo or Chester [Pennsylvania] or some other place, far away from New York," so that finding and arresting them "is not so easy."[26]

In the case of the *Kandahar*, Isbister wrote, Abdou had saved the day. The ship had originally signed on a full crew of sixty-one Indian seamen in Calcutta in September 1919 and had docked and unloaded in Brooklyn in June 1920. Just before it was about to continue onward from New York, nineteen members of its crew jumped ship, and Isbister turned to Mohammed Abdou, "who keeps a boarding house in West Street," to fill the sudden deficit of workers without delaying the *Kandahar*'s departure. Abdou had come through by quickly providing nineteen new "lascar" seamen for the outgoing ship, at double pay and with the promise that the nineteen men would be discharged in India. Isbister added, in Abdou's favor, that "since we have been dealing with Abdou, we have been able to get some of our own men back, as in the case of the '*City of Winchester*' six of her own men were returned on board before sailing."[27] It did not occur to Isbister at this time that Abdou may have been involved not just in supplying Indian seamen to replace those who had previously deserted but also in facilitating the original desertion. This, of course, was the implication of Captain Crome's later accusations—that Abdou had been involved in creating a shortage on the *Kandahar* as it was leaving port in New York, so that he could smuggle Indian "seditionists" and their propaganda onboard as part of a replacement crew.[28] While Crome's letters, with their alarmist tone, are difficult to take entirely at face value, his descriptions of Mohammed Abdou's "dealings" in New York bear a striking similarity to Sailendranath Ghose's description of the ruse that his middleman on the Calcutta waterfront used in this same period, to smuggle him onto an outgoing ship disguised as a seaman.

That Abdou was running some sort of scheme aimed at both aiding Indian seamen to desert and helping others get hired out of New York at higher wages becomes clearer in testimony elicited in an apparently unrelated case in 1924. In March of that year, the Special Branch of the Calcutta Police sent to the India Office in London information received in the interrogation of a Bengali seaman named Ishaque Mia, suggesting that this information be forwarded to the Foreign Office and eventually the British consul in New York for their attention. Because it corroborates much of the other evidence about desertion in New York, it is worth reproducing here at length. The Calcutta authorities wrote:

9th March 1924

One Ishaque Mia of village Ziapur in Sylhet returned to Calcutta from New York about 3 weeks ago. He said that he went on voyage about 2½ years ago in a Clan [Line] Ship and deserted the ship at New York. There he stopped for some time with M. Abdon [sic] of Messrs. Abdon and O. Daud & Co., the agent of the White Hall Employment Agency at 19 West Street, South Perry [sic]. M. Abdon assisted him in concealing his presence at New York. Ishaque Mia was [then] employed at some factory and after about 3 months, he...removed from the above-mentioned place to 689 Sixth Avenue, 42nd Street in New York....At this place, he used to meet with many Indians...who were also working in different factories and workshops there. There was a Bengali young man who works as a canvasser or broker for Messrs. M. Abdon & O. Daud & Co. This Bengali practically led the Indians at New York. It is said that the Bengali in course of conversation with Ishaque said that he ([the] Bengali) and the other Indians residing at New York were doing propaganda for the achievement of Indian independence, but Ishaque could not understand what they were doing.

12th March 1924

In course of conversation, he said that he did not know the names of the Bengali and the Punjabis who were said to have been doing something for the Indian independence at New York but he gave the following names and addresses as the principal abodes of those men:
(1) Messrs. M. Abdon & O. Daud & Co., agent to White Hall employment agency, 19 West Street, South Perry
(2) Mr. Moharam, 82 Lackawanna Street, Buffalo, New York
(3) Asad Ali, 14, 9th Avenue, Yengustan, U.S.A.
(4) Nasir Mohammed, 309 Bridge Road, Lackawanna, New York[29]

Allowing for variations in the pronunciation and transliteration of English/American words, names, and addresses (e.g., "South Perry" for South Ferry), it is striking how many of the details of Ishaque Mia's account match those that appear in other archival records. This is the case with most of the addresses that Mia gave his interrogators, for example: 19 West Street, near South Ferry, had been Abdou's living and work address since 1919 or 1920; "14, 9th Avenue, Yengustan, USA," an address which an official of the India Office in London dismissed as "highly doubtful," did in fact correspond exactly to an address—14, 9th Avenue, Youngstown, Ohio—where, according to the U.S. Census, several Indian steelworkers were still living in 1930; "309 Bridge Road, Lackawanna," is clearly a mistransliteration of an address on Ridge Road, the street on the edge of the Lackawanna Steel plant grounds where the vast majority of the plant's Indian workers were living in the 1920s.[30] Although the address that Mia gave for an Indian residence/boardinghouse in Manhattan—689 Sixth Avenue, Forty-Second Street—does not in fact correspond to a building anywhere near Forty-Second Street, this may have been an unintentional or intentional obfuscation of 689 Eighth Avenue, an address that was not only just above Forty-Second Street but less than a block away from the Ceylon India Restaurant, a key gathering place for Indians in New York and a center of expatriate nationalist activity.[31]

The most intriguing aspects of Mia's testimony are his descriptions, first, of an independent sphere of Indian nationalist activity within the community of Muslim seamen turned factory workers who resided in

or near New York in the 1920s, and, second, of the Egyptian Mohammed Abdou's role in helping Mia desert his ship, evade authorities,
and, as is implied, find factory work in one of the cities listed in his
testimony—Lackawanna, Buffalo, or Youngstown.[32] Added to the other
archival evidence, Mia's testimony gives us a clearer picture of Indian
maritime desertion in and through New York: confirming that seamen
were regularly jumping ship with the assistance and perhaps encouragement of middlemen like Abdou; that some were then guided to
other middlemen in factory towns farther inland who helped them find
jobs and accommodations; and that others stayed in—or returned to—
the city itself, where groups of ex-seamen were congregating in shared
apartments, working service-sector jobs, getting involved in expatriate nationalist activities, and going back out to sea at better wages than
they could obtain in Indian ports.

It is impossible to know exactly how many Indian seamen and ex-
seamen were living onshore in New York by the early 1920s, but these
men constituted a large enough presence to draw the attention of
some of the anti-imperialist expatriates who had made the city their
center of operations. Mohammed Abdou himself appears to have
been part of a larger circle of political exiles; he was an active member of New York City's Egyptian nationalist community in addition
to having ties to Sailendranath Ghose's New York–based organization,
the Friends of Freedom for India (FFI).[33] It is possible that Ghose was
in fact the "Bengali" that Ishaque Mia described to British authorities
as an associate of Abdou's who was "doing propaganda" work among
the city's Indian seamen.[34] Other evidence points in this direction;
both British surveillance documents and FFI correspondence suggest that Ghose and his comrades, Agnes Smedley and Taraknath
Das, had identified seamen as a key group to recruit to the cause of
Indian independence. In August 1920, when the U.S. Immigration
Service rounded up thirty-nine Indian workers from the steelworks
at Bethlehem, Pennsylvania, and sent them to Ellis Island to await
deportation hearings, Smedley turned up at the immigration station
with the FFI's legal counsel and began to argue for the men's release.
As a result of the FFI's efforts, it was discovered that twenty-nine of
the men had already been handed off to British ships, without any
official review of their cases, and the Department of Labor was forced

to open an inquiry "into possible collusion between immigration officers and British interests to shanghai Hindu seamen into the British merchant marine." In the weeks that followed, Das and the FFI's
lawyers traveled to Gloucester, New Jersey, to press for bail for the
remaining seamen and succeeded in having the men released. The
FFI also worked with local and federal officials to sponsor one of the
detained workers, a boy of only fourteen, and enroll him in school in
New York City.[35]

Such efforts did not go unrecognized by the Indian ex-seamen who
were working onshore in New York City and elsewhere. Amir Haider
Khan was particularly impressed by Agnes Smedley's commitments to
his community and to the larger cause of Indian independence. While
figures like Ghose, Das, and Basant Kumar Roy were the recognized
spokesmen of the FFI and garnered the attention of New York's political
circles, Smedley was, according to Khan, the person whose organizational work, alliance-building, and strategic decisions made the organization run. In the case of the men held at Ellis Island, Khan writes
that Smedley "moved every quarter to get these poor, illiterate workers
released from the clutches of the U.S. Immigration Department. First
they were released on bail, then she continued the fight until they were
permitted to live in the U.S. unconditionally." As a maritime worker,
Khan was clearly moved by the fact that Smedley could shift her political energies from pursuing the lofty goal of Indian independence to
addressing the everyday difficulties and concerns of Indian seafarers
in the United States—and that she could see, as he no doubt did, that
both efforts were part of the same struggle.[36] By the time the Friends of
Freedom for India held its first annual congress at the Hotel McAlpin
and the Lexington Theater in Manhattan in December 1920, Khan was
one of a group of seamen who circulated through the crowds dressed
in brightly colored turbans that Smedley had passed out to them to add
spectacle to the event.[37]

Khan and other seamen also mixed with Indian students and expatriate intellectuals at the Ceylon India Restaurant, on Eighth Avenue
and Forty-Third Street in Manhattan. Opened in 1913, the Ceylon
India was the first Indian restaurant in New York City owned and
operated by someone from the subcontinent. Its Sinhalese proprietor,
K. Y. Kira, had first traveled to the United States as a member of

circus and exhibition troupes, and by the late 1910s, he was a leading figure among New York's small Buddhist community and a committed anti-imperialist. Kira used the living space upstairs from his restaurant as a halfway house for recent arrivals from the subcontinent. The 1920 census, for instance, listed two boarders at the restaurant's address, Frank Buda, a twenty-nine-year-old Sinhalese sailor, and Jacob David, a Telegu-speaking hotel porter.[38] It is possible that Kira also provided work for ex-seamen as cooks, dishwashers, and waiters at his restaurant or helped them find such work elsewhere. The Ceylon India itself became a gathering place for Indian nationalists and their sympathizers in the city; the Friends of Freedom for India held meetings and functions at the restaurant throughout the early 1920s, and both British and U.S. intelligence had the establishment under surveillance.[39]

Amir Haider Khan's memoir *Chains to Lose* is perhaps the only first-hand account of this period written by an Indian seaman. Khan spent several years in New York and Detroit between 1918 and 1925 before returning to the subcontinent, via Moscow, to join the independence struggle as an organizer for the Communist Party of India. What is remarkable about Khan's memoir is its detailing of an arena of expatriate Indian nationalist organizing distinct from that of New York's elite expatriates. Khan refers to the Ceylon India Restaurant, for example, as a place where Indian students and intellectuals would meet and interact with the various seamen who were working for the FFI. At the same time, Khan makes a clear distinction between the restaurant's regular clientele and these maritime workers. While the Ceylon India was a place where "most of those Indians belonging to the educated classes would dine," Khan and other seafarers gathered at a separate restaurant run by a Goanese proprietor—likely a former steamship cook—"in a cheap locality on West 37th Street." In contrast to the Ceylon India, this was predominantly a workers' space, "an ideal spot," as Khan describes it, "to take one's evening meal, meet with other Indians, chat, discuss problems in India of mutual interest, and keep track of those Indians who were in New York at that time."[40] This and a number of other residences and establishments formed a network of spaces near the city's docklands within which Khan gradually came to be part of a group of "politically minded seafaring men" in New York. In 1920–1921, during a period in which Khan was shipping in and out of New York as an engine-room worker on American merchant ships, Khan's primary space of political community was a laundry run by his friend Azim; this was the place to which Khan would "rush" back whenever he returned from a job at sea. The laundry, writes Khan, "was one of the places where Indian [ex-seamen] would frequently meet and [where] one could get information regarding political developments in India." After returning from a short trip to Trinidad in 1920, for example, Khan went directly to Azim's shop and "met some of the members of this social group who gave me the most glowing and optimistic account of the progress of the National Anti-British Movement in India." Khan and these men had not only begun to come together in New York City around ties of kinship, language, and work, but now encouraged among one another a shared sense of possibility for an independent India. "Under normal circumstances, they would have no interest in politics," says Khan, "yet now these humble sons of India were living in anticipation and hope of momentous changes—changes that would shake off all the old fetters, the religious and caste prejudices . . . which had split our people into innumerable divisions."[41]

It was here at Azim's laundry that Khan also met the man who first led him to the Friends of Freedom for India. He describes the man simply as the "Gadar Sikh"[42]—a forty-year-old veteran member of the Ghadar Party whose background, like that of the city's ex-seamen, appears to have been rural and/or working-class, and who had come to New York to work among the Indian community there. The man Khan describes was quite likely the Ghadar Party organizer Bhagwan Singh. Through his friendship with this "Gadar Sikh," Khan went through a kind of political tutelage. According to Khan, the Gadar Sikh

> had devoted himself wholly to the cause of freedom for our people and could detail the litany of British misdeeds and episodes of brutality towards members of various revolutionary organizations. . . . He would often narrate stories of the struggles that were going on in various British colonies, particularly Ireland and Egypt. When he was not speaking to us, he used to sing or recite selected pieces from "the Gadar Ki Goonj."

What is significant here is that the "Gadar Sikh's" appeal to Khan and his group of ex-seamen relied on a specifically working-class text (*Ghadar di Gunj*) and modes of address (storytelling, singing, recitation). It was, in other words, from within their own radicalized working-class community, and through this representative of the Ghadar Party, that Khan and his cohort of ex-seamen came into the larger fold of Indian and other anti-British nationalist groups in New York City. Khan himself writes that he "became very attached to the 'Gadar Sikh' and would spend all [his] free time in his company," and it was as a result of this relationship that the Sikh "acquainted [Khan] with a variety of anti-British radical organizations and institutions and a number of personalities associated with these movements who were staying in New York at this time." This included Agnes Smedley, Sailendranath Ghose, and other members of the FFI.[43]

Although he lent some of his energies to the Friends of Freedom for India when he was ashore in New York City in 1920–1921, Amir Haider Khan followed the Gadar Sikh's example of political work when he shipped back out to sea. Smedley, Ghose, and their expatriate associates in the United States had, by 1921, begun to transition to a strategy of recruiting well-known American left and liberal writers, intellectuals, and religious and political figures to the cause of Indian independence; in subsequent years, their efforts would increasingly focus on the figure of Gandhi and his ideas of nonviolent resistance.[44] Khan, on the other hand, had been supplied by his Sikh compatriot with two Colt pistols and a footlocker full of copies of *Ghadar di Gunj* and now took to recruiting fellow workers as he moved from port to port as a fireman on a U.S. merchant ship. Khan used every stop along his ship's journey— from New York through the Caribbean and the Panama Canal to Japan and China—as an opportunity to find groups of Indians onshore, in port, and on other ships, and bring them into the nationalist fold. Khan writes of spending his spare moments in his cramped bunk, memorizing the movement's poems and songs so that, like his mentor in New York, he could most effectively engage his audiences, who were often farmers, workers, or sailors like him.[45] This trip marked the maturing of Khan as a political actor—it was the moment he made the transition from learning about, discussing, and protesting British imperialism to actually working as part of an expatriate movement for the overthrow of British colonial rule.

Khan was not alone. British surveillance documents from this time exhibit a growing concern not just over elite radicals' (such as Ghose's) use of the maritime trade to move in and out of India undetected but over the activities of Indian seamen who were smuggling small fire-arms from Europe and the United States to China and the subconti-nent, and the involvement of Indian ex-seamen in expatriate organiz-ing in the United States.[46] The latter was the case in Detroit, where the local British consul appears to have spent a good deal of energy in the 1920s trying to woo Indian students at the University of Michigan away both from radicalism and from the influence of ex-seamen. According to Khan, who went to Detroit in search of factory work in early 1925, the city's population of Indian ex-maritime workers consisted chiefly of men who had first jumped ship in New York and then made their way to Michigan to take up jobs in the auto industry. On arrival, Khan found a well-established network of friends and former acquaintances who had followed this path; his transition to living and working there was made almost effortless by the existence of this infrastructure of ex-seamen whom he had previously known in New York. After "getting out of the ferry boat station," Khan writes,

> I had hardly walked for about ten minutes when I met an Indian pass-erby in the street. From him I obtained the necessary information as to where the people from India were living. He directed me to a nearby poor locality where there was an Indian restaurant. There I enquired about the various individuals whom I knew intimately in New York. The proprietor of the little dingy eating place told me that the persons whom I wanted to see usually came there for evening meals....While I was wait-ing, there came an Indian worker...by the name of Nikkah Singh whom I knew at New York. From him I got information about all our other mutual friends and acquaintances from New York [who were now living in Detroit].

Khan's friend set out with him and quickly found him a place to stay in a nearby boardinghouse. "Most of our acquaintances also lived round about there," says Khan, and "it was near the centre of the city and the place where we could get Indian cooked food."[47]

The area Khan described was not merely the "centre of the city" but the center of Detroit's working-class African American population. Indian Muslim ex-seamen had settled, established group households and boardinghouses, and opened a restaurant amid the thousands of black men and women who had made their way to the city as part of the Great Migration. This was, in part, why the British consul in Detroit sought to distinguish the city's Indian students from the ex-seamen. A consular dispatch sent from Detroit to the British embassy in Washington, DC, in the year Khan arrived in Detroit describes the Indian population there as consisting of three distinct groups: "some two hundred students at the Michigan University, some hundred and fifty student-workers at the Ford plants, and about a hundred and fifty others, chiefly ex-lascars," who were also employed in the auto factories. The "student-workers," noted the report, were part of a Ford program in which a select group of young Indians was "being trained with a view to returning to their own country [to] be dispersed throughout the various Indian provinces." This group, the consul felt, "constitut[ed] a somewhat important body of opinion." The "ex-lascars," on the other hand, had "married coloured women" who were part of what the consul described as Detroit's "large influx of ignorant Coloured people from the south," and were, in his eyes, bringing disrepute and the negative attention of local authorities upon the Indian population as a whole. The British consul's primary focus at this moment was the Indian student-workers, who, because of the racial segregation of Detroit, often lived in the same neighborhoods as ex-lascars and southern black migrants; the consul sought to court this "important body of opinion" and advocate on their behalf to ensure that, racially and politically, they neither identified with nor became identified with the ex-lascars and African Americans among whom they lived.[48]

These fears were compounded by the fact that the students and workers had begun to mingle in Detroit's Indian nationalist organizations. British intelligence about the United India League of America and its later incarnation, the Independence League of India, identified seamen as the organizations' most radical members.[49] While one

British informant attributed this to the fact that the ex-seafarers had put down roots in the United States, and thus had "less to lose" than the students, it is clear that there was a class inflection to the political divisions among Detroit's Indian population. As "trainees" destined for midlevel management jobs in a series of planned Ford factories in India, the "student-workers" in Detroit arrived with a different relationship to India's future than the maritime workers who had labored first on British steamships and now on Henry Ford's assembly lines. Many if not most of the latter group, according to Khan, also owed their factory jobs to a middle-class Indian immigrant named Mathur, a metallurgical engineer in Ford's employ who had established a kind of patronage system in Detroit. Mathur had not only created the "special industrial student" program to train young members of the Indian "intelligentsia"—as Khan put it—to run Ford plants in India but set himself up as the middleman to whom Indian ex-seamen had to go in order to find manual labor in Ford factories.[50]

Khan's story suggests that some of Detroit's Indian ex-seamen found greater allies and inspiration among the other working-class communities with whom they shared neighborhoods, workplaces, and common experiences of racialization in the United States. For his own part, Khan became involved in the grassroots African American movement in support of Ossian Sweet, a black Detroit doctor who was on trial for murder after he defended his house in a segregated white suburb from a violent mob. Khan describes being swept into the cause, attending organizational and support meetings in black churches and community spaces much as he had attended similar events in support of Indian independence in New York five years earlier. He was deeply moved by what he saw. "Negroes in the U.S.A.," he writes, "rose to the occasion throughout the country. . . .Negro groups did not leave any stone unturned to rally the race in defence of the accused."[51] Khan's experience of this time, as an Indian autoworker living on the East Side of Detroit, deepened his understanding of both the violent and the institutional sides of American racism; it demonstrated to him what was possible when people came together around a common cause across various lines of difference (in this case class, age, gender, etc.); it consolidated his racial and political identification with African Americans; and, in doing so, it ultimately stretched his own politics to an internationalism deeply rooted in cross-racial identification. When Khan joined the Communist International later in 1925, his decision was catalyzed as much by this experience of African American antiracist organizing as by his experiences as a colonial subject and as an industrial and maritime worker.[52]

Dada Amir Haider Khan was clearly an extraordinary figure, both in terms of the breadth of his travels, encounters, and experiences over the course of the seven years that followed his desertion from the SS *Khiva* in 1918 and in terms of the written record he left behind. This is precisely why Khan's account is so useful—not because it represents, from beginning to end, the exact trajectory that other Indian Muslim seamen took after deserting British ships in the United States during this era but because it touches upon, and provides a firsthand account of, so many of the *different* trajectories that Indian seamen followed in these years. After he jumped ship in New York City on a cold night in February 1918, almost everywhere Khan went, there were other Indian ex-seamen who were there or who had been there before him. On the New York waterfront; in its boardinghouses and Indian-run restaurants and laundries; in the meetings of the Friends of Freedom for India in New York City and the United India League of America in Detroit; in the American merchant marine and its ships' crews; in munitions factories in New Jersey, railway workshops and steel foundries in New Jersey and upstate New York, and auto factories in Michigan; in Black Bottom rooming houses, black churches, UNIA meetings, and the prayer meetings of Duse Mohammed Ali's Islamic Society in Detroit—in all these spaces through which Khan's seven-year trajectory passed, there were other Indian ex-seamen. His story makes clear how ingrained Indian "seafaring men" were on the East Coast and in the Midwest of the United States in the 1910s and 1920s. Seamen and ex-seamen constituted both a clandestine population of industrial and service-sector workers and a semiautonomous arena of expatriate anticolonial activism. Our understanding of early twentieth-century Indian history must account for the pathways they followed and carved out for themselves; the spaces in which they lived, worked, and interacted; the encounters—both within and outside Indian communities—that were unique to their trajectories; and the transformations they underwent in the ways they saw themselves and the world.

NOTES

1. *New York Times*, "Hold American Girl as an India Plotter," Mar 19, 1918, 1; *Los Angeles Times*, "Nab California Girl with Hindu Plotter—San Francisco Co-conspirator of Bopp Caught in New York," Mar 19, 1918, 1; *New York Tribune*, "Two German Plots Exposed; Bernstorff's Hand Is Shown; 3 Women and 3 Men Seized," Mar 19, 1918, 1; "Hindu Plotters Had Two Marked for Death Here," Mar 28, 1918, 16. For a more recent consideration of this case, see Seema Sohi, "Echoes of Mutiny: Race, Empire, and Indian Revolutionaries on the Pacific Coast," PhD diss., University of Washington, 2007.

2. Sailendranath Ghose, "An Indian Revolutionary: The Story of a Bengali Boy in Flight from Physics Laboratory to Stoke-Hole," *Asia* 27 (September 1927): 736–742, 772–775.

3. Ghose, 775.

4. In this, Ghose was among the ranks of scores of nineteenth- and twentieth-century political figures who spent time either working as, or disguised as, seamen as they made their way from one part of the world to another. This group included Frederick Douglass, George Padmore, Claude McKay, and Ho Chi Minh, among others. Paul Gilroy, *The Black Atlantic: Modernity and Double Consciousness* (Cambridge: Harvard University Press, 1993), 13; Brent Hayes Edwards, "The Shadow of Shadows," *positions: east asia cultures critique* 11, no. 1 (2003): 14.

5. Laura Tabili, *"We Ask for British Justice": Workers and Racial Difference in Late Imperial Britain*, The Wilder House Series in Politics, History, and Culture (Ithaca: Cornell University Press, 1994); Rozina Visram, *Asians in Britain: 400 Years of History* (London: Pluto, 2002); G. Balachandran, "South Asian Seafarers and Their Worlds: c. 1870–1930s," paper presented at the Seascapes, Littoral Cultures, and Trans-Oceanic Exchanges Conference, Library of Congress, Washington, DC, February 12–15, 2003; Ravi Ahuja, "Mobility and Containment: The Voyages of South Asian Seamen, c. 1900–1960," *International Review of Social History* 51, no. S14 (2006): 111–141.

6. Historian Sucheta Mazumdar argues that in the late nineteenth century and early twentieth century, sojourning was in fact the more common mode by which migrants from all over the world engaged as workers in the United States. Sucheta Mazumdar, "What Happened to the Women? Chinese and Indian Male Migration to the United States in Global Perspective," in *Asian/Pacific Islander American Women: A Historical Anthology*, ed. Shirley Hune and Gail Nomura (New York: NYU Press, 2003), 58–74.

7. Those ex-seamen who did stay in the United States, moreover, quietly became part of working-class neighborhoods in New York, Detroit, and elsewhere, and lead us to a little-explored history of Indian Muslim intermarriage within Puerto Rican and African American communities that continued throughout the Asian exclusion period. This history parallels the development of Punjabi-Mexican communities in California and the Southwest over the same years, but

it points to different dynamics of racialization and cross-racial, cross-ethnic, and cross-religious encounter that were specific to East Coast urban contexts. Vivek Bald, "Overlapping Diasporas, Multiracial Lives: South Asian Muslims in U.S. Communities of Color, 1880–1950," in *Black Routes to Islam*, ed. Manning Marable and Hishaam Aidi (New York: Palgrave Macmillan, 2009); Vivek Bald, "Selling the East in the American South: Bengali Peddlers in New Orleans, 1880–1920," in *Asian Americans Down South*, ed. Khyati Y. Joshi and Jigna Desai (Champaign: University of Illinois Press, 2013).

8. These numbers are based on an analysis of ships records via search tools for the Ellis Island Arrivals Database developed by Dr. Stephen Morse, Gary Sandler, and Michael Tobias: U.S. Department of Labor, Immigration Service, *List or Manifest of Aliens Employed on the Ship as Crew* (hereafter USDL/IS/LMAC), various, 1914–1924, *Enhanced Ellis Island Database*, http://stevemorse.org/ellis2/ellisgold.html (accessed Apr 2–4, 2007).

9. The result of lobbying by British seafarers' unions, this "lascar line" provision attempted to secure a series of Atlantic routes as the exclusive province of white sailors—at least for half the year. Tabili, 77–78, 185–186; Ahuja, 127–128.

10. United Kingdom, India Office Records: IOR/P/10793, A 73–76, 243–248, 341–344.

11. USDL/IS/LMAC: *SS Carmania*, Jan 1, 1919; *SS Kasama*, Jan 2, 1919; *SS Lowther Castle*, Jan 4, 1919; *SS Karimata*, Jan 6, 1919; *SS Kandahar*, Jan 10, 1919; *SS Clan Macintyre*, Jan 13, 1919; *SS Malancha*, Jan 17, 1919; *SS Clan Cunningham*, Jan 19, 1919.

12. Visram, 196–197.

13. Dada Amir Haider Khan, *Chains to Lose: Life and Struggles of a Revolutionary* (New Delhi: Patriot Publishers, 1989), 126–128, 307, 314–315, 395, 399, 407.

14. U.S. Department of Commerce, Bureau of the Census (hereafter USDC/BC), *U.S. Census, 1920*, Population Schedules, Hillsboro Township, NJ: Sup. Dist. 204, Enum. Dist. 129, Sheets No. 23A, 23B, 57B; Bethlehem City, PA: Sup. Dist. 7, Enum. Dist. 82, Sheets No. 3B, 9B; Chester City, PA: Ward 3, Precinct 2, Sup. Dist. 2, Enum. Dist. 123, Sheets No. 2A, 9B; Youngstown, OH: Ward 2, Precinct D, Sup. Dist. 265, Enum. Dist. 157, Sheet No. 6A; Youngstown, OH: Ward 2, Precinct H, Sup. Dist. 265, Enum. Dist. 161, Sheets No. 7B, 8A; Detroit City, MI: Ward 3, Sup. Dist. 145, Enum. Dist. 90, Sheets No. 4B, 5A, 10B; Detroit City, MI: Ward 11, Precinct 1, Sup. Dist. 145, Enum. Dist. 327, Sheets No. 6A, 7B; Detroit City, MI: Sup. Dist. 145, Enum. Dist. 791, Sheet No. 7B; Detroit City, MI: Precinct 9, Sup. Dist. 145, Enum. Dist. 705, Sheet No. 3A.

15. Lackawanna Area Chamber of Commerce and Rev. Robert McArtney, *Lackawanna History*, http://ourworld.compuserve.com/homepages/rmcartney/lackawan.htm (accessed July 20, 2008).

16. USDC/BC, *U.S. Census, 1920*, Population Schedules, Lackawanna, NY: Ward 1, Sup. Dist. 21, Enum. Dist. 306, Sheets No. 43B, 53A, 62B.

17. The majority, for example, were unable to sign their names, instead marking the bottom of their draft cards with an "X" or a check mark. Eight of these workers signed their names in rough Bengali, while only one signed in clearly drawn English script.

18. U.S. Selective Service System, *World War I Selective Service System Draft Registration Cards*, 1917–1918 (hereafter USSS/DRC WWI), Local Registration Board, Erie County, NY (various; see especially the record for Hasmatula Serang).

19. USDC/BC, *U.S. Census, 1930*, Population Schedules, Lackawanna, NY: Ward 1, Sup. Dist. 7, Enum. Dist. 15-420, Sheets No. 3A, 8B, 9A, 9B; Dearborn City, MI: Precinct 13, Sup. Dist. 18, Enum. Dist. 82-896, Sheet No. 42B; Detroit City, MI: (various).

20. There is evidence in census records of at least two Indian and two Afghan rooming houses in this area of Detroit—at 570 Lafayette Street, 574 and 584 Fort Street East, and 569 Congress Street East. USDC/BC, *U.S. Census, 1930*, Population Schedules, Detroit City, MI: records for 566, 570, & 582 Lafayette Street E., 574 & 584 Fort Street E., and 569 Congress Street E. See also the testimony of Ishaque Mia, United Kingdom, *Foreign Office Correspondence* (hereafter UK/FOC): FO371/9614 (A2858), and Khan, 390–391.

21. Ibid.

22. The sweeps began with the July 1920 arrest of "27 Singhalese from the mining districts of Western Pennsylvania" who were transported to Ellis Island to await deportation. At the time, an item circulated in the U.S. press in which "Ellis Island officials" asserted that there were "now in the United States 2,000 Hindus and other natives of the barred zones…[who] have come ashore from ships on seamen's certificates…and have failed to return to their vessels." *Washington Post*, "Move to Oust Many Hindus," Jul 30, 1920, 6. Three weeks later, immigration officials captured thirty-nine more "Hindu seamen" in a sweep of a factory in Bethlehem, Pennsylvania. In this case, twenty-nine of the men were taken to Ellis Island, where an official secretly released them to a British shipping company in need of a crew for one of its outgoing vessels. *Washington Post*, "Probe of Hindu [*sic*] Arrests—Department of Labor Suspects Collusion with British Shipping Interests," Aug 17, 1920, 6.

23. *New York Times*, "Rail Shop Strike at Deadlock Here," Jul 9, 1922, 2; *New York Times*, "Strikers Migrate to Take Rail Jobs," Jul 12, 1922, 1–2.

24. "Strikers Migrate to Take Rail Jobs," 2.

25. Tabili, 135–151; Visram, 66–68, 196–205, 216–218, 254–269, 273–275; Balachandran.

26. Abdou's activities set off a flurry correspondence—between captains and their superiors at Ellerman & Bucknall, and between British officials in New York, London, and Calcutta. The correspondence that built up displays a certain degree of imperial paranoia, and often disagreement about how "dangerous" a character Abdou really was. Officials even had trouble deciding who Abdou was—he was sometimes described as a "native of India", sometimes as a Turk,

and sometimes as an Egyptian. This body of official correspondence is reveal-
ing in terms of what it suggests about the limits of British and U.S. control over
Indian sailors and revolutionaries. USDL/IS/LMAP: *SS Finland*, Feb 21, 1916;
New York City, *City Directory, 1916–17, 1920, 1922, 1924*, Municipal Archives,
New York, NY; USSS/DRC WWI, *Registration Card* for Mohammed Abdou,
Local Registration Board: New York, NY; USDC/BC, *Census of the United States:
1920—Population Schedule.* New York, NY: records for 18, 19, 21, 22 West Street;
UK/FOC: FO371/5675 (A3331, A4156); FO371/11169 (A2383).

27. UK/FOC: FO371/5675 (A3331).
28. "I have for some months suspected that certain Societies in the U.S. were using
shifting crews as intermediates for seditious purposes, both on our steamers
and others," Crome wrote after finding that Abdou's men were in possession of
Indian nationalist pamphlets, "[and] now my suspicions [are] fully confirmed."
Ibid.
29. UK/FOC: FO371/9614 (A2858).
30. USDC/BC, *Census of the United States: 1930—Population Schedule.* Youngstown,
OH: record for 14 9th Avenue; USSS/DRC WWI, Local Registration Board:
Lackawanna, NY (various).
31. For more on K. Y. Kira and the Ceylon India Restaurant, see Vivek Bald, "'Lost'
in the City: Spaces and Stories of South Asian New York, 1917–1965," *South
Asian Popular Culture* 5, no. 1 (2007): 59–76.
32. It is telling that, in his testimony, Mia could be seen to be shifting, perhaps
strategically, between being very specific and very vague. He remembered and
reported details only in relation to a few names and addresses, and these only
after three days, and unknown means of pressure, in police custody. While he
described activities that may have been violations of U.S. laws, he never provided any usable details about what the Calcutta police were after—anti-*British*
activities.
33. Abdou had traveled to Washington, DC, to testify before the Senate Foreign
Relations Committee, unsuccessfully urging the United States to not ratify the
Treaty of Versailles as long as it contained clauses that granted Great Britain
continued colonial control over Egypt and other territories. *New York Times*,
"Pleads for Egypt at Treaty Hearing: Folk Denounces British Protectorate as a
Piece of Highway Robbery," Aug 26, 1919, 4.
34. UK/FOC: FO371/5675 (A3331, A4156); FO371/9614 (A2858); FO371/11169
(A2383).
35. Letter from Agnes Smedley, Friends of Freedom for India, to Santokh Singh,
Ghadar Party, San Francisco, Sep 30, 1920; *Christian Science Monitor*, "Rounded
Up Hindus Go on British Boats," Aug 17, 1920, 10.
36. Khan, 211.
37. Khan, 212.
38. USDC/BC, *Census of the United States: 1920—Population Schedule* for New York,
NY, record for 672 Eighth Avenue; see also USSS/DRC WWI, Local Registration

Board: New York, NY, Registration Cards for Abraham Pira, A. Hussaine, S. M. D. Pereira, Stanley Lionel.

39. *New York Times*, "To Proclaim Republic Today," Jan 1, 1922, 3. In the 1930s, the Ceylon India Inn also became the regular meeting place for talks and functions organized by the All-World Gandhi Fellowship, a liberal pro-independence organization, organized in part by the Reverend Holmes: *New York Times*, "Hail Policies of Gandhi," Dec 5, 1930, 19; *New York Times*, "Dr. Wise Rebukes Gandhi on Zionism," Oct 3, 1931, 14; UK/FOC, British Embassy, Washington to Foreign Office, London, Dec 22, 1925, FO371/11169 (A42).

40. Khan, 167, 207–210.

41. Khan, 207.

42. Because Khan wrote this first volume of his memoir in 1942 while held in a British colonial jail, it is likely that he purposely withheld the name of this "Gadar Sikh" in case his writings fell into the hands of the authorities.

43. Khan, 207–210.

44. By early 1921, the FFI's letterhead included a listing of six Executive Committee members, including ACLU founder Roger Baldwin, and thirty National Council members, including Franz Boas, Upton Sinclair, and W. E. B. DuBois; letter from Taraknath Das, Friends of Freedom of India, New York, to Hakam Khan, President of Hindusthan Gadar Party, San Francisco, CA, Jan 18, 1921, Kartar Dhillon Papers, in possession of Professor Vijay Prashad, Trinity College, Hartford, Connecticut ; Khan, 210; Harold A. Gould, *Sikhs, Swamis, Students, and Spies: The India Lobby in the United States, 1900–1946* (New Delhi and Thousand Oaks, CA: Sage, 2006), 245–246.

45. Khan, 216–219, 220–245 passim.

46. U K/FOC, Mr. Ferrard (India Office) to R. Sperling, Esquire (Foreign Office), FO371/7300 (A7068). See also: FO371/5675 (A3331, A4156); FO371/9614 (A2858); FO371/11169 (A2383). UK/IOR, Copy of Secret Letter, dated September 16, 1929, from the Commissioner of Police, Bombay, to the Deputy Director, Intelligence Bureau, Simla, P&J(S) 1769/1929.

47. Khan, 390–391.

48. UK/FOC, Dispatch from British Consul, Detroit, MI, to the Rt. Hon. Austen Chamberlain, M.P., His Majesty's Principal Secretary for Foreign Affairs, Foreign Office, London, England, Dec 2, 1925, FO 371/10639 (A6330).

49. UK/FOC, Dispatch from British Consulate, Detroit, MI, to the British Embassy, Washington, DC, Sept 25, 1929, FO 371/13534 (A6872).

50. Khan, 395, 399, 407.

51. Khan, 417.

52. Khan, 456–462.

4

"The Hidden Hand"

Remapping Indian Nurse Immigration to the United States

SUJANI REDDY

I have a dozen ideas that I would like to put into the TNAI [Trained Nurses Association of India] but we have a number of "missionary" minded people that feel modern equipment is not necessary for an organisation; while I acknowledge the yeoman work done by the missionaries, I could almost wish that they would go back to their own countries and give the Indians a chance to think for themselves and to take the reins of nursing into their own hands. I feel so strongly about this that I clash with the TNAI Council at almost every turn....I, of course, know that I am emotionally involved, but is that a crime? I feel that you understand what I mean otherwise I would not tell you this. My visit to your country has done nothing but add fuel to the fire....I am more ambitious for India than ever, so maybe I should have stayed at home?[1]

These are the impassioned words of Kumari Lakshmi Devi, the TNAI's first general secretary of Indian origin and the editor of its signature publication, the *Nursing Journal of India*. Devi addresses herself here to Virginia Arnold, assistant director for medical education at the Rockefeller Foundation (RF). The year was 1959, and Devi had just returned from an RF-sponsored tour of nursing programs and professional organizations around the world—beginning with a brief stop in London before moving on through the continental United States, San Juan (Puerto Rico), Honolulu, and Manila.[2] After the Philippines, Devi used her around-the-world ticket to continue on to Fiji, Australia, and finally New Zealand, where she could visit with her natal family for the first time since 1947. This last leg aside, her itinerary followed what had, by that time, become professional nursing's standard international circuit.

It was a circuit whose purpose was the creation, cultivation, and coordination of a cadre of international nursing leaders. At mid-twentieth century, this was still relatively unprecedented terrain for an Indian, as the overwhelming majority of India's nurses labored in what remained an undervalued and underpaid *occupation*, without the esteem or accreditation of a *profession*. Their status as decidedly nonprofessional was a direct product of the colonization of their labor.

Working within the fabric of British colonial domination, Protestant medical missionaries were the primary force behind establishing (what we now know as) biomedical nursing among Indians. Their work took root in the late nineteenth century, as missions underwent a simultaneous professionalization and feminization. This combination made way for the arrival of single female medical missionaries, who were among the first women to graduate from medical schools in the United States and the United Kingdom. Colonial migration offered female physicians a degree of professional and institutional authority that was not yet available to them in their home markets. In India, they were not only able to practice their new profession but also able to found the schools and hospitals that would employ India's first substantial pool of Indian nursing labor. And yet, when female-led medical missions grew to a size that belied the capacity of a single woman's direction, leadership did not pass into the hands of the Indian nurses who made up the bulk of the mission workforce. Instead, an evolving division of labor opened up a space for mission nurses, who arrived at a time when professional nursing was still very much struggling for recognition in Great Britain and North America. Again, mission medical institutions became a space for metropolitan nurses to assert a professional authority that was tenuous, at best, at home. And again, theirs was an authority that relied on the subordination of Indian labor. Increasingly, it was colonial nurses' access to professional training—a training that was not available in India, or to Indians—that came to cement their authority. Thus it was that the "T" in TNAI was also an implicit announcement of the racialized barriers that constituted professionalization through colonization.

Given this history, Kumari Lakshmi Devi's ascension within the TNAI—India's oldest nursing organization and a bastion of India's colonial nursing leadership—was a clear sign of the transfer of power taking place within Indian nursing, a transfer that only began in earnest after the cessation of territorial colonization in 1947. At the same time, her access to the global field through the Rockefeller Foundation was a sign of the continued salience that imperial interests, and metropolitan-centered circuits, had to the ascension of Indian nurses in this process. Here it is important to note that Devi's impassioned letter was accompanied by a report that she filed with the RF detailing her impressions of graduate or university-based nursing programs where Indian nurses were either already studying or, in her opinion, should be studying. Following World War II, a small and selected number of Indian nurses had begun migrating to the United States to pursue graduate degrees that were not yet available in India. While abroad they were exchange visitors, participants in the first phase of foreign nurse migration to the United States. When they returned to India, the degrees they earned became their tickets into the nascent ranks of India's postcolonial nursing leadership. The relationship between this transnational transfer of power within Indian nursing and the beginning of Indian nurse immigration to the United States is the main subject of this chapter.

* * *

Nurses formed part of the mass movement of skilled labor from India to the United States during the Cold War. Their migration pattern was female dominated, and drew heavily from India's minority Christian communities, as well as its southernmost state, Kerala. Accounts of their immigration attribute it, primarily, to implementation of the 1965 Immigration and Nationality Act amendments (Hart-Cellar). Hart-Cellar included nurses in its occupational preference quotas while simultaneously lifting the race-based exclusion that had prevented Indian laborers from legal immigration since establishment of the Asiatic Barred Zone in 1917. Scholars have cited this combination as the key that unlocked the U.S. market to Indian nurses, alongside their professional-managerial compatriots.[3]

This focus on the explanatory power of immigration law erases the role played by the U.S. nation-state or U.S.-based interests globally in fostering such flows; leaves no room for considering the participation of the United States in global histories of capitalist imperialism; and offers no framework for synthesizing the complexities of migrants' decisions alongside their negotiation with the institutions of this global system. Instead, immigration to the United States begins when migrants are allowed to legally land on U.S. shores, and their decision to do so is based on economic considerations that coincide with the ideological premise of the American Dream. Ultimately, such a formulation plays into the paradigm of American exceptionalism: the view that the United States is a nation-in-isolation that stands apart from, even as it is a beacon for, the rest of the world. What is more, it does so to describe immigration at the onset of the Cold War, a moment when American exceptionalism gained new currency on the global stage. The historiography of Indian nurse migration to the United States thus serves as an uncritical mirror of this ideological project.

In contrast, by focusing on the Rockefeller Foundation, I introduce a global analytic framework that can account for the role that U.S.-based institutions played *in India* when Indian nurses began migrating to the United States. My argument is that the RF, in particular, functioned as the "hidden hand" turning decades marked by struggles for decolonization into a prelude to the eventual immigration of Indian nurses to the U.S.—and, in the process, patterning the particular regional emphasis of their immigration pattern. Our inability to see the importance of the foundation's role in this outcome is, in large part, due to the success of its own strategy—a strategy that stretches back to well before the RF invested, specifically, in Indian nurses or nursing. And yet, it was a strategy that was foundational to the global, imperial hegemony of what we now know as biomedicine and its related biomedical professions.

The Rockefeller Foundation Remakes the Map of Colonial Medicine

The Rockefeller Foundation formed in the aftermath of a national scandal. In 1911, following years of popular protest and action by various states, the U.S. Supreme Court invoked the Sherman Antitrust Act to rule that Standard Oil, the largest oil refining company in the world, was an illegal monopoly. The Court ordered the corporation to split into what became thirty-four separate companies. By the time of the ruling, John D. Rockefeller Sr., the founder of Standard Oil, had long since retired from his role as the company's head manager. Retirement, however, did not equal divestment. On the contrary, Rockefeller retained major holdings in the resulting companies, and he emerged from the breakup richer than ever, having increased his wealth to $900 million (a large sum even today—an astronomical one at the time).[4] Two years later, in the face of his public image as a "robber baron," Rockefeller received an official charter from the state of New York, and his foundation was born.

Rockefeller was a pioneer of corporate philanthropy, a form of giving that remains a key feature of civil society in the United States and around the world today. In the early twentieth century, coroporate industrialists turned philanthropists were at pains to distinguish their giving from the forms of Christian charity that had held sway up until that time. They emphasized that philanthropy is an investment, not a form of relief. Its goal is not ameliorative so much as productive. Philanthropic grants are meant to be of limited duration, with the intention of providing "seed money" that will continue to grow after the initial investment. The ideal outcome is the creation of a set of institutions and initiatives that will have a life beyond philanthropic funds, and, ideally, continue to carry out the aims that have already met with foundation approval. In this sense, the practice of corporate philanthropy premises itself on a type of "disappearing act." Recognizing this is critical for uncovering the role that the RF played in remaking colonial medicine's global infrastructure.

After receiving its official charter the RF immediately set about creating its International Health Division (IHD).[5] The IHD's mandate was "public health," and to this end it divided the world into four target areas: the U.S. South, Latin America, and British colonies in the West Indies and Far East. This mapping of British (as well as American) empire was purposeful. First, foundation officers publicly admired and approved of the global reach of Britain's rule. And yet, their focus on its colonies was not solely conciliatory or collaborative; it was also increasingly competitive. This tension was a product of larger shifts that turned the decades between World War I and World War II into a period of "imperial restructuring," marked by "a shift from the 'illusion of permanence' that characterized the high imperialism of the late nineteenth century to the recognition of the conspicuously altered state of metropolitan-colonial ties at the advent of the 'American Century.'"[6]

When the IHD took on health and medicine as its focus, it followed, specifically, in the footsteps of the Protestant medical missions that had already developed a global network of medical institutions across the stretch of Anglo-American empire. U.S. missionaries were at the vanguard of this movement, which had had its eye on the Indian subcontinent from the very beginning. The first medical missionary to work in India, the Reverend Dr. John D. Scudder Sr., was also the first medical missionary ever deputed by the American Board of Commissioners for Foreign Missions. His arrival heralded a movement that made U.S. missionaries second only to their British brethren in India.[7] Their long historical presence on the subcontinent is a reminder that the colonization of India was never solely a British affair but one where U.S.-based interests were involved from the very beginning. It also points to the critical, cumulative role that U.S.-based institutions played in connecting India and Indians to colonial medicine's global map.

The RF appeared on the global stage just as the ideological and financial fervor that had fueled medical missions' massive expansion over the turn of the century was running dry. Medical missions were in need of a new structure of support if their work was to continue. The IHD thus began by making monetary contributions to medical missions, but it quickly evolved into buying out mission boards and leveraging mission institutions toward its own ends. In the process, Rockefeller wealth pushed the seeds of secularization already contained within medical mission work. This is not the same thing as saying that it did away with the impulse to evangelize. Instead, scientific medicine and public health functioned as their own kind of theology within the foundation, and as "civilizing" tools when spread abroad. Foundation officers believed that scientific medicine in general and the scientific method in particular were key to opening the hearts and minds of the non-Western peoples within their purview.[8] Their belief persisted at a time when exactly what constituted "scientific medicine" was neither clear nor ascendant over other, competing health care systems in the United States or around the world. This was where their money mattered, as "Rockefeller wealth became the *largest single source of capital* for the development of *medical science* in the United States, the conversion of *medical education* to a scientific research basis, and the development of *public health* programs in the United States and abroad."[9]

What Rockefeller invested in, both in the United States and abroad, was a health care model that was research as opposed to clinically oriented, and university as opposed to hospital based. It trained students to privilege the pursuit of knowledge over its application, and it was explicitly elitist in intent, positioning a professional class of medical doctors as managers of the field.[10] Nurses were in a secondary, subordinate position. However, to the degree that nursing education did figure in the designs of Rockefeller's "medicine men,"[11] it too was to be university-based. The purpose was to train nursing leaders, as leadership was what the RF saw as its mandate across all its programs. Indeed, in the 1920s, foundation support provided critical leverage for the establishment of university-based nursing programs, which in turn helped to consolidate a professionalized nursing leadership that stood over and above the vast majority of working nurses in the United States.[12]

Once again, the foundation's vision was global from the beginning. The RF focused its investments on two model nursing programs: one at the London School of Hygiene and Tropical Medicine and the other at the University of Toronto. The idea was that these could serve as beacons for large swaths of the globe: Toronto for Canada and the Caribbean, London for the rest of the British Empire. Eventually, however, no program loomed larger than Toronto, as North America in general, and the United States in particular, became global centers in a nursing circuit fueled by RF international fellowships.[13] RF fellowships funded individuals to study in model metropolitan institutions, after which fellows would spread across the globe and, ideally, bring with them the methods they had learned. The function of these fellowships was and is a source of intense debate. Generally speaking, supporters praise the opportunities metropolitan programs provided and the achievements they enabled while critics focus instead on their essentially undemocratic and elite function.[14] What both sides concur on, however, is their impact:

> Anecdotal evidence has always suggested that the fellowships may have been the most important of all Rockefeller Foundation support in the long run. The awards were highly prized, and there were few alternative sources of support, especially for young researchers. Hence, almost any scientist who achieved prominence from the 1920s to the 1950s was likely to have been a Rockefeller fellow.[15]

The same can be said of Indian nursing leadership in the decades following Indian independence/partition and before the opening of immigration to the United States. In my research I found that many of India's first generation of Indian nursing leaders had been, at one time or another, Rockefeller fellows. Indeed, this was the terrain traversed by Kumari Lakshmi Devi. All the nursing programs, professional organizations, and individual nurses she visited were products of the RF model, even though the foundation itself may have had only a minor role in funding their operations at that point. The RF no longer needed to be the primary force behind promoting its version of biomedicine because it was in a moment of what I will call "philanthropic transition." This consisted of several converging dimensions.

By the mid-twentieth century, the RF-funded model of biomedicine was hegemonic in the United States. It had become the standard curriculum at U.S. universities and was the center against which all other models of medical education and health care practice had to contend. In addition, in 1951 the IHD merged with the RF's medical sciences program and ceased its existence as an independent entity. Success was a major reason for its dissolution. By this time much of the work it had pioneered had been taken over by a new set of agencies including, in the United States, the National Science Foundation, the National Institutes of Health, and, on the global stage, the World Health Organization. These organizations were not only largely modeled after the IHD but also were heavily staffed by former IHD administrators.[16] Finally, RF-style international fellowships had also become the standard model followed by other foundations, international agencies, and the U.S. State Department.

In 1948, the State Department launched its Exchange Visitor Program (EVP) as part of the Information and Educational Exchange Act. The act's stated objective is to promote understanding of the United States in the world. It contains two overarching provisions, one aimed at disseminating information about the United States, and the other meant to facilitate educational and technical exchange. With regard to nursing, the EVP allowed several thousand agencies to sponsor foreign nurses for study in the United States. The official expectation was that after earning their degrees they would return to their home countries to use their newfound technical expertise, thus serving as unofficial "goodwill ambassadors" for the United States. Exchange visitor nurses were thus one part of a much larger program grounded in the Cold War objectives of U.S. foreign policy, objectives that had their roots in the practices of U.S. industrial corporate philanthropy.[17]

By the time that the RF turned its attention to the status of nursing in India, this system of centers and circuits was fully in place. It provides the matrix through which we can analyze the foundation's investment in Indian nurses and nursing through the provision of international fellowships and the establishment of university-based nursing programs in India.

The RF and Establishing Professional Nursing in India

In 1946, the College of Nursing at the University of Delhi (Delhi)[18] and the Christian Medical College, Vellore (Vellore) each established a four-year degree course leading to a bachelor of science (honors) in nursing, the first of their kind in India. The RF was heavily involved in the development of both programs. When it opened, the College of Nursing at Delhi came equipped with a consultant from the RF, and its core staff consisted of six Indian nurses who had been RF fellows, two who had received RF travel grants, and two who were at the time studying at the University of Toronto.[19] Yet, in spite of these investments, RF assessments of the Delhi program were repeatedly troubled, noting staff shortages, improper placement of RF fellows, and problems with student retention. RF officers laid much of the blame for the inability to properly professionalize students on the low status afforded nurses in India. This was what kept *quality* students from entering nursing, and what made it difficult for the RF to produce adequate nursing leadership from among their ranks. Foundation officers' assessment of the situation in Delhi contrasted sharply with their view of Vellore: "Compared with the Delhi College of Nursing, the Vellore School has a larger and better qualified staff, which includes a group of Indian nurses who are being prepared to replace the European staff."[20]

Vellore's appeal to the Rockefeller Foundation was inextricable from its history as a U.S.-based mission. Indeed, it was the mission at Vellore that the Reverend Dr. John Scudder Sr. founded in 1836 as the aforementioned first medical missionary in India. The Christian Medical College, Vellore, began as the one-woman dispensary of his granddaughter, Dr. Ida Sophia Scudder, in 1900. Dr. Scudder was one of the first female graduates of Cornell's Medical College, and is an exemplar of the opportunities that single female medical missionaries found in the colonial field. Her practice grew into a forty-bed hospital (1902), the School of Nursing (1909), the Missionary Medical School for Women (1918), and, ultimately, a university-affiliated medical college (1942). Throughout this growth, professional mobility through international migration remained central to the evolution of Vellore's nursing curriculum. By the 1930s, Vera K. Pitman and Florence Taylor headed the School of Nursing. Pitman had trained at Guy's Hospital, generally regarded as the premier nursing program in England at the time. Meanwhile, Taylor was a Canadian educated at the University of Toronto. Both Taylor and Pitman were firm believers in the need to upgrade Vellore's nursing curriculum in ways that would register with Taylor's training at Toronto.

This reconstitution of medical and nursing education at Vellore cannot be considered outside of the institution's financial needs. As a U.S.-based medical mission, Vellore had always relied heavily on overseas funding. During the late nineteenth and early twentieth centuries, when the missionary movement was at its height, the Vellore boards in both the United States and the United Kingdom first formed, primarily for fund-raising purposes. However, as this movement lost its momentum in the years leading up to World War I, Vellore could not rely on these channels alone. And it was precisely at this time, as we have seen, that the RF emerged as a major player on the global health scene. Thus, it was no mere coincidence that Vellore conformed to the type of medical institution that would attract funding from the foundation. Vellore was a consistent recipient of Rockefeller grants throughout the period under consideration. So, for instance, in 1956 the RF provided grants for staff development, salary increases, research, and building construction[21] Examination of the documents attached to these grants reveals that they were donated with the understanding that, as with all RF monies, they would be considered short-term, and for the purposes of stimulating matching funds and, ultimately, of enabling self-supporting programs. A key to this last proposition was the creation of Indian leadership.

In spite of the fact that the RF had targeted Vellore on the basis of its educational standards and, concomitantly, the quality of its Indian staff, the transfer of leadership at the institution proceeded slowly. In 1952, five years after independence/partition, there were still no Indians in the top positions at Vellore.[22] Yet by this time the institution had graduated its first group of BSc nurses, creating a pool of prime candidates for promotion, if they continued on the path to professionalization. Vellore graduates thus became the primary source for RF nursing fellowships in India. Of the twenty-five RF Indian nursing fellows listed in *The Rockefeller Foundation Directory of Fellowships and Scholarships 1917–1970*, more than half were from Vellore.[23] One of these was Aleyamma Kuruvilla, who earned her master's degree at Columbia University in 1953 and was subsequently appointed the first Indian dean of the College of Nursing, Vellore. It was under her leadership that Vellore introduced its master of science program in 1967. Kuruvilla was also the first Indian to be president of the Board of Nursing Education, South India, a position she held from 1972 to 1974, and again from 1978 to 1994. She also served as president of the Christian Medical Association of India and the TNAI for four years each.

Clearly, if the RF were to judge its success in fostering Indian nursing leadership on the case of Aleyamma Kuruvilla alone, it would have to conclude that its investment was a smashing success. Yet she was not the only example of a Vellore grad turned Rockefeller fellow turned nursing leader. Violet Jayachandran, Kasturi Sunder Rao, Ann Rajan Sukumar, and Rachel Chacko were all RF fellows who went on to become professors and department deans at Vellore. Beyond the presence of these specific fellows were the other Indian nurses who received international scholarships or fellowships from other agencies (on the RF model), and who also went abroad to study, assuming leadership positions upon their return. Critically, the ascension of these international fellows was not limited to a changing of the guard at Vellore. In 1994, out of forty nursing colleges operative in India fully half were headed by Vellore grads.[24] This all-India spread was precisely what the RF aimed for with its investments. However, a closer look at the archives reveals that there was a decidedly regional emphasis to the influence of both the foundation's investments and the work of its fellows. Indeed, available evidence suggests that it was in the southernmost Indian state of Kerala, not in New Delhi, that the RF found its ideal government sponsor, and that this relationship took root in the decade preceding passage of Hart-Cellar.

From Migration to Immigration: The RF, Vellore, and Nursing Education in Kerala

If more than half of the Rockefeller Indian nursing fellows listed in the foundation's 1917–1979 directory had Vellore training, half of these went on almost immediately to work at the school (later, college) of nursing at Trivandrum, capital of Kerala state.[25] According to historian Meera Abraham, this was partly due to the fact that in the 1950s the government of Kerala began posting advertisements for BSc nurses to help in its push to establish nursing education in the state. The result was that many Vellore graduates (Vellore being the only institution in South India to offer the BSc in nursing at the time) went to work in Kerala, and "nursing education in Kerala was put on a firm footing by them."[26] The stamp of the RF was on this movement in that many of these nurses had been international fellows, Rockefeller or otherwise. Their migration in search of higher education and upward mobility was, however, only one prong in RF support of nursing education in Trivandrum.

By the time the nursing school at Trivandrum opened in 1943, the region had already caught the attention of RF officers. Again, this began with Vellore, where nursing students from Kerala, most of them Syrian Christian, had already filled the ranks of its nursing program. The presence of large Christian communities in Kerala, combined with the historical association between Indian Christians and colonial nursing on the subcontinent (due in no small part to the centrality of Protestant missions in this history), provides a partial explanation for their predominance. It was not, however, the whole story. Vellore also specifically recruited Syrian Christians, most notably under the leadership of Vera K. Pitman. This began as early as 1928, with its impact definitely felt by 1932. By the 1940s, Vellore thus had a ready-made pool of students from Kerala that the school at Trivandrum could draw from, and that the RF had noticed.[27]

The first director of Trivandrum's nursing school, Mrs. Rugmaniamma Iyengar, was both a Vellore graduate and the recipient of an RF fellowship prior to taking up the post. She was not alone. By 1951, RF officers noted with approval that all the teachers at Trivandrum were from Vellore, and that the school actually had more applicants than available slots.[28] In addition, it was government-supported, relatively new, in need of funds, and ripe for intervention in RF-preferred areas of development such as public health nursing.[29] All these reasons fed into the foundation's decision to invest in Trivandrum.[30] This began in the 1940s, with the provision of textbooks and educational materials as well as the aforementioned training of its first director. Over the years, the foundation also supplied the school with new buildings, model wards for clinical training and practice, and RF-appointed nursing advisers.

The first RF adviser, Lillian A. Johnson, arrived in 1952. She was appointed for a two-year residency at the school to work as a consultant alongside Iyengar. The arrangement was meant to emphasize RF policy regarding the promotion of Indian leadership and the discouragement of undue reliance on its foreign personnel. In spite of this distinction, Johnson's credentials would have certainly resonated with the historically familiar image of a colonial nursing leader. She was a white American woman who had been educated at Bellevue Hospital in New York. By the time she arrived in India, she had worked with U.S. company hospitals in Panama, Columbia, and Peru; served in the army in New Zealand, the Philippines, and New Guinea (earning the rank of captain); and worked with the Community Service Society in Puerto Rico.

Apparently Johnson's global/colonial credentials did not prepare her for the nursing situation in Kerala, which she found particularly tough going. In her detailed correspondence with RF officers in New York, she remarked, "Each day I absorb a bit of the depressed conditions of the nurses."[31] These conditions had much to do with the low pay and long bonds that nurses in Trivandrum were subjected to, as well as the general lack of respect for nurses in India, as she and other RF officers also consistently observed.[32] Yet again these rank-and-file issues were not the immediate concern of the foundation. Instead, its goal was to install professional Indian nursing leaders and, it was to be supposed, everything else would take care of itself. With regard to the former (though not, concomitantly, the latter), the foundation's goals were once again met in multiple.

One of Johnson's primary tasks upon arrival was to observe and recommend potential candidates for RF international fellowships. She recommended Miss Lucy Peters, who was a 1951 BSc graduate from Vellore. Peters received a RF fellowship to earn her master's in nursing at Boston University. When she returned to India, she initially went to work at the School of Nursing in Ernakulum, Kerala, but in 1959 she moved to Trivandrum to become the director of its School of Nursing, where she had the help of another RF-appointed nursing adviser, Jane R. Stewart, who was in Trivandrum from 1963 to 1965.

Stewart arrived at a time when the development of nursing education at Trivandrum, and indeed in Kerala, was no longer the task of two women, one an RF nursing adviser and the other a former RF fellow, as in the days of Mrs. Iyengar and Miss Johnson. Instead, by 1963 Trivandrum's entire nursing faculty had been RF fellows.[33] The influence of these nurses was not limited to nursing education at Trivandrum. When Peters took over, Iyengar was transferred to head the nursing program in Alleppy. And, by 1969, Govindan Balagopalan Chandramathy, a Rockefeller fellow who had studied at Syracuse University in New York from 1952 to 1953, was the nursing superintendent at the government hospital in Perurkada. Finally, in the 1980s, Mrs. Chellamma George, a Vellore BSc graduate and close colleague of Peters in both Ernakulum and Trivandrum, went on to start a four-year BSc nursing program in Calicut, Kerala.

The spread of professional nursing education across the state of Kerala linked the RF, RF fellows, and the government of Kerala in what was a by-then standard philanthropic manner. That is, the state accepted RF funding with the understanding that it had to raise and/or provide matching or partial funds and, in the case of international fellows in particular, ensure positions and promotion upon their return. In addition, with regard to fellowships, many of these would not officially go under the name of the RF per se but instead be labeled as coming from the particular school in question or the government of Kerala itself.[34] In light of these many layers, it is beyond my current capacity to provide a full accounting of the exact nature of the relationship between the RF and the government of Kerala with regard to nursing education in the critical two decades following Indian independence/partition. However, as confirmation that there was a close and continued relationship between the two, I quote a 1963 letter from A. Sethumadhava Menon, secretary, Health and Labour Department, Kerala State, to then director of medical and natural sciences at the RF, Dr. Robert S. Morrison. The letter is part of an application for a grant from the RF for the School of Nursing at Trivandrum:

The Nursing Education in the State has received great encouragement from the Rockefeller Foundation, U.S.A. which has provided Advisors to advise [the] Government in organizing the Nursing Education in the State. The Foundation also provided Fellowship for Nurses to get themselves trained in U.S.A. as teachers. They have also assisted the School of Nursing with books and equipments. As a result of this sympathetic and generous attitude of the Rockefeller Foundation, Nursing Education in the State has been largely developed in recent years. In addition to the certificate courses and diploma courses in Nursing, this Government are [sic] introducing the B.Sc. degree course also in Nursing in the Medical College, Trivandrum, which is expected to commence in a couple of months. As such, the assistance of the Foundation is essential. A large number of nurses who are qualified by undergoing courses in the different institutions in the State are serving in different parts of India. The degree course in Nursing is being introduced with a view to see that the services of highly qualified and well trained nurses are available not only in this State but also throughout India. The Foundation has already provided a Nursing Advisor. It is however necessary to seek the further assistance of the Foundation to push forward the programme in the field of Nursing Education in the State.[35]

Given the fact that they came attached to a request for more funds, the health secretary's words were meant to flatter and emphasize the foundation's contributions to nursing education in Kerala. The contributions he lists, however, were not an exaggeration. Indeed, they confirm much of what I have already cited. It is also of note that he wrote the letter in 1963, two years prior to Hart-Cellar's passage and the movement of Indian, in general, and Keralite, in particular, nurses to the United States as *immigrants*. Certainly, the long bonds and low wages described by Stewart contributed to the lure that the U.S. market would hold for Kerala's nurses. But also, in order to immigrate, Indian nurses would need a degree of certification that could translate in the U.S. market. It was precisely this that RF and RF-styled fellows and funds helped to establish in India. In addition, these nurses served as individual, institutional, and ideological models for what upward mobility could mean for Indian nurses who accessed the increasingly U.S.-centered international field. As Rajan (not her real name), a Vellore graduate and an immigrant nurse whom I interviewed in 2003 at a hospital in Queens, New York, put it:

> Most of our professors who had a master's degree got their degree in the United States. They were teaching you. They were a role model for you. So you wanted to become like one of them by going abroad and getting your education....It was so patterned at Vellore. At a certain level, after a certain year, they usually sent staff abroad to get educated and come back....That's how they maintained their standards.[36]

Rajan is from Tamil Nadu, where Vellore is located. Her perspective both takes us back to Vellore and reminds us that even as Kerala nurses become increasingly significant to this history, they were not the totality of nurses who were involved. What is more, her own *immigration* history signals the fact that in the case of postindependence India, the opportunity to study abroad did not always lead to the institution's or its international sponsors' preferred result. As we have seen, this was in large part the transfer of power from a colonial to a postcolonial nursing leadership. The question of placement upon return from an international fellowship was key to this process. In the case of the RF, it was also the final guarantee that the RF had that its investments would be put to their intended use. This was a point of repeated insistence among foundation officers, and RF fellowships to either the government or specific institutions came with the understanding that the fellow would be placed in an upgraded position upon their return. That there were difficulties with this mandate come across in the case of Atula Shroff, who was an RF fellow at the University of Washington in 1951.[37] In 1953 Shroff was offered a post at the College of Nursing at Delhi but refused, citing that she saw "no future prospects" in the position. RF correspondence detailing her refusal concludes:

> Apart from having an exaggerated idea of her own importance, my feeling is that Miss Shroff never had much intention of joining the College of Nursing, unless she could do so at her own convenience and terms, on her return to India....I think we may write Miss Shroff off as a bad fellowship investment.[38]

Here it is very clear what a "bad investment" is from the perspective of the RF: a nurse who exercised her own will rather than followed that of the foundation. This could of course come in many forms. Even nurses who did take up the posts prepared for them upon their return could act in ways that might not suit the tastes of RF officers or the interests they served. However, if such a thing did occur, the result would be largely the same as that which attached itself to Miss Shroff's refusal: the fellows and/or the program they headed would be dropped from consideration for further foundation support. For the RF, it was as simple as that. For the returned fellow, it was not. Instead, she faced a national field that was not, in the main, defined by the foundation's goal of instituting a model of professionalized nursing that was shaped by the international field and attached to university-based programs that would perpetuate elite leadership.

The RF's focus on professionalization positioned itself against state-sponsored plans that focused on addressing the massive health needs of a population that was emerging from long-term, systemic colonial neglect. Independent India's plans regarding nursing were based largely on the recommendations contained in the 1946 report of the Health Survey and Development Committee (Bhore Report). The report states that conditions for nurses were deplorable, and there existed an absolutely critical shortage of nursing personnel.[39] For the years 1941–1971, it recommends increasing the number of medical doctors by four times, but for nurses and health visitors (public health nurses), a hundred times.[40] After independence the government of India insisted, in its first two five-year plans, on the rapid training of more nurses to meet the massive demand. It linked this training to the rural and public health emphases of its plans.[41] While some of this may have fit with the RF's earlier goals under the IHD (particularly around public health), it did not meet with its focus on ensuring an Indian nursing leadership that met with international standards. Instead, it produced a context for Atula Shroff's refusal, and Kumari Lakshmi Devi's lament: "My visit to your country has done nothing but add fuel to the fire....I am more ambitious for India than ever, so maybe I should have stayed at home?"

Devi here raises the question of a disjuncture between the version of professionalized nursing established in the United States (and promoted by the RF), and the reality on the ground in India at mid-twentieth century. Her question also leads to the fact that, in spite of the aspirations that exposure to the U.S. market might evoke for Indian nurses, staying in India was what they had to do. In India, the RF worked with individual institutions, state governments, and the government of India to try to assure its fellows positions commensurate with their newly acquired training. This intention was not, however, limited to the foundation. It was also central to the EVP. The program issued exchange nurses temporary visas for a maximum of two years. Persons who overstayed their visa or engaged in political activity during their stay were subject to immediate deportation.[42] Thus, while the EVP inaugurated foreign nurse *migration* to the United States, it was explicitly not intended to enable foreign nurse *immigration*. And yet, it was precisely by *not* settling in the United States that exchange visitor nurses became key to the eventual immigration of Indian nurses when the possibility to do so opened up in 1965. This stemmed from the seemingly simple fact that they did their job and, in the process, helped to spread a version and vision of nursing education that was compatible with the U.S. market.[43] Recognizing this allows us to recast passage of Hart-Cellar as a turning point rather than an inauguration in the relationship between Indian nurses and a colonial medical map that had connected professional mobility to U.S. individuals, institutions, and ideologies since the nineteenth century.

NOTES

1. Lakshmi Devi to Virginia Arnold, April 17, 1959, folder 491, box 53, sub-series 464C, series 464, Record Group 1.2, Rockefeller Foundation Archives, Rockefeller Archive Center (hereafter RAC).

2. Kumari Lakshmi Devi, "Summary of Tour Undertaken by Kumari Lakshmi Devi under a Rockefeller Foundation Travel Grant—1959, to observe nursing education programmes and professional organizations," 1959, folder 491, box 53, sub-series 464C, series 464, Record Group 1.26, Rockefeller Foundation Archives, RAC.

3. George, Sheba Mariam, *When Women Come First: Gender and Class in Transnational Migration*, Berkeley: University of California Press, 2005; Williams, Raymond Brady, *Christian Pluralism in the United States: The Indian Immigrant Experience*, Cambridge: Cambridge University Press, 1996; Thomas, Annamma, and T. M., *Kerala Immigrants in America: A Sociological Study of the St. Thomas Christians*, Cochin: Simon Printers and Publishers, 1984; and DiCiccio-Bloom,

Barbara, "The Racial and Gendered Experiences of Immigrant Nurses from Kerala, India," *Journal of Transcultural Nursing* 15:1, January 2004: 26–33.

4. Yergin, Daniel, *The Prize: The Epic Quest for Oil, Money and Power* (New York: Simon and Schuster, 1991, p. 113.

5. Technically, this division was the International Health Commission from 1913 to 1916, the International Health Board from 1916 to 1927, and the International Health Division from 1927 to 1951. It is best known in this last incarnation, so for consistency I will use this name throughout.

6. Sinha, Mrinalini, *Specters of Mother India: The Global Restructuring of an Empire.* Durham, NC: Duke University Press, 2006, p. 4.

7. Pathak, Sunil Madhava, *American Missionaries and Hinduism (A Study of Their Contacts from 1813 to 1910)*, Delhi: Munshiram Manorhalal, 1967.

8. Ma, Quisha, "The Peking Union Medical College and the Rockefeller Foundation's Medical Programs in China," in *Rockefeller Philanthropy and Modern Biomedicine: International Initiatives from World War I to the Cold War*, ed. William H. Schneider, Bloomington: Indiana University Press, 2002, p. 165.

9. Brown, E. Richard, *Rockefeller Medicine Men: Medicine and Capitalism in America*, Berkeley: University of California Press, 1979, p. 104.

10. In the United States the model institution funded by the RF was the medical school at Johns Hopkins University. It was this model that the foundation exported around the world, beginning with its model non-U.S.-based institution the Peking Medical Union College in 1915.

11. Brown, *Rockefeller Medicine Men.*

12. Reverby, Susan *Ordered to Care: The Dilemma of American Nursing, 1850–1945*, Cambridge: Cambridge University Press, 1987; Melosh, Barbara, *"The Physician's Hand": Work Culture and Conflict in American Nursing*, Philadelphia: Temple University Press, 1982.

13. Abrams, Sarah E., "Brilliance and Bureaucracy: Nursing and Changes in the Rockefeller Foundation, 1915–1930," *Nursing History Review* 1 (1993): 119–137.

14. Fosdick, Raymond B., *The Story of the Rockefeller Foundation*, New York: Harper and Brothers, 1952; and Berman, Edward H., *The Influence of the Carnegie, Ford and Rockefeller Foundations on American Foreign Policy: The Ideology of Philanthropy*, Albany: State University of New York Press, 1983.

15. Schneider, William H., "The Men Who Followed Flexner: Richard Pearce, Alan Gregg, and the Rockefeller Foundation Medical Divisions, 1919–1951," in *Rockefeller Philanthropy and Modern Biomedicine: International Initiatives from World War I to the Cold War*, ed. William H. Schneider, Bloomington: Indiana University Press, 2002, p. 46.

16. Nielsen, Waldemar A., *The Big Foundations*, New York: Columbia University Press, 1972; Shaplen, Robert, *Toward the Well-Being of Mankind: Fifty Years of the Rockefeller Foundation*, Garden City, NY: Doubleday, 1964; Jonas, Gerald, *The Circuit Riders: Rockefeller Money and the Rise of Modern Science*, New York: Norton, 1989; and Farley, John, *To Cast Out Disease: A History of the International*

Health Division of the Rockefeller Foundation (1913–1951), Oxford: Oxford University Press, 2004.

17. Berman, *The Influence of the Carnegie, Ford and Rockefeller Foundations on American Foreign Policy.*
    Also, in the case of the EVP in particular, the Rockefeller Foundation funded the first major study of foreign nurses' experiences in the United States in 1962, Martha Jeanne Broadhurst's *Nurses from Abroad: Values in International Exchange of Persons*, New York: American Nurses' Foundation, 1962.

18. The Delhi College of Nursing is also known as the Rajkumari Amrit Kaur College of Nursing.

19. "India—Nursing—1st and 2nd Semi-Annual Reports," 1946, folder 2494, box 204, series 464C, record group 5.3, Rockefeller Foundation Archives, RAC.

20. "India—Nursing—1st Semi-Annual Report," 1948, p. 6, folder 2496, box 204, series 464C, record group 5.3, Rockefeller Foundation Archives, RAC.

21. "Vellore Christian Medical College," July 1, 1956, folder 488, box 51, series 464A: India, record group 1.2, Rockefeller Foundation Archives, RAC.

22. Abraham, Meera, *Religion, Caste and Gender: Missionaries and Nursing History in South India*, Bangalore: B I Publications, 1996.
    The highest-level Indian nurse was Anna Jacob, who was the first Indian to hold the post of nursing superintendent. Jacob had not been a Rockefeller fellow but nevertheless had been funded through another channel to attain her bachelor's degree in nursing at McGill University in Montreal, Canada. Her promotion thus reflected the institutional pattern linking upward mobility with higher education and international migration (and especially to North America).

23. *The Rockefeller Foundation Directory of Fellowships and Scholarships 1917–1970*, New York: Rockefeller Foundation, 1972. This covers grants given up until 1968. It is actually not possible to give an entirely accurate number. The entries are based on fellows' responses, some of which are vague. For example, Annamma Nattacheril Matthews Gupta received her BSc from Wayne State University in Detroit in 1952. She was appointed from the "Christian Medical College," to pursue her master's degree at Wayne State as well. She does not write "Vellore"; however, in this case it applies. For Annamma Matthews was the RF fellow originally slated to take the helm at Vellore, but who, according to the fellowship directory, took a position as a professor in Windsor, Ontario, Canada, instead. Another possibility, for other entries, is that a nurse received a diploma from Vellore and then a BSc elsewhere, and so Vellore does not appear on the record. In terms of the available evidence, I counted thirteen graduates of Vellore and/or the University of Madras (to which Vellore's College of Nursing was affiliated). It is entirely possible that a couple more of the entries have a Vellore connection.

24. Abraham, *Religion, Caste and Gender.*

25. In 1991, Trivandrum was renamed Thiruvananthapuram.

26. Abraham, *Religion, Caste and Gender*, 106.

27. Prior even to the opening of the school at Trivandrum, RF officers noted the predominance of students from the region at Vellore. Tennant, Mary Elizabeth , "Summary of Impressions of Nursing in India," 1941, folder 3816, box 561, series 464C, record group 2, stack material, Rockefeller Foundation Archives, RAC.

28. RBW to EWB 12/21/51 RF 1.2 464 C: India, 53, 492.

29. Elizabeth W. Brackett, Diary Excerpt, March 3, 1952, folder 403, box 44, series 2.1, record group 6.1, Rockefeller Foundation Archives, RAC.

30. In 1952, RF officer Dr. Robert Briggs Watson wrote to the principal of the Medical College at Trivandrum, Dr. C. O. Karunakaran, that the RF "is not content to support mediocrity...in the cooperative enterprise we hope to establish with the Trivandrum Medical Center, our objective would be to develop the Nurses Training School in such a way that not only would its graduates be better nurses than are now produced; but the School would serve as a model for the development of other hospital nursing schools, whose graduates would more nearly meet the nursing needs of India. Therefore, our first condition would be that the authorities concerned would accept as a principle that the Nursing School would be an experimental one, with a curriculum substantially different from that now being followed."
Robert Briggs Watson to Dr. Karunakaran, June 4, 1952, folder 492, box 53, sub-series 464C: India, series 464C, record group 1.2, Rockefeller Foundation Archives, RAC.

31. Lillian A. Johnson, January 23, 1953, folder 492, box 53, series 464C, record group 1.2, Rockefeller Foundation Archives, RAC.

32. This was a point of friction between the RF and the government of Kerala. Because of the fact that many of the fellows funded by the RF were actually also officially sponsored by the state, they incurred not only promotions upon return but also state bonds. For example, Rugmaniamma Iyengar had a fifteen-year bond to the state upon return from her year in Canada. The foundation explicitly sought to reduce the possibilities of producing such "indentured servants of the state." This is the language of Dr. Watson, in his 1951 letter to Elizabeth Brackett in the New York office. He continues by explaining that, in Kerala, "education by the State, at home or abroad, carries with it a bonded promise to serve the State for varying lengths of time. This used to be 12 years in the case of nurses; but due principally to our efforts this has been reduced to five." Robert B. Watson to Elizabeth W. Brackett, December 21, 1951, folder 492, box 53, series 464C, record group 1.2, Rockefeller Foundation Archives, RAC.

33. Trivandrum School of Nursing Scholarships 1963–1967, folder 495, box 54, series 464C, record group 1.2, Rockefeller Foundation Archives, RAC.

34. With regard to Kerala, Stewart wrote that the scholarships on offer should be advertised throughout India and labeled as coming from the sponsoring school, not the foundation.
Jane R. Stewart to Virginia Arnold, March 7, 1963, folder 495, box 54, series 464C, record group 1.2, Rockefeller Foundation Archives, RAC.

35. A. Sethumadhava Menon to Robert S. Morrison, August 8, 1963, folder 495, box 54, series 464C, record group 1.2, Rockefeller Foundation Archives, RAC.

36. Author's interview with Rajan, July 9, 2003.

37. Interestingly, her entry in *The Rockefeller Foundation Directory* states that Narjidas Shroff Derasari was appointed an IHD fellow from a position at Columbia University. In other words, she was already in the United States. It is not clear to me whether or not she was already at Columbia under the auspices of the RF or through another agency.

38. Robert Briggs Watson to E. W. Brackett, March 27, 1953, RF 6.1, 2.1, 44, 403.

39. Sood, Mrs. Raj Kumari, "Nursing Services in India: An Urgent Need for Reorganisation in View of the Goal Health for All by 2000 A.D.," *Nursing Journal of India* 79.11 (1988): 288–291.

40. Jeffery, Roger, *The Politics of Health in India*, Berkeley: University of California Press, 1988, p. 223.

41. Jeffery, *The Politics of Health in India*.

42. "United States Information and Educational Act of 1948," PL-CHS 36, January 27, 1948.

43. For a similar conclusion about the role of the RF in the Philippines, see Brush, Barbara, "The Rockefeller Agenda for American/Philippines Nursing Relations," *Western Journal of Nursing Research* 17.5 (1995): 540–555.

From Imperialism to Free-Market Fundamentalism

Changing Forms of Migration and Work

5

Putting "the Family" to Work

Managerial Discourses of Control in the Immigrant Service Sector

MIABI CHATTERJI

One blustery December evening in 2007, I went to a small Indian restaurant in Manhattan's "Curry Hill" neighborhood. This small neighborhood centered around Lexington Avenue is home to South Asian restaurants, grocery stores, clothing shops, and other immigrant-oriented businesses. That evening, I was speaking to four restaurant managers, men in their thirties and forties, all migrants from India, who currently run businesses in New York and New Jersey. All four have run ventures in South Asian commercial enclaves in the New York metropolitan area, from Jersey City to Curry Hill to Jackson Heights, Queens. While the manager of our host restaurant oversaw the dinner rush and stopped by our table to chat and make sure we were comfortable, the other three managers and I discussed their experiences in the United States and in the restaurant industry.

When asked how they would describe their managerial style, the four managers all used the word "family." This term emerges again and again when speaking to urban South Asian managers and business owners. It shows up on menus and websites that describe their kitchens and restaurants as warm and familial, and it is repeated to journalists who review Indian restaurants or profile South Asian neighborhoods. Describing their restaurant teams as functioning "like a family," these managers declare that they think of their employees as extended kin, or even as sons and daughters. Employees enjoy being part of such a close-knit team, my manager participants have told me—they love working for managers who treat them with familial kindness and respect.

The four managers spoke of the familial orientation of their businesses in different ways. Mannur said that people always think of him as "an uncle" and can "come to me with their problems, for advice." Bipin said that he likes to run his restaurants like families because then he can be more "close and comfortable with the staff. You don't want to let a family member down, and you have certain rules in a family." Shri laughed and said, "Sometimes it's like a real family, sometimes it's a forced family. But you have to make it work, you have to have the respect of the workers. Otherwise they'll walk right over you."[1]

In the contemporary urban South Asian context, the concept of family within the restaurant or ethnic retail store is likely to be used as a metaphor, not as a term referring to literal groups of kin-based relations. Even when South Asian business owners employ a handful of their relatives in their service-sector business, these family members almost never constitute the entirety of the workforce. Other people must "join the family," and in the urban U.S. service sector, those jobs are often filled by recent South Asian, Mexican, and Central American immigrants. The ethnic "family business" in the contemporary service sector, particularly in restaurants, small groceries, and ethnic retail stores, is changing rapidly.

In this chapter, I argue that in urban South Asian enclaves in the United States, small-business owners make use of the concept of the family as a managerial ideology that complements several dominant cultural narratives in the United States about family businesses, immigrant communities, and Asian cultures. As I studied the relationships between recently arrived immigrant employees and their employers in the service sector in New York City, I in turn studied the dynamics of this metaphorical family of the immigrant-run business. What kind of family is being invoked, and to whose benefit? I examine ways in which workers respond to the rhetoric of the family at work, variously resisting or accommodating this language. I argue that the family is not just a convenient metaphor but a managerial tool that attempts to privatize economic relations and screen them from public view and regulation. The family discourse is one strategy that managers employ to resist legal regulation and enforcement of standards in their industry. The lack of regulation and the level of informality in the service sector in the United States have deep effects on the kinds of work hierarchies that are able to emerge and remain in place over time—informal hierarchies that are usually based on race, national origin, gender, and other ascribed characteristics. Finally, I observe the ways that managers within South Asian ethnic enclaves in New York treat South Asian and Latino workers differently and, in turn, the ways that some groups of Latino and South Asian immigrant workers experience the same or parallel treatment and conditions at work, especially when other factors such as gender, immigration status, or job-prestige status divide employees at the same workplace.

For activists and scholars studying the growing service sector in the United States, in which laws and worker protections are laxly enforced, a central problem continues to be: How do we work toward increased enforcement of standards and a meritocratic system that provides opportunities for advancement for low-wage workers? In order to work toward that goal, we need to understand qualitatively how managers make use of their authority and how they are able to evade regulation and standardization of worker treatment. Only then will we be able to change policies, inequalities, and the possibilities available in the urban immigrant-led service sector.

As I sat with Bipin, Vinod, Shri, and Mannur in Curry Hill, servers, bussers, and the host were all busy at work in the restaurant around us, as the dinner rush picked up. I eventually spoke to several of these workers, all men in their twenties and thirties, from Nepal, Bangladesh, and India. They, like the many other low-wage service workers from South Asia, Mexico, and Central America with whom I speak in my research, rarely if ever use the term "family" when describing their work environment. They are much more likely to use the terms "oven," "prison," or "chaos" to refer to their workplaces, and if the concept of family comes up, it is usually when workers skeptically refer to the managerial tactic of couching business relationships in familial terms. Only a few of the workers with whom I spoke share the view that their workplace felt like a family. Clearly there is a significant conceptual divide here, one that can be mined for a deeper understanding of the moral economy of the contemporary service sector, the fastest-growing sector of the urban capitalist economy.[2]

The Ethnic Enclave Debate and Exploitation in the Service Sector

Just ten years ago, literature on urban immigrant labor brimmed with studies that argued that in the workforce, recent immigrants could find their best chances in ethnic enclaves, working for and with people from their same ethnic background. Prominent sociologists of immigration to the United States argued that "unskilled" immigrant workers can find many benefits in ethnic enclaves.[3] However, I found something quite different in my research. Critics of the ethnic enclave theory argue—and my data confirm—that many workers feel disassociated from their co-ethnic immigrant managers and owners in the low-wage service sector. This alienation is a result of several factors, including underpayment for their labor and a common feeling that co-ethnic managers make use of their shared racial or ethnic background in ways that exacerbate exploitation rather than lessen it.[4] While the informal perks of having a "flexible" workplace may create a more comfortable environment for some workers, this "flexibility" also allows for forms of managerial control that weaken worker power.[5]

Critics of the ethnic enclave theory analyze the ways that "flexibility" in the co-ethnic workplace is not always as beneficial as it might seem at first glance, and may entail, instead, getting employees to work longer hours for less pay than they would receive in the mainstream economy.[6] These scholars also argue that allowing employees to bring their children to work, for example, is a time-honored device of sweatshop overseers: if workers can take care of their children on the job, they can work much longer shifts. Such "flexibility" in the workplace can also lead to more unregulated spaces allowing for sexual harassment and violence, forms of worker control and coercion not uncommon in the low-wage service sector.[7] I argue that we must go further in analyzing the conditions of co-ethnic work in the contemporary ethnic enclave, especially in investigating the significance of race, gender presentation, and national origin in the running of the service sector.[8]

The family firm was a cornerstone of early U.S. capitalism, when family-based capital built entire industries, including industrial manufacturing, real estate, financial services, and insurance. This history comprises parts of the service sector as well, especially restaurants, where family networks and labor have gone hand in hand in the United States since the first restaurants emerged in the early nineteenth century. In immigrant and ethnic-minority communities, family businesses in the service sector have proved to be crucial to economic integration, allowing capital accumulation in some instances. As ideologies of immigrant assimilation and bootstrap-style class mobility were refined through the mid-twentieth century, the small family-run business emerged as a key part of these narratives.[9] While the family business is not particularly ethnic, South Asian, or immigrant in nature, the family firm has come to hold deep rhetorical and cultural significance in the dominant understanding of how "good" immigrants assimilate and access their part of the supposedly meritocratic American Dream.

Conditions of Work and Managerial Tactics of Division

"We immigrants, we've always had to rely on our families, the people we know, to run businesses here in America. It's the same with the Chinese, the Jewish. We have to work with our own. And that way, it's safer for everyone, and you can rely on each other. Yes, it's safer. It's much easier for everyone when you work like a family, same background, same life." These are the words of Shri, an Indian immigrant and former manager of restaurants and retail stores in the New York area. When discussing the work that the "back-of-the-house" staff do in restaurants (referring to cooks, food preparation staff, dishwashers, cleaners, and chefs), he told me that it was both "easy" and "simple." In this he echoed many of my manager respondents, presenting an image of the industry as a safe and secure space.

In fact, however, this sector offers many hazards; its difficult working conditions belie Shri's words. Most of the workers I spoke to had experienced racial or gender discrimination from at least one manager; the majority had been injured on the job in ways that could be traced to lax health and safety measures. The majority of these injured workers did not see a doctor or go to a hospital, either because they did not have health insurance or because they were encouraged by their managers to stay at work. Many explained that hygiene and safety standards at work were minimal, even at fine-dining restaurants. And three-quarters of the more than fifty workers I spoke to had experienced problems with getting paid in the past—they were not paid on time, or they were paid less than they were due.[10] More than a fifth of the workers I spoke to experienced some kind of unpaid "training time" at work, lasting up to a full month. Wages are, needless to say, difficult to live on: back-of-the-house staff can make as little as $200 a week. That is an annual salary of $9,600 if one was to work each week, with no vacations. Tipped staff working at the bar or as servers can make quite a bit more, depending on the style and prices at the restaurant and how many shifts a worker might be able to work—but most immigrant workers I interviewed take home less then $20,000 a year. I found little difference in wages between South Asian and Latino back-of-the-house staff, but there are discrepancies in who gets hired for front-of-the house jobs, leading to inequalities in wages. U.S.-born South Asian American workers were routinely paid more than any immigrants, and South Asian immigrant servers were paid slightly more than Latino servers.

These experiences are typical of the larger service industry. In a report on conditions in the restaurant industry in New York City in 2005, the Restaurant Opportunities Center of New York (ROC-NY) found that 21 percent of workers employed in back-of-the-house positions made less than the legal minimum wage; 83 percent did not have health insurance; 67 percent experienced overtime violations; 54 percent had to work in dangerously hot kitchens; 65 percent did not receive workplace safety training; and 35 percent had done something on the job, in the interest of time, that may have compromised the health and safety of customers.[11] Wage-law violations are particularly common in the restaurant industry. Many workers wait for days, weeks, and in some cases even months for their management to produce payment. One primary reason

for these endemic problems is the dearth of Department of Labor officials charged with investigating violations of minimum-wage, overtime, health, safety, and other laws. Over and above the understaffing
at the Department of Labor, a 2009 national report by the Government
Accountability Office found that the Department of Labor's Wage and
Hour Division "had mishandled 9 of the 10 cases brought by a team of
undercover agents posing as aggrieved workers."[12] What work does the
rhetoric and ideology of the family do in ethnic-enclave restaurants and
retail stores to mask, justify, and perpetuate such workplace violations?

Bipin and Vinod, two of my manager respondents, told me the family mentality of their workplaces is especially important because most
of the young men they employ do not have family here in the United
States. They live "bachelor lives," as Vinod put it. They are usually
anywhere from their late teens to their forties and often live with one
another or other male South Asian immigrant friends while saving
money to send home or to visit home—or they spend their wages supporting their families in New York and the surrounding area. The family bonds that form in the restaurants where they work, Vinod said to
me, are "very strong. These guys don't have anyone else to go to. Their
friends have only been here for a couple years. I've been here for thirty-
six years. I know New York, this country, better than any of them. They
need me, like a parent." Bipin nodded as he sipped his beer. "Yeah, that's
why they call me, you know, like a father sometimes."

Vinod's analysis reveals some of the core political-economic dynamics of the immigrant-run service sector. The first is the most basic: in
the service industries and other sectors of the workforce that employ
unskilled workers, employers hire recent immigrants in order to keep
labor costs down.[13] This basic economic imperative explains why immigrant workers dominate the restaurant and small-grocery industries
in New York City. As Vinod pointed out to me, the workers who have
been in the country for the shortest amount of time need his help and
guidance the most. Ostensibly, those workers who need him less, and
therefore may command higher wages, are native-born workers and
immigrants with greater seniority. Whereas Shri and Vinod's narrative
is that they treat their employees like kin out of a sense of co-ethnic caring and mutual benefit, the low-wage workers in my study largely dis-
agreed. Instead, the bonds Vinod describes can be interpreted as a form

of paternalistic exploitation disguised as community ties of duty. He can use his seniority, social and financial capital, and position of power to squeeze extra labor and effort from his employees. Rather than "looking out" for his workers, as he describes it, he can also be seen to be taking advantage of their lack of knowledge of worker-protection laws in the United States and industry wage standards. The "bachelor lives" that the newest members of the diaspora lead provide relatively few networks of support and information, a fact that management can use to keep workers in the dark about standards of treatment while at the same time arguing that they are the only ones taking care of co-ethnic immigrants.

Managers are also able, whether consciously or not, to call upon deeply entrenched notions of what subcontinental immigrant culture means to people in the United States. Orientalist notions that continue to circulate in popular culture affect immigrant business owners' ability to screen their business practices from public view. I heard, for example, a Pakistani business owner at a business-improvement-district meeting explain that it is important to him to maintain certain customs at his restaurant. "Tradition is very important to our culture," he told the multiracial, mostly native-born audience in Brooklyn. "We do things together, we observe Muslim holidays, and I always understand when the boys want to go home during the summer." This comment was part of a discussion on how to ensure that more businesses in the area were hiring workers in legal, above-board ways. This business owner was using disparate pieces of what he deemed "cultural traditions" to argue that he could not comply with employer tax and wage laws. Here we see a key Orientalist concept that the employer used to his benefit: that immigrants from the East look always to homeland customs; that they therefore do not need, or even want, U.S. worker protections. This discourse has followed Asian immigrant workers in the United States since at least the 1870s. It is also often combined with the idea that Eastern cultures are more patriarchal than U.S. mainstream culture: therefore, a business owner or manager can be rightfully seen as not only an employer but a figure of cultural and psychological authority who can speak for his employees. There is a particular kind of family being invoked, then, by managerial rhetoric. It is a reductive and Orientalist notion of a subcontinental family. Letting so-called old-world customs continue in the U.S. labor market, or justifying them, can even be seen by some urban policy makers and consumers as a way to be "cultur-ally sensitive" in the current multicultural, liberal version of U.S. race relations.

Hussein, a Pakistani immigrant in his late thirties with a gentle man-ner who worked for ten years in New York City movie theaters as an usher, concessions-stand cashier, and eventual manager before moving into the taxi industry as a driver, told me that with hindsight, he recog-nizes that his managers exploited his lack of knowledge when he was a very recent immigrant. He related an incident to me in which he had been robbed at gunpoint when working one of his first jobs, at a gas station in the Midwood area of Brooklyn. A couple of teenagers had robbed the gas station while he was working the late-night shift, and he laughed sadly at how little he had known, back then, about what to do. When I asked him how his boss, a fellow Pakistani immigrant, had responded, he said that the boss did not care about how traumatic the incident had been for Hussein. "I mean, most of the bosses, they try to use you, if they know that you are new, and don't know [better], or might be stupid or alone." He recalled another experience from that job: his boss had told Hussein that he had accepted a couple of counterfeit twenty-dollar bills from customers, and that Hussein would be respon-sible for paying the gas station back out of his own pocket.

> I said, "Uh…okay"! I mean, what do you want me to say, you know? Obviously, he's the manager… he said, "Well I'm going to the bank, and let's see if [the bills] work or not. If, you know, it's a fake, it's not gonna work!" And he never showed me the *receipt*, even, because later I found out that the bank usually issues a receipt for that, if there's something like a counterfeit bill. He never showed me.

Far from providing Hussein with training, familial care, or co-eth-nic solidarity, this manager exploited Hussein for his lack of knowl-edge in the United States, in a way that left it questionable whether or not Hussein had actually done something wrong. This incident reveals the many informal ways that managers are able to eke out extra work, hours, or even money from their recent-immigrant hires.

Hussein mentioned that he did not have many "activities" at that time, so he used his extra time working for extra pay: "Just go home, sleep, watch TV, come back to my job...that's the only thing I had." Hussein's lack of connections in the community, when he first arrived, meant that he had little opportunity to compare his experiences with those of veterans of the service sector and realize that his employers were maltreating him. Many scholars have also noted that recent immigrants tend to consider their wages in terms of their home currency, at first, and therefore accept a much lower rate than their more-senior peers.[14] Only when workers start to consider their wages in relation to their new cost of living in the United States do they begin to switch jobs in search of higher wages. Based on my observation of the service industry, this can take anywhere from a few weeks to several months. In the meantime, managers profit from the extremely low wages they can pay their newly arrived hires.

There are particular racialized consequences to managers' preference for recent immigrants, who can be paid the least. With the exception of chain retail stores and chain fast-food jobs, African American and U.S.-born Latino workers are disproportionately *not* employed in New York City's service sector, in comparison to immigrant Latinos and other immigrants such as South Asians and Chinese. Not only does this result in the disadvantaging of African American and Latino American low-wage workers, a phenomenon that others have examined, but this dynamic also means that immigrant workers have little leverage for improving their job conditions and wages, as they have relatively little connection to native-born workers who could advise them and work with them to effect change in their industries.[15] This lack of workplace interaction between native-born and recent-immigrant workers in the vital and growing service sector can also result in building resentments among these different groups, each mistrusting the other and having little personal experience with which to refute cultural and racist stereotypes.[16]

If service-sector managers tend to avoid hiring U.S.-born workers and recent immigrants at the same job sites, then why are South Asian and Latino immigrants, specifically Mexicans and Central Americans, so often working together in New York City and in many urban centers in North America? In 65 to 70 percent of the workplaces where I interviewed workers or managers, or observed customers on an extended basis, there were immigrant employees from more than one part of the world, including Asia and Latin America. The Latino workers are mostly immigrants from Mexico and Central America, with a smaller cohort from South America, which largely corresponds to the demographic makeup of so-called unskilled Latino labor in New York City. Latinos constitute the largest pool of "unskilled" immigrant workers in the city, and Department of Labor and Bureau of Labor Statistics records reveal that they dominate the service industries.[17] What is new about the workplaces I analyze in my project is that it is increasingly common for urban service-sector employers to hire immigrants from different regions of the world to do similar work at the same site.[18] Two related explanations for this shift are convenience and an acknowledgment of the changing demographics of working-class immigration to New York. At one business improvement district meeting that I attended along with small-business owners from the Flatbush and Kensington areas of Brooklyn, the conversation centered on the best ways to hire low-wage workers. Although "unskilled" workers are plentiful, managers talked about their goal of hiring reliable, fast, efficient workers who will get along with others and stay for a while, reducing the costs of turnover and training.

The South Asian managers I spoke with in Brooklyn, Queens, and Manhattan have various reasons for employing Latinos as well as South Asians. Many of them point simply to the fact that there are so many Latino workers available to hire, although a few mentioned to me that Latinos are "agreeable" and "don't demand raises" as much as the desis. My respondent Mannur, a manager of a restaurant in Curry Hill that opened in 2004, said that he did not hire Gujaratis, people from his part of India, because they tend to "take liberties with him," whereas people who don't consider themselves to be "like him" don't take advantage of him in the same way.

Workers, on the other hand, often see their managers' decisions to hire South Asians and Latinos in the same workplace as a dividing tactic, meant to create barriers between different groups of workers and prevent employee alliances. A number of workers told me they felt that they were played off against one another in the workplace by savvy managers who knew that hiring people from multiple communities would keep them from organizing—especially workers who could not communicate with one another easily because of language differences. The language barrier is, in fact, one of the most common complaints at all ranks of the service industry—from major business owners to entry-level workers. Martín, a clean-cut, earnest, ambitious young restaurant worker from a small town in Puebla, Mexico, with whom I spoke on several occasions, told me that language was one way that managers divided workers by race and made them compete with one another for favor. When Martín first started working as a busser in New York and his English was limited, one of his managers went out of his way to assign Spanish-speaking bussers to non-Spanish-speaking black servers. "It's going to cause problems sometimes," and those miscommunications kept the two groups of workers at odds with one another. In the instances when the servers and bussers did not get along, "the managers always blamed us, the Mexicans," Martín said. "We got reprimands, yelled at, or worse, and that just made the black people, the people who spoke English, feel like they were better than us, when they weren't." While there are practical issues regarding language differences in multiracial work settings that get in the way of efficiency, there are also creative ways to solve these problems, which service workers and advocates are quick to detail.[19] Martín pointed out, for example, that if servers and bussers had been paired more sensibly, with the few Spanish-speaking servers assigned to the Spanish-speaking bussers and runners, and those with relatively better English skills paired with English speakers, many of these communication problems could have been avoided.

It is clear that language is a common cause, but not the only source of arguments and tension in the workplace. Managers often tell me that workers pretend they understand managerial orders and then do not follow them, which they found frustrating and inefficient. Whether it is intentional or not on the part of managers and bosses, the religious, national, and color divides between Latino and South Asian workers provide further obstacles to the formation of worker alliances. It is not hard to see why some of the workers I spoke with voiced the opinion that managers hire different groups of workers in order to "divide and conquer" and to pay them different rates without being easily exposed for doing so. This is a managerial tactic with a very long history, and one that has been analyzed by social scientists in the United States for as long as our disciplines have existed, studying workplaces as different as factories, sweatshops, white-collar offices, plantations and farms, and entertainment studios.

Regulation, the Private Sphere, and Managerial Authority

If workers in urban South Asian–run businesses argue that managers strive to divide them on the basis of ethnicity or language, how and why is it that so many managers have talked to me about the strong familial bonds at work in their businesses? One answer to this question stems from the fact that the restaurant and small-grocery industries are *highly* unregulated—or, more accurately, the labor, health, and safety laws that govern them as workplaces are barely enforced. Business owners in New York City by and large fight to keep it that way, bonding together to oppose legislation regarding city regulation and enforcement of health, safety, wage, sanitation, tax, immigration, and other laws affecting their ventures. Employing the metaphor of the family allows business owners and managers to explain and justify their opposition to state regulation and law enforcement. In both Western and South Asian contexts, the family has long been considered a "private," "unregulated" sphere—one where legal and state interference is unnecessary and unwelcome. Theorists of gender have long explored the nature of what has been "public" (under various meanings of that term) and what has been "private" in civil society. Nancy Fraser, for example, points to several operational definitions of "the private." One of these refers to the arena of private property and market relations— an arena that would clearly include small service-sector businesses. The arena of property and market relations, however, is no longer considered entirely private in the West. Running a business entails allowing one's transactions and business practices to be opened up to public scrutiny and state regulation. Service-sector businesses have the additional exposure of the customer's gaze, as the consumer interacts with the employees and, in some cases, management. Another definition of the private, however, is that which "pertain[s] to intimate domestic or personal life, including sexual life."[20] I argue that by using the rhetoric of the family—the domestic, personal life—managers and business owners are attempting to invoke this second version of the private, and therefore to screen their economic interactions from public view. "[The] rhetoric of privacy . . . has historically been used to restrict the universe of legitimate public contestation," Fraser argues.

> The rhetoric of domestic privacy seeks to exclude some issues and interests from public debate by personalizing and/or familiarizing them: it casts these as private-domestic or personal-familial in contradistinction to public, political matters. The rhetoric of economic privacy, in contrast, seeks to exclude some issues and interests from public debate by economizing them: the issues in question here are cast as impersonal market imperatives or as "private" ownership prerogatives or as technical problems for managers and planners, all in contradistinction to public, political matters. In both cases, the result is to enclave certain matters in specialized discursive arenas and thereby to shield them from general public debate and contestation. This usually works to the benefit of dominant groups and individuals and to the disadvantage of their subordinates.... These notions, therefore, are vehicles through which gender and class disadvantages may continue to operate subtextually and informally even after explicit, formal restrictions have been rescinded.[21]

Both the rhetoric of domestic privacy and the rhetoric of economic privacy work to hide power dynamics from public contestation, then, but as a managerial technique, Indian business owners shrewdly blur the line between one (the economic) and the other (the domestic), shoring up a stronger argument against regulation and "interference" from the state or from the public. At the same time, through rhetorical use of the discourse of the family and treatment of workers in ways that echo normative patriarchal family dynamics, owners and managers become architects of a workplace ideology, one that expects all members of the business-based family to comply with its social rules and hierarchies. Managers themselves are conscripted in this workplace ideology, as we shall see later in the chapter.

What are the components of this ideology? First, we may look at the ways in which the patriarchal heteronormative family overlaps with the service-sector immigrant-owned business model. In both frameworks, the paternal figure is the head of the unit and the one in control, using age and seniority as legitimization of authority and influence. In the moral economy of the patriarchal family, experience and age are considered natural reasons for authority, and many of the managers who use family as their organizing framework call upon experience and age as the foundation for their authority as well. In conversations with business owners and managers about the reasons they have succeeded or stayed in the industry, experience, time in the United States, and relative comfort with English and U.S. customs emerge repeatedly. Of course, all work hierarchies in an industrialized and capitalist system position the manager or head of a work unit as the one in control, largely based on experience, skills, and time in the field. The familial ideology, however, constructs dependence on the patriarch or head as organic and natural rather than a structural power difference based on particular objective characteristics. We see this logic at work in Bipin's claim that his employees "call [him] . . . a father sometimes." Take, too, what one Jackson Heights store manager, Pandav, told me:

> I started out at this store about four years ago. I was really ambitious, wanting to get ahead. Some of the guys that I worked with never got promotions, moved on, or are still here, bagging groceries, cleaning up. But I had that something . . . they already looked up to me, even when I was doing the grunt work. Obviously I wasn't supposed to be doing the grunt work. I'm better as a manager. [The workers] see me, they give me respect. They know I'm the boss.

I asked Pandav if there were particular things that made him a good manager, rather than a grunt worker. "Sometimes it's just the way you are. The owners here, they can usually recognize who should be a manager, sometimes it's not something you can [put your finger on]. Sometimes, it's just because I can kick these boys in the ass, make them do what I tell them." In this comment, Pandav points out that his authority emerges not from workplace seniority or from particular managerially based tasks at which he proved to excel; rather, it is an ineffable, "natural" ability that does not have to be described, only used. Note that he calls his employees "boys," though many of them are older than he. His relationship to the workers he manages is one of disciplinarian rather than leader, reinforcing the idea of manager or entrepreneur as a father figure rather than a member of a team with particular abilities.

Managerial authority can also be blurred with paternal disciplinary authority in more extreme ways, as the quotation from Pandav implies. Shri, who started in the restaurant industry as a dishwasher before eventually moving up to become business manager and sometime co-owner, told me that Bangladeshis, as workers, are "a little scared" of managers, and "you have to kick their butt." He spoke with the wisdom and affection of a big brother or father, but the relationship he is describing could easily be seen as one of exploitation and threatened physical abuse of low-wage workers, especially considering the frequency with which such abuse takes place. In this instance, Shri equated his managerial authority with the authority to use fear to discipline subordinates. This is a traditionally patriarchal form of legitimation—the use of violence and other forms of discipline to maintain hierarchy.

South Asian managers in the ethnic enclave can call upon cultural scripts related to the concept of the family that affiliate it with privacy and informal, "natural" self-regulation. By attempting to set "the family" as the organizing rubric of the restaurant, managers and bosses are calling upon particular narratives of why regulation is unnecessary and why informal social dynamics can be relied upon to set rules and norms. Using family-based discourse to describe their businesses allows managers to use language and treat their workers in ways that a more formal workplace would not allow. In this way, the family can be seen as an ideology, a way of thinking that serves particular functions in the service sector to privatize, deregulate, and enshrine power relations.

Favors and Documents: Managerial Conceptions of Morality at Work

My ethnographic research reveals that the logic at work in the urban South Asian American service sector is based on a particular notion of the patriarchal family that makes an attempt to *privatize* and *make informal* what is more accurately a relationship of exchange—labor and client services for money. This effort to informalize labor relations includes the managerial tactic of injecting duty and moral obligation into hierarchical workplace relationships, with the worker in the position of being indebted to his manager. Let us take the example of employer sanctions. In 1986, the Immigration Reform and Control Act (IRCA) for the first time put into place a system of federal penalties for U.S. employers who were found knowingly to employ undocumented immigrants. Under IRCA, employers were required to fill out a form at the time of hiring, showing that they had seen their hires' identity documents. Employers were not requested to verify these documents, however. Employers, if they had the proper forms filed, were safe from much threat of penalty because, if questioned, they could make an "affirmative defense" that they did not know an individual was undocumented because the employee had produced counterfeit records.[22] In addition, part of the enforcement of the "employer sanctions" included warning employers at least three days before a workplace raid, in order to give them enough time to handle their personnel problems on their own.[23]

Analysts and interest groups on both the Right and the Left have criticized the employer sanctions program.[24] Immigrants' rights groups, many social justice groups, and some major labor unions point to several deleterious effects upon the lives of undocumented workers. First, the program has increased the market for counterfeit identity documents enormously since the 1986 law was passed. Second, there is no protection for workers against employers who exploit them on the basis of their immigration status. Because IRCA made it technically illegal for employers to hire undocumented workers, those who hire them are doing so under the table, with a wink and a nod—knowing that their employees are shouldering all the risk—and this can result in deeply exploitative situations. As we will see, this is not at all uncommon in the New York City service sector. Third, critics argue that IRCA's skewed version of "employer sanctions" drove undocumented workers underground in more ways than before; these workers are accepting harsher working conditions and lower wages, and are less frequently seeking out ways to ameliorate their situations or organize. This hurts native-born workers as well, critics argue, forcing many of them to compete for jobs with worsening wages and conditions. If the employer sanctions program was repealed, groups such as the Break the Chains Alliance argue, "employers [would] no longer have the same insatiable desire to seek out undocumented workers because [workers would] no longer be as vulnerable."[25] "Thus," Nicholas De Genova argues, "IRCA's provisions primarily served to introduce greater instability into the labor-market experiences of undocumented migrants and thereby instituted an internal revolving door. What are putatively employer sanctions, then, have actually aggravated the migrants' condition of vulnerability and imposed new penalties on the undocumented workers themselves."[26]

Because everyone must show identity documents to fill in an I-9 form, all employees who have filled out the forms are ostensibly in the United States legally, but managers know that many low-wage immigrant workers are, in fact, undocumented and using counterfeit documents. Some employers use this knowledge to treat workers as if they are doing them a favor by employing them. Many managers assume that the majority, if not all, of their Latino immigrant workers are undocumented. This deeply entrenched belief not only is inaccurate but also has had insidious effects on the treatment of Latino immigrants, on policy making, and on Latino immigrants' ability to access various kinds of citizenship.[27] So no matter what their Latino workers' I-9 forms say, many South Asian ethnic-enclave managers treat these workers as if they are undocumented, and therefore expendable.

For undocumented workers, the danger of being caught and reported is acute. Particularly after the attacks of 9/11 and the ensuing tightening of immigration, detention, and deportation laws, South Asian immigrants are particularly nervous and vigilant about their immigration status. Almost all of them have stories about the Special Registration Program in 2001–2003, which required all noncitizen and non-permanent-resident young men from nineteen "Muslim countries" (as well as North Korea) to register their presence with the government. Immigration raids have been carried out in South Asian communities in New York City regularly since 2001; though they have slowed considerably, they still occur, and many New York City South Asian cultural and religious institutions were surveilled and even infiltrated by the U.S. government, in the guise of either the Department of Homeland Security or Immigration and Customs Enforcement (ICE). Some managers inject the concept of moral debt and noble favors here, attempting to informalize a system that has very serious formal effects on undocumented workers—ranging from being fired to being deported.

It was incredibly difficult to discuss documentation status with my participants, whether they were young men who had been in the

United States for a couple of years or sixty-year-old women who had been working at the same store for twenty years. From bussers to large-business owners, everyone had legitimate reasons to be circumspect when discussing immigration. Though it was spoken about infrequently and only among friends and trusted advisers, the topic of legality still suffused the workplace. Whenever I broached the subject of immigration status with workers or managers, the tension and anxiety in my respondents' faces and bodies were palpable. Workers are not the only ones who are hesitant or unwilling to discuss immigration status. Many managers told me directly that all of their workers were documented, at the beginning of my conversations with them: legally, they *cannot* admit that they know or suspect that their employees are undocumented. Though managers were reluctant to talk about immigration status, their feelings about it, and their efforts to make it an operational issue at work, emerged in conversations about related topics. Two such topics were gratefulness and the morality of low-wage workers and their managers.

One manager, Sharod, told me that when he first started out in the restaurant business, he used to be personally generous with his workers: he would offer some of them housing for a few days when they did not have a place to stay, or he would give them basic tutorials on money, rent, calling home, and other essentials. He has largely stopped doing this, however, because the workers were not "grateful," and, he told me, one of them stole money from him while staying at his apartment. Just as Mannur talked about how Gujaratis took liberties with him, Sharod was concerned that his expressions of care or paternal guidance were not reciprocated through gratitude. The implication is that there is a moral duty between manager and worker, and that the worker, in the position of the child of the family, should be grateful for what the paternal figure provides. Devjit, a grocery manager in Manhattan, told me that his workers were "ungrateful":

> They don't seem to understand that look, I'm doing them a favor. They can't go out and get any job they want. They need this job. I don't have to hire them: there are a hundred guys for every job opening here. And I look the other way when, you know, sometimes they have a problem, their girlfriend comes to visit work a lot, or you know, maybe I don't

think they're legal. But they complain and complain. They're probably back there right now [gesturing to the stockroom, about five feet away] complaining.

In his commentary, Devjit describes a large employment pool of "unskilled" workers who, because of their limited English skills, immigration status, and/or formal education background, are limited to low-wage jobs in the service industry or other similar work. He has a great deal of power, then, in picking workers, though he might not be satisfied with the level of competence or enthusiasm he finds in the hiring pool. In these comments, though, he translates that hiring power and his workers' job limitations into a *favor* that he is doing his employees. This puts workers in situations where they feel obligated to their bosses just for being employed. Facts of life such as being undocumented, having children or dependent relatives, or not having strong English skills all become factors that managers can use to make workers feel even more indebted to them. This workplace philosophy states that the more a worker needs a particular job, the more he or she is obligated to be grateful for that job. The undefined and subjective nature of "gratitude," and how it should be shown, is a central part of the working of the moral economy. This uncertainty and flexibility gives the manager the power to continually redefine the terms of "gratitude" at will.

Erased in these scenarios are the real dynamics of power between ethnic-enclave managers, who have been in the United States longer, have better English skills, and have business and managerial experience and in some cases more educational training, and low-wage workers, who are often recent immigrants and do not have the educational and training resources that managers do. While workers do clearly contribute to the businesses they work for, managers often imply that they expect these workers to do more than offer their labor. They expect employees to relate to them in familial ways, out of filial duty or moral indebtedness. While restaurant and retail work is not often discussed in terms of requiring emotional labor in the ways that domestic work, sex work, and other forms of service work are, this familial expectation of gratitude reveals how restaurant and retail workers, too, are called upon to do additional and unpaid affective work in order to fulfill their managers' expectations. This is to say nothing of the emotional labor required to assuage customers. In some cases, if workers do not act grateful or indebted, they are penalized. When managers blur the lines between the relationship of exchange on the one hand and moral and familial obligation on the other, there are tangible effects on managers' authority and on workers' lives.

We're Not All in the Family: Racializing Latino Workers in the South Asian Enclave

Workers from Mexico and Central America face particular struggles in multiracial service-sector workplaces managed by South Asian immigrants. One practice I observed in more than one desi, or South Asian, business was the pattern of managers and owners calling all Latino workers by the same name. Mannur, the manager of a hip, relatively new restaurant in Curry Hill, called all his Latino workers "amigo." I noticed this from my first visit to the restaurant; while I was seated at a table eating food, I heard him call over to a busser, referring to him as "amigo." The Spanish word stood out in Mannur's sentence. I heard it again another day, when I was talking to a server by the bar after having paid my bill. Mannur rushed through the dining room on his way to the kitchen behind me. "Hey amigo!" he called to someone behind the kitchen door, then walked through the doors, continuing to speak in a loud voice to someone in the kitchen. When I interviewed Santiago, one of the dishwashers, a few days later, he told me that Mannur called all the Latino workers "amigo." "How did that start?" I asked him. He had no idea. It was like that when Santiago had started, about six months earlier.

Benny, who is one of the managers at an upscale Indian restaurant in the East Village—one of the few restaurants where I spent time that was not in a desi enclave—likewise calls all of his Latino workers "José." This nicknaming functions as a way to put workers in their place, communicating to the Latino workers that they are, on the one hand, different from the other, non-Latino workers and, on the other hand, exactly the same as one another within their own group. Benny was very protective of his employees and did not want me to talk to them. He said it was unnecessary for me to interview them because he could answer any questions I may have about his restaurant. This was not an uncommon response for managers when discussing their employees with me—and it was the reason I usually tried to begin a relationship with employees before I tried to speak to management—but Benny was more insistent than most. When I heard him calling more than one worker "José," I asked him, "Do you have more than one employee named José?" He took a moment to answer; then he laughed and said, "Ah, no, that's just my nickname for the Spanish guys. It's just a funny nickname."

This practice is neither coincidental nor nonchalant: these managers called their South Asian workers by their individual names or did not use their name at all in front of me. Calling all Latinos one stereotypical name puts a clear distance between management and staff; it also shows non-Latino workers that it is acceptable to treat Latinos—but not other workers—disrespectfully in this way. Moreover, it sends a distinct message to all involved that Latinos hold a particularly low position within the hierarchy of these workplaces—and of low-wage work in general. It is not only South Asian managers who use these techniques to build hierarchical relationships at work. When I asked Santiago how he felt about Mannur's blanket usage of the nickname "amigo," he shrugged it off unhappily as just a part of working in the service sector. "It's the same shit everywhere. If he's not calling us amigo, he calling us worse. They got nicknames for us at every restaurant—they only learn Spanish so they can swear at us!" Santiago had worked at several restaurants, including two fast-food places, in the past several years. The problem was not only with Mannur, or only in the desi ethnic enclaves. Insults and discrimination against Latino workers were widespread, he said. Other Latino workers agree with him.

Here, we see that managers are able to use simple techniques to distance themselves from their own workforce and establish their authority in the workplace hierarchy. In the context of the workplace family that seems so rhetorically important to ethnic-enclave management, non-co-ethnic immigrant workers, such as Latinos in the South Asian enclave, can be easily excluded from the family, hidden from view (in the back of the store or restaurant), and, notably, referred to as "friend" rather than family member. Though many low-wage South Asian employees argue that they do not benefit from this familial rhetoric, being expelled from the rhetorical family can hardly be better.

Conclusion

I have argued here that there is a relationship between exploitative practices in low-status service-sector jobs and the managerial rhetoric of the family. It is not, however, a causal argument. I am not claiming that managers who use familial ideology at work are then able to treat their workers in a particular way *because* of their use of the discourse of the family. Neither am I arguing that only ethnic-enclave managers make use of this discourse, or that only ethnic-enclave managers exploit workers, evade laws, or discriminate against particular communities of workers. Instead, I argue that ethnic-enclave managers are able to use this rhetoric in particular ways against their recently arrived employees. They call upon dominant narratives of the desirability of the immigrant entrepreneur in contrast to the backward nature of "unskilled" immigrant workers. Explanations for exploitation abound in the service sector, but many of them can devolve into the reductively economic (employers hire undocumented immigrants because they can pay them less than native-born workers; they make all decisions based on what will generate the most profit) or the dangerously culturally simplistic (immigrant employees are willing to take any job because their orientation is toward their homeland) and therefore do not help us understand the everyday workings of race, gender, nation, and class at work. I argue that business owners must be able to call upon a range of knowledges and powers in order to feel confident in paying workers too little, paying them late, firing them at will, or using racial epithets in their presence. The widespread violation of labor, health, safety, and immigration laws in the restaurant and ethnic grocery industries continues, under the noses of workers, labor activists, the media, the city, the state, and academics, because employers can be confident that there will be little enforcement. They know that they do not have to hew strictly to formal labor and health and safety laws because they will not be called upon to do so. I have repeatedly heard employers use the concept of the family, the close-knit bonds of the workplace, or the dependence between boss and worker to construct a moral economy of mutual indebtedness and informal guidance rather than a stark and impersonal sphere of exchange regulated by law and enforcement. It is more palatable for a manager to say that his workers are lucky to get a job at a low wage because they have just arrived in the United States and he is doing them a familial favor by hiring them at all than it is to explain that he does not have to pay the federal minimum wage because none of his competitors do so. The former narrative is one of private, familial, intracommunity relations, and can only benefit management if it is convincing.

For the past twenty years, scholars of the ethnic enclave have been interested in whether or not employment in such immigrant neighborhoods helps the career chances of unskilled immigrant workers, and this literature remains important to my work because of my interest in the treatment of immigrant workers in the service sector. However, we must go deeper than examining wage levels and access to entrepreneurship: we must ask what tools employers use in enclaves that are absent or inaccessible in the mainstream economy. We must try to understand, as I attempt to do here, how managers use the resources at their disposal to best manage and control their workers—and how they attempt to keep the state out of their workplaces so that they can run their businesses as they see fit.[28] This is a story of employer evasion of law and regulation; but it is also the story of employers creating and constructing influential scripts, reworking old ideologies, and constituting family in a new way in the burgeoning service sector, the heart of the neoliberal, deindustrialized U.S. economy. The operating conditions in the urban service sector and managerial practices will become more relevant to a larger portion of the population in the coming years, as more working-class people whose families once worked in manufacturing and heavy industries move to the service sector for employment. When managers energetically fight regulation of their service-sector workplaces, the condition of everyday life for a growing number of people is at stake. As we uncover workplace scripts about race, gender, and ethnicity, we may better understand what can create conditions of possibility and satisfaction at work.

NOTES

1. All of my respondents' names have been changed, as well as some identifying details where they would reveal someone's identity.

2. In this case, I use the term "moral economy" to refer not to E. P. Thompson's (1971) or James C. Scott's (1976) conceptual work on the moral economy but to the kinds of ethics and morality that operate in a particular setting of economic exchange. This can be seen in relation to Raymond Williams's (1977) concept of the "structures of feeling" at work.

3. Portes and Bach 1980; Portes and Jensen 1992; Waldinger 1993; Zhou 1995; Granovetter 1973; Borjas and Tienda 1985. Examples include bosses driving workers to and from work, allowing their workers to bring their children to work when child care is not available or after school hours, offering workers informal loans, allowing workers to speak in their native language at work, and providing workers with references and connections when they leave the job.

4. For other reasons that workers may be particularly sensitive to harsh treatment at the hands of co-ethnic managers, see Navarro 2006.

5. Theorists of neoliberal globalization and the restructuring of the U.S. economy in the late twentieth century discuss the changing nature of work as the "flexibilization" of the U.S. and global workplace. See Ong 1999.

6. Wilson and Martin 1982; Portes and Bach 1985; Sanders and Nee 1987; Bailey and Waldinger 1991; Bonacich 1993; Kwong 1997; Portes 1997; Hum 2001, Sanders, Nee, and Sernau 2002; Logan, Alba, and Stulus 2003.

7. ROC-NY 2009, 41: "Sexual harassment is so widespread in the restaurant industry that it is the norm, rather than the exception...virtually no workers we spoke to were able to deny its prevalence in restaurants. As one focus group participant explained, 'I just feel like [in the restaurant industry] it's more overt, it's more accepted, it's part of the culture.'" This study also notes that workers who register discomfort and resistance to harassment were often dismissed.

8. In the past two decades, scholars have attended more deeply to the ways that managers and business owners are adjusting to, and indeed creating, new kinds of workforces under neoliberal globalization, where workers from several different communities and identity categories seek employment in the same industry, thanks to changing flows of migration, shifting gender roles, and urbanization. It has been shown that employers use the multiple axes of minoritization existent in the workforce to differentially value and divide workers—based on, say, nation, gender, race, ethnicity, immigration status, or language. My field research is informed by this scholarship, especially as it reveals how the tactic of dividing low-status workers on the basis of race, ethnicity, and gender weakens worker power. Bourgois 1989; Bonacich 1994; Portes and Rumbaut 1996; Bohon 2000; Freeman 2000; Hondagneu-Sotelu 2001; Parreñas 2001; Hernández 2002; Mills 2003; Waldinger and Lichter 2003; Fink 2003; Ong 2006; Williams 2006; Sherman 2007.

9. Colli 2003.

10. The practice of managers taking part of the tip pool is rampant, though illegal. For servers, bartenders, and other tipped workers who rely on tips for the bulk of or even the entirety of their wages, managers taking part of the tip pool can mean a serious reduction in take-home pay. See Talwar 2002.

11. ROC-NY 2005, 32; Esbenshade 2006.

12. Greenhouse 2009.

13. Bonacich 1993.

14. De Genova 2005, chap. 4.

15. Grasmuck 1985; Bailey 1987; Ong and Valenzuela 1996; Waldinger and Lichter 2003.
16. See the rich literature on black-Korean tensions in the run-up to and aftermath of the post-Rodney-King-decision L.A. Rebellions: Kim-Gibson 1993; Abelmann and Lie 1995; Kim 2003, especially chap. 4, "The Red Apple Boycott."
17. U.S. Bureau of Labor Statistics, "Employment by Detailed Industry, Race, and Hispanic Ethnicity," ftp://ftp.bls.gov/pub/special.requests/lf/aat18.txt (accessed February 10, 2010).
18. Franklin Wilson (2003) notes that increasingly, many immigrant groups "share niches," so that there is more than one ethnicized group working in an ethnic economy or niche. In fact, he argues that in the contemporary moment, only African Americans, Hawaiians, and Mexicans have high proportions of workers in sectors where most of their coworkers are co-ethnic in the United States. Also see Lamphere 1994; Smith 1995; Kim 2003.
19. See ROC-NY 2009 for a list of best practices for the restaurant industry and policy recommendations to make treatment of workers more objectively based on merit rather than based on race, color, gender, or other ascribed characteristics.
20. Fraser 1990, 71.
21. Fraser 1990, 73, 74.
22. De Genova 2005, 235.
23. De Genova 2005, 236.
24. Two major examples would be the Federation for American Immigration Reform, a conservative group, which explains its critiques of employer sanctions at http://www.fairus.org/site/ PageServer?pagename=iic_immigrationissuecentersff8e (accessed October 15, 2008), and the coalition called Break the Chains!, made up of several left social-justice groups advocating for the repeal of employer sanctions. They lay out their argument at http://www.nmass.org/nmass/breakthechains/breakthechains.html (accessed October 15, 2008).
25. The Break the Chains Alliance, "Break the Chains! Repeal IRCA Now," http://www.nmass.org/nmass/ breakthechains/breakthechains.html (accessed October 15, 2008).
26. De Genova 2005, 236.
27. Ngai 2005, chap. 2; De Genova 2005.
28. It should be noted that the state does not always have low-wage workers' interests at heart. Most health, safety, health care, and wage laws are weak and business-friendly, and enforcement of these laws will not result in fairness or meritocracy. Regardless of whether these federal and state laws protect workers adequately, however, employers still work to evade these regulations, creating dynamics that affect workers on a day-to-day basis. Thank you to Sharmila Rudrappa and Arlene Dávila for this insight. My forthcoming work looks more deeply at the issues of the state as a site of both disciplining and devaluing low-wage workers as well as one of the only sources of worker protection.

REFERENCES

Abelmann, Nancy, and John Lie. *Blue Dreams: Korean Americans and the Los Angeles Riots*. Cambridge: Harvard University Press, 1995.

Bailey, Thomas. *Immigrant and Native Workers: Contrasts and Competition*. Boulder, CO: Westview Press, 1987.

Bailey, Thomas, and Roger Waldinger. "Primary, Secondary, and Enclave Labor Markets: A Training Systems Approach." *American Sociological Review* 56 (1991): 432–445.

Bohon, Stephanie. *Latinos in Ethnic Enclaves: Immigrant Workers and the Competition for Jobs*. New York: Routledge, 2000.

Bonacich, Edna. "The Other Side of Ethnic Entrepreneurship." *International Migration Review* 27 (1993): 685–692.

———. "Asians in the Los Angeles Garment Industry." In Paul Ong, Edna Bonacich, and Lucie Cheng, eds., *The New Asian Immigration in Los Angeles and Global Restructuring*. Philadelphia: Temple University Press, 1994.

Borjas, George, and Marta Tienda. *Hispanics in the World Economy*. Orlando, FL: Academic Press, 1985.

Bourgois, Philippe. *Ethnicity at Work: Divided Labor on a Central America Banana Plantation*. Baltimore: Johns Hopkins University Press, 1989.

Colli, Andrea. *The History of Family Business, 1850–2000*. Cambridge: Cambridge University Press, 2003.

De Genova, Nicholas. *Working the Boundaries: Race, Space, and "Illegality" in Mexican Chicago*. Durham, NC: Duke University Press, 2005.

Esbenshade, Jill, with Micah Mitrosky, Erica Morgan, Marilisa Navarro, Matthew Rotundi, and Cynthia Vasquez. "Profits, Pain, and Pillows: Hotels and Housekeepers in San Diego." *WorkingUSA: The Journal of Labor and Society* 9 (2006): 265–292.

Fink, Leon. *The Maya of Morganton: Work and Community in the Nuevo New South*. Chapel Hill: University of North Carolina Press, 2003.

Fraser, Nancy. "Rethinking the Public Sphere: A Contribution to the Critique of Actually Existing Democracy." *Social Text* 25/26 (1990): 56–80.

Freeman, Carla. *High Tech and High Heels in the Global Economy: Women, Work, and Pink-Collar Identities in the Caribbean*. Durham, NC: Duke University Press, 2000.

Granovetter, Mark. "The Strength of Weak Ties." *American Journal of Sociology* 78 (1973): 1360–1380.

Grasmuck, Sherri. "Immigration, Ethnic Stratification, and Native Working-Class Discipline." *International Migration Review* 18 (1985): 692–713.

Greenhouse, Steven. "Labor Enforcement Agency Is Failing Workers, Report Says." *New York Times*, Mar. 24, 2009, "Washington" Section.

Hernández, Ramona. *The Mobility of Workers under Advanced Capitalism: Dominican Migration to the United States*. New York: Columbia University Press, 2002.

Hondagneu-Sotelu, Pierrette. *Doméstica: Immigrant Workers Cleaning and Caring in the Shadows of Affluence*. Berkeley: University of California Press, 2001.

Hum, Tarry. "The Promises and Dilemmas of Immigrant Ethnic Economies." In Marta López-Garza and David R. Diaz, eds., *Asian and Latino Immigrants in a Restructuring Economy: The Metamorphosis of Southern California.* Stanford, CA: Stanford University Press, 2001.

Kim, Claire Jean. *Bitter Fruit: The Politics of Black-Korean Conflict in New York City.* New Haven: Yale University Press, 2003.

Kim-Gibson, Dai Sil. "Sa-i-Gu." San Francisco: National Asian American Telecommunications Association, 1993.

Kwong, Peter. *Forbidden Workers: Illegal Chinese Immigrants and American Labor.* New York: New Press, 1997.

Lamphere, Louise, Alex Stepick, and Guillermo Grenier, eds. *Newcomers in the Workplace: Immigrants and the Restructuring of the U.S. Economy.* Philadelphia: Temple University Press, 1994.

Logan, John, Richard Alba, and Brian Stulus. "Enclaves and Entrepreneurs: Assessing the Payoff for Immigrants and Minorities." *International Migration Review* 37 (2003): 344–388.

Mills, Mary Beth. "Gender and Inequality in the Global Labor Force." *Annual Review of Anthropology* 32 (2003): 41–62.

Navarro, Mireya. "For Latinos, Familiar Faces May Not Be Friendly Bosses." *New York Times,* Oct. 22, 2006.

Ngai, Mae. *Impossible Subjects: Illegal Aliens and the Making of Modern America.* Princeton: Princeton University Press, 2004.

Ong, Aihwa. *Flexible Citizenship: The Cultural Logics of Transnationality.* Durham, NC: Duke University Press, 1999.

———. *Neoliberalism as Exception: Mutations in Citizenship and Sovereignty.* Durham, NC: Duke University Press, 2006.

Ong, Paul, and Abel Valenzuela, Jr. "The Labor Market: Immigrant Effects and Racial Disparities." In Roger Waldinger and Mehdi Bozorgmehr, eds., *Ethnic L.A.,* 165–192. New York: Russell Sage Foundation, 1996.

Parreñas, Rhacel Salazar. *Servants of Globalization: Women, Migration and Domestic Work.* Stanford, CA: Stanford University Press, 2001.

Portes, Alejandro. "Immigration Theory for a New Century: Some Problems and Opportunities." *International Migration Review* 31 (1997): 799–825.

Portes, Alejandro, and Robert Bach. "Immigrant Earnings: Cuban and Mexican Immigrants in the United States." *International Migration Review* 14 (1980): 15–41.

———. *Latin Journey: Cuban and Mexican Immigrants in the United States.* Berkeley: University of California Press, 1985.

Portes, Alejandro, and Leif Jensen. "Disproving the Enclave Hypothesis: Reply." *American Sociological Review* 57 (1992): 418–420.

Portes, Alejandro, and Ruben Rumbaut. *Immigrant America: A Portrait.* Berkeley: University of California Press, 1996.

Restaurant Opportunities Center of New York (ROC-NY) and the New York City Restaurant Industry Coalition. "Behind the Kitchen Door: Pervasive Inequality in New

York City's Thriving Restaurant Industry." Jan. 25, 2005. http://www.urbanjustice.org/pdf/publications/BKDFinalReport.pdf.

———. "The Great Service Divide: Occupational Segregation and Inequality in the New York City Restaurant Industry." Mar. 31, 2009. http://www.rocunited.org/files/great-servicedivide.pdf.

Sanders, Jimy, and Victor Nee. "Limits of Ethnic Solidarity in the Enclave Economy." *American Sociological Review* 52 (1987): 745–773.

Sanders, Jimy, Victor Nee, and Scott Sernau. "Asian Immigrants' Reliance on Social Ties in a Multiethnic Labor Market." *Social Forces* 81 (2002): 281–314.

Scott, James C. *Moral Economy of the Peasant.* New Haven: Yale University Press, 1976.

Sherman, Rachel. *Class Acts: Service and Inequality in Luxury Hotels.* Berkeley: University of California Press, 2007.

Smith, Christopher. "Asian New York: The Geography and Politics of Diversity." *International Migration Review* 29 (1995): 59–84.

Talwar, Jennifer Parker. *Fast Food, Fast Track: Immigrants, Big Business, and the American Dream.* Boulder, CO: Westview Press, 2002.

Thompson, E. P. "The Moral Economy of the English Crowd in the Eighteenth Century." *Past and Present,* no. 50 (1971): 76–136.

Waldinger, Roger. "The Two Sides of Ethnic Entrepreneurship." *International Migration Review* 27 (1993): 692–701.

Waldinger, Roger, and Michael Lichter. *How the Other Half Works: Immigration and the Social Organization of Labor.* Berkeley: University of California Press, 2003.

Williams, Christine. *Inside Toyland: Working, Shopping, and Social Inequality.* Berkeley: University of California Press, 2006.

Williams, Raymond. *Marxism and Literature.* Oxford: Oxford University Press, 1977.

Wilson, Franklin. "Ethnic Niching and Metropolitan Labor Markets." *Social Science Research* 32 (2003): 429–466.

Wilson, Kenneth, and W. Allen Martin. "Ethnic Enclaves: A Comparison of the Cuban and Black Economies of Miami." *American Journal of Sociology* 88 (1982): 135–160.

Zhou, Min. *Chinatown: The Socioeconomic Potential of an Urban Enclave.* Philadelphia: Temple University Press, 1995.

6

Looking Home

Gender, Work, and the Domestic in Theorizations of the South Asian Diaspora

LINTA VARGHESE

The scale and impact of mobility must not obscure the role of place, of sedentariness, of reterritorialization.
—K. Tololyan, *Restoring the Logic of the Sedentary*, 2005

After a general meeting at the Worker's Awaaz office, Bala, a live-in domestic worker, approached Mona, a young lawyer who specialized in U.S. immigration law, and excitedly announced, "Meine LIFE Act ki bari mein abhi kuch soona hai" (I just heard about the LIFE Act). The Legal Immigration Family Equity (LIFE) Act of 2000 to which Bala referred offered the possibility of status adjustment to people who had been living without documentation in the United States. The particular provision that caught her attention was Section 245(i), which stated that a person in violation of immigration status could pay $1,000 and remain in the United States while that status was being adjusted, *provided* he or she had an immigration petition pending. After gathering some information about her petition history, however, Mona informed Bala that she did not qualify. Bala's employers, a wealthy Indian family, had failed to file a work permit for Bala, and thus she lacked the crucial component to qualify—a pending immigration petition.

Insecurity of place and its causes were frequent topics of discussion at Worker's Awaaz, a now defunct South Asian women's workers' center located in Queens, New York. Many members' ability to remain in the United States was structured by immigration and labor law, and the privatization of care work, all of which contributed to labor exploitation in their places of work, someone else's home and household. Life in this nexus produced quite different experiences of diaspora than that detailed in much contemporary literature on diaspora. Theories that assert diaspora as a state of multiple loyalties, as acts of border crossings, and as a series of flows have structured sites of inquiry that emphasize circulation over dwelling, movement rather than "the logic of the sedentary" (Tololyan 2005). This is buttressed by a methodology that focuses on macro-global processes in which attention to national and transnational scales elides those spaces where mobility is not the organizing logic. Worker's Awaaz members' palpable anxiety regarding the ability to stay put raised questions for me about the importance of dwelling in diaspora. Similarly, the fact that the abuse many domestic workers faced occurred in the private homes of their wealthier South Asian employers signaled the need to attend to "smaller" scales in diasporic formations.

The literal space of the home and household as a critical space in the articulation of South Asian diasporic life in the United States has been an area of intellectual focus for South Asian American feminist writers and activists, many of whom point to the gendered constructions of the national that are imbricated in heteronormative household formation. Collections such as *Our Feet Walk the Sky* (1993) and portions of *Dragon Ladies* (1997), *A Patchwork Shawl* (1998), and *Body Evidence* (2007) contain personal, political, and academic writings and provide a vehicle for women's voices and experiences to enter the collective creation of South Asian America. It is in this set of writings that the home as multiply gendered and sexually normative due to its location in the private sphere, its symbolic functioning in the production of diasporic nationalisms, and its association with women's work becomes apparent.[1]

Writing from her observations and experiences as one of the cofounders of Sakhi for South Asian Women, a domestic violence organization, and the recriminations of community betrayal that were often lobbed at the organization and those within it, Annanya Bhatacharjee provides an analysis of the household and its relationship to the constitution of home and nation in the South Asian diaspora in the United States. In "The Habit of Ex-nomination" (1998 [1992]), Bhattacharjee argues that for the Indian immigrant bourgeoisie, "the domestic sphere of the family" contains "the [home] nation's cultural essence" and is a space outside "contamination by dominant Western values" (178). Most important, it is in this private space that "the immigrant bourgeoisie recognizes the woman" (178) and attempts to reproduce what it deems to be Indian culture. Bhattacharjee (1997a) picks up on the constellation of the home, nation, and woman and pushes the interconnection further in her essay "The Public/Private Mirage: Mapping Homes and Undomesticating Violence Work in the South Asian Immigrant Community."[2] Here, she offers a complicated and multilayered discussion of home and its "multiple significations" as "conventional domestic sphere," "an extended ethnic community separate from other ethnic communities," and "nations of origin" (1997a, 313–314). In this tripartite casting, home refers to a set of contingent spaces that reference different formations depending on usage. In all three usages, home is constructed as widening spaces of the private through control over women's behavior and symbolic value as boundaries of authentic community formation. Though she focuses on the household as a site of heteronormative partner violence, and not labor exploitation,[3] her arguments highlight the home and household as an integral space to South Asian diasporic experiences, imaginaries, and formations. Further, her focus on the modes through which the heteronormative, middle-class South Asian home is a space produced through gendered notions of nation and culture signals not only that the home is a crucial site of analysis but also the necessity to excavate the relations of power that produce the very space of the home and household.

Using data gathered at Worker's Awaaz and the legal case of Ms. P., one of the organization's domestic worker members, this chapter examines the role of the home and the household as structuring forces in the lives of domestic workers. My analysis is informed by the multivalent modes through which the home and household shaped organizational work in Worker's Awaaz. As physical spaces of labor, the home and household were sites of economic relations to be brought under labor regulations. As targets of political struggle, they were spaces to be transformed. Both understandings recognized the ideological constitution of home and household as central to shaping quotidian diasporic life embedded in dominant notions of the private and the public.

My goals in centering the home and household as the unit of analysis, and the domestic worker within it, are multiple. By focusing on the home and household, I question the implicit, and generally unquestioned, analytical scalar units of the national and transnational that undergird contemporary theorizations of diaspora. I show how attention to smaller scales such as community organizations and the household is integral not only for our understanding of how people are placed in diaspora but to our theorizations of diaspora. The unmoving attention to larger scales and sites of circulation replicates gendered notions of the private and the public, and in doing so, constructs the male diasporan as the normative object of study. Thus, this essay asks us to reconsider two points of entry and placement: the mechanisms of entry and placement through which migrants become part of a diasporic formation, and our own intellectual entry and placement into the study of the South Asian diaspora.

* * *

Turn to the classified section of most South Asian newspapers published in the United States, and you will find numerous ads seeking live-in domestic workers. Requirements abound, as potential employers seek particular skills and qualifications that may include shared language and regional affiliation, child care skills, basic or specialized culinary repertoires; of course, it never hurts to have prior experience and good references. For potential employers, hiring a co-ethnic is a way to maintain and reproduce certain cultural, linguistic, and other ethnic practices in the household. For many domestic workers, working for a co-ethnic is thought to mitigate possible abuse and exploitation due to potential feelings of solidarity along national, regional, or religious lines. For many undocumented South Asian female migrants, domestic work is one of the few easily available jobs.

Coregional and co-ethnic employment is made possible by increasing class bifurcation in the South Asian community in the United States, in which established upper-class and recent migrant professionals coexist with a growing population of low-wage and working-class community members (Singh 2003). In contrast to the immediate wave of post-1965 immigration composed largely of white-collar professional men and their families,[4] mainly from India, who formed a community through state selection (Prashad 2001; Visweswaran 1997), most of the women who answer the ads found in South Asian press classifieds are part of subsequent streams of migration that include women who migrate alone, working-class or downwardly mobile migrants (Das Gupta 2006; Mathew 2005), and migrants from nations other than India. Some of them also arrive without documentation or remain in the United States after their immigration status lapses. Most, if not all, domestic worker members of Worker's Awaaz migrated after the initial post-1965 professional wave.

It is difficult to estimate the number of South Asian domestic workers in the New York metropolitan area. By its very nature, domestic work, which takes place in the employer's home, is generally invisible. Further, unlike other professions in which individuals labor together in public spaces such as stores and restaurants, domestic workers labor alone, behind the closed doors of a single family's residence. South Asian domestic workers generally secure employment through informal networks and means such as word of mouth or classified ads in the ethnic press, which makes official tracking through statistical counting vis-à-vis employment records nearly impossible. Added to the invisibility inherent in the profession, South Asian domestic workers are also concealed by the still-dominant discursive construction of the South Asian community as one composed of upper-middle-class and upper-class professionals.[5] This construction is also aided by the post-1965 professional migrants' ability to claim community representation (Bhattacharjee 1997b; Das Gupta 2006; Khandelwal 1997).

Home Is Where the Work Is: Inside New York's Domestic Work Industry, a 2006 report published by Domestic Workers United (DWU)[6] and the DataCenter,[7] provides a glimpse into the lives of domestic workers in New York City. The report combines historical and legal analysis with data gathered from 547 surveys of domestic workers, fourteen domestic worker testimonies, and interviews with seven employers. Though it focuses on domestic workers across nationality, race, and ethnicity, and does not disaggregate along these lines in the presentation of findings, much of the data resonates with the experiences of South Asian domestic workers in Worker's Awaaz.

The report estimates that there were 200,000 domestic workers in New York City in 2006, almost all immigrant women of color (DWU 2006, 2). This continues a long legacy of women of color and immigrant women providing domestic work in the United States starting with enslaved black women and, after the abolition of slavery, free black women and immigrant European women, to the current situation in which immigrant women of color constitute the bulk of this workforce (Amott and Matthaei 1996; Glenn 1992; Romero 2002).[8] As per the DWU and DataCenter report, 99 percent of domestic workers were women of color, while 77 percent of their employers were white. Due to this fact, the dynamics of race and ethnicity within the home between the women of color domestic worker and her white female employer is the focus of many studies of domestic work in the United States (Rollins 1987; Romero 1992; Chang 2000; Hondagneu-Soleto 2001; Tucker 2002). This aspect marks a point of difference in the employment patterns of South Asian domestic workers, who tend to work for wealthy South Asians, from domestic workers of other nationalities.

* * *

Ms. P.,[9] a domestic worker, joined Worker's Awaaz in 2001, two years after she left the household of her employers, an Indian doctor and a businessman, and five years after she migrated to the United States. Prior to her entry to the United States, she had been a domestic worker for a large, multifamily household in New Delhi, India, where she had slowly worked her way up to take charge of the kitchen. Her New Delhi employers knew that a friend's son and daughter-in-law, Dr. and Mr. Dutta, who lived in the United States, were looking for a domestic worker to help with the care of a newborn. They offered to approach Ms. P. and discuss the possibility of her migrating to the United States under the Duttas' employ. For Ms. P., the recommendation from her employers was a sign that they thought highly of her and her capabilities. In turn, she had placed a great deal of confidence in their belief that going to work in the United States as a domestic worker would be a good opportunity for her.

At the time of her interview and hiring in New Delhi by Mr. Dutta's parents, Ms. P. was told that her only responsibility would be the care of a newborn, the only child in the household. For this she would be paid 4,000 Indian rupees per month (at that time approximately $111) and would be provided with room and board in the family's Manhattan residence. The Duttas were to take care of all her needs in the United States, and hence she asked that her wages be sent to her husband, who remained in India. With her wages, he was to purchase property in their village in Bengal and begin construction on a house. An oral agreement was reached that Ms. P. would work for the Duttas for three years, then return to India.

With the help of the Duttas, Ms. P. obtained a visa to enter the United States as a personal attendant to Mr. Dutta's father and accompanied the elder Duttas to New York City. Soon after her arrival at the Duttas' residence, however, Ms. P. was told that she was responsible for the majority of household tasks, in addition to child care. The amount of time spent on household duties fluctuated according to the work schedule of the couple, increasing when Mr. Dutta traveled for business or his wife, Dr. Dutta, was on call at the hospital. In addition to day-to-day tasks, Ms. P. also catered numerous parties at the younger Duttas' residence as well as that of their parents. On average, she worked from 119 to 130 hours per week with no days off. The Duttas also confiscated her passport and other personal papers upon her arrival, and she was rarely allowed to leave the house without the accompaniment of one of her employers. Finally, with the exception of a monthly phone call to her family in India, Ms. P. was restricted from using the phone.

In 1999, after two and a half years of employment, Ms. P., a Christian, quit when she was denied permission to attend church on Easter Sunday. Though it was nighttime, she was told to pack her belongings and leave the Dutta residence; she was able, however, to convince Dr. Dutta to let her stay the night. She left the following morning, without her passport and other personal papers, which the Duttas refused to return to her.

At the start of the campaign seeking justice for Ms. P., Worker's Awaaz sent a letter to the Duttas on behalf of Ms. P., specifying the amount of back wages owed based on calculations of federal, state, and city law and demanding the return of her passport and other personal documents. The letter also detailed legal actions that would be initiated if the requests were not met. Although two phone conversations with the Duttas over the wages owed and the return of Ms. P.'s property did take place, they refused to honor the requests articulated in the letter.

In early December 2001, with the support of Worker's Awaaz and two lawyers from a New York City law clinic, Ms. P. filed a lawsuit against her former employers alleging violations of the Fair Labor Standards Act (FLSA) and the New York Wages and Hours Law, as well as breach of contract, fraud, false imprisonment, and wrongful discharge. The suit sought more than $100,000 for compensatory damages and unpaid wages based on calculations of 119 to 133 hours worked per week, and paid remuneration at roughly twenty-two cents per hour for the first eight months, and $50 total for the remaining seventeen months of employment. The complaint was later amended to include trafficking and involuntary servitude under the Alien Tort Claims Act (ATCA).

During the pretrial discovery phase, the Duttas' defense rested on the claim that Ms. P. was not an employee in their household. Rather, they depicted her as "a part-time babysitter" at most, and asserted that the work she performed was no different than that performed by other household members. If the Duttas' claims were found to be true, the case could not move to trial, since charges of labor law violations necessitate that an employer-employee relationship between the plaintiff and defendant be established beyond a doubt. Without formal documentation such as a written contract, pay stubs, deposit slips, or canceled checks providing evidence of employment, the pretrail discovery judge ruled that employment could not be proved or disproved, and left it to the court to decide this crucial material fact.

The Duttas' fashioning of their relationship with Ms. P. hinged on flexibility written into labor and wage laws regarding payment and protection of excluded categories. Under the FLSA, neither minimum-wage laws nor overtime pay requirements apply to those employed on a casual basis, such as some classes of babysitters. Likewise, protections guaranteed under New York labor law exempt part-time babysitters in the home of the employer, or babysitters who work more than part-time, but whose main duties do not include other housework. Fortunately, the judge assigned to establish the material fact of employment ruled in Ms. P.'s favor, stating that "as a matter of law" the services provided by Ms. P. to the Duttas were not casual, and that neither the FSLA nor New York State exemptions regarding part-time babysitters applied. The court further gave a restricted reading of part-time baby-sitter exemptions, interpreting it to apply to teenagers or others whose main source of income is not tied to "rendering such services." The judge also pointed out that during pretrial discovery depositions, the Duttas themselves often referred to Ms. P. as their domestic worker who resided with the family initially in Manhattan and later in their resi-dence in Secaucus, New Jersey. In addition, he highlighted the Duttas' own claim that they paid Ms. P. a salary of $150 per week from May 1997 to August 1998, and $200 per week after September 1998 when Dr. Dutta returned to full-time employment, thus establishing a pattern of employment and remuneration for services rendered.

Though unsuccessful, the Duttas' arguments regarding their rela-tionship with Ms. P., and Ms. P.'s relationship to their household, drew from the mutually reinforcing social and legal ideologies of the house-hold as private, feminine, and nonproductive, a space that does not contain relationships engendered by paid work and an institution that does not hold subjects outside of a family structure. The private sphere of domesticity and family cannot be the site of paid labor because it is seen as constructed through love-based kinship relationships: between heterosexual spouses, between parents and children, and between siblings. Indeed, these affective relationships are the hallmark of the "home." It is through this network of heteronormative love- and/or kin-based relationships that domestic workers enter the United States and the diaspora. This hegemonic notion of what is private and familial and what is public and nonfamilial shaped the lives of most Worker's Awaaz members, even as their very presence in the households of their employers blurred boundaries between the private (household) and the public (site of paid labor). As Bridget Andersen insightfully argues, "For the relations of the employment contract to hold, the domestic worker must be constructed as selling her labour power rather than her personhood—but this is extremely difficult within the private domain as it is currently imagined" (2000, 167).

The Duttas' defense during the pretrail discovery phase articulated their household as a space produced through relations of love and reciprocity between family members. They rendered their home, and Ms. P.'s presence within it, as a space of voluntary, shared care work and familial arrangements. Acts such as confiscation of Ms. P.'s passport and control of her movement outside the home, understood by Worker's Awaaz and Ms. P. as techniques of control, were explained away as gestures of protection from immigration authorities, since Ms. P.'s visa expired six months after her arrival, and this, according to the Duttas, was grounds for arrest should she be stopped by law enforcement while out of the house. Additionally, though the agreement to send her wages to her husband was instituted by Ms. P., the Duttas justified halting payments as arising from concerns over her husband's financial mismanagement and irresponsibility.

National labor laws that generally do not cover the private household as a worksite bolster constructions of the household as coming into being through family relations, literally and metaphorically. Numerous labor acts exclude domestic workers either by name, function, or work environment. The National Labor Relations Act (NLRA), passed in 1935 and since amended, forms the cornerstone of workers' rights to organize, petition for improved working conditions, and join unions. However, it does not extend to those who work in domestic service for any person or family in a private home. The FLSA, which sets the federal minimum wage, maximum work hours, and overtime pay, completely excluded domestic workers from its concern until 1974, when it added domestic workers to occupations covered under minimum-wage regulations. Overtime provisions contained in the FLSA still do not extend to domestic workers. Domestic workers are also not covered under the Occupational Safety and Health Act (OSHA) of 1970, which ensures safe and healthy working conditions and environments. In addition, Title VII of the Civil Rights Act, which pertains to discrimination in employment, is enforceable only in workplaces where there are fifteen or more employees. Given that most domestic workers are solitary employees in someone's household, they have no recourse to employment discrimination laws. The four acts, which form the foundational laws of employment and labor rights in the United States, exempt the household by name or scale from the rights guaranteed in each to workers, and, in doing so, position the household as outside the purview of state labor regulation, regardless of the forms of relationships contained within it. According to Monika Batra, "There is a belief that domestic workers do not need the protections afforded by the NLRA. This view rests on an assumption that the home shields paid household workers from the ills associated with industrial life" (2005, 127).

Supported by dominant conceptions of the home as containing only love-based familial relationships, and labor laws that erase the home as a workspace, the Duttas countered Ms. P.'s charges by positioning her labor as voluntary, emanating from her feelings for the members of the household and her own desire to care for their infant rather than from her duties as a domestic worker. The Duttas were not unique in using this line of defense. Defendants in labor exploitation cases initiated by domestic worker members in Worker's Awaaz often used the refrain of voluntary love and family to place the onus of overwork on the domestic worker, and to claim that some work performed by the domestic worker was driven by her emotional connection to the family. While many domestic workers did speak of their affection for the families they worked for, particularly for the young children under their care, employers' ability to revoke the affective relationship as desired signals the asymmetrical relationships of power between domestic workers and their employers. Instead of making the labor arrangements between the domestic worker and her employer more agreeable, the discursive incorporation of the domestic worker into familial arrangements "enforces and perpetuates unequal relations of power between domestic workers and employer" and further allows employers to "manipulate the use of family ideologies for the extraction of unpaid labor" (Parreñas 2001, 179; see also Romero 1992).

The incongruity in the dominant construction of the home and household as produced through familial relationships on the one hand and the reality of homes as a space of monetary-based relationships on the other proved to be a useful entry point for Worker's Awaaz. From their start at Sakhi for South Asian Women, Worker's Awaaz members recognized that a pivotal part of their struggle lay in challenging and recasting both commonsense and legal understandings of the home. It is worth noting that in its first incarnation as the Domestic Workers Committee in Sakhi, Worker's Awaaz was firmly situated in an organization that had confronted dominant conceptions of the private, the domestic, and the household in the framework of fighting domestic violence.

At its inception as an independent organization, Worker's Awaaz continued to organize domestic workers for better working conditions. In addition to this work, the organization held ESL classes to teach English and provide information about labor rights and collaborated with the National Employment Labor Project and the Asian American Legal Defense and Education Fund to publish a know-your-rights booklet titled *Rights Begin at Home: Protecting Yourself as a Domestic Worker*. Worker's Awaaz gradually expanded its analysis and work beyond a legal framework and placed the exploitation of domestic workers in a broader analysis of labor extraction and notions of gendered work. For a brief period, the organization joined with two other groups in the Ain't I a Woman Campaign, an effort that focused on the intersection of gender and labor exploitation. Though the membership of the organization was composed of women, and there was an implicit understanding that domestic work was partially devalued due to its status as "women's work," this campaign placed women's working conditions and leadership development at the center of a new labor movement. Worker's Awaaz also worked with these organizations in the Health and Safety Campaign, which highlighted the conditions leading to a loss of control over time and one's own body upon which current structures of labor extraction depend. All three campaigns—the case-by-case legal campaigns securing back wages (later named the Campaign against Workplace Servitude), Ain't I a Woman, and the Health and Safety Campaign—along with other temporary campaigns such as Beyond Ground Zero, which aided South Asian low-wage workers in the aftermath of 9/11, allowed for an analysis of the multiple forms and enactments of marginalization that fashioned the lives of Worker's Awaaz membership (Scott 1992).[10]

In line with the organization's structure as a workers' center, its strategies and tactics worked toward engendering the collective power of membership through analysis and action.[11] Nancy Fraser's (1990) concept of subaltern counterpublics, a reworking of the Habermasian public sphere, proves useful in grasping the intellectual functioning of Worker's Awaaz. According to Fraser, subaltern counterpublics

> signal . . . parallel discursive arenas where members of subordinated social groups invent and circulate counter-discourses, which in turn

permit them to formulate opposition interpretations of their identities, interests, and needs. . . . insofar as these counterpublics emerge in response to exclusions within dominant publics, they help expand discursive space. . . . in principle, assumptions that were previously exempt from contestation will . . . have to be publicly argued out. (1990, 67)

Thus Worker's Awaaz not only provided aid and advocacy but also consciously created alternative understandings of power dynamics and social relationships. Through campaigns, planning, and discussion, domestic workers were able to analyze dominant constructions of gendered work and challenge the notion that the household was a private space outside labor relations.

Two tactics for challenging constructions of the home and household as a site outside labor relations were tied to campaigns seeking wage redress. As mentioned earlier, the wages owed Ms. P. were calculated based on the hours she worked. However, as is the case with most domestic workers, Ms. P. did not keep records of her daily tasks or the number of hours she worked per day. The reconstruction of work done in the household was a critical early step in legal cases charging labor exploitation. Additionally, for live-in domestic workers, keeping a record of work was a way both to keep track of their labor time and, given their residency in the place of employment, to distinguish the tasks they undertook for themselves from those done for their employers.

Preparation for Ms. P.'s case included meetings attended by Ms. P., the Worker's Awaaz staff organizer, a few other members, and the lawyers from the New York City law clinic handling her case, and focused on reconstructing her average and not-so-average work days at the Duttas' home. The documentation of her work life served two distinct purposes. Legally, the recounted tasks and hours spent doing them provided the basis of calculating back wages owed. Organizationally, the reconstruction of how her time was spent showed that the duties domestic workers are expected to perform in their employers' household dictate the rhythm of their lives and are sites of labor and contestation.

The second tactic made the site of work, the ex-employers' home, a target of protest. Depending on the employer's residence, Worker's Awaaz organized protests outside the home or the employer's workplace, and sometimes both. Given the residential patterns of most of the professional segments of the South Asian community, protesting out-side of a home generally involved going to the suburbs of Long Island, New Jersey, or Connecticut. Due to the isolated nature of domestic work, there were no public or semipublic spaces—such as factories, res-taurants, or other places of work—in front of which to protest. Target-ing the employers' places of existence was crucial for naming the site of exploitation and recasting home and household as spaces of wage labor.

Outside of campaign-related tactics, Worker's Awaaz was itself a site where the meanings of domestic work, the causes of exploitation, and its solutions were generated and debated. This took place through dis-cussions of campaigns and the direction of the organization, political education, and social interaction among membership. The ability to come together and discuss members' lives as domestic workers in vari-ous forums was integral to the organization, and it was through these meetings, actions, classes, and workshops for both members and non-members that a counterdiscourse of the home and household as a site of labor struggle emerged.

* * *

Ms. P.'s legal case against the Duttas, and Workers' Awaaz's organiza-tional work offer an occasion to explore the units of analysis and scale that inform contemporary studies of diaspora. Recently, diaspora has become a dominant framework for analyzing South Asian experi-ences in the United States. This has been driven by larger academic and material shifts that have recognized transnational practices as an important process shaping migrant life (Edwards 2007; Maurer 2000; Tololyan 1996, 2005).[12] The national and transnational are the princi-pal spaces of analysis in this framework, and there is often a slippage between the national/local and the transnational/global. Diasporans are seen as crisscrossing the latter and, in doing so, as presenting a chal-lenge to the former. In neither pairing do smaller scales avail them-selves. An extremely abbreviated survey of three foundational texts will bear this out. In his essay "Diasporas" (1994), James Clifford states that "diasporas are caught up with and defined against . . . the norms of the nation-state" (307). Likewise, speaking of the contemporary global terrain, Arjun Appadurai writes, "The diasporic public spheres . . . are the crucibles of a postnational political order" (1996, 22). Finally, Paul Gilroy, in his groundbreaking work, *The Black Atlantic* (1993), claims that the African diaspora in England disrupts the isomorphism among English people, English culture, and the English nation, all imagined as racially white. All three works bring into stark relief the need to reconsider the notion that there is direct correspondence between a population, culture, and place, pushing scholars to consider the processes through which groups are deterritorialized from "home" nations and reterritorialized in "host" nations while still maintaining a sense of connection and collectivity.[13]

When home is referenced, it generally refers to the nation or national/regional space that has been left behind. Rarely is there an excavation of the multiple meanings and scales of home that are nested in the national, and further how men and women (and children) are positioned differently vis-à-vis the home nation as gendered, classed, or sexual subjects. Rather, the dominant deployment of home in diaspora theorization is premised on the notion that home is a space of belonging, and that the loss of home as a space of acceptance forms one aspect of diasporic existence.

One consequence of focus on the space of the national/transnational has been the implicit gendering of diaspora as male through attention to movement and rupture associated with men. Ironically, Clifford warns against this very tendency in his essay, saying, "When diasporic experience is viewed in terms of displacement rather than placement, traveling rather than dwelling, disarticulation rather than rearticulation, then the experiences of men will tend to predominate" (1994, 313). Though offered as a necessary corrective, Clifford's exhortation misses the mark. A corrective to this approach cannot remain at the level of making marginalized experiences known. Rather, we must devote sustained attention to the modalities through which power relations are produced, and how these place disparate diasporic subjects.[14]

Citing feminist scholars such as Chandra Mohanty and Jacqui Alexander, Monisha Das Gupta writes that "migration, from a radical Third World feminist perspective, is a direct result of displacement induced by structural adjustment programs and neoliberal policies forced on the Third World" (2006, 13). Though the reorganization of capital has produced country-specific effects in the various nations of South Asia,

liberalization of these economies has followed the general model dictated by the International Monetary Fund, World Bank, and donor
nations of curtailing programs that promoted social and rural development, and privatizing national holdings and infrastructure. In this
regime, migration, both internal and external, is turned to as a survival
strategy as the standard of living declines and the help citizens may
have received from public programs continues to shrink (Hondagneu-
Sotelo 2001, 2003; Sassen 1988, 1998; Wright 2006). These were often
the transnational dynamics instantiating diasporic movement for many
Worker's Awaaz members. Once in the United States, privatization of
care, which is managed differently based on household access to capital and social resources, worked to place them in wealthy South Asian
American households (Aranda 2003; Louie 2000; Parreñas 2001).

Relations of power arrange diaspora not only through the "pressures that produce movement and migration" but also in the ways
that people are placed in diasporic communities of settlement (Campt
and Thomas 2008, 2–3). The South Asian domestic worker, like most
domestic workers in the United States, is deterritorialized through gendered, raced, and classed migration, which is itself shaped by the flows
of global capital, and then reterritorialized in networks of raced and
gender labor market segmentation in which the home and household
become an index of "class, gender, and sexuality . . . [and] the terrain
for local negotiations of power" (Nassy Brown 1998, 297; see also Nassy
Brown 2005). Looking literally at the home and household as sites of
placement, and centering the struggle over its redefinition in Worker's
Awaaz show that attention devoted solely to the national and transnational misses smaller sites where diasporic life is created, lived, and
contested.

NOTES

1. See Gayatri Gopinath (2005, 61–186) and Martin Manalansan (2003, 89–125)
   for queer diasporic readings of home in South Asian and Filipino diasporic
   imaginary, respectively.
2. Though this essay does not appear in one of the collections listed above, it too
   draws from her work at Sakhi and considers similar questions.
3. Bhattacharjee does mention domestic workers in both essays, but they are
   marginal to her analysis, and she focuses mainly on Sakhi's work with domestic
   violence.

4. One exception to this was the migration of a significant number of female nurses, mainly from the South Indian state of Kerala. See George (2005) for a wonderful ethnography of this migration pattern, and Reddy in this collection.

5. In New York City, however, the taxicab driver and newspaper stand worker are two material and representational figures that disrupt the construction of a professional community. The increasing number of South Asian corner produce cart vendors also has the potential to do this work, though it remains to be seen if they will become iconic figures in the city's popular imaginary.

6. Domestic Workers United, founded in 2000, is a New York City–based multinational organization of careworkers (nannies, housekeepers, and elderly caregivers) "organizing for power, respect and fair labor standards." For information on Domestic Workers United, see http://www.domesticworkersunited.org/.

7. Following DataCenter's mission to provide research tools to community organizations and marginalized communities, researchers at DataCenter worked with domestic workers from DWU to develop a survey and train DWU membership in survey methods and data collection. For information on DataCenter, see http://www.datacenter.org/. For a full copy of the report, see http://www.data-center.org/reports/reports.htm.

8. The one historical exception has been the employment of Chinese men as domestic workers in the American West during the mid-nineteenth century and early twentieth century (Glenn 1986). However, Chinese men were already constructed as feminine, and thus the workings of gender and race in this instance served to mark them as appropriately suited for domestic tasks (see Lee 1999; Okihiro 2001).

9. Information, such as names and legal case titles, that would reveal the identity of Ms. P. has been changed.

10. For a history of Worker's Awaaz, see Mathew (1999/2000) and Varghese (2006).

11. Janice Fine's monograph on worker centers (2006) provides a good introduction and survey of this new organizational form.

12. Also see Natarajan (2007) for a related discussion about new sites of research in South Asian Studies.

13. Also see Hall (1990) and Mercer (1988).

14. See Minkah Makalani's guest-edited issue of *Social Text* for a discussion of "relations of difference" in the context of the African Diaspora.

REFERENCES

Amott, Teresa, and Julie Matthaei. 1996. *Race, Gender, and Work: A Multi-cultural Economic History of Women in the United States*. Boston: South End Press.

Andersen, Bridget. 2000. *Doing the Dirty Work: The Global Politics of Domestic Labour*. London: Zed Books.

Appadurai, Arjun. 1996. *Modernity at Large: Cultural Dimensions of Globalization*. Minneapolis: University of Minnesota Press.

Aranda, E. M. 2003. Global Care Work and Gendered Constraints: The Case of Puerto Rican Transmigrants. *Gender & Society* 17(4): 609–626.

Batra, Monika. 2005. Organizing in the South Asian Domestic Worker Community: Pushing the Boundaries of the Law and Organizing Project. In *The New Urban Immigrant Workforce: Innovative Models for Labor Organizing*, ed. Sarumathi Jayaraman and Immanuel Ness, 118–142. Armonk, NY: M. E. Sharpe.

Bhattacharjee, Anannya. 1992. The Habit of Ex-nomination: Nation, Woman, and the Indian Immigrant Bourgeoisie. *Public Culture* 5(1): 19–44.

———. 1997a. The Public/Private Mirage: Mapping Homes and Undomesticating Violence Work in the South Asian Immigrant Community. In *Feminist Genealogies, Colonial Legacies, Democratic Futures*, ed. M. Jacqui Alexander and Chandra Talpade Mohanty, 308–329. New York: Routledge.

———. 1997b. A Slippery Path: Organizing Resistance to Violence against Women. In *Dragon Ladies: Asian American Feminists Breathe Fire*, ed. Sonis Shah, 29–45. Boston: South End Press.

Campt, Deborah, and Linda Thomas. 2008. Gendering Diaspora: Transnational Feminism, Diaspora and Its Hegemonies. *Feminist Review* 90:1–8.

Chang, Grace. 2000. *Disposable Domestics: Immigrant Women Workers in the Global Economy*. Cambridge, MA: South End Press.

Clifford, James. 1994. Diasporas. *Cultural Anthropology* 9(3): 302–338.

Das Gupta, Monisha. 2006. *Unruly Immigrants: Rights, Activism and Transnational South Asian Politics in the United States*. Durham, NC: Duke University Press.

Das Dasgupta, Shamita, ed. 1998. *A Patchwork Shawl: Chronicles of South Asian Women in America*. New Brunswick, NJ: Rutgers University Press.

———. 2007. *Body Evidence: Intimate Violence against South Asian Women in America*. New Brunswick, NJ: Rutgers University Press.

Domestic Workers United and DataCenter. 2006. *Home Is Where the Work Is: Inside New York's Domestic Work Industry*. http://www.datacenter.org/reports/reports.htm.

Edwards, Brent Hayes. 2001. The Uses of Diaspora. *Social Text* 66:46–73.

———. 2007. Diaspora. In *Keywords for American Cultural Studies*, ed. Bruce Burgett and Glenn Hendler, 81–84. New York: NYU Press.

Fine, Janice. 2006. *Worker Centers: Organizing Communities at the Edge of the Dream*. Ithaca: Cornell University Press.

Fraser, Nancy. 1990. Rethinking the Public Sphere: A Contribution to the Critique of Actually Existing Democracy. *Social Text* 25/26:56–80.

George, Sheba. 2005. *When Women Come First: Gender and Class in Transnational Migration*. Berkeley: University of California Press.

Gilroy, Paul. 1993. *The Black Atlantic: Modernity and Double Consciousness*. Cambridge: Harvard University Press.

Glenn, Evelyn Nakano. 1986. *Issei, Nisei, War Bride: Three Generations of Japanese American Women*. Philadelphia: Temple University Press.

———. 1992. From Servitude to Service Work: Historical Continuities in the Racial Division of Paid Reproductive Labor. *Signs: Journal of Women in Culture and Society* 18(1): 1–43.

Gopinath, Gayatri. 2005. *Impossible Desires: Queer Diasporas and South Asian Public Cultures*. Durham, NC: Duke University Press.

Hall, Stuart. 1990. "Cultural Identity and Diaspora" *in* J. Rutherford ed, 222-237. *Identity: Community, Culture, Difference*. London: Lawrence and Wishart.

Hondagneu-Sotelo, Pierrette. 2001. *Doméstica: Immigrant Workers Cleaning and Caring in the Shadows of Affluence*. Berkeley: University of California Press.

———. 2003. *Gender and U.S. Immigration: Contemporary Trends*. Berkeley: University of California Press.

Khandelwal, Madhulika. 1997. Community Organizing in an Asian Group: Asian Indians in New York City. *Another Side* 5(1): 23–32.

Lee, Robert. 1999. *Orientals: Asian Americans in Popular Culture*. Philadelphia: Temple University Press.

Louie, Mariam Ching Yoon. 2001. *Sweatshop Warriors: Immigrant Women Workers Take on the Global Factory*. Cambridge, MA: South End Press.

Makalani, Minkah, ed. 2009. *Social Text*. Special issue on Diaspora and the Localities of Race.

Manalansan, Martin. 2003. *Global Divas: Filipino Gay Men in the Diaspora*. Durham, NC: Duke University Press.

Mathew, Biju, 2005. *Taxi! Cabs and Capitalism in New York City*. New York: New Press.

Mathew, Biju. 1999/2000. Loud and Clear: A Conversation with Workers' Awaaz. *Amerasia Journal* 25(3): 183–193.

Maurer, Bill, 2000. A Fish Story: Rethinking Globalization on Virgin Gorda, British Virgin Islands. *American Ethnologist* 27(3): 670–701.

Mercer, Kobena. 1988. Diaspora Culture and the Dialogic Imagination: The Aesthetics of Black Independent Film in Britain. In *Blackframes: Critical Perspectives on Black Independent Cinema*, ed. Mbye Cham and Claire Andrade-Watkins, 41–50. Cambridge: MIT Press.

Nassy Brown, Jacqueline. 1998. Black Liverpool, Black America and the Gendering of Diasporic Space. *Cultural Anthropology* 13(3): 291–325.

———. 2005. *Dropping Anchor, Setting Sail: Geographies of Race in Black Liverpool*. Princeton: Princeton University Press.

Natarajan, Nalini. 2007. South Asian Area Studies in Transatlantic Dialogue. *Comparative Studies of South Asia, Africa and the Middle East* 27(3): 591–600.

Okihiro, Gary. 2001. *Common Ground: Reimagining American History*. Princeton: Princeton University Press.

Parreñas, Rhacel Salazar. 2001. *Servants of Globalization: Women, Migration and Domestic Work*. Stanford, CA: Stanford University Press.

Prashad, Vijay. 2000. *The Karma of Brown Folk*. Minneapolis: University of Minnesota Press.

Rollins, Judith. 1987. *Between Women: Domestics and Their Employers*. Philadelphia: Temple University Press.

Romero, Mary. 1992. *Maid in the USA*. New York: Routledge.

Sassen, Saskia. 1988. *The Mobility of Labor and Capital: A Study in International Investment and Labor*. New York: Cambridge University Press.

———. 1998. *Globalization and Its Discontents: Essays on the New Mobility of People and Money*. New York: New Press.

Scott, Joan. 1992. Experience. In *Feminists Theorize the Political*, ed. Judith Butler and Joan W. Scott, 22–40. New York: Routledge.

Shah, Sonia, ed. 1997. *Dragon Ladies: Asian American Feminists Breathe Fire*. Boston: South End Press.

Singh, J. 2003. South Asians (Including Bangladeshi, Nepalese, Pakistani, and Sri Lankan). In *The New Face of Asian Pacific America: Numbers, Diversity, and Change in the 21st Century*, ed. Eric Yo Ping Lai and Dennis Arguelles, 105–112. Los Angeles: AsiaWeek.

Tololyan, Khachig. 1996. Rethinking Diaspora(s): Stateless Power in the Transnational Moment. *Diaspora* 5(1): 3–36.

———. 2005. Restoring the Logic of the Sedentary to Diaspora Studies. In *Les Diasporas: 2000 Ans d'histoire*, ed. Lisa Anteby-Yemeni, William Berthomiere, and Gabriel Sheffer, 137–148. Rennes: Presses Universitaires de Rennes.

Tucker, Susan. 2002. *Telling Memories among Southern Women: Domestic Workers and Their Employers in the Segregated South*. Baton Rouge: Louisiana State University Press.

Varghese, Linta. 2006. "Constructing a Worker Identity: Class, Experience and Organizing in Workers' Awaaz." *Cultural Dynamics* 18(2): 189–211.

Visweswaran, Kamala. 1997. Diaspora by Design: Flexible Citizenship and South Asians in U.S. Racial Formations. *Diaspora* 6(1): 5–29.

Women of South Asian Descent Collective. 1993. *Our Feet Walk the Sky: Women of the South Asian Diaspora*. San Francisco: Aunt Lute Books.

Wright, Melissa. 2006. Differences That Matter. In *David Harvey: A Critical Reader*, ed. Noel Castree and Derek Gregory, 80–101. New York: Wiley Blackwell.

7

India's Global and Internal Labor Migration and Resistance

A Case Study of Hyderabad

IMMANUEL NESS

A traffic accident causes all vehicles on a two-lane road to screech to a halt. Suddenly the traffic begins to move in the right lane—the traffic in the left lane remains at a standstill. People in the left lane will veer to the right lane or will become highly irritated and angry. In India, poor conditions are widespread but if the general level of inequality changes dramatically, a relative peace can turn into mass conflict as people move out of their social station.
—Debdas Banerjee (2005)

On September 29, 2005, Indian unions waged a general strike to protest a national government plan to privatize airline, railroad, and banking industries. The strike was a blow to foreign and domestic investors who had been pushing the Congress Party–Left Front coalition government to privatize India's transportation network. The government, however, did not waver. In January 2006, despite several such mass industry strikes, the government put forward a privatization plan for the Delhi and Bombay airports, demonstrating to international investors that they were serious about opening the country to foreign capital. The privatization plan did not include provisions for saving jobs and maintaining wages, so in early February 2006, most airport workers went on strike again. After a prolonged conflict and several unsuccessful strike actions, the Indian government moved forward with its plan and privatized the two airports in 2008.

The battle over airport privatization is but one chapter in what has become an ongoing conflict between Indian and international capital interests and Indian labor. The liberalization of India's economy has become the grounds for unending political struggles between wealthier segments of Indian society, who stand to gain from opening up the country's economy, and growing numbers of workers who find themselves pushed into deeper poverty and destitution. The strikes are but one manifestation of the standoff between foreign and national capitalist interests seeking to privatize all state infrastructure and an increasingly militant working class and peasantry fighting to maintain even a basic level of subsistence. In 2006, *Economic and Political Weekly* reported that 80 percent of India's nonagricultural economy consisted of informal (unorganized) employment outside of state-regulated control. In the organized sector, continuous industry-wide and nationwide strikes in the first decade of the new century by unions in rival Indian labor federations have shuttered a range of manufacturing, service, and public-sector industries and slowed the wave of privatization (Sakthivel and Joddar 2006).

Through neoliberal economic development, skilled workers in India's formal economy—whether they choose to stay in the country and enter its expanding information technology (IT) and/or business services sectors or instead attempt to travel to the United States or Europe as guest workers—face a number of challenges. First, through either outsourcing or guest worker programs, capital is striking down traditional labor union accords by removing workers from established jobs in old labor markets and replacing them with lower-wage workers who are not subject to government labor laws and protections. Indian and multinational corporate proponents of international migration view migration as a development strategy and advantageous to both Indian and foreign capitalists. Neoliberal global economic organizations falsely conclude that India is poised to become one of the world's leading economic powers—especially if internal and international migration is unleashed (World Bank Group 2008, 163), but in reality, most Indians are growing more restless as rural poverty, urban slums in the major metropolitan areas, and child labor dramatically grow. Finally, the increasing use of Indian guest workers by U.S. corporations in discrete labor markets where job shortages were deliberately created generates a need for new pliable and lower-cost labor and hurts both U.S. and Indian workers in the long run.

In this chapter, I trace the background of neoliberal reform in India and the effects of global capitalism on India's class divide and economic development in order to understand the connection between the United States and India in the neoliberal global system that expanded dramatically in the 1990s. I look at two case studies: First, I focus on the fate of technology workers who stay in India through a close examination of Hyderabad, a city that is modernizing yet facing growing levels of poverty. I then contrast the Hyderabad situation with that of Indian guest workers who travel to the United States to find jobs in the low-wage industrial labor market sectors.

Background of Neoliberal Reform in India

From the 1970s onward, the neoliberal economic order has directed the global economy—a trend accelerated by the breakup of the Soviet Union in 1991. This multilateral free-market system, framed in the Washington Consensus of 1989, opens up markets for leading corporations and multilateral economic organizations and reduces the capacity of governments to regulate their own economies, forcing countries in the Global South, such as India, to shift from the import-substitution industrialization (ISI) promoted in the postwar era to export promotion advocated by neoliberal economists (Harvey 2006). The penalty for nonconformity is exclusion from participation in the international system of trade that generates revenues that are crucial for the national capitalist classes.[1] Indian political and labor economists such as Amiya Kumar Bagchi (2002) argue that these market reforms are devastating to the vast majority of the population, but Indian capitalists have been incubating a squad of propagandists known as "enthusiasts" to defend their neoliberal efforts (Das 2002; Sheshabalaya 2005).

The IT sector best illustrates the ways in which the neoliberal "partnership" between capitalists in India and the United States hurts workers in both countries. By shifting work to offshore contractors in India and elsewhere in the Global South, multinational IT firms primarily based in the United States avoid national social welfare mandates and extract greater surplus value from the labor exchange process. Since 2000, the U.S. IT industry has been transforming its labor market by purging workers in the United States, increasing contract work, and outsourcing to Indian contractors, thereby providing a windfall in profits. Global outsourcing consultants calculate that businesses save between 35 and 65 percent of their IT and telecommunications labor costs by circumventing U.S. labor standards (Morstead and Blount 2003).

Instead of hiring full-time workers subject to prevailing standards, the IT and business services industries have formed a global labor market of temporary workers hired only on demand. The expansion of India's IT and business service capacity coincided with the initiation of market reforms in 1985. Government-sponsored high-technology, business, and engineering education expanded substantially at Indian universities and polytechnic institutions. Consequently, the domestic software industry has soared from 6,800 workers in 1986 to 650,000 in 2003. The Indian National Association of Software and Service Companies (NASSCOM 2010) attributes this growth to expanding global demand for Indian software services and actively promotes such services to IT industry leaders in the United States, the United Kingdom, and Western Europe.[2]

Sensing a synergy between U.S. corporate goals and Indian labor capacities, some American business interests sought to boost profits in the industry by convincing government officials that the shortage in IT and software workers in the United States placed the nation at risk of losing global sales. Indian business leaders echoed this sentiment, and since the initiation of the U.S. H-1B visa in 1982, India has provided a preponderant proportion of guest workers to the United States in the IT sector, in effect forming a wholly new contract labor market. From 1982 to 2007, India has sent some 5 million H-1B skilled guest workers to the United States, primarily due to a greater commitment to investing in higher education in India as well as China (Freeman 2007, 132–140). The vast majority return to India, while others go back and forth, directly or through third countries.

India is by far the largest source of migrant IT consultants for U.S. high-tech companies, due to its considerable cost advantages. First, H-1B computer programmers in the United States are paid 10 to 25 percent of the typical wages of U.S. programmers. Moreover, Indian programmers do not receive Social Security benefits while working in the United States, since they are foreign guest workers. IT companies, by some estimates, pay their workers as little as $200 a month plus living expenses and also profit from renting company housing to contract laborers. Indian IT professionals may work six-day weeks and sometimes sixteen hours per day. India also provides a large pool of high-skilled workers who are often fluent in English. By 2004, the Indian Institute of Technology, for example, produced 215,000 sub-baccalaureate and baccalaureate graduates in the IT and engineering fields, the most worldwide after China and the United States (see Arora and Athreye 2002; Friedman 2005; Gereffi and Wadhwa 2005; Zakaria 2008).

There is evidence that the U.S. presence in the Indian market is growing, as more U.S.-based multinational IT firms relocate corporate facilities to Hyderabad and other Indian high-tech centers. Since 2002, Adobe Computer Associates, Intel, Microsoft, Oracle, and Sun Micro-systems have established presences in India, and as recently as 2006, in response to growing opposition from U.S. migration opponents, the U.S. Congress increased this trend by authorizing the U.S. Citizenship and Immigration Service (USCIS) to issue fewer H-1B visas to foreign skilled laborers. This activated lobbyists for IT contractors to request variances and caused firms to send more work offshore as a viable and appealing alternative to hiring American workers full-time.[3]

Global Capitalism and the Class Divide

India's high-technology boom exemplifies a pattern of new industry replacing old stable communities by introducing new technology and securing low-wage labor. To undermine the power of labor unions, the government assists businesses in closing older factories that once provided living wages and in opening new enterprises that receive financial, technical, and logistical support from the state, while paying workers lower wages and repressing labor unions. A consensus among political economists in India is that new installations do not pay competitive wages and thus undermine the economic stability of entire communities (Bagchi 2002, 2005; Banerjee 2005; Bhatt 2005; Joshi 2005; Nayyar and Sharma 2005). Thus, while the "outside world" (or free-market economists in the Global North) views India as a first-rate model for economic development, only a small segment—the nation's capitalist class—profits from these technological advances.

As India opens its economy to the world, the country possesses the advantage of a democratic tradition, but the effects of India's failure to advance at China's pace are palpable. Some argue that the Chinese Communist Party's one-party rule has fueled its economic advance, a contention that contradicts the neoliberal relationship between democracy and free markets as a means to the capital class's prosperity and growth (Garnaut and Song 2005; Preston and Haacke 2003).

Outside of the leading high-technology centers, dependable electrical power is the exception rather than the rule. Thus, the technological boom in India has not set in motion broad access to the Internet. Even the World Bank reluctantly concedes that the unreliability of electricity and frequent blackouts stymie economic growth (World Bank 2009b). To compensate for the routine power outages, most small and medium-sized companies must run their own power generators because energy shortages are endemic to businesses and civilians (Baldauf 2005).

The few IT entrepreneurs who exist establish their own businesses in India or secure lucrative employment among five or six Indian private-sector companies. Whenever possible, multinational contractors invest in new high-technology facilities, undercutting unionized workers in garment, steel, and other basic industries. In opposition to policies favoring corporate interests over workers, leftist parties reject foreign and domestic investments that undermine trade unions, and welcome ventures benefiting a broader range of the population without weakening organized labor. Still, contractors for global corporations invest in capital-friendly regions and unorganized new sectors of the economy (Bagchi 2002).

Meanwhile, since the 1990s, federal government agencies have reduced services and funding programs beneficial to the poor and working class while targeting resources to private interests in core high-technology hubs with high concentrations of workers. In turn, the Indian federal social programs and initiatives in poverty-stricken regions that are crucial for the rural and urban poor are starving for resources. As a result, internal migration from India's rural regions has become crucial to building, maintaining, and serving new technology corporations. Most internal migrants work as construction workers, landscapers, security guards, and hospitality workers in the new IT complexes in Hyderabad and beyond. The caste system buttresses the contracting of labor, creating a food chain in which those from more privileged castes may hire and fire those below them. The caste system shapes exploitation, ideal for creating what I call a "contractor regime." Thus, the convergence of Hinduism and capitalism consigns the Dalit and Other Backward Classes (OBCs) to work for privileged-caste contractors, who take a cut out of their salaries, much in the same way global corporate contractors earn billions on their IT workers overseas (Bagchi 2002, 2005; Srinivas 2008; interview, Arun Patnaik, December 17, 2008).

Even if only 3 percent of India's inhabitants benefit from neoliberalism, they constitute 30 million residents, a considerable number of people for domestic and foreign consumer markets. Beyond the middle-income bracket, however, is a growing low-wage working class in urban and rural areas that fails to benefit from economic reform but works longer hours for low pay. Even by the inflated World Bank statistics, from 1981 to 2005, the number of people in India living on less than $1.25 a day increased from 421 million to 456 million (World Bank 2009a).

Indian Skilled Migrant Laborers in the United States

The growth in the number of skilled Indian guest workers in the United States reflects the rise in corporate demand for flexible contract laborers, used to reduce labor costs for multinational corporations through providing services on demand. After their contracts expire, migrant laborers must find new jobs in host countries or are unceremoniously deported. In the first decade of the twenty-first century, the United States imported more IT workers than any other country in the world (OECD 2001). The shifting of workers across the world like pieces on a chessboard has left both India and the United States with genuine job shortages in key labor markets. The elimination of labor markets for U.S.-born workers and their replacement with lower-wage foreign-born workers have led to a job shortage in the United States for professional and, more recently, less skilled workers. At the same time, India has become a site of innovation in several key skilled service sectors of the economy, each relatively new and interconnected: IT, software, business services, and call centers. The process of migration to the United States is driven by economic circumstance even for middle-income Indians. Even for those with skills, jobs in India are extremely difficult to find and demanding for those lucky enough to find them. At the same time, Indian high-technology workers contracted in the United States are shamefully exploited, laboring as much as sixteen to eighteen hours a day with almost no down time. It is true that there is an emerging "IT elite" nexus among Indians in the United States and South Asia, but while the industry is growing, those entering its top end already come from the middle and upper classes that, as noted, constitute a small fraction of India's population (Sona Shah, interview, March 18, 2005).

Even if Indian contractors charge high hourly rates for skilled guest workers, U.S. firms profit immensely by making use of unrestricted discretionary labor services rather than hiring full-time workers. As nonemployees, guest workers provide a distinct advantage for corporations, which do not have to contribute government-mandated Social Security, unemployment, and disability benefits or prevailing pensions and other benefits. For U.S. companies in IT and business services, Indian guest workers provide a clear advantage over U.S.-born workers, since the government does not monitor working conditions and wage and hour standards. Labor contractors in India also profit. Corporations and labor contractors in the United States and India draw closer to one another through the capacity to establish reciprocal facilities in each country where workers are interchangeable. Indian contractors expand corporate flexibility and profits by providing the equivalent of global temporary agencies selling skilled laborers for IT and business services jobs. In 2005, Indian contractors commenced trade in lower-wage H-2B labor. Upon returning from the United States, Europe, or Japan, Indian IT workers recall disturbing stories of lives that revolve around work and the promise of a better life (interviews, September 28–October 9, 2005, Hyderabad). One IT worker returned to India from the United States after paying most of his salary to a contractor who promised a green card. In effect, even skilled workers are paying contractors for work. The contractors and companies confine most migrant laborers working in the United States to workplaces and housing complexes controlled by contractors—the equivalent of modern-day indentured servitude.

Even with this expansion of U.S. guest worker programs, it would be inaccurate to conclude that massive waves of Indian and other workers in the Global South procure "good jobs" at the expense of U.S.

workers—rather, corporations willingly pay Indian contractors, who provide low-wage labor, to take responsibility for ensuring that work is completed according to specifications. U.S. capital is indifferent to the abysmal wages and conditions of foreign guest workers. The widening use of Indian guest workers among U.S. corporations in diverse industries illustrates how capital deliberately creates job shortages through undermining established labor market relations, generating a need for new pliable and lower-cost labor. In turn, by introducing guest workers, U.S. labor markets slacken, wage rates decline, and corporate profitability grows. The result is a direct correlation between corporate downsizing and Indian guest worker programs in several labor markets, turning erstwhile good jobs into bad ones. One important example is the trucking industry.

Indian Labor Exportation: Low-Wage Manufacturing and Support Services

Since 1980, when President Jimmy Carter deregulated trucking, the U.S. industry has eroded the labor power of long-haul drivers. Deregulation in U.S. trucking gradually reduced worker power through allowing companies to operate in all states without consent from the Interstate Commerce Commission (ICC). The North American Free Trade Agreement (NAFTA) regional accords that became law in 1994 further reduced the labor power of truck drivers by permitting Mexican and Canadian haulers to enter the United States without prior authorization. Consequently, long-distance trucking companies have sharply reduced wage rates to drivers by hiring workers in states and countries that pay lower wages. NAFTA has allowed Mexican drivers to compete with U.S. workers, and efforts to import Indian truckers trained in Andhra Pradesh have set in motion a process of lowering wage costs even further.

In May 2005, the American Trucking Association (ATA) issued a report prepared by Global Insight, a research organization. "US Truck Driver Shortage: Analysis and Forecasts" is an industry study that contends that the country has too few long-haul drivers, and that the shortage will reach 114,000 by 2014. It concludes that the decline in drivers is a result of high turnover, the arduous work of long-haul trucking, the long hours away from home, and expectations that the number of male workers, who predominate in the industry, will drastically decline. The report notes that "demographic trends will turn against the industry over the next 10 years" as "white male" truck drivers between thirty-five and fifty-four years of age leave the industry and wage rates in the industry continue to decline (Global Insight 2005). To ameliorate the dearth of drivers, the industry is advocating introduction of the H-2B guest worker program.

In June 2007, two years after issuance of the ATA report, *The Hindu*, a nationwide newspaper of record in India, reported that 217 truck drivers were undergoing training by the Overseas Manpower Company of Andhra Pradesh (OMCAP) in Hyderabad in order to work as guest workers in the U.S. long-haul trucking industry on H-2B visas. The article continued: "Of these, 79 had been cleared by the trainers of the United States as eligible for obtaining Commercial Driving License in the US" (Rajeev 2007). Within a year, Indian contractors began establishing a broader presence in the United States to channel truckers through the H-2B visa. In the spring of 2007 they signed a memorandum of understanding with USCIS to recruit 200 drivers of heavy trucks to the United States.

The effort to extend guest worker visas to low-wage Indian laborers reveals the corporate economic interests behind political efforts to establish comprehensive immigration reform. The Teamsters seek to restrict the importation of foreign truckers into the United States, while the trucking industry lobbies the government to increase visas for foreigners as a new means to lower labor costs. The initial opening of opportunities for Indian labor contractors to appropriate export labor into the U.S. trucking labor market and other industries at low wages reveals that in all locations, capitalists seek to expand profitability through repressing labor unionization. Neoliberalism and the government-sponsored attack against workers and labor unions are now as prevalent in India as in the United States, though the union organizations differ dramatically in political and economic power. The case study of Hyderabad migration reveals the government effort to use guest work as a development strategy that fails to address sustainability and the needs of the overwhelming numbers of working-class and poor Indians.

A Case Study of Hyderabad: Modernization, Migration, and Poverty

Geography, religion, class, and caste divide Hyderabad, a sprawling city in the heart of the state of Andhra Pradesh on the southeastern coast of India, separations exaggerated by the investment in and growth of high-technology industries. Hyderabad is the core urban center of Telangana, the northwestern region of Andhra Pradesh that was incorporated into the state in the aftermath of independence and which, since the late 1960s, has sought autonomy as an independent state, in part on account of its distinctive Telegu language and culture. The Telangana independence movement, which would make Hyderabad its capital, strengthened with the support of Congress Party leaders in 2004 but is opposed by Andhra and Rayalseema, the coastal regions of Andhra Pradesh, leading to growing political tensions. Independence for Telangana could erode revenue that the region produces for the economy of the two other regions of Andhra Pradesh, further undermining living standards.

Hyderabad is divided into two cities: one high-tech, and the other the old, established core. In addition to a booming IT sector, Hyderabad is home to garment production and the production of luxury goods deriving from the region's abundance of pearls and precious stones. The city is also a leading producer of pharmaceuticals and medicine and is emerging as a banking center. Bangalore's economy relies on the presence of leading corporations and the aeronautic industry. Both cities have large working classes and displaced peasants, but Hyderabad's economy is considerably more diverse. In Hyderabad, the expansion of an urban underclass of precarious laborers creates a severe housing crisis. The villages of peasant laborers are displaced by high-technology complexes in the Genome Valley technology cluster and the concurrent dramatic rise in contract and bonded labor. Between 1995 and 2008, Hyderabad and Bangalore have been experiencing vast and dramatic expansion in high-technology sectors, spreading the construction of new complexes to the hinterland of the cities.

An increasing number of workers in rural regions of Andhra Pradesh are forced to migrate to Hyderabad due to economic necessity, as the growth in market-based corporate farming is driving down living standards. Once in Hyderabad, the typical rural migrant is employed as a construction worker or in a similarly unsafe job, is paid low wages, and lives in a tent without access to potable water.

Slum Growth

There are roughly 1,607 slums throughout Hyderabad and its twin city, Secunderabad, and they are home to just over 2.8 million people. Most of the residents fall below the poverty line and have no access to medical or eye care services. In the absence of developed land and clear policies to address their problems, the poor suffer from many inadequacies in terms of access to basic services.

The numbers of slums and the slum population in the Municipal Corporation of Hyderabad (MCH) have been increasing at a faster pace over the past few decades. In addition, in the municipalities around the MCH constituting the Hyderabad Urban Agglomeration (HUA), there are around 500 slums. As these municipalities were constituted only in the late 1980s, the slum population is clearly extremely high. In Quthbullahpur, Alwal, and Rajendranagar, slums constitute about 60 percent of the total population, highlighting the enormity of the problem. The slum population in HUA is heterogeneous in character—with Hindus, Muslims, and Christians having migrated from different neighboring districts. The languages predominantly spoken in slums in Hyderabad and Secunderabad are Telugu and Urdu, followed by a smattering of Marathi and Kannada. A similar pattern exists in surrounding municipalities as well.

Slums in HUA are controlled by municipal, state, and central authorities on quasi- government-owned, private, and unclaimed lands. The state government of Andhra Pradesh classified all the slums on its land as either "objectionable" or "unobjectionable" in 1985. Categorization as "objectionable" was based on location and land use—location in riverbeds, low-lying areas, drains, road margins, and so forth. Only a few slums were deemed "unobjectionable." In the case of surrounding municipalities, they were the small and scattered villages inhabited by the poor, particularly laborers from the industrial areas. The absence of physical and social amenities contributes to lower living standards and even greater economic deprivation (Greater Hyderabad Municipal Corporation 2010).

Hyderabad and the High-Technology Industry

As India modernizes its economic base, the state privileges nonunion firms, leading to the growing marginalization of organized labor. As a consequence, the most modern industries are likely to be free of union representation. Hyderabad's unions are struggling to organize new industries: engineering, IT, and business services that seek to avoid organized labor. The largest trade unions in Hyderabad represent public-sector workers who are already under assault by government agencies. Meanwhile, the World Bank guest worker development policy privileges a policy that views migrant labor as the primary development policy.

High-technology workers earning middle-income wages are employed in the new corporate complexes swallowing up land in Hyderabad. These new buildings are constructed by low-wage Indian temporary laborers. While the new Indian and multinational firms are primed to enter the global economy, working conditions for white-collar IT workers are arduous and despotic. College-educated workers employed in high-technology development as programmers, business service specialists, and call center operators work long hours in facilities that resemble prison blocs rather than corporate offices. At the Center for Economic and Social Studies, political economists note that IT companies keep employees in separate buildings and prohibit them from interacting or mingling with fellow workers in the same complexes (interview, Arun Patnaik, December 17, 2008).

Indian neoliberal proponents saw market reforms as a means of reducing communal divisions and directing the country to the international market, according to Prakash C. Sarangi, professor of political science at the University of Hyderabad. Instead, Sarangi argues, over the two decades from 1985 to 2005, neoliberalism has only reinforced caste, communal, and gender divisions in society, which in turn has obscured class divisions: "Only the cream of students goes to careers in the IT sector while the rest work in supportive roles as cleaners, security, and landscaping" (interview, October 6, 2005). IT guest workers may earn low salaries in the United States, but when their wages are converted into the Indian rupee, they are a substantial amount of money.

Sarangi asserts that training IT workers to the exclusion of other skills is not in India's best interest: "We need a full range of skills to promote development. It is almost a requirement to have a family member working in the U.S. to enter upper-middle-class status in the state of Andhra Pradesh." He adds that many IT guest workers return to India with the intention of "living like a king—employing servants, owning a beautiful house, car, et cetera. There they are part of the middle class—part of the elite" (interview, Prakash C. Sarangi, October 8, 2005). For working-class Indians in steel, apparel, and other manufacturing industries, the neoliberal reforms are leading to the closure of older factories and the building of modern factories that employ fewer workers at considerably lower wages (Bagchi 2002).

The perception that India is a technological giant is misleading, and the country bears the genuine cost of an ongoing brain drain of necessary expertise. When IT, software, and business service workers return to India, they are not equipped with the diverse skills needed to serve the vital needs of the population. Also, despite the naïve argument that India is poised to compete worldwide in business service professions, the 2001 government census reports that 35 percent of its population, including more than 54 percent of women, is illiterate. Pankaj Mishra, an Indian writer and essayist living in the West, argues that the official literacy rate "includes many who can barely write their names" (2006, A21). Only a small proportion of India's overall population stands to gain from the growth in IT professions from 1990 to 2010, which account for 1.3 million of the national population. Moreover, a growing number of highly educated students with graduate degrees in the social sciences from regional universities are excluded from growth industries and gainful employment (interviews, Arun Patnaik, October 7, 2005; December 17, 2009). Others will find work in call centers servicing Western consumers—jobs that require twelve to sixteen hours of work each shift, usually starting at night and ending in the late morning of the next day. Intel, Microsoft, IBM, Siemens, and other leading multinational firms prime workers to travel to the United States and Europe as guest workers in the IT sector.

The political economy of Hyderabad, like the IT center of Bangalore, is bifurcated between an upper class of corporate officers, contractors, and other business owners and a growing working class laboring as food-service workers, car service drivers, security guards, building cleaners, and day laborers in the construction industry. The informal sector marginalizes workers into jobs with little prospect of earning enough to survive. In Hyderabad, many construction workers are displaced former peasants who live in the city's slums. While cities grow more prosperous for those employed in the IT and business services sectors, workers and peasant farmers in the countryside are displaced and left without adequate housing, education, and public services.

Contractors frequently hire these same displaced laborers to build and maintain the new high-technology centers on former agricultural land expropriated by Indian technology firms. The vast majority of those working as contract labor now live in tent communities near the high-technology centers. Upon completion of their work, most must move on to new construction sites, continuing the process of dispossession and labor exploitation. In interviews with thirty-eight workers living in makeshift housing and tents laboring in Hyderabad construction sites from November 2006 to February 2007, the vast majority indicated that they had no choice but to work as contractors and subcontractors building and maintaining the buildings and grounds of high-technology complexes and residences for those laboring in the industry (interviews, Arun Kumar, November 2006–February 2007).

The rise of high technology in Hyderabad provides an unqualified example of Bagchi's contention that the capitalist class and multinationals make use of caste, communal, and gender divisions in order to diminish the living standards and suppress the expression of workers and peasants (2002, 263–291). The divisions are an expedient means to contain working-class dissent and protest against superexploitation and economic destitution.

The Yagar family is a prototype of the tens of thousands of rural workers forced to work in Hyderabad who can no longer survive as agricultural workers, due to growing inequality. In an interview, Yagar, a Dalit, one of Hinduism's lowest castes, said he was forced to migrate to Hyderabad from the city's hinterland with his wife and daughter due to their inability to survive as agricultural laborers. As tenant farmers, the family accumulated a huge debt to landowners cultivating chili in a rural area of the state. Due to the accumulated debt and anxiety, they could not afford the dowry for their daughter's marriage, and therefore the family moved to Hyderabad.

The husband and wife landed jobs as joint temporary laborers in the garden of Larsen & Toubro Limited, a Mumbai-based technology, engineering, construction, and manufacturing firm, one of India's largest companies. Because the couple belongs to a "backward caste," contractors filter payments to them through another contractor and two subcontractors, reducing the money allocated by the company.[4] While typical wages for couples working in similar jobs are 200 to 230 rupees a week, Yagar and his wife earned only 150 rupees combined (80 rupees for Yagar and 70 for his wife). The Hindu hierarchical system prohibits privileged-caste Indians at the construction company from interacting with Yagar. The hierarchy in the caste system serves to marginalize Yagar through the capitalist system of subcontractors, who each take a commission of the original wages.[5]

Yagar and his family live in makeshift tents constructed of pieces of plastic, for which they are charged 150 rupees per month. The family lives in an area with no sanitation and no sewage system. The construction company provides the couple with a meager supply of water for drinking and cooking. Although all the family members work in Hyderabad, the higher cost of shelter and food in the city offsets their gains in income, and their lot is only marginally improved. Yagar said that due to the strenuous nature of the work and little hope of improving the family's standard of living, most of the remaining income is used to pay for alcoholic beverages.

Indian Union Avoidance Schemes

Hyderabad is a major business hub for Infosys, one of India's leading high-technology firms. The company has a huge facility of six separate buildings, which employs about 3,000 high-technology workers and some 400 security, maintenance, and support personnel. The support staffs at the complex, dormitories, cafeteria, and health club are all contractors working an average of fifteen to sixteen hours a day.

Satyam, one of India's four largest high-technology firms, also has extensive operations in Hyderabad, within the Hyderabad Information Technology Engineering Consultancy, a gated business, residential, and hotel zone in the city. Satyam prevents workers from interacting or mingling at the conclusion of their shifts, ostensibly for security purposes. Workers in each structure are employed in different segments of the company. The operation reflects the caste system itself, as some buildings house workers with specialized skills who earn higher wages and have better working conditions, while other blocks employ workers in other segments of the company that may pay lower wages. Recognizing the hierarchy in skill and wages, to keep workers apart, Satyam uses a sophisticated security system, staggers the hours of workers, and prevents access through use of security and barriers between parking lots.

The fate of workers who remain in India is different in some ways than the fate of those who join the ranks of guest workers seeking jobs in other countries. Though exploitation is endemic in both systems of labor relations, variant regional conditions lead to differing outcomes.

Conclusion: Mobile Workers and Resistance

The most important factor in U.S. high-technology and service jobs moving offshore to India is the capacity to recruit foreign workers who earn significantly lower wages, to perform services identical to those performed by U.S. workers. Forrester, a technology research company based in Cambridge, Massachusetts, argues that the job loss will continue unabated. This research company, influential in the IT industry, released a study in May 2004 projecting that 400,000 IT and service jobs will move offshore in 2004, and by the year 2015, about 3.3 million jobs in the industry will move to low-wage foreign competitors or guest workers in the United States (McCarthy 2004).

Corporate executives in the United States persistently demand more global guest workers while ignoring India's public health disaster, illiteracy, and the rigid caste system that consigns nearly 300 million Dalit (formerly known as untouchables) and OBCs to wretched and persistent poverty.[6] In June 2008, the Indo-Asian News Service reported that contrary to the propaganda that represents India as a wealthy and prosperous country, 900 million Indians live on less than two dollars (eighty-five rupees) a day (De Sarkar 2008). Fewer than 1 million people out of more than 1 billion Indians are fluent enough in English to work at call center jobs, considered among the best jobs in the country. True enough, IT services in Hyderabad, Mumbai, and Bangalore can compete with those in the United States, but they do so amid the human tragedy that is growing ever more rapidly as open markets and the ending of hard-won government benefits challenge both Americans and Indians. The endemic poverty in India, China, and most of the Global South is ravaging stable communities by exposing workers and peasants to market forces without even minimal safeguards.

From 2000 to 2010, leading U.S. academics, investors, and media pundits have portrayed India as the site of the next wave of technological growth and economic prosperity (Friedman 2005; Rajan 2009). This logic hinges on the belief that as a democratic society, India will permit greater innovation through unfettered capitalism. The reality is that India's market reforms have solidified the power of the upper classes while further marginalizing workers and peasants. According to most Indian economists, the imposition of neoliberalism in 1985 has dispossessed the working poor and peasants of their jobs and property (Bagchi 2002, 2005; Banerjee 2005; Deshpande, Sharma, Sarkar, and Karan 2006; Joshi 2005; Lieten and Sharma forthcoming).

While India "enthusiasts" boast that the model Indian is an IT worker earning enough to own a large house and fancy cars, they conceal the fact that this model Indian depends on several low-wage servants to cook, clean, and care for children. Many more are displaced by economic crises in old industries and agriculture and are working in low-wage sectors in conditions of poverty (Srinivasulu, Kumar, and Sekhar 2004; Kumar 2005). Development economists willingly admit that such conditions exist during what they describe as an "economic transition." They insist that during a short period of economic crisis the poor majority will suffer as the economy transforms. Contrary to what they predict, however, the vast majority of Indians are not joining the middle class as the reforms take effect. If poverty is indeed a necessary stage to development, how long must it last?

The notion that the country's enduring democratic institutions provide an advantage over other countries persuades many to assert that the nation's economy will adapt to neoliberal capitalism more swiftly than China's erstwhile socialist economy (Das 2002). India is not superseding China economically, however. Unlike India, a middle class is emerging in China. In 2005, India's GDP per capita is estimated at $3,300—less than half that of China's $6,800 (CIA 2006).

Indian political economists are challenging the prevailing consensus among U.S. enthusiasts. The core empirical evidence is that market reform creates homogenization of labor in specific labor markets in India and a drive to the bottom. As this collection makes clear, Indian migration is not exclusively composed of high-wage educated workers going to the United States and Europe, despite the media's focus on H-1B high-technology laborers. Most are low-wage internal migrants from poverty-stricken urban and rural areas and low-wage manual-labor migrants to the Gulf States and, increasingly, the Global North.

Whether in the United States, Western Europe, or India, Indians must work long hours at low wages even in the high-technology sector. According to Banerjee, "We are seeing the onerous conditions of work found in early capitalism. IT and call center workers are employed for twelve-hour days and are monitored and subject to constant surveillance. We are seeing the return of sweatshop conditions, only now in the high-technology sector" (interviews, Debdas Banerjee, October 5, 2005; December 18, 2008). Similarly, working conditions in U.S. IT facilities are also requiring employees to work long hours and forcing them into onerous working conditions (Benner 2002; Pellow and Park 2002).

Proponents of expanding the supply of guest workers fail to recognize the poverty that export-promotion policies create in India and the Global South. As shown in this chapter, it is more likely that Indians will work in menial jobs, whether in India or as guest workers in the United States. While only a small share of India's huge labor force includes skilled laborers primed to go abroad to work in the IT and business service industries, they are now generating an unprecedentedly large share of foreign revenue for the country. India does not have an infinite number of knowledge industry workers, though the false idea that it does is promoted by experts like Thomas Friedman of the *New York Times* and Nandan Nilekani (2009), who point exclusively to IT hubs while neglecting to evaluate the nation as a whole.

Gurcharan Das, bourgeois ideologue, one of India's leading neoliberal enthusiasts, and former CEO of Procter & Gamble India, has asserted that the temporary migrant labor system benefits India. Expanding guest worker programs worldwide, he argues, is necessary, since Indian college graduates have training in the newest corporate high technology (Das 2002, 331). In turn, Indians working in the United States will promote the new growth of India's IT sector. This assessment, however, is incorrect. First, the country boasts only 2 million college graduates every year, nowhere near enough to validate Indian enthusiasts' false image of an emerging large middle class. In reality, in a country of more than 1 billion inhabitants, just a small fraction of about 2 percent of the population can qualify as middle-class, less than half as many as in China (Srinivas 2008).

Worse still, this emphasis on IT encourages colleges to steer students into this field as the pathway to wealth. This will cripple India in the long term, leaving the country lacking in health care workers, engineers, agronomists, educators, and skilled workers in other sectors crucial for the nation's development.

While some argue that the Indian middle class expanded to 250 million by 2006 (nearly 20 percent of the national population), in that year the Indian National Sample Survey Organization reported that monthly per capita consumption expenditures in 2004–2005 in urban India were 1,052 rupees (US$23) in urban areas and 559 rupees (US$12) in rural areas, revealing the narrow size of the Indian middle class and the persistence of poverty in urban and rural regions. Even the World Bank (2005) estimates that only 4.5 percent of India's population owns personal computers, though in 2003, 17.5 percent of the population used the Internet. By contrast, 15.9 percent of Chinese owned computers in 2005, and 63 percent used the Internet. It is therefore absurd to claim that IT is transforming India—rather, India is a hub in the global economy for trained and mobile IT workers.

Some benefit from this system, but most fall further behind. Predictably, India's minute upper and even middle classes benefit from the market transition, thanks in part to a new urban proletariat migrating from rural India to the new high-technology centers. At the top of the contracting chain are multinational IT companies that contract out virtually all services. Next come young Indian workers sent to the United States and the Global North, earning comparatively higher salaries that provide a modest nest egg with which many hope to marry and raise a family. Upon their return, they frequently work in the IT and business complexes sprawling throughout India's major cities. Notably, however, the majority of Indian migrants work arduous construction and hospitality jobs in Saudi Arabia, the Persian Gulf, and increasingly, the United States. Jagdish Bhagwati, an Indian American economist and spokesperson for U.S. neoliberal reform, insists that only young protesters from the wealthy countries in the Global North oppose market reforms, while most in the impoverished Global South support greater global integration. Bhagwati and his acolytes fail to report the even-more-organized opposition to neoliberalism among protesters from the Global South and India in particular. The World Social Forum, held in Mumbai from January 16 to 21, 2004, raised global awareness of the grassroots opposition to neoliberal programs in India, including peasants' resistance in 2007 to the placement of a Special Economic Zone (SEZ) in Nandigram, a rural region in the East Midnapur district of West Bengal. Moreover, protest has grown against plans by the national government to privatize airports and education, and to increase commodification of agriculture (Kumar 2008). Bhagwati (2004) and Das (2002), along with other global apologists for neoliberal capitalism, argue that human misery is a necessary sacrifice in the process of moving to a market economy. As they make excuses, the proportion of the population falling hopelessly into poverty increases.

The radically disparate narratives outlined in this chapter and the hard evidence of growing poverty in the Global South prove false the fiction generated by multinational corporations and India's capitalist class. Capitalists in India and the United States ignore stultifying poverty and focus on their own economic gains, the modernization of two or three economic sectors, and growing foreign interest in India as beneficial to the country overall, when that is simply not the case. New roads and infrastructure are linking India's rapidly expanding IT centers, airports, hotels, and affluent communities, while urban and rural transport and intercity railways rust away. Meanwhile, the market-based economy neglects basic needs such as sanitation, clean water, electricity, medicine, and food for the majority of the population. Even if global capital is generating a fictional account of India's economic development as approaching the level of industrialized countries, a congruent labor struggle is emerging in shared yet distinctive resistance among workers and the poor in the North and South.

NOTES

1. The Washington Consensus, directed by the International Monetary Fund (IMF), World Bank (WB), and World Trade Organization (WTO), was formed in 1989 to implement neoliberal reforms advocated by leading global corporations.

2. A growing number of foreign labor contractors in the United States are becoming known as "body shops," given that they trade in people and control the work lives of foreign workers in the United States. Moreover, foreign contractors are crucial in securing the housing and health care needs of foreign nonimmigrant workers. Three Indian contractors provide a large segment of the U.S. IT and business services market: Tata Consultancy Services, Infosys Technologies Ltd., and Wipro Technologies. These are Indian companies that provide IT, business consulting, and accounting services on an international basis. The companies primarily employ Indian programmers. An ongoing complaint by opponents is that U.S. government authorities do not enforce the law and permit contractors to replace American workers and fraudulently file labor applications at lower rates than U.S. workers.

    While India's IT firms emerged in the last decade to eclipse most other companies in the global software services marketplace, the leading companies are branches of large companies that have controlled the Indian economy for many years. Tata Consultancy Services (TCS), a unit of Tata Group, the leading Indian software consulting company in the United States, was founded by Jamsetji Tata in 1869 as a family-owned cotton and steel manufacturing company. Just in the last decade, the company's profile has transformed into a multinational high-technology firm that provides banking, accounting, insurance, and IT services in fifty-five countries. Sixty-six percent of Tata capital is held by the family through philanthropic trusts, while the Tata Group is now a public company. TCS, founded in 1968, is the firm's largest division, employing 24,000 software, engineering, and computer architecture consultants globally, with more than $1 billion in annual revenue in fiscal year 2002–2003. IT services are outsourced, and the firm has formed joint ventures with leading U.S. software, manufacturing, and financial services firms.

    TCS's client list reads like a who's who of the leading manufacturing, energy, telecommunications, financial services, and software multinationals in the world: AT&T, AXA Insurance, British Telecom, Canadian Mutual Life, ChevronTexaco, Citicorp, Deutsche Bank, General Motors, Ford, General Electric, IBM, Lucent Technologies, Nike, Nortel Networks, P&O Nedlloyd, Qwest Communications, UBS, and Verizon Communications. The firm has formed strong relationships with educational institutions in India and throughout the world, including the Indian Institute of Technology; University of California; University of Wisconsin; Carnegie Mellon University; University of Humberside; University of Waterloo; and the Rotterdam School of Management.

Infosys Technologies Ltd., founded in 1981, is now one of the world's leading IT software contractors, with 28,000 international employees and annual revenue exceeding $1 billion. Based in Bangalore—considered India's Silicon Valley—Infosys expanded rapidly only under the neoliberal reforms. In 1987, the company entered the U.S. market, opening offices in Fremont, California. By 1999, Infosys became the first Indian company to be listed on the NASDAQ stock exchange. Infosys has rapidly increased its U.S. presence, opening five development centers in 1999 and 2000 as the H-1B guest worker program expanded dramatically. The company serves clients in North America, Western Europe, and East Asia—including Oracle, Intel, Siebel, Interwoven, Informatica, BEA, Star Partner, MatrixOne, Mantas, and SAP Partner Services.

Founded in 1945, Wipro Ltd. is a diversified global software outsourcing and global contracting company, with 75 percent of its revenue derived from offshore IT business services. In 2003, *Business Week* ranked Wipro Information Technology as the twenty-first-largest software services company in the world. To meet global outsourcing and offshoring demands, Wipro employs 15,000 IT and business service workers worldwide. The company operates IT facilities in North America, Western Europe, and Japan, as well as in India, to meet projections for dramatic growth in offshore demand for software services in the event that on-site outsourcing declines. The firm is also a leading operator of call centers serving advanced economies.

The history of Wipro reveals the shift from domestic production to export promotion through information services, taking advantage of India's plethora of IT workers trained by the country's state-sponsored high-technology institutions. In the wake of Indian independence from Britain in 1947, Wipro began as a family-owned producer of hydrogenated cooking oil for the domestic market. In 1975, the firm branched out into manufacturing hydraulic and pneumatic cylinders for storage and transport of the oil and cooking products. In 1980, Wipro established IT production operations targeted to the domestic Indian market. In 1989, the company changed course dramatically, establishing a joint venture with General Electric for the production of medical systems technology. The same year, Wipro disbanded its software production business while expanding into IT services for the domestic market. By 1992, the Bangalore-based company established a global services division that has grown exponentially over the ensuing decades.

By 2000, Wipro Ltd. was listed on the New York Stock Exchange, with consolidated operations in global IT services and products. Wipro, which claims to have the highest market capitalization of any company in India, also operates a consumer care and lighting division. In fiscal year 2003–2004, Wipro's revenues exceeded $1 billion. The company projects that future operations will focus on two major areas: outsourcing services on a global scale and facilitating offshoring operations by leading multinationals in India. As more and more U.S. and Western European high-technology firms move to India, Wipro is expanding operations in its home country to retain a competitive advantage over Accenture, IBM Global Services, and EDS by providing outsourcing software services to industries globally. This "global delivery model," according to Wipro, requires more than U.S. IT firms offshoring back-office operations to India; it also necessitates retaining "high value services" that compete with the global IT companies in high-end consulting services in India.

Satyam Computer Services, founded in 1987, is taking an increasingly larger share of the U.S. market. One of the five largest software service outsourcing firms in India, Satyam provides global consulting to an array of multinational firms for which software services are not central to the company's operations. The Hyderabad-based firm, listed on the NASDAQ stock exchange, provides software professionals to U.S., Western European, and East Asian automotive, banking, financial services, insurance, health care, manufacturing, telecommunications, media, and entertainment firms. In 2002–2003, 99 percent of the firm's revenue was derived from foreign operations, 76 percent of that in the United States. Satyam maintains five domestic and thirteen global development centers with nearly 10,000 employees, the vast majority stationed in the United States.

The company is more reliant on outsourcing in the United States and Western Europe than its competitors now diversifying into offshoring operations, and thus is more dependent on the condition of the global economy. Satyam is not as well positioned as its competitors to take advantage of offshoring operations and is vulnerable to caps being placed on foreign guest workers. Even after the collapse of the high-technology bubble in 2000, American firms retained access to 195,000 foreign workers under the H-1B program, three times the rate of preceding years. However, when the guest worker program was capped at 65,000 in 2004, Satyam's foreign revenues, so highly dependent on the U.S. market, peaked and began to level off. Concurrently, employment growth has leveled off from 8,593 in 2000–2001 to 9,759 in 2002–2003.

3. On average, programmers in India and China earn a fraction of the average U.S. wage of $60,000 per year. As H-1B authorizations declined in 2006 and 2007, Internet Technology Association of America (ITAA) is successfully lobbying Congress on behalf of the IT industry to provide exemptions to allow more than 85,000 workers to enter the United States. Concomitantly, IT contractors elude the cap of 85,000 by sending workers to the United States through a consortium of third countries (ITAA 2004, 2006, 2007).

4. Because Yagar and his wife are members of a low caste, employers may not remunerate them directly but instead pay contractors and subcontractors, who take large cuts out of the salary.

5. Dalit is not a single caste. The lowest castes, those that used to be treated socially, if not legally, as untouchables, are even now treated as outcasts; they call themselves Dalits, meaning the oppressed.

6. OBC includes not only a number of castes but also other groupings (Ramaiah 1992).

REFERENCES

Arora, Ashish, and Suma Athreye. 2002. "The Software Industry and India's Economic Development." *Information Economics and Policy* 14(2): 253–273.

Bagchi, Amiya Kumar. 2002. *Capital and Labour Redefined: India and the Third World.* London: Anthem Press.

———. 2005. *Perilous Passage: Mankind and the Global Ascendancy of Capital.* Lanham, MD: Rowman and Littlefield.

Baldauf, Scott. 2005. "Power Shortages Threaten India's Boom." *Christian Science Monitor*, June 1.

Banerjee, Debdas. 2005. *Globalisation, Industrial Restructuring and Labour Standards: Where India Meets the Global.* New Delhi: Sage.

Benner, Chris. 2002. *Work in the New Economy: Flexible Labor Markets in Silicon Valley.* Malden, MA: Blackwell.

Bhagwati, Jagdish. 2004. *In Defense of Globalization.* Oxford: Oxford University Press.

Bhatt, Ela Ramesh. 2005. *We Are Poor But So Many: The Story of Self-Employed Women in India.* New York: Oxford University Press.

CIA. 2006. *The World Factbook.* https://www.cia.gov/library/publications/the-world-factbook/geos/in.html. Accessed March 18, 2010.

Das, Gurcharan. 2002. *India Unbound: The Social and Economic Revolution from Independence to the Global Information Age.* New York: Anchor Books.

De Sarkar, Dipanka. 2008. "900 million Indians Live on Less Than $2 a Day." *Indo-Asian News Service*, June 12.

Deshpande, L. K., N. Sharma, Sandip Sarkar, and Anup K. Karan. 2006. *Liberalisation and Labour: Labour Flexibility in Indian Manufacturing.* New Delhi: Institute for Human Development.

Freeman, Richard B. 2007. *America Works: The Exceptional U.S. Labor Market.* New York: Russell Sage Foundation.

Friedman, Thomas. 2005. *The World Is Flat: A Brief History of the Twenty-First Century.* New York: Farrar, Straus and Giroux.

Garnaut, Ross, and Ligang Song. 2005. *China Boom and Its Discontents.* Canberra: Asia Pacific Press.

Gereffi, G., and W. Wadhwa. 2005. "Framing the Engineering Outsourcing Debate: Placing the United States on a Level Playing Field with China and India." Master of Engineering and Management Program, Duke University.

Global Insight. 2005. "US Truck Driver Shortage: Analysis and Forecasts." May. http://advancedmaritimetechnology.aticorp.org/short-sea-shipping/ATADriverShortageStudy05.pdf. Accessed March 7, 2010.

Greater Hyderabad Municipal Corporation. 2010. *Hyderabad: City Development Plan.* Hyderabad, India.

Harvey, David. 2006. *A Brief History of Neoliberalism.* Oxford: Oxford University Press.

Joshi, Chitra. 2005. *Lost Worlds: Indian Labour and Its Forgotten Histories.* London: Anthem Press.

Kumar, Ravi. 2008. "Against Neoliberal Assault on Education in India: A Counternarrative of Resistance." *Journal of Critical Education Policy Studies* 6(1).

Kumar, V. Anil. 2005. *Farmers' Suicides in Andhra Pradesh: The Response of Political Institutions*. Hyderabad, India: Centre for Economic and Social Studies.

Jing Wang. 2008. *Brand New China: Advertising, Media, and Commercial Culture*. Cambridge: Harvard University Press.

Lieten, G. K., and Alakh N. Sharma. Forthcoming. *Globalization and Social Exclusion*. New Delhi: Institute for Human Development.

McCarthy, J. C. 2004. *Near-Term Growth of Offshoring Accelerating: Resizing US Services Jobs Going Offshore*. Cambridge, MA: Forrester Research.

Mishra, Pankaj. 2006. "The Myth of the New India." *New York Times*, July 6, A21.

Morstead, Stuart, and Greg Blount. 2003. *Offshore Ready: Strategies to Plan and Profit from Offshore IT-Enabled Services*. Flower Mound, TX: ISANI Press.

National Sample Survey Organisation. 2006. Ministry of Statistics and Programme Implementation, Government of India. "Press Note on Level and Pattern of Consumption Expenditure, 2004–05." Report No. 508, December 27.

NASSCOM. 2010. http://www.nasscom.in/. Accessed March 8, 2010.

Nayyar, Rohini, and Alakh N. Sharma. 2005. *Rural Transformation in India: The Role of Non-farm Sector*. New Delhi: Institute for Human Development.

Nilekani, Nandan. 2009. *Imagining India: The Idea of a Renewed Nation*. New York: Penguin.

OECD. 2001. *International Mobility and the Highly Skilled*. Paris: Organization for Economic Co-operation and Development.

Pellow, David N., and Lisa Sun Hee Park. 2002. *The Silicon Valley of Dreams: Environmental Injustice, Immigrant Workers and the High-Tech Global Economy*. New York: NYU Press.

Preston, Peter Wallace, and Jürgen Haacke. 2003. *Contemporary China: The Dynamics of Change at the Start of the New Millennium*. London: Routledge.

Rajan, Ramkishen S. 2009. *Monetary Investment and Trade Issues in India*. New York: Oxford University Press.

Rajeev, M. 2007. "Fresh Way of Hope for Trained Truckers." *The Hindu*, May 6. http://www.thehindu.com/2007/05/06/stories/2007050617000100.htm. Accessed August 20, 2007.

Ramaiah, A. 1992. "Identifying Other Backward Classes." *Economic and Political Weekly*, June, 1203–1207.

Sakthivel S., and Pinaki Joddar. 2006. "Unorganized Sector Workforce in India: Trends, Patterns and Social Security Coverage." *Economic and Political Weekly*, May 27, 2107–2114.

Sheshabalaya, Ashutosh. 2005. *Rising Elephant: The Growing Clash with India over White-Collar Jobs and Its Challenge to America and the World*. Monroe, ME: Common Courage Press.

Srinivas, Alam. 2008. *The Indian Consumer: One Billion Myths, One Billion Realities*. Singapore: Wiley.

Srinivasulu, K., V. Anil Kumar, and K. S. Vijaya Sekhar. 2004. *Crisis in Handloom Sector in Andhra Pradesh: The Ways Forward*. Hyderabad, India: Centre for Economic and Social Studies.

World Bank. 2005. *World Development Indicators Database*. Washington, DC: World Bank Group. http://web.worldbank.org/WBSITE/EXTERNAL/COUNTRIEShttp://web.worldbank.org/WBSITE/EXTERNAL/COUNTRIES EASTASIAPACIFICEXT/CHINAEXTNEASTASIAPACIFICEXT/CHINAEXTN/0,,menuPK:318956~pagePK:141159~piPK:141110~theSite PK:318950,00.html. Accessed March 19, 2006.

———. 2009a. *New Global Poverty Estimates: What It Means for India*. http://www.worldbank.org.in/WBSITE/EXTERNAL/COUNTRIES/SOUTHASIAEXT/INDIAEXTN/0,,contentMDK:21880725~pagePK:141137~piPK:141127~theSitePK:295584,00.html. Accessed April 8, 2009.

———. 2009b. *Regional Cooperation and Integration—Energy: Opportunity for Trade*. http://web.worldbank.org/WBSITE/EXTERNAL/COUNTRIES/SOUTHASIAEXT/0,,contentMDK:21510953~pagePK:146736~piPK:146830~theSitePK:223547,00.html. Accessed April 8, 2009.

World Bank Group. 2008. *World Development Report 2009: Reshaping Economic Geography*. Washington, DC: World Bank Publications.

Zakaria, Fareed. 2008. *The Post-American World*. New York: Norton.

8

Water for Life, Not for Coca-Cola

Transnational Systems of Capital and Activism

AMANDA CIAFONE

Over the last decade, several rural communities around Coca-Cola plants exploded in protest against the company's exploitation of groundwater in the production of bottled drinks amid a growing national crisis of water scarcity. As demonstrated in the vibrant ongoing struggle in Mehndiganj, Uttar Pradesh, these mobilizations articulated a powerful critique of corporate globalization and Indian neoliberalism, illuminating the dispossession of the resources of the rural poor for consumption by those on the other side of a widening economic divide in the nation's vaunted new freer marketplace. After local political and economic elites failed to respond to these resource struggles, activists created links to disparate sites of protest against Coca-Cola and distant allies. This network remapped Coke's corporate world system, allowing local activists to bring multinational pressure against the multinational corporation. To do so, activists on the ground in India and those acting in solidarity in other parts of the world mobilized the symbolic capital of the branded commodity to subversively resignify Coca-Cola and hail people who speak its language to join their struggle for "water for life, not for profit."

These corporate and activist systems of Coke are constituted within the larger geopolitical world, both critical of and shaped by the changes in economic, cultural, and social power concurrent with neoliberalism. Within that world, corporate executives and local activists did not encounter each other on an equal field of power. For activists, transnational mobilization depended on such problematic things as the existence of mobile, multilingual, resourced activists, the support of international NGOs, members of the diaspora convinced to care about the issue, and consumers in the Global North willing to revalue the Coca-Cola Company's brands and take action within the market. Seen through the curvy glass of a Coca-Cola bottle, the company's history in India—dramatically exiled under state socialism, returning with headlines in the free market 1990s, and embattled in the 2000s—offers lucid reflections on these larger shifts of power in the last quarter century.

Through the Looking Glass Bottle of Coke: Reflections on Neoliberal India

After just a few years of operation, residents of Mehndiganj had had enough of the Coca-Cola plant in their village outside the city of Benares in the northern state of Uttar Pradesh. Farmers, landless agricultural workers and their families, many Dalits (low caste), mobilized against the plant, denouncing the corporation's dispossession and privatization of an environmental commons that traverses property lines and is essential to all human life: water. The plant, they charged, improperly disposed of manufacturing by-product "sludge" material, flooded surrounding lands with effluent water, and exacerbated falling groundwater levels. Neighboring wells had dried up, and the remaining water became salty, bitter, and hard, as each day truck after truck took hundreds of thousands of bottled drinks from the plant.

In 1993, after sixteen years of self-imposed exile to avoid the restrictions on multinationals by the postcolonial socialist state, the

Coca-Cola Company dramatically reentered an India opening itself up to foreign corporations through economic liberalization. The government launched a wave of economic reforms in the early 1990s curbing the role of the state in the market, including the approval of foreign investment, privatizations in the public sector, dissolution of the "license raj" regulatory regime, and removal of restrictions on multinational corporations, including the prohibition of the sale of products under international trademarks. The Coca-Cola Company had long been eager to return to India, one of the largest markets of the "sweat belt," as company executives called the hot, developing countries of the Global South with large Muslim and/or Hindu populations that looked down on alcohol consumption and thus held vast potential profits for the soft drink industry.[1] Now was the company's chance: it spent $1 billion in the following ten years buying out the largest Indian soft drink producer and reestablishing its global brands and bottling system in one of the country's largest foreign investments.[2] With Coca-Cola's sudden, almost ubiquitous reappearance at the moment of liberalization, it became both an aspirational sign of global consumer citizenship for India's urban middle classes and an emblematic brand of neoliberal globalization for those dispossessed of resources to fuel their consumption.

The Coca-Cola Company located much of its production in places like Mehndiganj, rural communities outside of larger metropolitan areas, to access reserves of water as well as cheap labor. This was in line with the Indian government's greater reliance on market-led forces to fuel the economic development of rural India, as it disavowed previous rural social and economic welfare policies and overlooked the lack of existing environmental regulations. In this context, state and local governments compete to attract corporations by creating industrial areas and offering financial incentives, such as tax exemptions, to encourage industries to invest in "backward" areas.[3] Here the majority of residents are landless or land-poor agricultural workers who are under extreme economic and environmental stress, part of what has been called an agrarian crisis in India.[4] The roots of this crisis are deep: the earlier socialist state's agrarian planned economy, which fed India's large population and reduced its vulnerability to famine, also overexploited water and land with intensive irrigation and agrochemical application. Liberalization has since compounded this toll on rural India with unrestrained and uneven industrial growth, resulting in "environmental degradation and social dislocation" that have disproportionately affected marginalized groups.[5] Higher costs for electricity (to run water pumps), seeds, fertilizers, and pesticides needed to cultivate environmentally degrading land, and the deregulation of the banking sector and subsequent credit crunch for farmers seeking loans to pay for these inputs, have led to extreme indebtedness.[6] The resulting agrarian crisis is most shockingly visible in the large number of farmer suicides in the last decade—between 22,000 and 25,000 by several estimates.[7]

The shift from statist development's emphasis on poverty alleviation in rural India to liberalization's market-directed consumerist focus on the interests of the middle class has exacerbated disparities in economic and cultural power,[8] contributed to environmental strain, and incited new class formations and struggles, in the places it has not completely devastated. Through the 1990s the population grew by almost one-third in the Mehndiganj area as people who could no longer work the land sought out marginal labor in the service sector of these growing villages. Such a surge in population density, like the precipitous rise in industrialization and urbanization expected over the next decades in India, markedly aggravates water use.[9] Still, agriculture is the primary use of water in Mehndiganj, and executives have argued that the farmers are sucking their own wells dry. Farmers have expanded their cultivation of water-intensive rice in their search for economically viable yields, and often flood their lands with as much water as possible because of its irrigation demands, the infrequent electricity to the area, and the need to rent time on wealthier neighbors' deeper wells and more powerful pumps. But villagers argue that vastly more of the water for agricultural and daily use seeps back into the groundwater. If farmers must make their own water use more sustainable, they concede, there should also be a reconsideration of the location of a water-intensive industry like Coca-Cola in areas with already depleting aquifers, which profits by drawing up and privatizing large amounts of water, shipping its liquid commodities far outside original watersheds.

At its Mehndiganj plant the Coca-Cola Company uses roughly three liters of water to produce each liter of soft drink or bottled water. From 100-meter-deep bore wells, with an independent twenty-four-hour supply of electricity from their own generators, hundreds of thousands of liters of water are extracted each day, constituting what villagers and activists call "water mining."[10] Withdrawal is far higher during the hot months when more soft drinks are sold, coinciding with the time of year when farmers' lands and wells become parched in advance of the increasingly erratic monsoon rains.[11] Groundwater extraction is virtually unregulated as a colonial-era law gives landowners private property rights not only to their land but to whatever groundwater lies underneath.[12] Although national and Uttar Pradesh state water policy statements acknowledge worsening water scarcity and disparity, and specify that drinking water and irrigation are higher priorities than industrial uses, few states have implemented water resources legislation.[13] Thus, the Coca-Cola Company was not required to provide assessments of the potential environmental impact of its proposed plants on water resources, while the company's proprietary internal studies were focused solely "on ensuring a sustained supply of water for business operations" and were never made public.[14] The local *panchayat* (village council) granted a procedural permission for the plant's operation with no conditions on the amount of groundwater withdrawn, only requiring payment of minimal annual taxes and license fees.[15] While a cess is collected on water consumed by industry, the charges are so minuscule that heavy water users like Coca-Cola can draw groundwater virtually for free.[16]

Extraction and pollution of this shared water resource affect all who rely upon it but most fundamentally, the peasants who are dependent on it for their lives (for drinking, cooking, bathing) and their livelihoods (for irrigating their crops). Water shortages disproportionately affect "weaker sections" of these communities: landless agricultural workers who lose work in the fields, Dalits who face discrimination around access to water sources, women who are responsible for most of the labor around water (collection, cooking, washing, bathing, cleaning). Faced with the devastating prospect of water scarcity in Mehndiganj and surrounding villages, community members held dharnas (sit-in fasts) on effluent flooded lands, marched on the plant, and dumped by-product sludge on the desks of pollution control regulators. In the past few years, they have mobilized through the local community organization Lok Samiti (People's Committee) to host conferences on water rights and climate change, dig public water ponds in the village, and set up free drinking water stops in places where bottled water and soft drinks are sold, like the Benares train station, to inform people of their struggle and garner interest in public water programs. The movement in Mehndiganj, in its organizers' own words, rejects the way "water is seen as an asset and a commodity by the Indian government, the international institutions…and the multinational corporations." Instead, residents assert that water is "an inalienable right which cannot be sold for profit," requiring the community's say in its "participatory development."[17]

"Water for Life, Not for Profit": Transnational Mobilizations against Coca-Cola

By challenging Coca-Cola's water use, villagers dispute market and state development of rural India without their say, contesting the version of industrialization that uses environmental resources to benefit some by negatively impacting others. In this way, they enact what has been called an "environmentalism of the poor,"[18] similar to struggles around the world for environmental justice and against environmental racism.[19] These struggles, according to Indian environmental thinker Anil Agarwal, are acts of the "'victims of development,' the poor peasants and tribals who have thus far had to unwillingly make way for the dams, steel mills, and highways that . . . intensified social inequalities as well as devastated the natural environment."[20] In India, these movements have challenged both state and private development plans, but the shift to the free-market logic of the last twenty years has engendered protests against the urban-industrial complex's encroachment on the natural resources of village communities for the country's growing consumer culture of the urban middle and upper classes.[21] Thus, the effects of neoliberalism have galvanized a movement that unites an awkward and even sometimes antagonistic[22] coalition of Indian Marxism and environmentalism to fight privatization, exploitation of resources, and pollution.

After several protests by groups of farmers opposing the plant's water exploitation and pollution of their lands and local workers frustrated by the lack of secure employment or benefits at the plant, the Mehndiganj community organizing group Lok Samiti and its cadre of young local social workers became a central force in the growing mobilization. Through Lok Samiti's work in "strengthening people's democracy"

through education, Dalit and women's empowerment, and government accountability, it had become active with the National Alliance of
People's Movements (NAPM), an alliance of autonomous grassroots
struggles dedicated to an alternative and democratic, "just and sustainable," "people based development."[23] This movement of movements arose
in the immediate wake of India's economic reforms as diverse groups
came together "to save their common natural resources like forests and
pastures from privatization and exploitation for short-term profits...for
their right to life and livelihood."[24] While NAPM took an anti-neoliberal
globalization position, it proscribed the virulent nationalist response by
also critiquing the intensifying ethnic and religious communalism that
emerged from both the resulting socioeconomic upheaval and India's
self-promotion in the global economy. The NAPM's early mobilizations
to stop the Narmada River damming and Enron power projects brought
forth one of the alliance's leaders, Medha Patkar, who articulated to
national and international audiences the alliance's critique of the collusion of the Indian state and transnational capital in development that hurt
the poor. From NAPM's founding, just as the Coca-Cola Company was
dramatically reentering the Indian market, its member groups expressed
concern about the arrival of soft drink multinationals and their privatization of water while much of India was without sources of public drinking
water, calling for "a sustained and intense campaign against MNCs with
the slogan 'Not Pepsi/Coke—we want water' [and a] vigorous campaign
for Swadeshi [domestic self-sufficiency] with the actions like smearing
the posters/hoardings [billboards] of Pepsi/Coke."[25]

As Mehndiganj residents mobilized against their local plant, the primarily Adivasi (indigenous) and Dalit residents in Plachimada, Kerala,
were a few years into a permanent protest in demand of the closure of
the Coca-Cola plant in their village, in what would become the best
known of the Indian anti-Coca-Cola struggles and one of the iconic
Global South movements against water privatization. The NAPM provided support to the Plachimada protesters, organizing marches—with
the now famous Patkar crucially drawing media attention—and linking
the local struggle with similar fights in other parts of India. Through
the NAPM, Mehndiganj activists became involved in the struggle in
Plachimada, bringing back strategies, allies, as well as inspiration from
the eventual Keralan victory in closing its Coca-Cola plant in 2004. As

a result, the groups began to imagine a connection between villages with Coca-Cola plants that could be mobilized to multiply the points of pressure on the company. Mehndiganj activists began working with committees of residents in Ballia, Uttar Pradesh, and Kala Dera, Rajasthan, where the water has been so overexploited that the company was advised to truck water in from outside sources or close the plant entirely.[26] These groups enacted a network of places, concerns, and communities linked through the capital and commodities of the Coca-Cola Company.

When the persistent protests of the grassroots committees[27] were met with inaction by the economic and political powers in their states, as well as the distant nodes of power of the multinational corporation in Atlanta, Georgia, and its Indian subsidiary in Gurgaon, India, the movement reached beyond local elites' traditional control to national and international allies and nongovernmental organizations. Transnational activists became mediators between the local Indian struggles and distant supporters, garnering the struggles international solidarity

Protestor at the "Right to Water National Conference and Protest against Coca-Cola," Mehndiganj, Uttar Pradesh, March 30, 2008. Photograph by author.

and media attention. Nationally, the NAPM connected the similar struggles in Plachimada and Mehndiganj, across language barriers and a broad geographic distance, as well as internationally, introducing the movement in Mehndiganj to allies among South Asians in the diaspora. Lok Samiti's work in education and community organizing attracted the attention of the transnational nonprofit Asha for Education, cofounded by Sandeep Pandey (a leader in NAPM).[28] Through the donations and

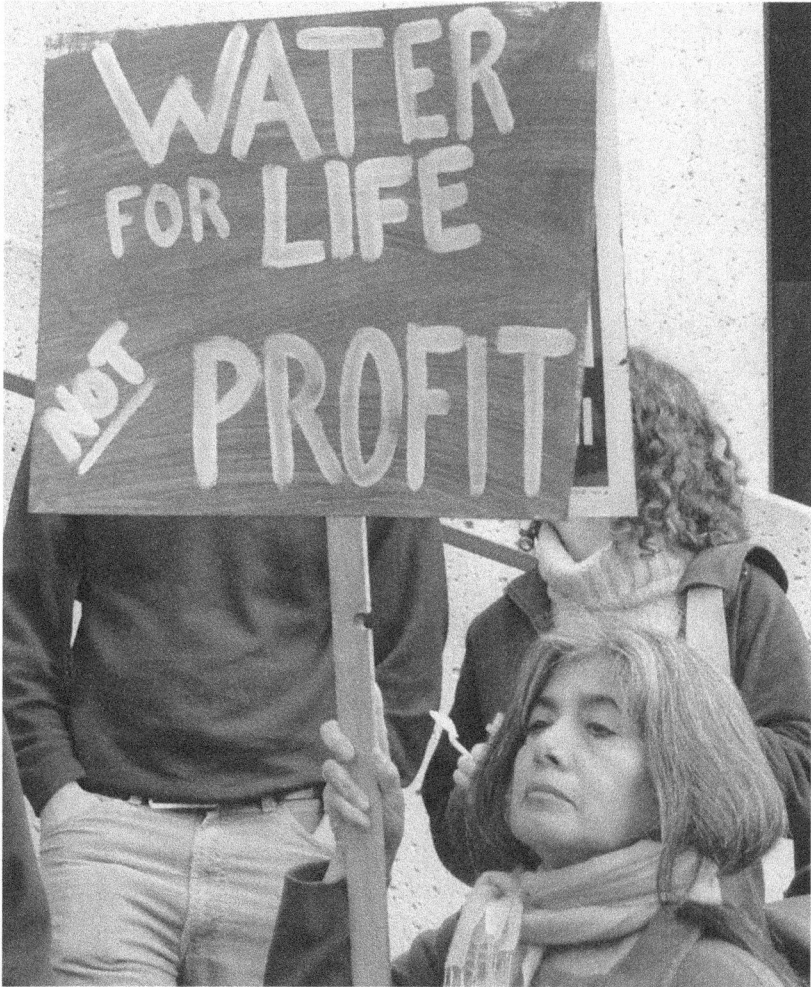

Activists protesting the Coca-Cola Company at the conference "Corporate Water Foot-printing: Towards a Sustainable Water Strategy" in San Francisco, California, December 2 and 3, 2008. Photograph by Amit Srivastava, India Resource Center.

volunteerism of its primarily upper-middle-class, South Asian members in the United States, Europe, and India, Asha has supported Lok Samiti's education and water rights programs.

North American alter-globalization activists concerned with corporate capitalism's effect on the environment in India brought the fights in Plachimada and Mehndiganj to international activists, consumers, and investors. The web-based nonprofit India Resource Center offered itself as the transnational "platform" for the communication and representation of the Indian Coca-Cola struggles to international media and allies, to "create a dialogue with Indian movements and those around the world in order to share information, skills and strategies for organizing in order to strengthen the global movement for holding corporations accountable to human rights, environmental justice and labor rights." The India Resource Center also imagined a more active role for itself, aiming "to mobilize a key constituency in the US and around the world that will take action in support of movements in India—by applying pressure in the home countries of the corporations where they are more susceptible to public pressure."[29] The India Resource Center's founder and lone full-time employee, Amit Srivastava, had organized around environmental justice causes in the United States and was researching and publicizing corporations' environmental practices in international contexts for the U.S.-based corporate watchdog group CorpWatch when the Plachimada protesters sought assistance in 2002.[30] He planned his first transnational protest around the issue by urging CorpWatch's web visitors to send a fax to the Coca-Cola Company demanding it close its plant in Plachimada.[31] When financial constraints forced CorpWatch to cut back its work, Srivastava launched the India Resource Center "to support movements against corporate globalization in India."[32] As the movements against Coca-Cola's water use in India grew and Srivastava became committed to garnering them global attention, the India Resource Center began focusing almost entirely on their struggles, launching an international campaign to hold Coca-Cola accountable to its practices in India, and drawing about 20,000 visitors a month to the site.[33] CorpWatch and the India Resource Center's reporting on the Indian movements against Coca-Cola led to mainstream international media coverage. In 2003, the BBC radio program *Face the Facts* broke the story of water depletion and pollution in Plachimada to mainstream

British audiences, revealing tests that found dangerous levels of carcinogenic toxic metals in the manufacturing by-product "sludge" that the company was disposing on its grounds and giving away to neighboring farmers as a fertilizer and land filler. In a follow-up story the next year, the BBC correspondent asked a Coca-Cola India executive to drink a sip of water from a Plachimada well and broadcast his wary reaction to audiences.[34]

While the Indian government celebrates its Non Resident Indian (NRI) professional success stories for attracting foreign investment and sending billions of dollars in remittances to the country, Srivastava is one of "other NRIs," the many Indian diaspora activists, nonprofit workers, academics, and cultural producers who have little financial clout but are deeply engaged with Indian concerns and have mobilized international constituencies to address them.[35] Maintaining frequent contact with the local organizing groups and often in India himself, Srivastava represented the Indian organizing against Coca-Cola through the website and in these major news sources, as well as on speaking tours to college campuses and activist groups in North America and Great Britain. Srivastava is self-reflective about his role as a Global North participant in a southern movement, going only to locales with struggles interested in his collaboration and consciously situating his organization in a supportive rather than leading role. But his success in internationalizing the Coca-Cola campaign by identifying points of leverage against the company and mediating the local Indian struggles to new publics has made him the focus of media attention and brought to the fore not only the challenges of constructing a movement across the vast differences in power between mobile, multilingual, media-savvy, resourced transnational activists and rural peasants but also the challenges of representation when Global North audiences assume a lack of agency or sophistication among tremendously adept social movements in the Global South.

On the other side of the world, a Colombian union and its allies in U.S. and European labor and solidarity movements had launched a similar transnational mobilization against the Coca-Cola Company. In the context of ongoing civil war in Colombia, for decades paramilitaries had waged a campaign of intimidation and violence against leftist labor and human rights activists, including several murders in the 1990s against the largest union of Coca-Cola workers in the country, the leftist

Sindicato Nacional de Trabajadores de la Industria de Alimentos (Sinal-trainal). The union was a vocal critic of the Colombian neoliberal labor regime, facilitated by the free-market economic reforms that swept through the country and around the world in the early 1990s, which had enabled corporations like the Coca-Cola Company to downsize and underemploy its workforce, resulting in economic and social inse-curity for workers. Sinaltrainal accused U.S. multinationals of exploit-ing Colombian workers and natural resources and being a threat to Colombian sovereignty, a biting critique coming from a union that rep-resented workers at high-profile multinationals like Coca-Cola and one that attracted significant attention from paramilitaries who violently opposed this view. Mobilizing the international discourse of human and labor rights violations, Sinaltrainal denounced the complicity and collusion of multinational corporations like the Coca-Cola Company that benefited from the resulting loss of the union's labor power in such a climate of fear. International labor allies mobilized to support the Colombian union and draw international public attention to its cause in order to pressure the Coca-Cola Company in some of its larger markets. The United Steelworkers of America and the International Labor Rights Fund assisted Sinaltrainal in bringing a case against the Coca-Cola Company and its Colombian bottlers in U.S. courts for their alleged involvement in the violence. Several unions in the United States and Europe pledged to boycott Coca-Cola products. Colombia soli-darity groups and peace activists, long concerned with U.S. economic and military influence and the struggles of marginalized groups in the country, brought Sinaltrainal activists to North America and Europe for speaking tours.[36] The transnational mobilization around Sinaltrainal took on even larger significance in the context of the proposed U.S.-Colombian free trade agreement, which Sinaltrainal and many of its international allies challenged by providing evidence of continued vio-lations of labor rights in Colombia. Sinaltrainal appealed to U.S.-based labor consultant Ray Rogers to create a corporate campaign against Coca-Cola highlighting the union's labor and human rights struggles in Colombia as it demanded that the company change its labor practices and compensate the victims of the violence. The resulting Campaign to Stop Killer Coke used research on the Coca-Cola Company's corporate workings and financial interests in order to target them, trenchantly manipulated the brand image to resignify Coke products, and mobilized U.S. supporters in public protest to "move the fight to the doorsteps and into the boardrooms of Coca-Cola."[37]

The recent emergence of international social movement forums provided venues for these different groups organizing against the Coca-Cola Company to encounter each other and work together in transnational solidarity. The World Social Forum, with its ideal as a movement of movements where disparate groups can maintain their autonomy but coalesce around common concerns, was formative as both a place and a practice, allowing for labor unions, corporate watchdog groups, environmentalists, and community organizers from different campaigns, and with distinct critiques of Coca-Cola, to come together. Activists from the Indian Coca-Cola struggles, including hundreds of Mehndiganj residents who traveled to Mumbai in 2004, participated in the World Social Forum, where they met with representatives of international allies and other environmental social movements and NGOs working against corporate water privatization. Similar international forums focused specifically on water rights, including the World Water Conference hosted by Plachimada in 2004, brought global anti-water-privatization activists like Maude Barlow together with the Indian movements against Coca-Cola, garnering them international media attention. North American NGOs like Corporate Accountability International and the Polaris Institute brought back information about the Indian struggle to their supporters and rallied support for protests against Coca-Cola. These groups concurrently launched their own related campaigns against the corporatization of water, targeting bottled water giants Coca-Cola and PepsiCo in the United States, Canada, and Britain because of the industry's environmental, social, and economic impacts. Their campaigns caused a media sensation resulting in calls for boycotts of bottled water and renewed attention to public water systems when they revealed that the branded commodities were little more than the water that comes from the tap.

In these international venues, the trade unionists of Sinaltrainal, Indian villagers, and their Global North allies shared their experiences, goals, and strategies and began to enact simultaneous and loosely related struggles organized around the commodities and capital of the same corporation, even across differences in political cultures and histories. But a union in Colombia determined to save jobs in Coca-Cola plants and peasant activists in India committed to shutting down plants not only have different formations and contexts but also could be materially at odds with each other. But their different positionalities have resulted in a productive tension in the interaction between the two movements. Both campaigns produced larger critiques of neoliberal capitalist globalization beyond the single issues of water and jobs and thus identified points of common cause. In India, the environmentalism of the poor is concerned with environmental justice for marginalized peoples and their rights to livelihood and thus is grounded in a materialist critique of corporate capitalism in contrast to middle-class environmentalisms. In Colombia, a revolutionary trade unionism critiques corporate capitalism's varied extractive powers and challenges it through constant contestation, rather than corporate unionism, toward equitable redistribution of the varied forms of the world's resources. Remarkably, these Indian and Colombian activists have learned from each other's struggles and imagined an interrelation between them. From its exposure to the Indian movement, as well as its involvement with Colombian campaigns against the extraction and enclosure of resources by multinational corporations, Sinaltrainal has begun to organize around issues of corporate water use, pollution, and privatization. But the interactions of these two campaigns are primarily mediated through U.S.-based transnational activists who have the languages and resources to translate the struggles, and represented in the grassroots groups in the United States and Europe that mobilize based on their understanding of their own interrelation with India and Colombia in the Coca-Cola world system.

Informed by the transnational advocacy of Srivastava's India Resource Center, the Campaign against Killer Coke, and other activist networks, as well as coverage from the mainstream press, North American and European college and university students became concerned about the Coca-Cola Company's record on the environment in India and labor and human rights practices in Colombia. They took up these international struggles against Coca-Cola, protesting the corporation's practices and challenging both the general sale of Coca-Cola products and Coca-Cola bottlers' significant financial contracts for exclusive provision of beverages on their campuses. Student groups organized events with Srivastava, Rogers, and the Sinaltrainal trade unionists, mobilized protests that prominently deployed the Coca-Cola brand to hail prospective consumers as part of the international struggles, and lobbied their university administrations to cut their contracts with the company. As of 2007, students at some 200 colleges and universities in the United States, Canada, Ireland, the United Kingdom, Italy, and India had protested against the Coca-Cola Company, with 45 schools ending exclusive contracts with Coca-Cola on their campuses.[38] These students organized from their local positions within global networks of commodities and capital, identifying their consumptive relationship within the corporate system of labor and environmental exploitation, however distant geographically from Indian villagers and Colombian trade unionists.

Students mobilized through existing social justice groups, formed new student organizations specific to the Coke cause, and created campus alliances like the University of Michigan's Coalition to Cut Contracts with Coca-Cola. To draw an array of activists to the cause, Srivastava and student activists emphasized the "broad coalition" of concerns and groups that converge around the issue—South Asian student organizations and Latin American student organizations (with interests in India and Colombia); organizations of students of color (concerned with environmental racism); human rights groups (as labor and environmental issues have increasingly been taken up under the rubric of human rights); women's groups (as women are disproportionately affected); as well as environmental, labor, and broad-based social justice organizations.[39] As a result of the wave of student mobilizations against the Coca-Cola Company, in 2005 the *Nation* declared it "the largest anti-corporate movement since the campaign against Nike,"[40] in reference to the student activism of the late 1990s, which leveraged college and university apparel contracts to target labor abuses at the factories of companies like Nike. Anti-Coke activists were descendants of the antisweatshop movement, benefiting from its legacy both politically and organizationally with United Students against Sweatshops prominently articulating a national campaign strategy and mobilizing their campus chapters against the Coca-Cola Company. Coca-Cola executives insisted that these student efforts were misguided because of the fundamental difference between the commodity chains of the apparel and Coca-Cola industries. Whereas the former had brought sweated goods directly to campuses for sale, Coca-Cola products are typically sold in the same regions where they are produced; the Coca-Cola bottled in areas with falling water tables in India is sold in India, that bottled in the antiunion climate in Colombia is sold in Colombia, and that purchased by consumers in the United States and Europe is bottled in those regions, they explained. But student activists were unconvinced, seeing themselves as materially and symbolically connected through the Coca-Cola system: in buying a Coke product, they would be supporting a company that also profits from the plant in Mehndiganj (in fact, owns it) and continuing to participate in the sign system that encodes Coca-Cola as happiness would enable suffering to go on under its brand name. Many students were impelled to take action in solidarity with others in distant places, or else be complicit with Coca-Cola's water use and labor practices wherever they happened in that system.

In addition to concerns about the environmental practices in India and labor practices in Colombia, students voiced a local critique from their own position within the Coca-Cola world system. They criticized the Coca-Cola Company's contracts for exclusive soft drink sales on campuses and the use of college names in marketing. These financial arrangements were "emblematic of the growing corporatization of education."[41] As activists at Rutgers University described, their university's contract with the soft drink company "delivers corporate gains through the use, branding, and manipulation of a public education institution."[42] Students organized against the Coca-Cola Company's contracts on their campuses to simultaneously challenge neoliberalism far and near: the dispossession and privatization of water in India, regimes of labor insecurity and violence in Colombia, and the corporatization of education right where they were.

Brand Battles: Revaluing Coca-Cola's Symbolic Capital

The symbolic capital of the Coca-Cola Company's heavily branded products—in 2006, Coca-Cola was the most globally recognized brand, with a value of $67 billion[43]—reflected the power of the corporation to endow fizzy drinks with signification across global publics. For activists, this brand value became the means by which they envisioned and represented a common target while fighting from their own geographic

Cartoon by Brazilian activist Carlos Latuff, 2009.

position in solidarity with struggles on different continents. Student activists redeployed the company's symbolic capital—Coca-Cola products' ubiquity, iconicity, and intimate corporeality (as it is physically imbibed)—in various forms of culture jamming to subvert brand connotations with new political meanings and hail prospective consumers to join with the international struggles. Activists turned vending machines into crime scenes by wrapping them with police "CAUTION" tape, they inflated a giant blow-up Coca-Cola bottle bearing the words "College-Control" to dominate a campus green, they performed street theater dressed as "Killer Cokes" or Coca-Cola pinup girls selling bottled public water to onlookers, they made the advertised image of thirst-quenching bottles of Coke repulsive by adding dripping blood and "Toxic" labels, created images like radical cartoonist Carlos Latuff's illustration of a Coca-Cola executive sucking out the water from an Indian well with a straw, and reproduced "Water for Life, Not for Profit" signs that Indian protesters themselves used to connect their struggles to a global environmental justice movement.

These activists use the brand, known to people all over the world, to create what anthropologist Robert Foster has called a "critical fetishism," in other words, the identification and valuation of the conditions of a commodity's production and consumption.[44] Because the material product of Coca-Cola is mostly caffeinated sugar water, when consumers purchase a Coca-Cola drink, they are paying as much for the immaterial value imbued in the commodity through the meaning of the brand. But this symbolic capital of the Coca-Cola brand is not the product of the Coca-Cola Company alone; rather, the brand relies on the endowment of qualities and associations by consumers' own production and recognition of these meanings (happiness, coolness, modernity, familiarity, etc.). Revelations that the Coca-Cola Company is dispossessing and polluting water resources contradicts and challenges the meanings of the brand, and thus also the collaborative relationship in this semiotics between consumer and producer.[45] Even more powerfully, the production of new meanings or associations for brands by activists can lay bare this system of consumerist meaning-making and produce new systems of solidarity relations among those connected through the corporate brand's own symbols and language.[46] The Coca-Cola Company executives have a name for this process as well, accusing the Indian Resource Center, NAPM, and local Indian organizers like Lok Samiti of "brand-jacking." Brand-jacking, as defined by a report by an international business organization that includes the Coca-Cola Company as one of its most prominent members, is "when a third party hitches a ride on a brand's fame, positioning and slogan" to attract attention to their issues or agenda, "whilst undermining the brand's reputation in the process."[47] In response to this suggestion that the "issues or agenda" is tangential to the brands that are "jacked" to relay them, Indian villagers and activists contend there is nothing more central to the Coca-Cola Company's business practices than the sustainability and safety of the resource that is its primary ingredient: water. The corporations' argument about "brand-jacking" is not, however, far from that of this chapter. Activists use the corporation's material and symbolic capital to connect different people, places, and struggles to produce a politics that is at once local and global, much like the multinational itself.

As protests emerged in different parts of North America, Europe, and India, the business press brooded over this multinational network of activists organizing against Coca-Cola's environmental practices in India. On its front page the *Wall Street Journal* portrayed California-based Amit Srivastava as the individual at the center of the movement's communications web. In this representation he embodied a new kind of challenge to global corporations, mobilizing transnationally through a globally connected counterpower network with little organizational structure, threatening the cultural significance of a brand through a communications campaign without the political legitimacy of mainstream media:[48] "That a one-man NGO armed with just a laptop computer, a Web site and a telephone calling card can, with his allies, influence a huge multinational corporation illustrates the role social activists can play in a world that's going increasingly online."[49] While the business press focused on him, overlooking on-the-ground activists in India, Srivastava consciously identified his role as supportive, as a Global North member of a transnational movement, providing a means for the grassroots movements in India to communicate their struggles, while not dictating their direction or putting himself visibly in the forefront.[50]

This anti-Coca-Cola activist network could be seen as an element of neoliberal globalization itself, as transnational activists, NGOs, and corporations have become central actors in a political sphere that transcends state borders and is organized through the market. There are thus some real political predicaments to global consumer campaigns around branded commodities and multinational corporations. Social justice movements' focus on hypervisible branded consumer goods produced by multinationals can overlook less well-known egregious offenders of environmental or labor standards. The use of a brand, then, to produce a "critical fetishism"[51] can risk contributing to a refetishization of the branded commodity (or, even different actors in the commodity chain, like the noble Indian peasantry). Corporate campaigns often risk moving political action away from the state to the market, where consumers and corporations become the agents for piecemeal, unenforceable social change. Some student activist groups have even engaged a free-market logic to critique their colleges' and universities' exclusivity contracts with the Coca-Cola Company, as "monopolistic arrangement[s]"[52] that "impede fair competition by promoting local monopolies."[53] Similarly, a consumer campaign strategy that highlights boycotting or "buycotting"[54] (a vote of support through purchasing) moves political power to the act of consumption. Concerned about the political ramifications of this campaign strategy, the Indian anti-Coca-Cola activists contend that it "disenfranchises poorer consumers, often the ones most affected by Coke's actions, by linking political power to purchasing power—one dollar, one vote."[55]

Activist groups have also appealed to Coca-Cola shareholders and prospective investors to pressure the corporation through the discourse of socially responsible investing and shareholder activism. The argument against consumption-based activism becomes even more persuasive when applied to these calls for investor activism where only those with shares, for whom the ultimate motivation is profit, get a vote. At the annual shareholders' meeting of the Coca-Cola Company, activist investors make public statements or offer resolutions to the vote of stock owners informing them of the concerns and organizing in places like Mehndiganj, and demanding greater transparency and better business practices from the corporation. They frame demands with the rationale that the company's environmental and human rights practices will affect its financial performance (disrupt production, diminish sales, ward off future investors). In doing so in such a forum, they draw the attention of the media and their fellow shareholders to these issues and, in effect, enact the threat of dissuading investment. In effect, these models of social change bolster neoliberal ideologies of market solutions like consumer choice and corporate profitability: by choosing to buy a commodity other than Coke, or by a profit-driven ethics of investor relations where the more "responsible" corporation will make more money for investors. Corporations can easily co-opt movements by creating new markets in corporate social responsibility or philanthropy in which to compete for consumer loyalty and profit.

As transnational activism around the company's water practices in India grew and the media began to focus on the probability of future water crises around the world, it became evident that the Coca-Cola Company's own long-term corporate "sustainability" was vulnerable to both water scarcity and environmental critiques. Even the business press began to point out Coca-Cola's water problem; an article in the *Economist* entitled "In Hot Water" argued that because water was so essential to the Coca-Cola Company's business model, over the long term its battle over environmental sustainability would be more fierce than Big Oil's.[56] Thus, with a market logic of both ensuring the existence of future exploitable reserves of a major ingredient and constructing itself as an environmentally conscious business to concerned consumers, the Coca-Cola Company launched a global corporate social responsibility campaign around water. Over the past decade, companies like Coca-Cola have begun to define and self-regulate the terms of corporate environmental responsibility in order to "'immunize" themselves against activist criticism[57] and get out in front of governments' demands for accounts of their water footprints.[58]

The Coca-Cola Company began a major public relations and operations campaign to reduce and recycle water used in the production process, and to "replenish" watersheds, pledging to become "water neutral" by putting back as much water as it uses through more than 100 conservation projects in forty-nine countries in partnership with the World Wildlife Fund at a cost of more than $20 million to the company.[59] The company has instituted several philanthropic initiatives in the area of Varanasi; in Mehndiganj the company has invested in rainwater harvesting and recharging units to capture more rain for the aquifer, providing new hand pumps, and funded a local research project on drip irrigation to conserve more water in farming certain types of crops. But environmental activists cried "Greenwash!" over the vagueness of the phrase "water neutral," the associated practices of water offsets, and the lack of workable methodology for measuring its effects.[60] Mehndiganj residents doubt that the Coca-Cola Company recharges as much water into the aquifer with the nineteen rainwater harvesting sites in the area as the plant uses. This analysis belies a problem with the "water neutral" pledge generally: even if the Coca-Cola Company is able to put back as much water as it uses over its entire global corporate system, it would be offsetting its water use in certain areas with conservation projects on different continents, not putting back the water from the specific locales it took it from, leaving bottling plant communities dry.[61] Mehndiganj residents have numerous outstanding questions: What water is the company taking credit for having replenished: water that would have reached the aquifer anyway? How can all the previous years' water use be accounted for? With erratic monsoons and global warming, how well will rainwater harvesting and recharging work? Can Coca-Cola make it rain? If not, will it stop bottling? The company's large-scale environmental responsibility initiatives may have positive environmental effects and are surely better than "irresponsible" alternatives. But, in classic neoliberal terms, the responsibility for ensuring the security of public water has been turned over to a private corporation, one that sells that very resource. The activists of Lok Samiti ask: What happens when Coca-Cola no longer deems it necessary or financially justifiable to continue these corporate social responsibility initiatives, or when the company leaves entirely?

Through the ubiquity of the Coca-Cola Company's world system of capital—both material and symbolic—diverse movements and their international supporters were able to mobilize around a common and familiar target from their own location and critique, and in solidarity with struggles on different continents. This transnational activism retraced connections within the world system of the corporation, which in its powerful multinational form necessitated an activist politics that extended beyond the nation-state, the traditional bounds for the political. Mobilizations in North America and Europe increased the leverage of the Indian movement by creating new points of pressure closer to the centers of power of the corporation otherwise out of the reach of activists in India. The transnational networks of activism and solidarity linking seemingly distant groups—village farmers, workers, consumers, investors—made visible the relations of people and power within the world system of the corporation. The nodes of intersection of disparate localized movements—Indian villagers' fight against the privatization and commodification of water, Colombian trade unionists' challenge to regimes of labor insecurity and violence, and college and university students' anger about these issues as well as the corporatization of their institutions—articulated a broader critique of the Coca-Cola Company and neoliberal corporate globalization. As activists re-created a transnational system from the power of Coca-Cola's own global capital—the ubiquity of its material commodities and brand signs—they produced a critical fetishism of the commodity. So that Lok Samiti can invoke Indian and international listeners in its protest song in Mehndiganj: "Now come out from the circle of people who speak the language of Coca-Cola. And do something."[62]

NOTES

1. Quoting Mark Pendergrast in Sonia Shah, "Coke in Your Faucet?," *Progressive*, August, 2001, 29–30.

2. Jonathan Hills and Richard Welford, "Case Study: Coca-Cola and Water in India," *Corporate Social Responsibility and Environmental Management* 12 (2005): 168.

3. This was true of Plachimada, Kerala, and Kaladera, Rajasthan, where new plants were built; the Mehndiganj, Uttar Pradesh, plant was a brownfield acquisition by Coca-Cola subsidiary Hindustan Coca-Cola Beverages Pvt. Ltd. of Kejriwal Beverages Pvt. Ltd., a Parle franchisee bottling plant.

4. Anthropologist Ananthakrishnan Aiyer argues that the struggles against Coca-Cola should be interpreted in the context of the larger "agrarian crisis." Ananthakrishnan Aiyer, "The Allure of the Transnational: Notes on Some Aspects of the Political Economy of Water in India," *Cultural Anthropology* 22, no. 4 (2007): 650–652.

5. See Neeraj Vedwan, "Pesticides in Coca-Cola and Pepsi: Consumerism, Brand Image, and Public Interest in a Globalizing India, *Cultural Anthropology* 22, no. 4 (2007): 661–662.

6. Aiyer, "Allure of the Transnational," 650–651.

7. Ibid., 650.

8. Vedwan, "Pesticides in Coca-Cola and Pepsi," 661–662.

9. The Energy and Resources Institute (TERI), *Independent Third Party Assessment of Coca-Cola Facilities in India* (2008), 199.

10. This chapter builds upon interviews with residents and activists of Mehndiganj, Uttar Pradesh, Kala Dera, Rajasthan, and Plachimada, Kerala, in the spring of 2008. While the history of the movement against the Coca-Cola Company in Plachimada has been well documented, the focus of this chapter is on the active and underresearched mobilization in Mehndiganj.

11. TERI, *Independent Third Party Assessment*, 206–207. Maximum daily average intake for the Mehndiganj plants is around 600,000 liters, but the plant has averaged more than 900,000 liters a day in some months.

12. Ibid., 220.

13. Ibid.

14. Ibid., 6.

15. The Mehndiganj plant pays the *gram panchayat* Rs. 6,000 (US$136.36) in annual taxes and Rs. 2,500 (US$56.82) in license to operate fees. Ibid., 222.

16. The Easement Act of 1882, as discussed in TERI, *Independent Third Party Assessment*, 90. For all the water it withdrew in Mehndiganj during 2005–2006, the plant paid a water cess of just Rs. 31,573.00, or $717.57, with an average exchange rate of around Rs. 44.00 to the dollar in 2005–2006. Ibid., 223.

17. R. Chandrika, *To Protect Our Right over Our Water: On the Movement against Coca-Cola in Mehndiganj Varanasi, U.P.* (Benares, U.P.: Lok Samiti, 2007), 15–16. Interviews with Nandlal Master, Mehndiganj, India, March–April, 2008.

18. A phrase from Joan Martinez-Alier used in Ramachandra Guha's, *How Much Should a Person Consume? Environmentalism in India and the United States* (Berkeley: University of California Press, 2006), 59.

19. Ibid., 57–70. Some of the most prominent Indian examples are the struggles of the Chipko forest dwellers against logging and for rights to land, the Narmada Bachao Andolan's mobilization against the construction of the Narmada Dam and the flooding out of 425 villages, and Keralan fisherfolk's challenge to coastal development and unsustainable fishing methods.

20. Guha quoting Indian environmentalist Anil Agarwal, Ibid., 70.

21. Ibid., 63.

22. Ibid. C. R. Neelakandan interview with author, Ernakulam, India, March 21, 2008.

23. Rajni Bakshi, "'Development, Not Destruction': Alternative Politics in the Making," *Economic and Political Weekly*, 31, no. 5 (February 3, 1996), 255–257; Christine Keating, "Developmental Democracy and Its Inclusions: Globalization and the Transformation of Participation," *Signs: Journal of Women in Culture and Society* 29 (2003): 427–428.

24. National Alliance of People's Movements (NAPM), "National Alliance of People's Movements" (1996), http://www.proxsa.org/politics/napm.html.

25. Ibid.

26. TERI, *Independent Third Party Assessment*, 22.

27. Lok Samiti (People's Committee) and earlier Gaon Bachao Sangharsh Samiti (Save the Village Committee) in Mehndiganj, Uttar Pradesh; Coca-Cola Virudha Samara Samithi (Anti-Coca-Cola Struggle Committee) and earlier Adivasi Samrakshna Samithi (Tribal Protection Committee) in Plachimada, Kerala; Jan Sangharsh Samiti (People's Committee for Struggle) in Kala Dera, Rajasthan; and Coca-Cola Bhagao, Krishi Bachao Sangharsh Samiti (Get Rid of Coke, Save Farming Struggle Committee) in Ballia, Uttar Pradesh.

28. Asha for Education was cofounded by Sandeep Pandey and a group of nonresident Indians in the United States to support the education of underprivileged children as a catalyst for socioeconomic change in India. "About Asha for Education: Mission Statement," https://www.ashanet.org/index.php?page=about-asha-mission (accessed March 23, 2009).

29. "About India Resource Center," http://www.indiaresource.org/about/index.html (accessed November 22, 2009).

30. Interview with Amit Srivastava, Mehndiganj, India, March 29, 2008.

31. Steve Stecklow, "Virtual Battle: How a Global Web of Activists Gives Coke Problems in India," *Wall Street Journal*, June 7, 2005.

32. "About India Resource Center."

33. Stecklow, "Virtual Battle."

34. Sevanti Ninan, "The Plachimada Saga," *The Hindu*, June 19, 2005.

35. Naeem Mohaiemen, "The Other NRIs Come to India," *Subcontinental: The Journal of South Asian American Public Affairs*, January 22, 2004, http://www.

thesubcontinental.org/naeem/wsf01.22.2004.html; Srivastava cites his own diasporic experience growing up in the United States, India, and Tanzania as formative of his understanding of global inequality and environmental justice; interview with Amit Srivastava.

36. This kind of transnational mobilization around Coca-Cola workers had happened before, providing a historical precedent for the Colombian unionists and their allies: when, in the late 1970s and early 1980s, workers at the Coca-Cola bottling plant in Guatemala City faced the repression of their union, violence, and the closure of their plant, North American and European solidarity activists and labor unions made it an international issue by threatening a boycott and pressuring the headquarters of the multinational in Atlanta to intervene with the Guatemalan bottler.

37. Javier Correa, President, Sinaltrainal, William Mendoza, President of Sinaltrainal–Barrancabermeja, and Ray Rogers, Director, Campaign to Stop Killer Coke, "Dear Brothers and Sisters," http://www.killercoke.org/who.htm (accessed July 10, 2006).

38. "Colleges, Universities and High Schools Active in the Campaign to Stop Killer Coke," http://www.killercoke.org/active-in-campaign.htm.

39. Amit Srivastava, interview with Lori Serb, *Prairie Grassroots*, WEFT, November 4, 2005.

40. Michael Blanding, "Coke: The New Nike," *Nation*, March 24, 2005, http://www.thenation.com/article/coke-new-nike#.

41. Faiza Zafar and Shivali Tukdeo, University of Illinois–Urbana-Champaign's Coalition against Coke Contracts, "Coca-Cola Kicked Out of University of Illinois," August 6, 2007, http://caccuc.blogspot.com/ (accessed June 12, 2008).

42. "End Exclusivity Contracts at Rutgers University," http://www.petitiononline.com/RUCoke/petition.html (accessed June 12, 2008).

43. Interbrand and *BusinessWeek*, "Best Global Brands 2006: A Ranking by Brand Value," *www.interbrand.com/images/studies/BGB06Report_072706.pdf*.

44. Robert J. Foster, "Show and Tell: Teaching Critical Fetishism with a Bottle of Coke®," *Anthropology News* 49, no. 4 (2008): 38.

45. Robert Foster, *Coca-Globalization: Following Soft Drinks from New York to New Guinea* (New York: Palgrave Macmillan, 2008), 231.

46. Naomi Klein's analysis of branding and activist resistance to it, *No Logo: No Space, No Choice, No Jobs* (New York: Picador, 2002), is now a classic, referenced even in corporate texts like the International Business Leaders Forum's "Brand-Jacking and How to Avoid It."

47. Alan Mitchell, "Brand-Jacking and How to Avoid It," in *Issues: A Publication for Brand and Identity Decision Makers*, ed. Enterprise IG and in collaboration with the International Business Leaders Forum (London, 2004), 5.

48. Manuel Castells, "Communication, Power and Counter-power in the Network Society," *International Journal of Communication* 1 (2007): 238–259.

49. Steve Stecklow, "Virtual Battle: How a Global Web of Activists Gives Coke Problems in India," *Wall Street Journal*, June 7, 2005.

50. Interview with Amit Srivastava, Mehndiganj, India, March 29, 2008.

51. Foster, "Show and Tell," 38.

52. Zafar and Tukdeo, "Coca-Cola Kicked Out."

53. "End Exclusivity Contracts at Rutgers University."

54. For a similar critique, see Anand Giridharadas's editorial, "Boycotts Minus the Pain," *New York Times*, October 11, 2009.

55. Himanshu Upadhyaya, "Let Them Drink Coke: The Commodification of Thirst and the Monopolization of Hydration," *Ghadar: A Publication of the Forum of Inquilabi Leftists* 10 (November 2006), http://ghadar.insaf.net/September2006/MainPages/editorial.htm.

56. "In Hot Water," *Economist*, October 6, 2005, http://www.economist.com/businessfinance/displaystory.cfm?story_id=4492835.

57. Mitchell, "Brand-Jacking and How to Avoid It," 7.

58. A concept paper sponsored by the Coca-Cola Company predicts as much as it outlines ways to legitimize terminology and practices like "water neutrality" and "water offsets" for corporations. Winnie Gerbens-Leenes et al., "Water Neutrality: A Concept Paper," November 20, 2007, 4.

59. The Coca-Cola Company, "Replenish Report: Achieving Water Balance through Community Water Partnerships" (2008); E. Neville Isdell, chairman and CEO, the Coca-Cola Company, "Remarks at the WWF Annual Conference," Beijing, China, June 5, 2007.

60. Fred Pearce, "Greenwash: Are Coke's Green Claims the Real Thing?," *Guardian*, December 4, 2008, http://www.guardian.co.uk/environment/2008/dec/04/coca-cola-coke-water-neutral.

61. Ibid.

62. Lok Samiti, *Jahar Ba* (c. 2005).

9

When an Interpreter Could Not Be Found

NAEEM MOHAIEMEN

The Visible Collective was a coalition of artists, educators, and legal activists exploring contested migrant identities, including religion as an externally imposed, imperfect proxy for ethnicity, within the context of post-2001 security panic. The collective's first projects (*Casual Fresh American Style* and *Nahnu Wahaad, but really are we one?*) were part of the group show *Fatal Love: South Asian American Art Now* (2005) at the Queens Museum of Art in New York. Curated by Jaishri Abhichandani and Prerana Reddy, *Fatal Love* was a response (and perhaps rebuke) to the narrow framing of the India-centric, "blockbuster" show *Edge of Desire*, premiering that same year at the Queens Museum and the Asia Society. *Fatal Love* was also a platform for a generation of South Asian artists in the diaspora, including Asma Ahmed Shikoh (*Vanwyck Blvd*, featured elsewhere in this anthology), Anna Bhushan, Iftikhar and

Elizabeth Dadi, Chitra Ganesh, Vandana Jain, Swati Khurana, Nitin Mukul, Prema Murthy, Yamini Nayar, Sa'dia Rehman, Jaret Vadera, Visible Collective, and many others.

Between 1994 and 2001, members of Visible had participated in various platforms, including Youth Solidarity Summer, Coalition Against Anti-Asian Violence (CAAAV), 3rd I South Asian Film, the Mutiny club night, and *South Asian Magazine for Action and Reflection* (*SAMAR*). After reaching a natural conclusion with some of these organizations, Visible Collective coalesced in 2004 with an intention to directly intervene into art spaces. After the Queens Museum *Fatal Love* show, Visible continued to build projects in numerous venues, including the 2006 Whitney Biennial of American Art (within the *Wrong Gallery's* "Down by Law"), evolving into a platform for members to work in museums, galleries, universities, and public spaces, through installations, film screenings, and workshops.

Given the autobiographical turn in image production, some audiences wanted to think of Visible as "representing" post-2001 vulnerable groups—namely, immigrants and/or Muslims. Contrary to this enforced homogeneity, collective members' individual experiences were actually mediated by class privilege, citizenship, and access. To underscore these enabling conditions, the collective would present a "Privilege Matrix" slide at lectures, which showed, via bar charts, the birthplace and U.S. citizenship status of each member. A quick glance would show that although birthplaces ranged from Kolkata to Los Angeles, each collective member was either a birthright citizen, a naturalized citizen, or a legal permanent resident (green card holder) of the United States. These citizenship statuses allowed collective members to be vocal, while vulnerable immigrants are those in varying legal states ("processing papers," "out of status," or "undocumented") and therefore less likely to access public spaces.

Meanwhile, in popular culture, members of a new South Asian elite were being highlighted, as if to draw a distinction between "good" and "bad" immigrants. *Newsweek International* editor Fareed Zakaria, when asked about his status by Jon Stewart on *The Daily Show*, replied "I am 100 percent legal."[1] In the finance industry, Fareed's brother Arshad Zakaria became the youngest copresident of Merrill Lynch.[2] The Zakarias' institutional privilege made it possible for them to work in accelerated careers even at a time of intensified scapegoating of Muslim immigrants. While Fareed Zakaria's cachet rose with his ability to explain "what do *they* think," his successor at *Newsweek*, Tunku Varadarajan, went a step further when he wrote in the *Wall Street Journal* that he was willing to go through racial profiling.[3] Working-class migrants, lacking class privilege, experienced racial profiling very differently from all this. When border security looks at "Muslim" identity, it is of course a mirage of a category (defined usually, and often incorrectly, by visual appearance, surname, place of origin, and passport), but to the extent such screening measures are deployed, those most likely to be racially profiled are low-income migrants, not high-skill financiers, journalists, and technocrats.

* * *

Right-wing anti-immigrant groups were able, after 2001, to rebrand themselves as superpatriots. The rise of the Minutemen militia came about in this context. At the same time, American nativism was tempered, even after 2001, by a pro-immigrant sentiment that seemingly (perhaps temporarily) had sturdier roots here than it does in Europe. Consider in this context the Reagan era, when a 1986 law[4] gave amnesty and a path to legalization for undocumented migrants who had been in the United States since 1982, or had worked on a farm as seasonal labor. The political process, in this instance, rewarded those immigrants who were willing to give labor, especially on the farm—a landscape of labor deficit and symbolism, as well as a source for subsidised agribusiness. But in more recent times, such laws seem less likely (although the DREAM Act is an exception) because undocumented migrants are now paired with the idea of a "security threat," in spite of counterexamples such as the Timothy McVeigh, Theodore Kaczinsky, Aryan Nation, and Earth Liberation Front cases.

In Europe, anti-immigrant groups had trajectory and resonance as far back as the 1970s. In Germany, church and antiracist groups had tried to popularize the slogan "Kein Mensch ist illegal" (no human is illegal) with mixed success. They also joined forces with other European coalitions pressing for the rights of "sans papiers" (those without papers). But these concepts became much harder to argue in the last decade. After the 2005 London bombings, antimigrant sentiment intensified as the right-wing British National Party released flyers proclaiming "maybe now it's time to start listening to the BNP" and Tony Blair reminded the British people that immigration was no longer a right but rather a privilege.

Many of the new debates revolved around concepts of legality. "Loyalty" and "belonging" were being framed through instruments such as a proposed "Britishness" test and a specialized German citizenship test in the province of Baden-Württemberg.[5] Back in 1990, British politician Norman Tebbitt had said that the true test of the "Britishness" of British Asians was whether they cheered for India/Pakistan or England in a cricket match. Tebbitt's views became popular again after the London bombing. But there were also attempts to problematize this simplistic concept of patriotism, as shown in BBC viewers' responses to the "Britishness" test in the form of suggested alternative questions:[6] "Is binge drinking a good idea?"; " If the plural of 'mouse' is 'mice,' what is the plural of 'house'?"; "If someone bumped into you in the corridor and it was not your fault, would you still say sorry?"; "What side should the port be passed on?"; "Which breed of dog does the Queen favour?" and, of course, "Shepherd's Pie with ale or Lamb Bhuna with Cobra?"

* * *

In the Visible Collective's projects, a throughline was the idea of hypervisibility (as undesirables) twinned with continued invisibility (as marginal, working-class populations). In cities such as New York, low-income South Asian migrants drive taxis, sell newspapers and coffee, clean restaurant tables, and work in the kitchens. In the Middle East and elsewhere with similar fragile labor conditions, they work in cleaning, child care, construction, and everything in between. Migrants are therefore intimately present in our physical space (the "our" also includes the city's South Asian middle class and elite), but absent from the broader consciousness. Only when migrants become suspects do they acquire hypervisibility as "your mysterious neighbors." From this impulse come a *New Yorker* cover with an Osama bin Laden lookalike studying the subway map over the heads of dozing passengers,[7] and a *Village Voice* cover with another bin Laden clone looking back from a taxi driver's seat.[8]

These processes of hypervisibility and "othering" are not unique to South Asian, Arab, or other (presumed "Muslim") migrant groups, nor are they new developments after 2001. An ongoing history of demonization of immigrant groups might include racial epithets ("wop," "dago," "spic"); signage ("No Niggers, No Irish, No Dogs"); popular culture (corrosive anti-Semitism, especially up to World War II); the psuedo-science of racial physiognomy (a magazine feature during World War II that identified "differences" between a "Jap" as enemy and "Chink" as ally); whispering campaigns (targeting German Americans during both world wars); incarceration (Japanese American internment); public hearings (the Second Red Scare and House Un-American Activities Committee); and profiling ("driving while black").

While there has been a continued evolution of "suspect" groups within the body politic, it is to be noted that as one minority group becomes the target population, some members of other minority groups can become cheerleaders for this new policing. Juan Williams and Michelle Malkin are two examples of people of color who are public advocates for profiling tactics. This is a familiar strain within race-divisive politics, revealed also in the fractures over affirmative action battles in California, where Asian American, Latino/a, and African American communities at times diverged, based on a calculus of what did or did not directly harm or benefit each community. At the same time, this has to be juxtaposed with the many examples of solidarity across the lines, for example, with independent black hip-hop artists, one of the voices of solidarity for scapegoated migrants.

Taking blockbuster multiplex cinema as another weathervane, we can look at the stoner-humor *Harold & Kumar* franchise for some hints of the shifting positions of Asian American identities. This is both in terms of how Asians are self-identifying (via the actors, as well as a portion of the audience), and how majority culture (i.e., the creators of the series) is repositioning ideas of racialized behavior. This is both at the level of the explicit intentions of the filmmakers and in the postscreening close reading given by cultural critics. Like Slavoj Zizek[9] and Camille Paglia's[10] rereading of Hitchcock, much of what we excavate is not necessarily what was originally intended, but what can be projected to be other meanings at a distance of several years and intervening cultural milestones.

The *H&K* franchise started in 2004, and the third installment came out in 2011, by now within a very different political context (but not necessarily a better one). In 2004, Kumar (played by Kal Penn, who said in an interview he received 50 percent more "callbacks" after he shortened his name from Kalpen Suresh Modi) taunts the white racists who torment Asian 7-Eleven clerks. But by 2008, Kumar clashes with a black security guard, accusing him of racial profiling. Finally, by 2011, there are miscegnation quips, underlining a simplistic rendering of "Muslim(/brown) is the new black."

Harold & Kumar Go to White Castle (2004)

KUMAR [MOCKING WHITE RACISTS IN HIS MOCK ASIAN "ACCENT"]: "Thank you, come again!"

Harold & Kumar Escape from Guantanamo Bay (2008)

LIGHT-SKINNED BLACK SECURITY GUARD: Just a random security check. If you can just step aside, please.
KUMAR: Random, huh? . . . So this has nothing to do with my ethnicity?
SECURITY: Sir, it's our job as airport security to search for all possible weapons or illegal drugs.
KUMAR: So just because of the color of my skin you assume that I have drugs on me? Are you a racist?
SECURITY: Racist? Dude, I'm black!
KUMAR: Please, dude. You're barely even brown. Compared to me, you look like Matthew Perry.

A Very Harold & Kumar Christmas (2011)

BLONDE WOMAN: Do you want to see my room?
HAROLD: Uhh . . . married. He's single though [points at Kumar].
KUMAR: Hi! Kumar.
WOMAN: Sorry . . . I don't date black guys!

We note here that Harold Lee remains mostly constant, and it is Kumar Patel whose position shifts (in the second installment, he is the reason for

the arrest, and Harold is collateral damage). This underscores the fluc-
tuating and unstable racialization of South Asian American identities,
shaped sharply by the crisis politics of the last decade. Even the passage
of a few years has changed how the audience rereads these films. In 2004,
the South Asian Womens Creative Collective (SAWCC) hosted a heated
debate about whether to boycott the first *H&K* film. At that time, it was
considered groundbreaking to have the two main leads be Asian men,
within the frame of raunch, men-behaving-badly comedy (historically
the province of white males, from *Porky's* to *The Hangover*) as a dramatic
contrast to the usual orientalist or "peril" roles. But even so, the specter
of Asian American men engaging in misogynist humor made many in
the community uncomfortable. But, by the time the second installment
came out, culture wars over the "dangerous immigrant" had heated up
and the *Guantanamo* installment was embraced as a shot across the bow
of racial profiling. The film inspired many other riffs, including, most
famously, Das Racist's song "Rainbow in the Dark," which included the
lyric: "Tried to go to Amsterdam they threw us in Guantanamo."

By 2011, the latest installment shows some visible consternation
at their easy acceptance into the mainstream. Harold is a successful
banker, and the film opens with anticapitalist demonstrations in which
Harold's assistant takes the bullet (or rather the egg), going down in a
hail of fire like the last urban warrior in a John Woo film. Kumar too
knowingly twigs his establishment status as an official in the Obama
administration (on leave of absence to finish this film), when the party
crasher says, "Told them you work in the White House," and he replies,
"Yeah, like anyone is going to believe that."

Indeed, who would imagine that pot-smoking, bong-reengineering,
trash-talking Kal Penn would make it through the media screenings
required for this particularly friction-averse White House administration? Perhaps he is the future Manchurian candidate. . . .

* * *

Parsing through hypervisibility in news media, election year discourse,
and TV entertainment (*24*, *Sleeper Cell*, and *Homeland*), Visible Collective was interested in subverting media spaces, especially advertising forms that burrow their way into public consciousness. One of the

first projects at the Queens Museum was a satire of the giant billboards for a Gap clothing campaign, featuring *Sex and the City*'s Sarah Jessica Parker. The sheer size of these billboards contrasted with everyday representations of immigrant populations: blurred micro-images seen through weathered vendor IDs, or taxi licenses lodged between scratched glass partitions. Visible's first outing in Queens inserted studio shots of migrants who had been targets of racial profiling into a larger-than-life billboard format. A slogan underneath repeated the Gap tagline: "Casual Fresh American Style."

Later, the *Really Steven?* project reappropriated Steven Meisel's unintentionally sublime 2006 fashion shoot for *Vogue Italia*. In that magazine spread, Meisel set up a tableau of waifish white models being patted down, strip-searched, pinned to the floor, and arrested by security guards at airports and riot police on the street. Our response was primarily to imagine and speculate how we would have fared going through those same checkpoints. But, again, who is that "we"? That remains the position in flux.

Finally, *When an Interpreter Could Not Be Found*, the larger piece that is excerpted in this anthology and that provides the title for this chapter, was a monthy calendar of case studies, in the form of cinema posters. The title is a variation of what is offered to immigration asylum applicants, but the motif of text on image borrowed from contemporary advertising campaigns and the 1980s cult sci-fi film *They Live* (subliminal messages revealed only when wearing "special" sunglasses, later inspiring Shephard Fairey's "Obey" graffitti). This was also the period when the collective consciously moved outside North American borders and started documenting cases in Europe, the Middle East, and Asia. When the project traveled outside the United States (e.g., *Homeworks* in Beirut, *FACT* in Liverpool, *Kiasma* in Helsinki), there was subtle resistance to exploring the shared global conditions of migrants. Audiences seemed more at ease when the examples were from the American context (seen as exceptional when, in fact, increasingly, they were not). But since migrant lives and conditions are global, for us it was essential to expand conversations about hyphenated and fractured spaces of living beyond a mono-critique. There is a need to evolve our future pedagogy and organizing beyond a singular focus on conditions in one country or continent (though the United States, as the largest recipient and host of new immigrants, will remain a global signifier). Future stages of work about migrant lives have to draw linkages between shared struggles of immigrants, especially working-class labor, across the globe.

Within the Visible Collective, there were debates about what we should work on and where to focus limited energies. These questions became channels for concerns about the impact of museum projects: What was the ripple effect? What were we accomplishing? Friction and concerns about use-value came up repeatedly in our discussions. By 2011, some members are working in spaces that are more removed from the context of cultural production. Aimara Lin, Visible member and antiwar organizer, is now in law school. Aziz Huq is a law professor at the University of Chicago. Others have also shifted energy and efforts. Conversations in visual spaces were valued by Visible for the possibility of a "butterfly wing effect"—the possibility of influencing public thought in slow, unpredictable ways and generating more open-ended conversations. But we also became increasingly aware that, in the decade after 2001, many of the positive changes in migrant lives came because of legal cases and legislative victories. Therefore, a more results-based path (law, teaching, electoral politics) has become a focus for some of our energies—taking priority, at least for now, over more ephemeral museum projects.

* * *

Visible Collective's members included Naeem Mohaiemen, Anandaroop Roy, Jee-Yun Ha, Donna Golden, Aimara Lin, Vivek Bald, Kristofer Dan-Bergman, J. T. Nimoy, Sehban Zaidi, Anjali Malhotra, Aziz Huq, Sarah Olson, and Ibrahim Quraishi. The collective's projects are archived at disappearedinamerica.org.

DECEMBER 2002

Hundreds of Iranian men
arrested in California when
they come forward to
comply with 'Special Reg-
istration' program which
requires fingerprinting of
men from Muslim coun-
tries. Three more rounds
of Registration happen
over next year, covering
all Muslim countries, and
North Korea. After national protests, the program is
finally shut down.

This and all other images taken from the series *When an Interpreter Could Not Be Found*
(© 2006 Visible Collective).

APRIL 2003

On season two of Emmy-award winning hit TV show "24", Middle Eastern intelligence agent Yusuf Auda is beaten to death by a group of white racists. During the same season, Arab terrorist Syed Ali is shot dead. The show is criticized for its good Arab vs. bad Arab dichotomies, attracting the attention of Slavoj Zizek. "24" runs for eight seasons.

AUGUST 2004

ACLU of Northern California files Freedom Of Information requests with the FBI and local Joint Terrorism Task Forces seeking documents related to the questioning of American Muslims, as well as any surveillance of political and religious activity. This follows newspaper reports of an aggressive surveillance plan focused on Muslims and mosques.

APRIL 2005

Death of Fred Korematsu, who sued US to challenge internment during WW II. Korematsu was arrested for refusing to go to a center where 100,000 Japanese-Americans were detained. In 1983, the US admitted wrongdoing and began reparation payments to Japanese-Americans. In 2004, Korematsu made statements condemning detention of Muslims.

MAY 2005

FBI drops case against two 16-year old girls held as "suicide bombers." Adema Bah, from Guinea, is released. Tashnuba Hyder, from Bangladesh, is deported to her native country with her parents. Part of the alleged evidence against Tashnuba was an essay she wrote in school, in which she discussed the Islamic view of suicide bombing.

AUGUST 2005

London police data shows 600% rise in anti-Muslim hate crimes since bombing. Police say minorities now more likely to be searched, but Home Office 2004 statistics already show Asians 1.9 times more likely to be searched. In New York, two politicians say police are "wasting time" with random checks, and Middle Easterners should be targeted.

NOVEMBER 2005

Nobel laureate and University of Chicago Economics professor Gary Becker advocates racial profiling to prevent admission into US of students and skilled workers from countries like Saudi Arabia and Pakistan. In an editorial for *The Wall Street Journal*, he writes, "terrorists come from a relatively small number of countries and backgrounds, unfortunately mainly of the Islamic faith."

DECEMBER 2005

Showtime's new series *Sleeper Cell* has four faces on posters with the tagline: "Friends. Neighbors. Husbands. Terrorists." The hero is Darwyn, a Black Muslim FBI agent infiltrating a terrorist cell. The cell members are Arabs, Bosnians and other Muslims, all with "normal" jobs, "blending into" America. Producers insist they're not "defaming" Muslims.

APRIL 2006

Latino DJs join forces with activists, bringing out 500,000 protestors against HR 4437, which would criminalize illegal migrants. One protestor says, "It was my grandfather's sweat that built the city of LA!" As freeways choke up and schools empty out, Lou Dobbs takes the other side on CNN and Minutemen vigilantes guard borders. The Senate is debating the bill and the final outcome is unclear.

JULY 2006

Rumors fly that Zinedine Zidane's head-butt was in response to a racist comment by Materazzi. Although Alain Finkielkraut called the French team "black-black-black", others celebrated the "black, blanc, beur" combination as a model of integration. But by 2010, that same diversity (including Muslim convert Ribery) was being blamed for World Cup defeat.

NOTES

1. *The Daily Show* with Jon Stewart, March 28, 2006.
2. "Arshad Zakaria Appointed Merrill Lynch Co-president," *Rediff*, October 8, 2001; Fran Hawthorne, "40 under Forty," *Crain's New York*, 2002. Later Zakaria was ousted during palace intrigues against Stanley O'Neal (coincidentally the first African American CEO of a major bank at this level). The firing is detailed in Bethany McLean and Joe Nocera, *All the Devils Are Here: The Hidden History of the Financial Crisis* (reprint; New York: Penguin USA, 2011).
3. Tunku Varadarajan, "That Feeling of Being under Suspicion," *Wall Street Journal*, July 29, 2005.
4. Immigration Reform and Control Act (IRCA), Pub. L. No. 99-603, 100 Stat. 3359, enacted November 6, 1986, also known as the Simpson-Mazzoli Act.
5. David Sells, "German Citizenship Test Causes Uproar," BBC, February 17, 2006.
6. "Q&A: The Road to UK Citizenship," BBC, February 25, 2004. Viewer comments at news.bbc.co.uk/2/hi/uk_news/3078690.stm.
7. Edward Sorel, cover illustration for the *New Yorker*, March 3, 2002.
8. Sarah Goodyear, "I Thought My Cabbie Was a Terrorist... So I Called the FBI," *Village Voice*, September 24, 2002.
9. Slavoj Zizek, ed., *Everything You Always Wanted to Know about Lacan: But Were Afraid to Ask Hitchcock* (London: Verso, 1992).
10. Camille Paglia, *The Birds* (London: British Film Institute, 1998).

PART III

Geographies of Migration, Settlement, and Self

10

Intertwined Violence

Implications of State Responses to Domestic Violence
in South Asian Immigrant Communities

SONIYA MUNSHI

To study the intimate is not to turn away from structures of domination but to
relocate their conditions of possibility and relations and forces of production.
—Ann Laura Stoler, "Intimidations of Empire:
Predicaments of the Tactile and Unseen," 2006

GR is a South Asian immigrant woman who is being abused by her hus-
band and his parents. Through safety planning with an advocate at a local
South Asian Women's Organization (SAWO), GR moves into a women's
shelter. A week later, GR, accompanied by the SAWO advocate, GR's hus-
band, and GR's in-laws appear in court for a final restraining order hear-
ing. The judge grants GR a restraining order legally prohibiting her hus-
band and his parents from having any contact with her. If the terms of the
order are violated, she can call the police and have them arrested. How do
we evaluate whether this was a successful outcome?[1]

Introduction

Over the past twenty-five years, South Asian communities in the United
States have responded to the issue of domestic violence. Manavi, the

first SAWO in the United States to explicitly grapple with gender-based violence against South Asian women,[2] was founded in 1985. Since then, more than twenty-five formal organizations,[3] and countless informal configurations, have emerged to work against domestic violence in the South Asian community. These groups generally work from a platform that articulates culturally specific needs of South Asian women experiencing domestic violence. To do so, SAWOs implement multipronged strategies such as providing supportive services to survivors, conducting educational programs in the community, and advocating for policy reform, among other activities. Community-based efforts to counter domestic violence have become one of the most institutionalized forms of activism in South Asian immigrant communities in the United States.[4] Nearly every metropolitan area in the United States houses a SAWO; these organizations work on local, national, and transnational levels, both independently and in collaboration with one another. SAWOs also play a leadership role in broader South Asian social movement politics; indeed, almost half of the organizations in the National Coalition of South Asian Organizations name the provision of domestic violence support services as one of their principal activities.[5]

SAWOs' work in the United States is situated in a broader sociopolitical landscape. In the last two decades, various federal and state mandates, such as the Violence Against Women Act (VAWA), have recognized and institutionalized violence against women as a law enforcement priority in the United States. Efforts by advocates for immigrant survivors have expanded dominant definitions of domestic violence, including specific attention in VAWA to "battered immigrant women." The development of state recognition of, and legal response to, domestic violence is often heralded as a success by some social movement efforts to end violence against women; yet, for many immigrant survivors of violence, the increased reliance on state/legal interventions does not help to create conditions of safety or well-being in their lives. Approaching the state/legal system for assistance may be an especially complicated strategy for survivors who belong to communities that are at risk for detention and deportation and/or antiterrorist profiling, given that the last two decades have also included new and continued forms of repression of immigrant communities, most notably from the 1996 immigration reform laws to post-9/11 "War on Terror" policies. As such, the state and its legal system may not be safe sites for all immigrant survivors of domestic violence. SAWOs, due to their constituencies of South Asian women, are positioned to engage with the complexities that have emerged from the increased reliance on legal interventions as solutions to domestic violence.[6]

This essay discusses the logics of exceptional violence and the logics of punishment that are deployed in order to produce violence that is legible to the state. To do this, it takes a closer look at two components of state responses to domestic violence that directly affect South Asian immigrant survivors: (1) the furthering of criminalization as a solution to the problem of domestic violence, and (2) the institutionalization of a legally recognized "battered immigrant woman" in VAWA and the limitations that transpire for immigrant survivors of domestic violence who are ineligible for membership in this category. This essay also discusses the dilemmas that emerge in South Asian immigrant survivors' negotiations of safety amid these parameters, suggesting a shift from a paradigm of inclusion to one of recentering survivors who are left out of existing responses to domestic violence.

Academic research about domestic violence in South Asian communities has generally worked to describe dynamics of intimate violence in the micropolitical realm. It has focused attention on (1) refuting model-minority stereotypes about South Asians in order to affirm that social problems, such as domestic violence, do plague our communities, and (2) articulating culturally specific dynamics of intimate violence and needs of South Asian survivors to challenge assumptions of a universal experience of domestic violence.[7] This essay, on the other hand, joins the growing body of literature that is focused on state, institutional, and community-based responses to domestic violence, recognizing the complexities of providing effective advocacy to South Asian women experiencing domestic violence.[8]

Domestic Violence as Exceptional Violence: Criminalization and Logics of Punishment

Contemporary antiviolence work in the United States can trace its origins to feminist social movements in the early 1970s, which notably called attention to violence in intimate relationships through articulating that the private sphere is, in fact, a political realm as well. Within this discourse, feminists concerned with multi-issue social justice asserted that violence in intimate relationships can only be understood within larger sociopolitical and economic contexts that produce different arrangements of power. In this view, a comprehensive definition of violence in intimate relationships holds that interpersonal dynamics of abuse are demonstrations of unequal intimate relationships, and that these inequalities are located in oppressive systems, such as capitalism, racism, patriarchy, and heteronormativity, which require imbalances of power to sustain themselves. These varied forms of violence coconstitute one another, and domestic violence, then, is the manifestation that appears in the intimate realm.[9]

This complex and critical understanding of intimate violence, although still thriving in many social movement sectors, has been increasingly displaced by a decontextualized definition of domestic violence. This shift has been facilitated by the development of an antiviolence movement—which included some segments of the feminist movement but also transcended it—that both looked to the state for intervention in domestic violence and was then produced by the state as well. It was through these early alliances between the antiviolence movement and the state that domestic violence was reconfigured as an individual behavioral, criminal, and/or medical problem; intervention and prevention strategies have thus been developed at the level of the individual as well.[10] Of course, domestic violence can involve matters of life and death; this critique of the move toward analysis of domestic violence as an individualized problem does not discount the tremendous need for services and support for individual survivors. Rather, it asks what is lost through the shift in understanding domestic violence as a form of exceptional violence.

Beginning in the 1970s, federal governmental agencies, such as the Law Enforcement Assistance Administration and the Department of Labor, along with state agencies, started to allocate monies to fund telephone hotlines, shelters, and advocacy groups for survivors of domestic violence. State financial support affected the scope of early anti-domestic violence efforts and, perhaps, allowed them to even grow at all.[11] Besides allocating governmental monies to fund social services for people experiencing domestic violence, the state also, beginning in the 1970s, actively initiated a process of criminalizing domestic violence. In 1978, officials from medical and criminal institutions, along with anti–domestic violence activists and academics, participated in the U.S.

Commission on Civil Rights' "Consultation on Battered Women: Issues of Public Policy." This meeting was the first state-coordinated assessment of domestic violence. It led to policies enabling and regulating social service delivery, new funding allocations to support anti–domestic violence work, and varied anti–domestic violence criminal legislation on the state level.[12] The meeting also signaled the emergence of models of "policing and arrest, prosecution and punishment, and mandated treatment of individual men newly demarcated as deviant criminals."[13] These early alliances have also served to produce a professionalized antiviolence movement, led by experts such as lawyers, doctors, social workers, and academic researchers, that has been institutionalized in a "non-profit industrial complex."[14]

Over the past three decades, the criminalization of domestic violence has become institutionalized, most directly through mandatory arrest policies that remove discretion; when police officers respond to a "domestic violence" call where there is probable cause that a crime existed, they are required to arrest an offending party. Mandatory arrest polices are often accompanied by "no drop" prosecution practices, which limit prosecutorial discretion with respect to reduction of charges or dismissal of cases.[15] These policies mean that the agents of the state make the decision to arrest and/or prosecute the abusive person, even if the survivor does not want this to happen. Currently, at least thirty states have implemented mandatory or pro-arrest policies.[16]

The prioritization of a criminal legal response to domestic violence has been most facilitated by the funding allocations for policing/prosecution activities included in all versions of VAWA, which was first passed in 1994, was reauthorized in 2000 and 2005, and was up for reauthorization in 2011. The monies for these activities are growing, both in actual amounts and in percentages of the overall VAWA budgets: the most recent version (2005) increases funding allocations for Grants to Encourage Arrest Policies to $75 million per year (2007–2011), a growth from VAWA 2000, which allowed $65 million per year (2001–2005); the original VAWA allocated, on average, $40 million per year (1996–1998). The VAWA STOP block grants, which are distributed to states to administer locally, have consistently required more than 50 percent of funds to be distributed to policing/prosecutorial efforts.[17] In addition, VAWA institutionalized funding to enhance collaborative efforts between state institutions (e.g., law enforcement) and nonstate institutions (e.g., nonprofit organizations).

The creation of criminal legal solutions to domestic violence exemplifies what critical race theorist Alan David Freeman calls the "perpetrator perspective."[18] In his writings about anti–racial discrimination laws, Freeman states that the perpetrator perspective interprets discrimination as an action or series of actions that have been inflicted upon a victim by a perpetrator. In contrast, the "victim perspective" sees racial discrimination as an overall life situation produced by a set of conditions, including objective conditions (e.g., lack of job, money, housing) and nonmaterial conditions, such as consciousness about one's self and available options. Freeman asserts that the legal system's utilization of the perpetrator perspective, and consequent emphasis on perpetrator intent, has undermined the ability of antidiscrimination law to change overall conditions of discrimination that are experienced by people of color.[19]

Criminal legal responses to domestic violence operate through this same paradigm. Feminist advocacy efforts have generally been able to successfully institute an analysis of domestic violence as a form of gender-based discrimination. Legislative responses, such as the Violence Against Women Act, do consider domestic violence a form of gender-based violence (albeit through utilization of transphobic and heterosexist understandings of gender binaries, gender identities, and gender roles). Criminal legal responses to domestic violence, then, recognize these incidences of gender-based violence that can be directly attributed to an individual perpetrator. They simultaneously help to obscure contextual conditions that may both contribute to the dynamics of violence in the intimate relationship as well as contribute to overall conditions of violence and oppression in the life of the survivor. These responses, for example, make visible economic abuse within an intimate relationship, where one person can be punished for exerting control over the familial finances. They do not, however, account for how the elimination of welfare benefits adversely affects survivors who may otherwise be supported in economic independence from their abusers. Criminal legal responses can punish an abuser for physical violence in the home but do not recognize, for example, violence perpetrated by state agents, like immigration enforcement agents, in the home as violence, or how the fear of being targeted by immigration enforcement can contribute to more tensions within an intimate relationship. As such, they produce an understanding of domestic violence as exceptional violence, where this particular manifestation of violence is wrong or unfair;[20] the ongoing conditions of violence that may coconstitute abuse in an intimate relationship are left uninterrogated. This approach also provides the necessary conditions for the professionalized antiviolence movement's emphasis on strategies for attaining safety for individual women in individual relationships.

The increased reliance on criminal legal solutions to domestic violence also illustrates critical race scholar Derrick Bell's principle of "interest convergence." Bell, in discussing the barriers in *Brown v. Board of Education*'s ability to change unequal conditions in public education, explains that the possibilities of advancing racial justice through legal strategies are limited by the need for these efforts to converge with powerful interests and ideologies (e.g., whiteness); remedies that actually threaten existing unequal structures of resource distribution will not be accommodated by the legal system.[21] Reading legislation such as VAWA through this analysis of interest convergence reveals that while it is limited in changing conditions of inequality, it is useful in the state's deployment of a "double discourse" on violence.[22] The process of making domestic violence a crime allows the state to, on the one hand, make a public declaration of concern for survivors of violence and facilitate intervention.[23] On the other hand, it is able to dismiss or negate other forms of violence. As Ana Clarissa Rojas Durazo argues, violence that is produced by the state, and its institutions, becomes excluded from the realm of possibility; this maneuver constructs violence as oppositional to the state.[24] In protecting survivors of domestic violence, the state is allied with them against the perpetrators, who become held solely responsible for violence.[25] The state's interest in excluding itself from responsibility in producing conditions of violence has been able to converge, repeatedly, with the antiviolence movement's concern for safety for survivors; it is this convergence that has sustained and increased attention to domestic violence as an individualized problem by both the state and the accompanying nonprofit industries. Criminalization of domestic violence also is produced through another convergence of interests: the state can use domestic violence as a mode through which to increase prosecution, arrests, and imprisonment of individual perpetrators of violence, thus necessitating the growth in technologies of imprisonment and policing, a necessary feature of state-building projects in post-Keynesian neoliberal times.[26]

Criminalization of Domestic Violence: Possibilities for South Asian Immigrant Survivors

When GR expresses concern for her safety, the SAWO advocate assures her that domestic violence is a crime, and the restraining order legally prohibits her abusers from contacting her. If she is in a situation where she does not feel safe, she can call the police. If her husband and/or in-laws abuse her, they will be arrested. How does the criminalization of domestic violence create and/or preclude conditions for safety in GR's life?

Many feminist of color critiques situate the growth in policing and prosecution of domestic violence in concerns for immigrant and non-immigrant communities of color who have historically been and/or currently are targeted by state policies; these analyses refuse to configure domestic violence as an individualized problem outside of socio-political, cultural, and economic institutions of violence. As such, these critiques also argue that, even at the individual level, conditions of safety may be worsened for survivors who may be vulnerable in engagement with state institutions and their agents.[27] In the contemporary moment, for South Asian immigrant survivors in the United States, the increase in immigration enforcement activities, as well as the development of formal relationships between law enforcement and immigration enforcement, heightens these concerns.

In the time since VAWA (1994) was first passed, restrictive immigration policies and immigration enforcement activities have grown in the United States. The 1996 Illegal Immigration Reform and Immigrant Responsibility Act (IIRAIRA) implemented a series of changes that have had grave impacts on immigrants, especially undocumented people, and established the foundation for further curtailments of immigrant rights after 9/11. Since 9/11, up to 300,000 immigrants have been detained each year;[28] immigrants are the fastest-growing prison population, representing a 400 percent increase between 1994 and 2006.[29] In 2003, immigration concerns became formally situated in the newly formed Department of Homeland Security, which absorbed and reorganized the responsibilities of the former Immigration and Naturalization Service (INS). Policies that have emerged under the guise of antiterrorism security have particularly affected South Asian/Muslim/Arab communities, especially men with temporary or no legal immigration status. For example, the National Security Entry-Exit Registration System (NSEERS) (2002), commonly known as Special Registration, required nonimmigrant men from twenty-five countries to register in person with Immigration and Customs Enforcement (ICE), resulting in more than 290,000 registrations.[30] Although formally implemented as an antiterrorism measure, the registration process actually was most effective in identifying, detaining, and deporting people who had committed minor immigration violations. Another example is the growth in Section 287(g), which enables the Department of Homeland Security to enter into agreements with local law enforcement agencies to train them to serve as immigration enforcement agents. Under 287(g), local law enforcement agents become empowered with authority that was formerly limited to the federal realm.[31] Although created in 1996 as part of IIRAIRA, 287(g) was not in effect until 2002. By 2006, however, fifty-five law enforcement agencies had entered into 287(g) agreements, and in July 2009, the Obama administration announced that it would continue expansion of the program.[32]

Immigration enforcement activities, and collaborations between law and immigration enforcement, have many possible repercussions for immigrant survivors of domestic violence, as there is an increase in potential risks involved in any engagement with the police, including police responses to domestic violence. Additionally, increased conditions of fear and insecurity around state/institutional violence can create complications for domestic violence survivors. For example, reports indicate that despite increased domestic violence during the post-9/11 period, social service organizations noticed fewer calls from South Asian/Muslim/Arab women, likely due to apprehensions of seeking assistance from outside the community.[33] As such, a South Asian immigrant survivor may be concerned about interacting with law enforcement, particularly if the survivor and/or her partner is, or is perceived to be, undocumented, queer, trans, disabled, working-class, Muslim, and/or identified with other characteristics that may increase their vulnerability to police violence. The survivor may be unwilling to expose her abusive partner to risks involved in engagement with the police, or she may be dependent on her spouse for immigration status such that a criminal conviction would prompt a loss of his status followed by hers. And, of course, she may not want the abuser arrested, for reasons as varied and complicated as love, economic dependence, dependence for mobility, fear of retaliation by the abuser/extended family/community, shame, or embarrassment. Immigrant survivors of domestic violence, then, simultaneously grapple with the impacts of state policies that can harm their community as well as with the dynamics of violence in their familial relationships, which are often worsened during times of increased repression.

Another concern is that the criminalization of domestic violence, especially under mandatory arrest laws, has meant that increasing numbers of women are being arrested and sent into batterer programs for inflicting violence on their intimate partners. This trend reveals the inability of the criminal legal framework to hold the complexity of dynamics of domestic violence. It privileges quantifiable, evidence-based analyses (e.g., visible injuries) that do not reveal information about actual power dynamics within a relationship; police officers are often unable or unwilling to see beyond evidence. A survivor may inflict violence upon someone in an act of self-defense, or she may utilize physical violence for retaliation. However, these enactments of physical violence do not necessarily mean that she has the ability to induce fear in her partner, making these incidents distinct from ongoing patterns of abuse of power in situations of intimate partner violence.[34] For South Asian immigrant survivors, other factors can contribute to arrest, such as limited English proficiency that enables the abusive partner to convince the police of his narrative. Domestic violence arrests and prosecution can have adverse consequences for an immigrant survivor. An arrest can present problems for her immigration status, cue deportation proceedings, require jail time, cause retaliation from her abuser or her family or community, jeopardize her employment, or adversely affect child custody. The risks that are made possible through the criminalization of domestic violence can produce more violence in survivors' lives, through possible consequences in the intimate relationship and/or the community as well as through direct engagement with state agents such as police officers.

The Production and Circulation of "Battered Immigrant Women"

The SAWO advocate informs GR that, due to her experiences of domestic violence, she is eligible to self-petition for her own green card. Because GR's dependence on her husband for green card sponsorship is one of the main reasons she has not left her abusive marriage, this information helps GR to decide to leave her husband.

Feminist of color critiques, insisting on the immigration system as a potential site of institutional violence, have articulated the many ways in which this violence is inextricable from that in interpersonal dynamics in the intimate realm. For example, an abuser can hide or destroy a survivor's immigration documents; report an undocumented survivor to ICE; refuse to sponsor a visa or green card (legal permanent resident) petition; and/or threaten to do any of these things. These tactics illustrate the intertwined relationship between state power and domestic violence: the state, through the immigration system, empowers abusive people with a method to inflict violence at the interpersonal level.[35]

However, the specific form of immigration violence that has been recognized by the state is that which occurs within marriages where the abusive partner uses his position as a green card sponsor to exert control over his spouse.[36] The Immigration Marriage Fraud Amendments (IMFA; 1986) established a two-year conditional status on all green card through spousal sponsorship. After two years, if the U.S. Citizenship and Immigration Services (USCIS) is convinced that the marriage is a legitimate "good faith" marriage, the conditional status is removed. In a case of domestic violence, the survivor may have entered the marriage in "good faith," but if she leaves the marriage for safety reasons during those first two years, she risks losing her green card. To address this mechanism of control in intimate relationships, the Immigration Act of 1990 created the battered spouse waiver, which exempts survivors of domestic violence from the conditional period. This precedent enabled the cementing of a legally recognized category, "battered immigrant women," in the Violence Against Women Act. As indicated earlier, through VAWA, federal funding was designated to enable a state-based response to violence against women through allocations for policing and prosecution, as well as services for assorted priority issue areas and constituent groups, including "battered immigrant women."

VAWA defines "battered immigrant women" as domestic violence survivors who are married to U.S. citizens or green card holders and entered their marriages in "good faith." They must also prove that they have "good moral character" by demonstrating a lack of criminal history. A survivor who fits this definition is able to access immigration relief by self-petitioning (applying for her own green card without spousal sponsorship) or obtaining cancellation of removal (through which pending deportation processes can be suspended with proof that the abusive spouse's refusal to sponsor her green card rendered her undocumented).

Despite VAWA's claim to protect "battered immigrant women," these remedies are very limited: only a subset of immigrant domestic violence survivors, who are married to U.S. citizens or green card holders, are eligible. Domestic violence survivors who experience immigration violence due to the power dynamics of spousal sponsorship (e.g., visa holders on dependent visas) but who are not already on a clear path to a green card are not offered immigration status relief through VAWA. Survivors whose experience of immigration violence in their intimate relationship is unrelated to marriage-based sponsorship (e.g., unmarried, undocumented, queer, or trans people) are not offered relief either. Also illegible is the possibility that the process of migration itself may have been affected by domestic violence; for example, a survivor may be without status because her limited options within the abusive relationship led to a nonconsensual migration.

The legal category of "battered immigrant women" serves to produce a population of legitimate victims in a demonstration of biopolitical governance, or how "power relations are played out in how [and which] bodies are aggregated [into populations] and individuated, healed, buried, made indistinguishable and marked";[37] some populations are folded into life while others are left to die. Jasbir Puar, in articulating how these biopolitical processes occur, argues that queer subjects move from being figures of death (e.g., through associations with AIDS) to becoming figures of life (e.g., gay marriage), such that deviance itself, being queer, is a requirement for the process of normativization. State expressions of benevolence, such as pro-gay legislation, facilitate this process.[38] The production and circulation of "battered immigrant women" follows these same logics: as survivors of violence, their experiences deviated from scripts of happy and safe marriages, and it is this deviance itself that serves to normalize them into a population. "Battered immigrant women" move from proximity to (literal) death and are folded into life, as they are given possibilities to rebuild their lives, legally work, remarry, and move forward on a path to U.S. citizenship. VAWA provisions, then, implement biopolitical governance through which immigrant populations are disciplined to enable the production of compliant citizens who will contribute to, and not drain from, the nation.[39] Through this process, violence is again reified as aberrant and enacted by individual perpetrators upon good victim-subjects who are appeased by benevolent state gestures.

Although the population of "battered immigrant women" is created through VAWA, it circulates in other realms of state governance. For example, in 1996, the U.S. welfare system was dismantled and replaced with Temporary Assistance for Needy Families (TANF). Undocumented people and nonimmigrant visa holders were cut off from all benefits except emergency medical care, and recent legal immigrants were blocked from accessing public benefits during their first five years of residence.[40] Additionally, TANF instituted a lifetime sixty-month limit and work requirements for all recipients of public assistance. Yet, TANF also offered states the option of adopting a Family Violence Option (FVO) for domestic violence survivors, which relaxes work requirements and "stops the clock" on the sixty-month lifetime limit on public assistance. "Qualified immigrants" who meet VAWA's "battered immigrant women" standards can apply for the FVO. Immigrant survivors of domestic violence who are ineligible for consideration as "battered immigrant women" are excluded from the FVO. Immigrant survivors of domestic violence who are in economically unstable positions but ineligible for the FVO are left in a bind of negotiating safety against economic survival.

Implications for SAWOs' Advocacy Work

After obtaining the final restraining order, GR continues to live in the women's shelter. The SAWO advocate helps her to self-petition her green card. Meanwhile, as she waits for her legal work authorization, GR participates in support groups and job readiness programs to prepare for her future once her shelter stay has expired. The SAWO advocate provides ongoing support to GR.

GR's story illustrates some of the individual-level forms of relief that have been made to support immigrant survivors of domestic violence, particularly through the Violence Against Women Act. First, as an eligible "battered immigrant woman," GR is able to sever ties of immigration dependence on her husband by filing a self-petition for a green card. VAWA monies likely fund the domestic violence shelter and its services and perhaps even the SAWO itself. Criminalization of domestic violence, funded through VAWA, means that GR's restraining order is enforceable through the power of arrest. One analysis of GR's story is that it is an illustration of a successful intervention, especially because, presumably, GR is on the path to lead a safe, economically independent life as a legal permanent resident in the United States. GR's story may be a familiar one; descriptions of interventions, along with first-person survivor narratives, are often deployed by SAWOs and other social service organizations for purposes such as community education, fundraising support, and/or policy advocacy. These narratives solicit attention to detailed experiences of domestic violence at the micropolitical level. They can inadvertently, or intentionally, distract attention from the larger context within which domestic violence and different interventions occur.

While waiting for the hearing to begin, the SAWO advocate notices worrisome interactions between GR's parents-in-law. GR confirms that her father-in-law has been physically and emotionally violent toward her mother-in-law. She also reveals that her parents-in-law overstayed their visas and, due to disabilities, are physically and economically dependent on her husband. GR also reasserts that her mother-in-law has been physically and emotionally abusive toward her since she entered the marital home.

Attention to GR's mother-in-law helps to further expose the limits of strategies of state responses to domestic violence. First, the logics of punishment produce a set of questions: Is GR's mother-in-law a survivor of domestic violence or an abuser, or can she be both simultaneously? Criminalization of domestic violence is predicated upon a mutually exclusive binary of victim and perpetrator, where some people need protection and other people need punishment. If GR's mother-in-law is named as an abusive party on the restraining order, she will be recognized as a perpetrator. Her own experience of victimization may not be legible. Her history of perpetrating violence may preclude her from accessing support groups, shelters, or other services that are geared toward victims of domestic violence. These obstacles are greatened especially given that she is undocumented, has disabilities, may or may not speak English, and may or may not want to leave her husband. The logics of punishment and the consequent reductive analysis of violence serve as an obstacle for social service programs' abilities to adequately address the complexities of experiences of domestic violence.

Even if GR's mother-in-law is considered an immigrant domestic violence survivor, as an undocumented person married to another undocumented person, she is not a "battered immigrant woman." She is unable to gain any legal immigration status through the exceptions created by VAWA. She is unable to access any public benefits except for emergency medical care. Her physical and economic dependence on her son make her return to South Asia an unviable option because this would add more difficulties to her everyday life conditions.

And, what happens if the police are called to the house to intervene in an incident of violence? Her husband may be arrested, but he could claim that she is the one who abused him, potentially resulting in her arrest or dual arrests, which would put her or them at risk for deportation. If her husband is arrested, GR's mother-in-law may be able to apply for a U visa, a temporary visa created through VAWA 2000 for immigrant crime victims who have information that can help prosecute the crime. The U visa, unlike other provisions for a "battered immigrant woman," is not a legal remedy; it is not a gesture by the state to even purportedly alleviate conditions of violence. Here, the state uses the survivor as an accomplice in prosecution and offers the U visa in exchange for service. The U visa enables the state to offer the possibility of immigration relief to survivors who are willing to participate in policing and prosecution. In this case, GR's mother-in-law would likely be eligible for a U visa; it is, formally, an option. Whether it seems like a possible option for her is a different issue. Would she be willing to support the criminal legal system to prosecute her husband, especially if there is a risk of retaliation from her son? Would a U visa, which provides work authorization and access to some public benefits, be sufficient for her to live an economically independent life in the United States? What would she gain and lose if she pursued this option?

Attention to GR's mother-in-law also exposes critical questions for SAWOs' advocacy work: Which forms of violence are recognized and acted upon? How has the expansion of legal solutions to end domestic violence actually produced limitations, especially with respect to what forms of violence are visible and obscured? In this case, GR is actively seeking support from the SAWO; she wants to leave her marital home and get a restraining order against her husband and in-laws. On the other hand, there is no indication that GR's mother-in-law is interested in addressing her experience of domestic violence at this time. But her evaluation of what is even possible, the legibility of violence, and available resources to support her might be shaped by the limited frameworks that are created through the institutionalization of responses to domestic violence.

Conclusion

In Monisha Das Gupta's ethnographic study of South Asian organizations in the late 1990s, she distinguishes between two types of community politics: (1) "place-taking politics," which refuse to mar the model-minority image of the community, and (2) "space-making politics," which work to "create structures and resources that transform daily life into an arena of political contest" by "struggl[ing] to transform oppressive institutions and systems through collective action and empowerment."[41] Das Gupta argues that SAWOs illustrate space-making politics, through their disruption of community silences about violence and other social problems, their refusal to claim rights for their constituencies on the basis of citizenship, and their attempts to practice intersectional politics through complex analyses of structural oppression.[42] When pondering the future of activism and organizing in South Asian communities, she asks whether they will "replicate the limitations of the second wave of U.S. feminism despite the fact that they themselves are the result of resisting white women's exclusionary practices."[43]

Das Gupta's question is an important one given the implications of state recognition of domestic violence over the past two decades. Theoretically, most SAWOs' constituencies transcend legally recognized "battered immigrant women" to include all immigrant survivors of domestic violence, and of course, SAWOs do not just provide support to those community members who are eligible for VAWA. Yet, logics of punishment and exceptional violence entrenched in institutionalized responses to domestic violence can serve to normalize conditions of violence[44] and limit collective imaginations of the possibilities of processes of social change. For example, liberal interpretations of VAWA's trajectory suggest that each reauthorization of this legislation is an improvement, as each renewal has expanded the remedies available to immigrant women;[45] more and more women are included and offered this invitation into life with future possibilities.

Recent advocacy efforts to gain legal protections for H-4 visa holders experiencing domestic violence illuminate how SAWOs and South Asian activists/advocates ourselves can be situated in biopolitical governance. Although in the United States legally, H-4 visa holders are structurally in a similar position to undocumented immigrants in that they are unable to avail themselves of public resources; as a result, they are economically dependent on their H-1 sponsoring spouses. H-1 visa holders are employed in economic sectors that are considered "professional," and they, along with their dependent spouses, generally are formally educated, have had the means and privileges to migrate to and remain in the United States through legal mechanisms, and lead middle-class lives in the United States.[46] These characteristics may oversimplify the biographies of these subsets of the community, but class-related privileges distinguish most H-1/H-4 visa holders from most undocumented immigrants.

In advocating for survivors holding H-4 visas, one strategy that circulated drew parallels between undocumented women and H-4 visa holders, analogizing their limited work options, the likelihood of working illegally, and the lack of legal remedies available to them because they are not eligible for consideration as "battered immigrant women."[47] This call to reconceptualize legal nonimmigrants and undocumented

immigrants as sharing experiences of vulnerability to structural violence offered potential in disrupting hegemonic understandings of
migration, globalization, and economic access. It also potentially served
to challenge narratives that punish undocumented immigrants for the
circumstances of their lives and to center these survivors who are often
illegible in discourses about domestic violence in South Asian communities. By doing so, this reconceptualization brought seemingly disparate subsets of South Asian communities into an alliance. This alliance,
however, was temporary; the advocacy argument ultimately recuperated H-4 visa holders from association with undocumented survivors
by pressing for their inclusion in VAWA. Citing precedents that provide
work authorizations for other dependent spouses, and claiming that
the underlying principle of VAWA acknowledges that battered women
have human rights, this advocacy argument challenged the exclusion of
H-4 visa holders by relying on model-minority ideas of H-4 visa holders as educated, middle-class, and good professional workers (if only
given the opportunity to legally work). The 2005 version of VAWA did
include H-4 visa holders; although they are not eligible for immigration
relief, survivors became eligible for work authorization.

Strategies of inclusion rely upon the logics of exceptional violence:
violence in the intimate realm is extracted from other forms of systemic
violence (e.g., economic violence, immigration violence) in order to
create eligibility into a population of victim-subjects. Experiences of
intimate violence with specific kinds of perpetrators (e.g., green card
holders, H-1 visa holders, or a perpetrator who the state is interested in
prosecuting) are a requirement to gain membership into these populations. But if a contextualized understanding of domestic violence holds
that the state and legal systems can be intertwined with violence in
the intimate realm, then there is a limit to the change that can emerge
from within these systems. Recontexualizing domestic violence within
a broader understanding of violence can open up more possibilities for
transformational politics that do not locate solutions in state responses
that further violence in communities, like policing and incarceration/
detention. As the relationship between law enforcement and immigration enforcement grows, and immigrant communities are increasingly
managed under a framework of national security, the risks of depending on criminal legal solutions for domestic violence become harder to

avoid. Community-based responses that critically question the state as a safe entity and assess the risks of state involvement in the domestic realm can offer options for survivors such as GR's mother-in-law whose complex experiences are often obscured.

NOTES

1. This is a composite story that has been developed through my different experiences, over fifteen years, of working with immigrant survivors of domestic violence.

2. SAWOs usually define South Asians as descendants of Bangladesh, India, Nepal, Pakistan, and Sri Lanka. Because most SAWOs work primarily with constituencies of women, and most recognized survivors of domestic violence are heterosexual women, I will be using female pronouns to refer to survivors of violence and male pronouns to refer to abusers. These language choices serve for ease but are not adequate to encompass the complexity of experiences of gender, gender identity, sexuality, and/or relationship to violence.

3. See http://maitri.org/res_usa.html for a current list of SAWOs.

4. Although "immigrant" is a legal designation for migrants who have gained permanent residence in the United States, I use "immigrant" to refer to migrants regardless of their legal status.

5. South Asian Americans Leading Together 2008.

6. See, e.g., Richie 1995; Bhattacharjee 2001; Smith 2005; Sudbury 2005; Das Gupta 2006.

7. See, e.g., Dasgupta and Warrier 1996; Preisser 1999; Abraham 2000; Raj and Silverman 2002.

8. See, e.g., Abraham 2000; Rudrappa 2004; Bhuyan 2006; Das Gupta 2006.

9. Rojas Durazo 2006.

10. Ibid.

11. See Fine 1985.

12. Rojas Durazo 2006.

13. Adelman 2004: 47.

14. INCITE! 2006.

15. See Miccio 2005.

16. American Bar Association Commission on Domestic Violence 2008.

17. National Coalition Against Domestic Violence 2008.

18. Freeman 1995.

19. Ibid.; Arkles, Gehi, and Redfield 2010.

20. Spade 2009.

21. Bell 1995.

22. Rojas Durazo 2007.

23. Haritaworn 2010; Rojas Durazo 2007.

24. Rojas Durazo 2007.

25. Haritaworn 2010; Rojas Durazo 2007.
26. Gilmore 2007.
27. See, e.g., Richie 1995; Bhattacharjee 2001; Smith 2005; Sudbury 2005; Das Gupta 2006.
28. Bhuyan 2007: 241–242.
29. National Network for Immigrant and Refugee Rights 2008.
30. ICE 2008. ICE reports that more than 20 percent of registrants were referred for investigation (including those then detained), but it does not report how many men were deported.
31. Ibid.
32. See Shahani and Greene 2009.
33. Sthanki 2007: 68–69.
34. Dasgupta 2002; Osthoff 2002.
35. Abraham 2000: 36.
36. Ibid.
37. Stoler 2006, 13–14.
38. Puar 2007.
39. See Bhuyan 2006 for a fuller discussion of these mechanisms of governmentality, domestic violence, and immigration.
40. NOW Legal Defense and Education Fund 2008.
41. Das Gupta 2006: 9.
42. Ibid.
43. Ibid., 157.
44. Arkles, Gehi, and Redfield 2010.
45. Bhuyan 2007.
46. Shah 2007.
47. Ibid.

REFERENCES

Abraham, Margaret. 2000. *Speaking the Unspeakable: Marital Violence against South Asian Immigrants in the United States.* New Brunswick, NJ: Rutgers University Press.

Adelman, Madelaine. 2004. "The Battering State: Towards a Political Economy of Domestic Violence." *Journal of Poverty* 8(3): 45–64.

American Bar Assocation Commission on Domestic Violence. 2008. "Domestic Violence Arrest Polices by State 11/07." http://www.abanet.org/domviol/docs/Domestic_Violence_Arrest_Policies_by_State_11_07.pdf. (accessed December 20, 2008).

Arkles, Gabriel, Pooja Gehi, and Elana Redfield. 2010. "The Role of Lawyers in Trans Liberation: Building a Transformative Movement for Social Change." *Seattle Journal for Social Justice* 8(2): 579–641.

Bell, Derrick A., Jr. 1995. "*Brown v. Board Of Education* and the Interest Convergence Dilemma." In *Critical Race Theory: Key Writings That Formed the Movement*, ed. K. Crenshaw, N. Gotanda, G. Peller, and K. Thomas. New York: New Press.

Bhattacharjee, Anannya. 2001. *Whose Safety? Women of Color and the Violence of Law Enforcement*. Philadelphia: American Friends Service Committee.

Bhuyan, Rupaleem. 2006. "Disciplining through the Promise of 'Freedom': The Production of the Battered Immigrant Woman in Public Policy and Domestic Violence Advocacy." PhD diss., University of Washington.

———. 2007. "Navigating Gender, Immigration, and Domestic Violence: Advocacy with Work Visa Holders." In *Body Evidence: Intimate Violence against South Asian Women in America*, ed. Shamita Das Dasgupta. New Brunswick, NJ: Rutgers University Press.

Dasgupta, Shamita Das. 2002. "A Framework for Understanding Women's Use of Nonlethal Violence in Intimate Heterosexual Relationships." *Violence against Women* 8(11): 1364–1389

———. 2007. "Battered South Asian Women in U.S. Courts." In *Body Evidence: Intimate Violence against South Asian Women in America*, ed. Shamita Das Dasgupta. New Brunswick, NJ: Rutgers University Press.

Dasgupta, Shamita Das, and Sujata Warrier. 1996. "In the Footsteps of 'Arundhati': Asian Indian Women's Experience of Domestic Violence in the United States." *Violence against Women* 2(3): 238–259.

Das Gupta, Monisha. 2006. *Unruly Immigrants: Rights, Activism, and Transnational South Asian Politics in the United States*. Durham, NC: Duke University Press.

Fine, Michelle. 1985. "Unearthing Contradictions: An Essay Inspired by 'Women and Male Violence.'" *Feminist Studies* 11(2): 391–407.

Freeman, Alan David. 1995. "Legitimizing Racial Discrimination through Antidiscrimination Law: A Critical Review of Supreme Court Doctrine." In *Critical Race Theory: Key Writings That Formed the Movement*, ed. K. Crenshaw, N. Gotanda, G. Peller, and K. Thomas. New York: New Press.

Gilmore, Ruth Wilson. 2007. *Golden Gulag: Prisons, Surplus, Crisis, and Opposition in Globalizing California*. Berkeley: University of California.

Green, Boaz. 2006. "The Identity Victim." *Georgetown Journal of Gender and the Law* 7: 255–283.

Haritaworn, Jin. 2010. "Queer Injuries: The Cultural Politics of "Hate Crimes" in Germany." *Social Justice*. Special issue on "Criminalization and Sexuality." 37(1): 69–85.

ICE. "Special Registration." 2008. http://www.ice.gov/pi/specialregistration/ (accessed December 20, 2008).

INCITE! Women of Color against Violence. 2006. *Color of Violence: The INCITE! Anthology*. Cambridge, MA: South End Press.

Maitri. "Resources." 2009. http://www.maitri.org/res_usa.html (accessed January 12, 2009).

Miccio, Kristian G. 2005. "A House Divided: Mandatory Arrest, Domestic Violence, and the Conservatization of the Battered Women's Movement." *Houston Law Review* 42: 237.

National Coalition against Domestic Violence. 2008. "Comparison of VAWA 1994, VAWA 2000, VAWA 2005 Reauthorization Bill 1/16/06." http://www.ncadv.org/publicpolicy/VAWA2005_179.html (accessed December 20, 2008).

National Network for Immigrant and Refugee Rights. 2008. "Over-raided, Under Siege: U.S. Immigration Laws and Enforcement Destroy the Rights of Immigrants." http://www.nnirr.org/resources/index.php?op=list&type=10 (accessed December 20, 2008).

NOW Legal Defense and Education Fund. 2008. "Medicaid and Temporary Assistance for Needy Families Access for Battered Immigrant Women and Children." http://www.legalmomentum.org/assets/pdfs/tanfemfactsheet.pdf (accessed December 20, 2008).(accessed December 20, 2008).

Osthoff, Sue. 2002. "But, Gertrude, I Beg to Differ, a Hit Is Not a Hit Is Not a Hit: When Battered Women Are Arrested for Assaulting Their Partners." *Violence against Women* 8(12): 1521–1544.

Preisser, Amita B. 1999. "Domestic Violence in South Asian Communities in America: Advocacy and Intervention." *Violence against Women* 5(6): 684–699.

Puar, Jasbir. 2007. *Terrorist Assemblages: Homonationalism in Queer Times.* Durham, NC: Duke University Press.

Raj, Anita, and J. G. Silverman. 2002. "Intimate Partner Violence against South Asian Women in Greater Boston." *Journal of American Medical Women's Association* 57: 111–114.

Richie, Beth. 1995. *Compelled to Crime: The Gender Entrapment of Black, Battered Women.* New York: Routledge.

Rojas Durazo, Ana Clarissa. 2006. "The Medicalization of Domestic Violence." In *Color of Violence: The INCITE! Anthology.* Boston: South End Press.

———. 2007. "'We were never meant to survive': Fighting Violence against Women and the Fourth World War." In *The Revolution Will Not Be Funded: Beyond the Non-profit Industrial Complex*, ed. Incite! Women of Color against Violence. Boston: South End Press.

Rudrappa, Sharmila. 2004. *Ethnic Routes to Becoming American: Indian Immigrants and the Cultures of Citizenship.* New Brunswick, NJ: Rutgers University Press.

Shah, Shivali. 2007. "Middle Class, Documented, and Helpless: The H-4 Visa Bind." In *Body Evidence: Intimate Violence against South Asian Women in America*, ed. Shamita Das Dasgupta. New Brunswick, NJ: Rutgers University Press.

Shahani, Aarti, and Judith Greene. 2009. *Democracy on Ice: Why State and Local Governments Have No Business in Federal Immigration Law Enforcement.* New York: Justice Strategies.

Smith, Andrea. 2005. *Conquest: Sexual Violence and American Indian Genocide.* Cambridge, MA: South End Press.

South Asian Americans Leading Together. 2008. "Meet the National Coalition." http://www.saalt.org/pages/Meet-the-National-Coalition.html (accessed December 20, 2008).

Spade, Dean. 2005. "Sex, Gender, and Crime: The Politics of the State as Protector and Punisher." Georgetown University Law Center.

Sthanki, Maunica. 2007. "The Aftermath of September 11: An Anti–Domestic Violence Perspective." In *Body Evidence: Intimate Violence against South Asian Women in America*, ed. Shamita Das Dasgupta. New Brunswick, NJ: Rutgers University Press.

Stoler, Ann Laura. 2006. "Intimidations of Empire: Predicaments of the Tactile and Unseen." In *Haunted by Empire: Geographies of Intimacy in North American History*, ed. Ann Laura Stoler. Durham, NC: Duke University Press.

Sudbury, Julia. 2005. "Feminist Critiques, Transnational Landscapes, Abolitionist Visions." In *Global Lockdown: Race, Gender and the Prison Industrial Complex*, ed. Julia Sudbury, xi–xxviii. New York: Routledge.

11

Who's Your Daddy?

Queer Diasporic Framings of the Region

GAYATRI GOPINATH

This essay is part of an ongoing project of thinking through the uses of the region in producing new forms of queer scholarship. As such it is broadly concerned with the relation between queer studies, diaspora studies, and area studies; I explore the possibilities for a comparative queer studies project that is routed and rooted in and through each of these fields. The notion of the region, I suggest, may be a way of troubling the boundaries and presumptions of these bodies of knowledge and can offer us a particularly productive spatial metaphor to map sexual topographies in this transnational moment. This understanding of region is a heuristic device that allows us to see the "queer" of queer studies, the "diaspora" of diaspora studies, and the "area" of area studies in novel and unexpected ways.

An essay by renowned anthropologist of South Asia Bernard Cohn written some forty years ago bears revisiting as we seek to move the notion of the region into new realms. Cohn, in his essay "Regions Subjective and Objective," was responding to the growing interest in studying India through the "region" on the part of South Asia scholars and issued the following caution:

> Regions, even the assumed enduring ones…are of a changing nature through time. Various kinds of circumstances can rapidly alter the boundaries and the very nature and conception of a region.…Regions are far from fixed, enduring things, especially if any historical perspective is taken. They are not absolutes and they are difficult, if not impossible, to define by objective criteria.[1]

Cohn warned against reifying the region at a time when the region was in fact being fixed within area studies scholarship in precisely the ways that he was cautioning against, instead urging the field of South Asian studies to recognize how the region is constituted through an interplay of spatial and temporal logics.

In recent years we have seen a reanimation of the concept of the region along the lines of Cohn's definition, one that stresses and in fact embraces the slipperiness of the term and that understands it as shifting and mobile, rather than as fixed or static. New articulations of the region have emerged most notably from area studies scholars interested in pushing against nation-centered models by insisting on the malleability of the concept. This renewed interest in thinking through the region points to dissatisfaction on the part of many area studies scholars with frameworks that continue to privilege either the nation or the global as primary units of analysis. They suggest that we cannot fully comprehend the local through a reference to its apparent Other, the global, but that there are indeed other spatial scales at work in producing the local. In other words, the region may encompass the local, but while the local is often posited as a fixed and stable entity, the region avoids this reification precisely due to its multivalent connotations. There is a plasticity to the term, in that it references both subnational and supranational formations simultaneously, which allows it to trouble both the global/local dyad and a dominant nationalist frame.[2] The region thus emerges as a useful category in that it allows for a simultaneous consideration of the local, the national, the transnational, and the global.

This turn to the region is part of a collective project that is being undertaken by postcolonial scholars in order to provincialize the West through a focus on the traffic and travel within and between locations in the Global South. One exemplary recent instance of such scholarship is Indian literary scholar Tejaswini Niranjana's *Mobilizing India: Women, Music and Migration between India and Trinidad*. Here Niranjana engages in an ambitious comparative analysis of the discursive production of "Indian womanhood" in Trinidad and India. She situates within the same frame regions that have been thought to be geographically distinct (in this case the Caribbean and South Asia) but that are in fact mutually constitutive and intimately connected. As she eloquently puts it, "To recognize that there exist outside our everyday sphere geographic and political spaces other than the West, spaces that have always intersected with our history but by the very logic of colonialism cannot be acknowledged in their mutual imbrication with our past, is a first step toward rewriting our histories as well as …enlarging our futures."[3] By showing the centrality of the "subaltern diaspora" (by which she means the labor diaspora of Indian indentured workers and their descendants in Trinidad) in the constitution of modern Indian nationhood, she makes a crucial intervention into conventional area studies scholarship on South Asia that still, as she points out, is marked by a limiting nation-centrism. Instead, Niranjana calls for "South-South comparative work." She writes, "While such comparisons might produce new shadows, new regions will simultaneously be cast into relief."[4]

I would like to suggest that these reformulations of the region have much to offer queer studies. In a recent overview essay that maps the way in which the region is in fact gaining critical currency within queer studies, anthropologist Ara Wilson argues that a renewed attention to the gender and sexual economies of supranational regions such as "Asia" or the "Pacific Rim" has the potential to challenge the hegemony of Eurocentric and U.S.-based models of queerness. Pointing to the 2005 conference on Asian sexualities in Bangkok, Thailand, as one instance of this turn toward the region in queer studies, she argues that a "critical regionalism" allows us to provincialize Euro-American queer formations while stressing "the transnational nature of 'Asia' itself." Wilson situates "critical regionalism" as a corrective to queer diaspora studies, which she characterizes as privileging those in the Global North. She writes:

> Diasporic studies...have been criticized for recentring the analysis of cultural struggles on those subjects who migrated to the neglect of those...who remained in the home country....While such analyses create alternative queer narratives within the global north, diasporic queer critiques of Western hegemony still pivot on the first world.

Instead she asks, "Is there a way to make queer life in the complex modernities of the non-West, third world and global south itself the centre of transnational queer analysis?" She answers this question by calling for an increase in "empirical and situated studies of the many cross-border flows that provide conditions for queer life in the region," which can provide an antidote to the continuing hegemony of Euro-American queer formations.[5]

This call for a new queer regional studies that centers the Global South is echoed by other anthropologists working on sexuality and Southeast Asia such as Mark Johnson, Peter Jackson, and Gil Herdt; these scholars use a regional perspective to trace the similarities and dissonances between gender and sexual formations in sites as disparate as Thailand and Indonesia.[6] Critical regionality, for these scholars, makes multiple interventions. First, it challenges the Eurocentrism of dominant queer studies scholarship by focusing on alternative sexual and gendered logics that are not reducible to hegemonic Euro-American notions of gay identity. Second, it challenges area studies scholarship that remains overly nation-centric and that elides the function of transnational and diasporic flows as they remake even the most apparently "local" of sites. Finally, critical regionality challenges a theory of globalization that presumes homogeneity and that fails to adequately address how discourses of a "global gay identity" are transformed and negotiated within local sites.

I place Niranjana's work in conversation with the recent queer studies work on critical regionality as both are particularly compelling recent examples of how regional analyses can be used to foreground alternative solidarities and affiliations in the shadow of resurgent nationalisms, on the one hand, and globalization, on the other. Situating these texts in relation to one another also foregrounds the ways in which postcolonial and queer studies scholarship on the region can productively extend and inform one another. Like Wilson, Niranjana defines the region in its supranational rather than subnational sense: the axis upon which Niranjana's analysis rests situates the region (the Caribbean) in relation to the nation (India). This inadvertently replicates and reasserts precisely the hierarchy between the subaltern diaspora (in Trinidad) and the (Indian) nation that her work is trying to dislodge. To a certain extent, in Niranjana's text, Trinidad gains meaning only as much as it serves as the occluded Other to the Indian nation. She writes, "The East Indian [in Trinidad] could unsettle profoundly for us the sense of who is 'Indian' and why."[7] The "us" here clearly references Indians from India; this is her intended readership. As such, Trinidad functions purely instrumentally, in the sense that it tells us something about the formation of the Indian nation, Indian nationalism, and Indian womanhood. This implicit valorization of India over and against its diaspora, even in a project that explicitly seeks to undo such hierarchies, speaks to the challenges inherent in this project of seeking solidarity between different southern locations. Not all "Souths," after all, occupy the same playing field, and some Souths are more equal than others. To put it simply, power hierarchies operate not only between the West and the rest but also within and between regions in the Global South. I would argue that one way out of this trap of continuing to recenter the nation in relation to "its" diaspora, as Niranjana does, is to dislodge the nation from the diaspora-nation nexus. Instead, it may be more fruitful to think not in terms of diaspora-nation but diaspora-region, or region-to-region connectivities.

Niranjana's book also shares with Wilson's essay an implicit critique of dominant models of diaspora studies as recentering the Global North. Niranjana convincingly argues that "Indian" identities in the subaltern diasporas of the Caribbean, East and South Africa, and Fiji, for instance, have quite a different relationship to the Indian nation than do the moneyed and propertied nonresident Indian (NRI) diasporas in the metropoles of North America, the United Kingdom, and Australia. While this is inarguably the case, I would also suggest that such a critique risks fixing and homogenizing what constitutes the "West" in the first place. Indeed, one of the main projects of queer diaspora studies, and U.S. queer of color scholarship, has been to point to the fractured and heterogeneous nature of the West, the First World, and the Global North, by pointing to the many subaltern formations that inhabit these spaces. Ultimately it may be unproductive to articulate a comparative project of the Global South against a diaspora studies that is characterized as recentering the Global North. Rather than assert such a binary opposition between the two projects, what is needed is a comparative regional analysis of sexuality that redefines what constitutes the "South" in the first place. In other words, I suggest that a comparativist South-South project, or one on sexualities of regions in the Global South, is not antithetical to diasporic or U.S. queer of color scholarship situated in the Global North. These are in fact commensurate and overlapping projects, and situating them in opposition to one another risks stabilizing the meaning of the "West" that both diasporic scholarship and queer of color scholarship have worked hard to undo. Instead, I am interested in placing in relation to one another regions in the Global South alongside those "Souths" that exist in the Global North.

Furthermore, it seems crucial to explore the potential of a regional analysis not only by looking at the supranational but also by simultaneously considering the gender and sexual logics of the subnational, and how the regional logics in one subnational location may resonate with those in another in both the Global South and the Global North. This is, I think, what is most fruitful and exciting about the notion of the region: that it enables us to animate both of these spatial scales concurrently. Such an understanding of the region paves the way for a comparative project on the sexual economies of different regions within, between, *and* outside the Global South. This project is capacious enough to include within its rubric an analysis of rural sexuality in the U.S. South, as one particular subregional formation, in relation to, for instance, rural sexuality in South India.

This revisioning of the Global North to reveal the multiple "Souths" within it is apparent in a lyrical autobiographical essay by queer studies scholar Roderick Ferguson. The essay, entitled "Sissies at the Picnic," details the particular logic of race, class, gender, and sexuality that characterized his hometown of Manchester, in west-central Georgia in the U.S. South, in the 1970s.[8] Ferguson remembers Manchester as queer both temporally and spatially: temporally in its blurring of past and present, its refusal to enter into the modern time of the nation; and spatially in its gender and sexual heterogeneity, emblematized most dramatically in the body of the black sissies, the men deemed "funny" or "odd" who were nevertheless an intrinsic and valued part of the neighborhood. Ferguson poignantly recounts the demise of the black sissy in the early 1980s, with the advent of AIDS, the rise of right-wing Christianity, and the emergence of a black bourgeoisie invested in sexual respectability, as Manchester fell in step with the nation in the name of progress and integration.

I mention Ferguson's autobiographical tale here because it shows quite clearly the ways in which his "South" and its relation to the larger U.S. nation echo the relation of certain subnational regions in the Global South to their respective nations. As such his essay points to the productive conversations and overlapping investments between U.S. queer of color scholarship, queer diasporic scholarship, and a South-South comparative project. Indeed, Ferguson's characterization of this particular community in the rural U.S. South has remarkable resonance with my own interest in representations of the regional logic of gender and sexuality in rural Kerala. Here, too, as I will discuss, Kerala's entrance into the modern time of the (Indian) nation was purchased through the effacement of gender and sexual arrangements deemed "perverse," first by the colonial British state and then by the postcolonial Indian state. Juxtaposing rural Kerala to rural Georgia suggests a transregional mode of analysis that mines the connection between different "Souths," both globally and locally inscribed. This is not to suggest that these different "Souths" are in any way the same: clearly, a subaltern region in the Global North occupies a very different power position from a subaltern region in the Global South, given the legacies of colonialism and the exigencies of global capital. But the fact that we can hear resonances between projects that are situated in vastly different geographic and historical contexts suggests the uses and scope of theorizing queer sexualities from a regional perspective; it is worth mining the comparison between these different locations because it allows us to make meaningful connections between sites that would initially seem utterly discrete and incommensurate. Such a perspective provides us with an alternative mapping of sexual geographies that links disparate locations and that allows new models of sexual subjectivity to come into focus. Clearly, this kind of comparative project is a risky proposition, one that can easily fall into ahistoricity and a flattening out of the specificities of each location. A comparative project such as this in a

sense demands and requires collaboration in order to avoid these pit-
falls, since many scholars are trained only in the histories and cultures
of particular regions. Despite their dangers, however, these comparative
regional analyses are well worth taking on, in that they challenge us to
think ambitiously about the future directions of both area studies and
queer studies. Indeed, I would suggest that this model of queer comparative regional studies offers an important critique of conventional
area studies and the balkanized forms of knowledge production that it
encourages, even as it pushes queer studies outside of a Euro-Ameri-
can-centric frame and toward a deep engagement with questions of globalization and diaspora.

I want to turn now to the particular regional logic of gender and
sexuality in Kerala, South India, and its representation, translation, and
circulation in national and transnational circuits. I believe it offers us a
useful case study that makes apparent the way in which the region as
a subnational formation has a complicated and contradictory relation
to both the nation and the global. On the one hand, the region may
act as a counterpoint or challenge to nationalist progress narratives; on
the other hand, the region can very well be recuperated into nationalist narratives and serve to bolster and sustain them.[9] Indeed, the very
framing of Kerala as a region replicates the logic of the Nehruvian
nationalist project: modern-day Kerala came into existence in 1956,
when the three different political units of Malabar, Kochi, and Tiruvitamkoor were merged into a single, linguistically defined state by the
central government. Thus I am not suggesting that there is something
intrinsically queer and oppositional about the region, but rather that it
has the potential to both disrupt and reinforce hegemonic state nationalist discourses simultaneously. This becomes particularly clear when
we look at how Kerala at different historical moments has been made
representative of the Indian nation even as it has been fixed as marginal and ex-centric to a nationalist project. Bernard Cohn's observation again comes to mind here, in that the Kerala example makes very
clear the ways in which the region is a temporally and spatially defined
category, one that shifts meaning across both space and time. Anthropologist Ritty Lukose, for instance, critiques what she terms a discourse
of "Kerala exceptionalism" through which the region has been evoked
within both popular and scholarly discourses. Lukose points to the

ways in which both the Kerala state government and global development studies scholars are invested in producing Kerala as singular and
exceptional. She writes:

> While this discourse [of exceptionalism] has many registers, it is note-
> worthy that they oscillate between the idea of Kerala as a space of exotic
> "tradition," marked as exceptional by its tropical beauty, unique matri-
> lineal kinship patterns, and rigid caste system, and Kerala as uniquely
> "modern" and revolutionary, indexed as exceptional by high levels of lit-
> eracy and its communist traditions....Specifically, one important thread
> within the construction of Kerala as exceptional is the trope of devel-
> opment, in which the so-called "Kerala Model of Development" is held
> up as an example for other parts of the world. This literature narrates a
> heroic story of a progressive march from "tradition" to "modernity."[10]

Writing against this discourse of exceptionalism, Lukose's analysis rejects "standard spatial imaginaries of social scales and globalization" that would "nest the region within the nation and then within the
world." Instead, she suggests that we must understand how "regional
histories are part of a flexible articulation between region, nation, and
globe; one that does not make Kerala exceptional but points to specificities that mediate Kerala's experience of globalization."[11] Lukose underscores here the necessity of situating regional particularities within a
broader context of globalization rather than seeing such particularities
as markers of Kerala's anomalous status. I find Lukose's framing of the
region in relation to the nation and globe compelling, in that it insists
upon the dynamic interplay of these different spatial scales even as it
remains attuned to the specificities of regional histories.

This essay is similarly attuned to the shifting meanings of Kerala, as
a subnational region, in a nationalist and transnational imaginary, and
counters the reification of the region that Lukose cautions us against.
I am specifically interested in how contemporary queer South Asian
diasporic artists evoke the specificities of regional histories to articulate new modes of sexual, racial, and gendered subjectivity in the diaspora, even as they resituate the region outside of a narrative of exceptionalism. Queer diasporic reframings of the region, I suggest, provide
us with precisely the more nuanced mapping of the relation between

region, nation, and globe that Lukose calls for. In their engagement with questions of gender and sexual alterity, the work of queer South Asian diasporic artists radically disrupts the "heroic march from 'tradition' to 'modernity,'" as Lukose phrases it, enshrined within developmentalist and state nationalist discourses. Moreover, these queer art practices offer a useful counterpoint to both Niranjana's and Wilson's analyses: they point to the uses of framing the region as subnational rather than solely as supranational, and they mobilize a diaspora-region axis, rather than the more conventional diaspora-nation axis evident in Niranjana's work.

The double negotiation enabled by the region-diaspora axis, where both the nation and the transnational are simultaneously contested and reconstituted, is particularly apparent in the work of a queer diasporic artist such as David Dasharath Kalal, to whose work I now want to turn. Kalal is an Irish Indian artist whose hometown is New York City and who is currently based in Stockholm, Sweden. In a series of five paintings that is part of a larger multimedia project entitled *Kalalabad*, Kalal digitally remakes the canonized oil paintings of Raja Ravi Varma, the best-known Indian artist of the late nineteenth century and early twentieth century, who is commonly termed the "father of modern Indian art." In order to fully appreciate Kalal's queer diasporic revisioning of Varma's images, however, and the way in which it negotiates the regional, the national, and the transnational simultaneously, it is necessary to first situate Varma's work in the context of early Indian nationalism in the late nineteenth century.

Varma was born into an aristocratic family in Kerala in 1848. Significantly, he rose to prominence as an oil painter not by going through the system of British arts schools that were set up in India in the mid-nineteenth century as a way of shaping the tastes and sensibilities of a newly emergent Indian bourgeoisie. Varma instead was largely home-schooled in the art of oil painting (learning from a resident British oil painter at work in the Travancore palace in the 1860s); this fact would endear him to Indian nationalists who saw him, as art historian Saloni Mathur puts it, as "stealing the fire [that is, western techniques of representation such as oil and easel] for his own people."[12] In a fascinating discussion of Varma in relation to a comparative, contrapuntal history of oil painting in Britain and India, Mathur locates Varma as part of the first generation of Indian artists who were seen as "gentleman painters" rather than as "native craftsmen" in the eyes of both the British colonizers and the Indian elite who were the subjects of his work. Elevating the profession of the artist to one that was deemed respectable and refined, Varma paradoxically toward the end of his life opened a printing press, producing mass-market lithographs of Hindu mythological themes. These reproductions circulated widely and acted as the precursor of modern visual forms such as the cinema and photography that would come to dominate the visual field in India in the ensuing decades.

Varma is a contradictory figure, both lauded and derided at various moments in history by Indian nationalists. On the one hand, his mastery of a "foreign" mode of representation and the recognition he attained both within India and abroad were seen as a victory for a fledgling nationalist movement. On the other hand, his adherence to the conventions of Western academic realism and his subsumption of an indigenous aesthetic tradition were derided by subsequent nationalists, particularly after his death in 1906, as wholly derivative and imitative of British art. These charges of inauthenticity and mimeticism continue to haunt his work to the present day. Indeed, over the years his work has been dismissed as debased, mass-market kitsch by art critics who nevertheless concede to his enduring influence on visual culture in contemporary India. Recently, however, there has been a reassessment of his work by postcolonial art historians, who read him and his artwork as hybrid and syncretic. As art critic Geeta Kapur notes, Varma's work and its reception underscore multiple tensions of early Indian modernity: between the regional and the national, the indigenous and the foreign, the aristocratic and the bourgeois, "high" art and "low" art.[13] Varma was "as much an imperialist as he was a nationalist," in that his work spoke to a burgeoning nationalist sentiment as much as it confirmed a colonial, orientalizing view of the so-called East, particularly in its depiction of Indian women. As art critic Christopher Pinney writes, Varma's works then stand as "masterpieces of liminality, positioned as they are between different audiences, both Indian nationalists and the British elite, and between secular ideals and Hindu thematics."[14]

I am especially interested in the status of the regional, and particularly of Kerala, in Varma's work. The subjects of many of his oil paintings were drawn from his own social milieu: these are portraits of the regional elite of Kerala, many of them belonging to the Nair community. The Nairs historically constituted the dominant landowning caste community in Kerala and followed a matrilineal system of social organization and property inheritance. A vast majority of Varma's portraits are of women, and a significant number of these are specifically of idealized Nair women; Saloni Mathur notes that the "European-like grace, neo-classical features and ivory skin" of these figures are conjoined with their regionally inflected clothing, hairstyles, and jewelry.[15] Varma's mapping of regional difference onto the bodies of women is particularly apparent in the consignment of paintings that he sent to the 1893 World's Fair in Chicago. Here he showed a series of ten paintings, which he named *Native Peoples of India*, all of them portraits of Indian women from various regions and of different religious affiliations. His work was extremely well received at the World's Fair, and the prize that he subsequently won was heralded in India as both a regional and a national victory. Significantly, Varma's work was displayed not in the fine arts section but in the ethnographic section, and the prize was for the work's "ethnological value" rather than its artistic merit. Mathur argues that Varma's experience at the World's Fair makes clear how he was both trapped by and challenged the terms of orientalist discourse even as he attempted to produce a nationalist visual iconography. His painting *A Galaxy of Musicians* (1899), for instance, depicts a band of female musicians representing the different regions of India. A number of critics have noted that the portrait provides the visual equivalent of the nationalist slogan of "unity in diversity." This motto is "one the foundational myths of the modern secular democracy…mobilized to support the creation of a sovereign state out of the disparate remnants of British colonialism."[16] The regional, embodied in the idealized and orientalized figures of women, is evoked only to be contained in the service of the larger Indian nation. The painting is symptomatic of how Varma's work in general acknowledged and simultaneously disavowed regional, linguistic, and religious difference. Furthermore, the "India" that emerges in his work is based on a Hindu ideal, once again embodied in his images of feminine respectability and devotion, that effectively wipes out Islamic, Christian, and Buddhist histories in the making of an Indian past and present.[17]

Ravi Varma, *A Galaxy of Musicians* (1889).

Varma continuously indexes and resolves the region/nation tension by subsuming the region to the nation. This is particularly clear in his portrait *There Comes Papa* (1893), one of the ten paintings exhibited at the Chicago World's Fair. Crucially, the transformation of the region into an entity that buttresses rather than challenges a nationalist project hinges on the simultaneous transformation of gender and sexual ideologies. The portrait depicts an upper-class Nair woman holding her infant son and gesturing to the arrival of the father, who is out of the frame but around which the entire scene is organized. We can read this image as speaking quite directly to the rapidly changing gender and sexual norms of turn-of-the-century Kerala, as the system of matriliny that governed the Nairs and other communities in Kerala up to the mid-nineteenth century gave way to a patriarchal, patrilineal nuclear family structure. Matriliny was in fact legislated out of existence in Kerala through a series of laws enacted between 1887 and 1976, first by the British colonial government and then by the postcolonial Indian state.[18] There is a remarkable consonance and continuity in the language

Ravi Varma, *There Comes Papa* (1893).

and logic deployed by Indian reformers and British authorities during the colonial period, and by postindependence Indian lawmakers, in their zeal to transform existing gender and sexual norms in Kerala. For all these state actors, matriliny and the system of female-centered households around which it was organized were deemed barbarous, primitive, immoral, and uncivilized, archaic social forms that had to be abolished in order for Kerala to enter into the temporality of the modern nation. In other words, Kerala's modernity and its entrance into the national imaginary were purchased quite explicitly through excising its matrilineal past and establishing the primacy of what historian J. Devika terms the "ideal monogamous conjugal patrifocal unit" in its stead.[19] As Ritty Lukose writes:

> Among a variety of caste-based movements with different and overlapping traditions of kinship and inheritance, the nuclear family ideal, founded on monogamous sexual arrangements, became the focus of reform. Each group subordinated women's roles to the production of a new kind of modern family and its attendant domestic arrangements. Each understood this ideal as the "liberation" of women from barbaric caste practices through the workings of a modern and progressive public.[20]

As Lukose implies, the critique of matriliny was part of a broader, widespread critique of class and caste hierarchies on the part of these social reformers. A full discussion of the complexities of the history and politics of social reform in Kerala is beyond the scope of this essay. Here I want merely to underscore the ways in which the disparate interests of various social groups coalesced around a vision of modernity that entailed the production of conjugal domesticity and the nuclear family as the norm, one that strategically deployed Victorian notions of sexual and gender respectability.[21]

There Comes Papa, then, must be read within this contested history; the painting marks the precise moment when the particular sexual and gendered logics of the region were being translated into the more intelligible, patriarchal logic of the nation. Indeed, the painting itself enacts and colludes in this transformation. As historian G. Anurima writes in her reading of the portrait:

> The absent yet approaching Papa signifies the crisis in Nayar matriliny in the late nineteenth century. The fact that Ravi Varma chose to celebrate conjugal domesticity and the nuclear family at a time when these were comparatively unknown amongst large sections of the matrilineal population reveals his growing patrilineal sensibilities. *There Comes Papa* becomes akin to a clarion call for the end of matriliny.[22]

In marking this shift from matriliny to conjugal domesticity that the painting thematizes, I do not mean to suggest that there was a corresponding, neat shift from female empowerment and freedom to the strictures of patriarchal oppression. Indeed, feminist historians of Kerala such as G. Anurima have carefully detailed how matriliny functioned in tandem with, not in opposition to, patriarchy and caste and class hierarchies.[23] My intent here is not to imply that there existed, prior to the establishment of colonial and postcolonial gender and sexual norms, a kind of "golden age" of sexual and gender freedom in Kerala. However, as I argue in greater detail elsewhere, emerging queer scholarship on Kerala suggests that the particular sexual and gendered logic of matriliny may have opened up spaces for nonnormative sexual practices and same-sex intimacies in the past that counter contemporary, hegemonic narratives of gender and sexual normativity enshrined within nationalist modernity.[24] As I will discuss, it is the evocation of this past that is forcefully conjured into the present by queer diasporic art practices.

I have spent some time situating the work of Ravi Varma in the complex history of Indian modernity, because it is only by recognizing how his work colluded in a nationalist project that shut down regional differences, even as it seemed to celebrate them, that we can understand the wry interventions being made by a queer diasporic artist such as David Dasharath Kalal. Kalal's reworkings of three of Varma's most celebrated paintings of Nair women dismantle Varma's region/nation equation. In all three remakes, Kalal superimposes onto the bodies of the demure Indian women of the nationalist imagination the faces of queer diasporic Indian women, all of whom are progressive activists/academics from Kerala/Nair backgrounds. In Kalal's witty and quite brilliant remake of Varma's *There Comes Papa*, for instance, the entire gravitational pull of the painting has shifted away from the father's impending entrance into the scene. The woman's eyes are no longer gazing demurely downward at her son, schooling him in the locus of patriarchal authority. In Kalal's image, the woman gazes directly at the viewer, as does the collie, which has been transformed into a pit bull held by a chain. Neither is waiting for the inevitable entry of the father. Only the child remains static. The upper-middle-class interior of the Nair household in Varma's painting is utterly disaggregated here: only a piece of the original background remains visible to the right. The rest of the background is in shards and connotes exterior landscapes in motion; there also appear to be triangular fragments of what may be the borders of an Islamic miniature above and to the left of the figures. It would be a mistake, however, to read Kalal's composite image as decontextualized postmodern pastiche. Instead, we can read the painting's title, *Not Gonna*, as a refusal to celebrate the advent of patrilineal, conjugal domesticity as the hallmark of a new nationalist subjectivity. It is also a refusal of a nationalist narrative of progress and integration that wipes out regional logics of gender and sexual alterity in its inexorable march toward "national unity." Finally, it is a refusal of the reproductive imperative that bears down on women's bodies, as they are enjoined to (re)produce male nationalist subjects.

In its critique of the nationalist paradigm of "unity in diversity," Kalal's work must also be situated alongside that of contemporary feminist Indian visual artists such as Nalini Malani and Pushpamala N., who have specifically taken on the legacy of Ravi Varma in their work. Malani is a multimedia artist whose work has long been concerned with the gendering of Indian national identity, history, and religious identity. Her initial, explicit engagement with Ravi Varma was in the form of a watercolor entitled *Re-thinking Raja Ravi Varma* (1989), where, as art critic Chaitanya Sambrani writes, "Quoted figures from [Varma's *Galaxy of Musicians*] were presented as being pushed into the margin by the massively articulate form of a female nude that represents an animated conversation with normative notions of Indian womanhood."[25] Malani returned to Varma's *Galaxy of Musicians* in her 2003 video installation entitled *Unity in Diversity*, which responded directly to the horrific 2002 Gujarat massacre where Muslims were slaughtered by Hindu extremists with the tacit and at times explicit complicity of the state government. The ghostly outlines of the orientalized female figures in Varma's painting and quotations from Varma himself overlie the images of contemporary political violence, which are accompanied by spoken testimony describing the atrocities by eyewitnesses. Here, as Sambrani puts it, "The fragile fabric of the national ideal [of "unity in diversity"] is quite literally stretched, torn apart."[26] In both the earlier watercolor and the video installation, Malani uses Varma's work to underscore the contradictions of a secular, modern nationalist project, and the ways in which both women and religious minorities pay the deadly cost of its failure.

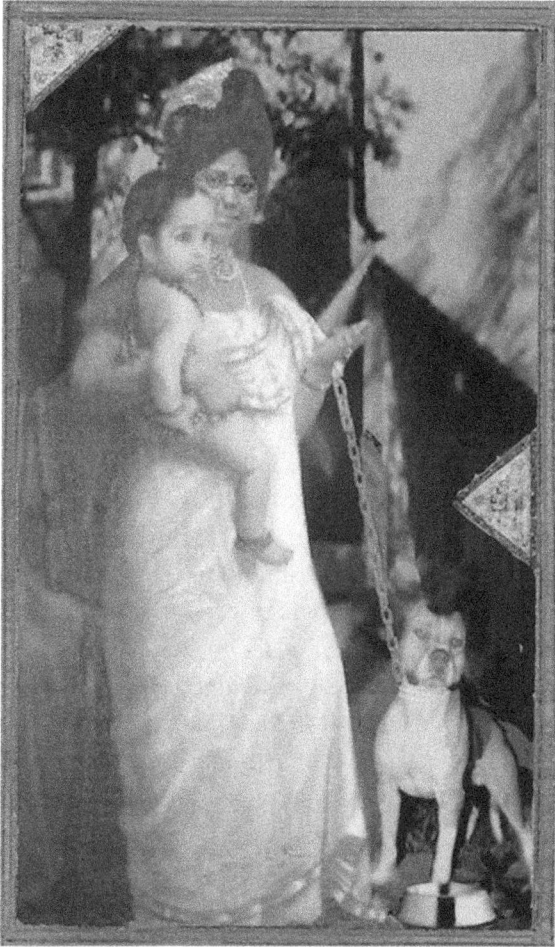

David Dasharath Kalal,
Not Gonna (2005). Image
courtesy of the artist.

Similarly, in a series of photographs entitled *Native Women of South India: Manners and Customs*, the photographer and multimedia artist Pushpamala N. elaborately restages Varma's *Native Peoples of India* paintings by substituting her own body into the frame. As in Malani's work, Pushpamala's photographs ironically comment on the gendered logic of the "unity in diversity" model of the modern Indian nation, but they also respond to the legacies of the orientalizing and classificatory gaze of the colonial state, particularly in terms of an ethnographic project that seeks to document and "know" the natives. As such, Pushpamala's citation practice, as feminist critic Susie Tharu writes, "draws

attention to the continuing presence of colonialism and its schemes in
'free' India."[27] In other words, Pushpamala's restaging of Varma's work
points to the complicity of a modern nationalist project with an earlier
colonial project that disciplines disparate bodies under the surveilling
gaze of the state.[28]

Kalal's project clearly shares with these feminist engagements of
Varma's legacy an interest in pointing to the fissures and violences of
a nationalist project. But while a critique of the nation remains the primary focus of Malani's and Pushpamala's feminist citations of Varma,
Kalal's work parts ways with this work in that the nation is not only
critiqued but radically disaggregated. The axis that Kalal's reworkings
of Varma mobilize is not nation/region as much as it is diaspora/region:
the nation is worked in and through, but is not the singular or primary frame of reference at work in the images. Instead, Kalal's images
in a sense offer us a queer diasporic countervision of the region: the
image dis-integrates the region from its subsumption into the nation.
In this dis-aggregation of the nationalist logic of gender and sexuality
that Varma's paintings so clearly thematize, Kalal's images obliquely reference Kerala's matrilineal history and the particular sexual and gendered logics to which it gave rise. But rather than fixing or fetishizing
this history within a nostalgic narrative of regional exceptionalism,
Kalal evokes this history in the service of what queer critic José Esteban
Muñoz terms "queer utopian memory."

Muñoz understands the "utopian longings" articulated by queer artists and writers, in their evocations of past moments of gay sex and
relationality, to "do the work of letting us critique the present, to see
beyond its 'what is' to worlds of political possibility, of 'what might
be.'"[29] Likewise, we can read Kalal's evocation of a fantasied matrilineal past as an instance of what Muñoz identifies as "a backward glance
that enacts a future vision."[30] This reconstituted past—one that reani-
mates the complex gendered and sexual arrangements that mark Kerala's history prior to the reformist movements of the nineteenth and
twentieth centuries—provides the raw material that forms the present
for the queer diasporic female subject that is at the center of the frame.
As such, Kalal's images suggest a queer, feminist genealogy that resitu-
ates the region as the locus of queer desire, practices, and subjectivity
within a diasporic imaginary. Clearly, Kalal is not interested in bringing

to light a heretofore buried history of Kerala "as it really was": his is not so much a recuperative project as much as it is one that allows us to reflect upon the ways in which, within queer utopian memory, the region suggests alternative formations of desire and relationality that are deemed impossible within the dominant nationalist and diasporic discourses that structure the present moment. Kalal's work thus allows us to access what Muñoz would term a "queer visuality"; in order to do so, writes Muñoz, "we may need to squint, to strain our vision and force it to see otherwise, beyond the limited vista of the here and now."[31] This intimation of another, more capacious future is particularly apparent in Kalal's re-creation of Varma's 1890 portrait, *Lady with Garland*. Here the original background, the domestic interior of a Nair household, is transformed into the interior of an aircraft, the painting's original flower tray into the tray of an airline seat, and the face of Varma's female figure, dressed in traditional Nair garb, is substituted with that of a contemporary queer diasporic academic/activist: the image thus literalizes the region-diaspora axis that I have been referencing throughout this essay. The (Indian) nation ceases to exert quite as strong a gravitational pull on the female subject, suspended as she is between diaspora and region, suggesting alternative horizons of possibility.

The queer diasporic re-visioning of nationalist iconography that we see in Kalal's images emerges specifically from a very particular moment of South Asian queer organizing in New York City in the 1990s in which Kalal was involved: the subjects of all three images are in fact fellow activists and academics who were central to the progressive South Asian social and political landscape of the time. The queer temporality of these images—where a heteronormative nationalist past butts up against a queer diasporic present—disorganizes that inexorable linearity of developmental narratives of modernity. In their apparently anachronistic quality, Kalal's images allow us to see the past queerly; indeed, they allow the queerness of the past to come into focus. This past, situated as it is in the particularities of regional logics of gender and sexuality, is one that the heteronormative logic of both the nation and diaspora seeks to obliterate. Kalal's queer diasporic framing of the region, then, allows for the intimate touching of multiple times and spaces. His work speaks to what queer literary scholar Carolyn Dinshaw terms "the possibility of touching across time, collapsing time

through affective contact between marginalized people now and then";
Dinshaw suggests that these "queer historical touches" enable the formation of " communities across time."³² Kalal's work produces precisely
a kind of affective genealogy and transtemporal sense of community
that links contemporary queer diasporic subjects to the queer(ed) past
of the region. In so doing, his work allows us to approach those alternative sexual and gendered logics that exist in the interstices of hegemonic
nationalist, diasporic, and transnational formations. It is also from the
vantage point of a queer diasporic present that we can place multiple
geographic locations within a shared conceptual space. Kalal's queer
diasporic reframing of the region allows us to place rural Kerala and,
say, Roderick Ferguson's rural Georgia into a single frame: it does so
by suggesting that there are fruitful connections to be drawn between
these disparate "southern" regions, marked as they are by an ex-centric
relation to dominant nationalist and transnational narratives of progress and development.

In closing, I want to reflect on the centrality of the autobiographical
and the place of the self, as artist, as subject, and as critic, to the project of queering the region. We can think here of Ferguson's turn to the
autobiographical in his detailing of the specificities of place and region
as moments of recalcitrance to the logic of the nation, and of Pushpamala's insertion of her own body into the frame of Varma's images.
Kalal's queer diasporic re-visioning of Varma also mobilizes the autobiographical in crucial ways. In one of his remakes of Varma's popular lithographs of Hindu mythology, Kalal substitutes his own face for
that of the god Krishna. The original Varma image, entitled *Gorgeous
Krishna*, is now rebaptized *Who's Your Daddy?* Kalal disrupts Varma's
idealization of the Indian nation as implicitly Hindu with the insertion
of a Jesus figure at the bottom of the image, as well as with his evocation
of Islamic miniature art in the image's framing. The title can be read
as referencing Kalal's own search for an alternative personal, aesthetic,
and artistic genealogy. As a queer diasporic artist, Kalal grapples with
the legacy of Ravi Varma as the "daddy" of modern Indian art and as a
central figure in the production of nationalist iconography. We can see
Kalal's act of placing himself in the center of the frame as his rejection
of a patrilineal nationalist genealogy and a suggestion of an alternative

David Dasharath Kalal,
Who's Your Daddy? (2005).
Image courtesy of the artist.

one that foregrounds the non-Hindu, the perverse, the nonreproductive, the female, the diasporic.

As I was entering into the research for this essay, I was startled to come across Ravi Varma's very first oil painting, a portrait commissioned in 1870 by a prominent Nair family. The image, *The Kazhikke Palat Krishna Menon Family*, portrays the family of Krishna Menon, a subjudge in the Tiruvitamkoor district of Kerala and a member of a wealthy landowning family from north Kerala. Aesthetically, Varma has not yet developed his distinctive style that combines Western academic realism with "indigenous" subject matter. The perspective here is flat, more in keeping with the indigenous art forms that preceded the establishment of colonial art education in India. Yet like the later *There Comes Papa*, the painting grants an ontological certainty to a patrilineal conjugal household that was only just coming into existence in Kerala in 1870. As G. Anurima writes in her reading of the painting:

> How strange…that this portrait was painted in matrilineal Kerala at a time when most of the Nayars, Krishna Menon's caste, would have been unused to living in patrilocal nuclear families, let alone anything that remotely resembled the western bourgeois family. The gravity given to this form of the family by Ravi Varma, himself a matrilineal man, points…to a changing sensibility within Kerala regarding matriliny.[33]

I was taken aback to realize that the Krishna Menon portrayed in the image is in fact my own great-great-great-grandfather. My great-great-grandmother is the little girl in the image. She went on to marry one C. Sankaran Nair, my great-great-grandfather, who, I found out, was the architect of the Malabar marriage bill that some twenty years later sought to legislate matriliny out of existence in Kerala. Like Krishna Menon, both Sankaran Nair and his son, R. M. Palat, were civil servants in the British colonial administration. Palat, my great-granduncle, went on to be the architect of the 1933 bill that further dismantled the matrilineal system. This essay, then, is in a sense a response to and negotiation with this past from the vantage point of a diasporic present. Kalal's

Ravi Varma, *The Kazhikke Palat Krishna Menon Family* (1870).

images force me to grapple with my own particular patrilineal genealogy; they allow me to make sense of this past and reframe it in terms of
a queer diasporic genealogy, one that negotiates between the region, the
nation, and the diasporic in novel ways. Thinking through the autobiographical demands that we map the connections between the personal,
the regional, and the diasporic as they take shape over various bodily,
psychic, and geographic landscapes.

As I have suggested, the category of "queer" in Kalal's work names a
way of reading the past so that the perverse and the antinormative come
into view. It is a way of resignifying histories, practices, and desires that
are systematically effaced by both heteronormative nationalist and diasporic narratives. There is, following Muñoz, a kind of utopian strain
in the work, in that it is reaching back to an occluded past (which may
never have really been) in order to imagine a queer diasporic present.
What does it mean to insist on the queer, the female, the diasporic, the
impure, and the inauthentic at this particular historical moment, when
South Asian diasporic communities have been subjected to unprecedented forms of state terror? To my mind it speaks to the endlessly creative ways in which queer of color/queer diasporic communities continue to insist on the possibility of other ways of imagining collectivity,
desire, and relationality.

NOTES

I am grateful to Miabi Chatterji and Manu Vimalassery for their careful and
incisive readings of earlier versions of this essay; I have incorporated many of
their suggestions here. My thanks also to David Dasharath Kalal for sharing his
work with me, to Manijeh Moradian for her able research assistance, and to Tei
Okamoto for his invaluable feedback and support.

1. Bernard Cohn, "Regions Subjective and Objective," in *An Anthropologist among
Historians and Other Essays* (New York: Oxford University Press, 1987), 113. I am
grateful to Saloni Mathur for pointing me to Cohn's essay.
2. See Gayatri Gopinath, "Queer Regions: Locating Lesbians in *Sancharram*," in *A
Companion to Lesbian, Gay, Bisexual, Transgender, and Queer Studies*, ed. George
Haggerty and Molly McGarry (New York: Routledge, 2008), 341–353, for a more
detailed discussion of the use of the "region" within recent area studies scholarship. In these rearticulations of the region, the region is a preferred term over
the "local," as the latter is often framed as a stable, transparent, and parochial
entity, as opposed to the fluidity and cosmopolitanism of the "global." The

region, for these scholars, importantly avoids replicating this global/local binary and instead stresses the relational aspect of all notions of space and scale.

3. Tejaswini Niranjana, *Mobilizing India: Women, Music and Migration between India and Trinidad* (Durham, NC: Duke University Press, 2006), 13.

4. Niranjana, 1.

5. Ara Wilson, "Queering Asia," *Intersections: Gender, History and Culture in Asian Contexts* no. 14 (November 2006), intersections.anu.edu.au/issue14/Wilson.html.

6. Mark Johnson et al., "Critical Regionalities and the Study of Sex and Gender in South and South East and East Asia," *Culture, Health and Sexuality* 2, no. 4 (2000): 361–375.

7. Niranjana, 38.

8. Roderick Ferguson, "Sissies at the Picnic," in *Think Again* (New York: New York State Black Gay Network, 2003), apla.org/publications/think_again/think_again.pdf.

9. For instance, recent critical work on the U.S. South illuminates the ways in which "the South" is represented as an abjected, atavistic regional other to the modern space of the nation. This work thus points to the ways in which the region can both undermine and buttress national progress narratives simultaneously. See Gopinath for a more thorough engagement with this work in "new Southern studies."

10. Ritty Lukose, *Liberalization's Children: Gender, Youth, and Consumer Citizenship in India* (Durham, NC: Duke University Press, 2010), 24.

11. Lukose, 25.

12. Saloni Mathur, *India by Design: Colonial History and Cultural Display* (Berkeley: University of California Press, 2007), 103.

13. Geeta Kapur, as quoted in Mathur, 104.

14. Christopher Pinney, as quoted in Mathur, 103.

15. Mathur, 104.

16. Chaitanya Sambrani, "Apocalypse Recalled: The Historical Discourse of Nalini Malani," in *Nalini Malani: Stories Retold* (New York: Bose Pacia Gallery, 2004), np.

17. Geeta Kapur, as quoted in Mathur, 103.

18. Gopinath, 350.

19. For an extended discussion of how reformist movements focused not only on the establishment of conjugal domesticity but also on the disciplining of the female body in particular, see J. Devika, "The Aesthetic Woman: Re-forming Female Bodies and Minds in Early Twentieth Century Keralam," *Modern Asian Studies* 39, no. 2 (2005): 461–487.

20. Lukose, 13.

21. G. Anurima, *There Comes Papa: Colonialism and the Transformation of Matriliny in Kerala, Malabar c. 1850–1940* (New Delhi: Orient Longman, 2003), 22.

22. Anurima, 1.

23. See Anurima for a detailed social history of matriliny in Kerala and its multiple implications for women's rights and empowerment. She writes, "Matrilineal

families were not characterised by 'mother right' or women's power in any uncomplicated sense. Equally, the contention that matrilineal communities were merely an avuncular form of patriarchy, where the figure of the uncle replaced the husband/father, is also untenable." Anurima, 13.

24. Gopinath, 350. For an exemplary instance of innovative queer regional scholarship, see in particular T. Muraleedharan, "The Writing on Absent (Stone) Walls: Pleasurable Intimacies in Southern India," *Thamyris* 5, no. 1 (Spring 1998): 41–57.

25. Sambrani, np.

26. Sambrani, np.

27. Susie Tharu, "This Is Not an Inventory: Norms and Performance in Everyday Femininity," in *Native Women of South India: Manners and Customs*, ed. Pushpamala N. and Clare Arni (Bangalore: India Foundation for the Arts, 2004), 13.

28. My thanks to Saloni Mathur for pointing me to the work of both Malani and Pushpamala.

29. José Esteban Muñoz, *Cruising Utopia: The Then and There of Queer Futurity* (New York: NYU Press, 2010), 38.

30. Muñoz, 5.

31. Muñoz, 22.

32. Carolyn Dinshaw et al., "Theorizing Queer Temporalities: A Roundtable Discussion," *GLQ* 13, nos. 2–3 (2007): 178.

33. G. Anurima, "Face Value: Ravi Varma's Portraiture and the Project of Colonial Modernity," *Indian Economic Social History Review* 40, no. 57 (2003): 60.

REFERENCES

Anurima, G. "Face Value: Ravi Varma's Portraiture and the Project of Colonial Modernity." *Indian Economic Social History Review* 40, no. 57 (2003): 57–79.

———. *There Comes Papa: Colonialism and the Transformation of Matriliny in Kerala, Malabar c. 1850–1940.* New Delhi: Orient Longman, 2003.

Cohn, Bernard. *An Anthropologist among Historians and Other Essays.* New York: Oxford University Press, 1987.

Devika, J. "The Aesthetic Woman: Re-forming Female Bodies and Minds in Early Twentieth Century Keralam." *Modern Asian Studies* 39, no. 2 (2005): 461–487.

Dinshaw, Carolyn, et al. "Theorizing Queer Temporalities: A Roundtable Discussion." *GLQ* 13, nos. 2–3 (2007): 177–195.

Ferguson, Roderick. "Sissies at the Picnic." In *Think Again.* New York: New York State Black Gay Network (2003). apla.org/publications/think_again/think_again.pdf.

Gopinath, Gayatri. "Queer Regions: Locating Lesbians in *Sancharram*." In *A Companion to Lesbian, Gay, Bisexual, Transgender, and Queer Studies*, edited by George Haggerty and Molly McGarry. New York: Routledge, 2008.

Johnson, Mark, et al. "Critical Regionalities and the Study of Sex and Gender in South and South East and East Asia." *Culture, Health and Sexuality* 2, no. 4 (2000): 361–375.

Lukose, Ritty. *Liberalization's Children: Gender, Youth, and Consumer Citizenship in India*. Durham, NC: Duke University Press, 2010.

Mathur, Saloni. *India by Design: Colonial History and Cultural Display*. Berkeley: University of California Press, 2007.

Muñoz, José Esteban. *Cruising Utopia: The Then and There of Queer Futurity*. New York: NYU Press, 2010.

Muraleedharan, T. "The Writing on Absent (Stone) Walls: Pleasurable Intimacies in Southern India." *Thamyris* 5, no. 1 (Spring 1998): 41–57.

Niranjana, Tejaswini. *Mobilizing India: Women, Music and Migration between India and Trinidad*. Durham, NC: Duke University Press, 2006.

Sambrani, Chaitanya. "Apocalypse Recalled: The Historical Discourse of Nalini Malani." In *Nalini Malani: Stories Retold*, edited by Rhana Devenport and Chaitanya Sambrani. New York: Bose Pacia Gallery, 2004.

Tharu, Susie. "This Is Not an Inventory: Norms and Performance in Everyday Femininity." In *Native Women of South India: Manners and Customs*, edited by Pushpamala N. and Clare Arni. Bangalore: India Foundation for the Arts, 2004.

Wilson, Ara. "Queering Asia." *Intersections: Gender, History and Culture in Asian Contexts* 14 (November 2006). intersections.anu.edu.au/issue14/Wilson.html.

12

Awaiting the Twelfth Imam in the United States

South Asian Shia Immigrants and the Fragmented American Dream

RAZA MIR AND FARAH HASAN

On September 11, 2007, the phone in our house rang too early to bear any good news. On the line was Kulsoom, the daughter of Kazim Bhai and Batool Aapa,[1] friends from Jersey City. Apparently, as they had slept in their illegally sublet basement, their landlord had been awakened by members of the Department of Homeland Security, who had demanded to know who else was living in the house. The petrified landlord had led them to the basement. The officers had asked the entire family to produce proof that they were legal residents of the United States. Only Kulsoom, who was a student at a New York college, had a valid visa. Kazim Bhai and Batool Aapa had then been arrested and taken to a detention center in downtown New York, where they were being held for "processing."

In the subsequent weeks, we were to become intimately acquainted with the protocols to which detained undocumented immigrants in the

United States were subjected. The process, while far more humane than we had feared, was nonetheless terrifying to this couple. Batool Aapa was released that very afternoon, in a paternalistic act of generosity by the officials, who (rightly) assumed that with her husband behind bars, she was not a flight risk. Kazim Bhai was quickly convicted of the offense of illegally overstaying in the United States and was transported to an immigration detention center in northern New Jersey. It took us one full week to bail him out, by which time he was a nervous wreck, having lost several pounds (among other things, he tried not to eat anything that might contain non-halal meat products).

In the year and more since this event, we have continuously tried to figure out ways in which this couple, who have lived in the United States for a decade, can avoid being deported. While we have, in many different ways, tried to persuade them to begin accepting the possibility that they may have to return to the economic uncertainty that characterized their life in India, their attitude appears almost irrationally optimistic. But one day, a few things fell into place. Responding to our frustrations at their inability to make contingency plans, they shyly admitted we were not the only people helping them with their case. Apparently, they had invoked "higher authorities," who were really the source of their optimism. On the 20th of Jamadussani,[2] Batool Aapa had been to the Astaana-e-Zehra,[3] a Shia *imambargah*[4] in central Jersey. That is a very special day in the Shia calendar, denoting the birthday of Bibi Fatima, the daughter of the prophet Muhammad. Women were especially active during its observances. In the Astaana-e-Zehra, Batool Aapa had lit a special lamp and made a direct request to Bibi Fatima to intercede on behalf of her condition. Likewise, Kazim Bhai had performed a special *maatam*[5] on the day of Ashoora[6] at the Al-Khoei Center in Queens, New York,[7] and was steadfast in his conviction that Imam Husain would intercede on his behalf with whoever it was that was making decisions on his case.

Irrespective of the eventual decision in their case, three things were clear. First, there was some truth to the couple's claim that their Shia faith was their bulwark against deportation. After all, it was the emerging social network of South Asian Shias in the United States that had fostered our own relationship with this couple. Thus, while we may discount the spiritual causality produced by Kazim Bhai and Batool Aapa between their faith and their ability to engage in a legal argument with the Department of Homeland Security (despite being unlettered in English and undocumented in status), their Shia identity had proved advantageous to the process. Second, despite any secular reservations we may have about their faith, it was evident that their belief in divine intercession had guaranteed that they went about their affairs with a modicum of confidence. Kazim Bhai drove his car past police cruisers with a prayer on his lips, and Batool Aapa managed to find a job as a nanny. Finally, despite its transcendent aspects, their faith was locally anchored. The rituals at the Astaana-e-Zehra and the Al-Khoei Center carried a sense of tangible and liminal materiality, and evoked a cultural continuity with an identifiable spiritual tradition. Their invocations for direct intercession were immeasurably strengthened by the artifacts from South Asia that were deployed, such as prayers (*munajaat*) chanted in Urdu, foods that carried the remembered significance of spiritual gathering, and collectively shared rituals. It is safe to say that the Shia experience played a major role in instilling a coping ability in Kazim Bhai and Batool Aapa.

Our empirical explorations have provided us with two interrelated conclusions. First, the greatest challenge to the community emerges not so much from its ability to deal with cultural heterogeneity across its immigrant congregation, but from the heterogeneities of economic class, which play out in subtle ways in the cultural dynamics of its rituals. Second, the general climate of Islamophobia in the broader U.S. sphere has produced new tensions within the community. The dialogue between those who advocate that the community create a safe cultural space for itself by acquiescing to U.S. policy and those who prefer an adversarial, civil rights–oriented engagement with the U.S. mainstream is intensifying and is bound to become contentious over time.

In the rest of this chapter, we attempt three interrelated tasks. First, we offer a brief history of the South Asian Shia community. We then describe a *majlis*[8] in New Jersey, which represents some of the important cultural practices of the community. Finally, we discuss the Shia community response to the pressures of transnationalism.[9]

Shias in the United States

It has been estimated that Shias constitute around 1.7 percent of the world population (Momen, 1985: 282), which would put their current population at around 115 million. A surprisingly large proportion of these Shias have South Asian origins. While Shias form the majority of the population in three nations, namely, Iran (88 percent), Iraq (57 percent), and Bahrain (54 percent), they are relatively underrepresented in much of the rest of the Middle East and in Southeast Asia. In South Asia, Shias are a significant minority in India (around 1.8 percent of the total population), Pakistan (14.5 percent), and Afghanistan (5.9 percent). Based on these ratios and the current estimate of the populations of these three countries (Central Intelligence Agency, 2008), one arrives at a tentative figure of around 60 million South Asian Shias, not counting the diasporic populations of the Middle East, East Africa, the United Kingdom, and the United States.

The history of Shias in the United States must be understood in the context of the broader contours of Muslim migration across the Atlantic, which presents a tale of continuous adaptation and negotiation. No surviving Muslim identities remain from the time that African Muslim slaves reached the shores of North America (Diouf, 1998), but Muslim identity began to take tentative root after the initial Arab migrations of the late nineteenth century (Haddad and Lumis, 1987). Over time, the Muslim community in the United States has grown substantially, through migration, conversions, and the emergence of second and third generations. Population estimates of U.S. Muslims are widely divergent; while the CIA factbook suggests that 2 million citizens of the United States identify as Muslim, the Council of American Islamic Relations declared in 2001 that U.S. Muslims numbered 6 million (Bagby, 2001). Based on the CIA factbook estimates, it would be reasonable to conclude that around 300,000 people in the estimate identify as Shia, but internal estimates place the Shia population in the United States at 1.8 million.[10]

The first Shia community in the United States emerged among the Arab immigrants of Dearborn, Michigan. Gravitating to the automobile plants of the Detroit area in the post–World War I era, Arab Americans began to create a social and cultural space for themselves. In the 1950s and beyond, Shias of Lebanese descent began to distance themselves from the pan-Islamic community under the charismatic leadership of Sheikh Jawad Chirri, culminating in the establishment of the first Shia mosque, the Islamic Center of America, in 1953 (Takim, 2002; Walbridge, 1997).[11] This observant community contrasts with Iranians in California, who are mostly nonobservant[12] and have taken great pains to distance themselves both from the public and demonstrative Shiism that characterizes the political landscape of current Iran, and from the more devout but politically quiet South Asian Shias (Bozorgmehr, 1997).

While the influx of educated South Asians into the United States following the 1965 initiatives is well documented,[13] a relatively recent phenomenon also concerns the immigration of "refugees from neoliberalism," or people who were dispossessed and rendered economic refugees in their lands after the green revolution and structural adjustment policies redistributed their meager earnings upward.[14] For example, Mathew (2008: 147–176) makes a clear link between the changes in landholding patterns created by the green revolution in Pakistan and India and the larger presence of South Asian taxi drivers in Manhattan. Many dispossessed South Asians ended up in the United States through a variety of circuits, from relatively tame ones like family-reunification initiatives by their U.S. citizen relatives and the green card lotteries of Pakistan and Bangladesh, to more perilous voyages, and many among them occupy the uncertain terrain inhabited by "illegals" in the U.S. economy. The Shias among them, of whom Batool Aapa, Kazim Bhai, and many such form a part, are also integral participants in the social and cultural landscape of the community.[15] While engaging with the mainstream in highly tentative fashion, they use institutions such as the network of New York–New Jersey *imambargahs* as spaces to enact a more self-possessed identity.

Shab-e-Ashoor at the Astaana-e-Zehra

It is nearly midnight at the Astaana-e-Zehra in Englishtown on the night of January 18, 2008. But the hall is packed with people, most certainly to the point where a visit by the fire marshal could lead to the event being shut down. The congregation is gender-segregated and extremely emotional as a *majlis* proceeds through its traditionally determined segments, some of which involve group chanting, contributing substantially to the decibel level in the hall. Around 400 men gather in a hall that would appear full with 200. A similar number of women crowd the basement. The air is redolent with odors of flowers and incense. It is *Shab-e-Ashoor*, the night before Ashoora, the holiest of days in the Shia calendar. In faraway Iraq, the shrine of Imam Husain in Karbala must already be bathed in the morning light, crowded with millions of mourning pilgrims.[16]

Sarfaraz Naqvi, one of the founder-trustees of the Astaana (as it is known by its congregation), appears tense. It is his unenviable job (along with other organizers and volunteers) to herd the community and ensure a space of decorum in a manner that does not attract the wrath of the residents of this quiet borough in central New Jersey. The 300 or so cars have to be parked in an orderly fashion; the community has to be exhorted to remain quiet when on the road, for fear of disturbing the citizens of the assisted-living facility that is the Astaana's neighbor. Today's gathering is about one-third the size of the entire population (1,764) of Englishtown,[17] once one of the headquarters for the American army in the Revolutionary War. The Astaana lies less than half a mile away from the still-standing Village Inn, where George Washington prepared papers in 1778 court-martialing Charles Lee, the general whose tactical errors had cost the Continental Army a sure victory in the Battle of Monmouth.[18] In 1778, Sarfaraz Naqvi's paternal ancestors had been living in Iraq, while his maternal ancestors had been residents of Iran. Their migratory patterns eventually took them through Central Asia to the South Indian city of Vellore, where his great-grandfather founded an *imambargah* also called the Astaana-e-Zehra. Mr. Naqvi's father, Mohammed Ali, then migrated to the city of Hyderabad, where he served as the president of the All India Shia Conference, a national clearinghouse of *imambargahs* in India. Mr. Mohammed Ali Naqvi migrated to the United States in the 1970s with his seven children and immediately began to mobilize community support around building an *imambargah*. His initial efforts led to the foundation of a religious school in 1984, which began its activities at the Saint Thomas Lutheran Church in Manalapan. In 1989, with support from the community, he formed a nonprofit organization called the Ahle Baith Foundation. The foundation found that an existing religious establishment, a Pentecostal church called the Bethlehem Prayer House, was for sale and mobilized the collective energy among the Shias of New Jersey to purchase it.[19] In the tradition of his ancestral *imambargah*, he named it Astaana-e-Zehra as well. Over time, the space at the Astaana has become far too small for the congregation it supports, and the organizers have begun an ambitious drive to collect money for a new building.[20]

These series of accidents of personal history have led to tonight's gathering of South Asian Shias in Englishtown. Many in the gathering have driven here from far away, for no observant Shia can abide being anywhere but at a *majlis* on *Shab-e-Ashoor*. The night is bitterly cold, but several people simply cannot squeeze into the hall. They huddle outside, and the din of ambient conversation increases—further convincing the organizers that they need to think of moving to more spacious premises soon.

The *majlis* proceeds based on a template established over centuries in South Asia, and from earlier Iranian templates. First, we have the *sozkhwani*, or the recitation of poetry, sung to familiar rhythms, extolling the wisdom and the valor of the twelve Imams, the prophet Muhammad, his daughter Bibi Fatima, and other spiritual leaders. The poems typically move from exuberant praises of the holy figures to laments about their plight as they faced death with bravery and honor. Tonight's *majlis* is dedicated to the memory of Shahzada Ali Asghar, Imam Husain's six-month-old infant son, whose death at Karbala is one of the most evocative symbols of Imam Husain's helplessness, as well as the implacable brutality of his enemies, members of the army of Yazid, the tyrant Umayyad ruler of Damascus.

As the poems move into the grieving stage with the chanting of the *marsiya* (a form of lament poem),[21] the atmosphere during the *sozkhwani* quickly dissolves into a frank expression of sadness by the crowd that would be difficult to explain to a Western audience, among whom public displays of grief are rare. Several men cry loudly and unselfconsciously, and their wails mix with similar sounds emerging from the women's section. Miraculously, the audience composes itself for the next session, a scheduled speech of about an hour by a *maulvi*,[22] who has, in this case, especially flown in from the United Kingdom for the observances of the first ten days of Mohurrum. Syed Ali Raza Rizvi, a tall, slight man in his early thirties, was born in Lahore, Pakistan, and is fluently bilingual. As he begins in English, volunteers herd in a large number of boys aged between seven and sixteen into the crowded room. These youngsters often stay outside the hall during the *majlis*, protesting that the Urdu proceedings do not make much sense to them. Now, an informal deal between them and their parents allows them to play outside during the stage of *sozkhwani*, but their presence is mandated when the proceedings are in English. The bilingual character of the *majlis* is primarily a nod to the younger generation, but it does have the effect of accommodating other immigrants in the congregation who do not speak Urdu well. Ali Raza Rizvi's bilingual speeches have been identified as a coup of sorts by the Astaana administrators, for he has managed to engage the interest of the youth not just because of his fluency in English but also because of his even more uncommon ability to engage with them in their idiom, and his sensitivity to the fact that their concerns may not be the same as those of their parents' generation.

Typically, a *maulvi*'s speech has two components. The first, termed *fazail* in South Asian circles, involves a mixture of Koranic exegesis, praising the Prophet and his progeny, and exuberant affirmations of Shia identity. The second, referred to as *masaib*, take the listeners back into the zone of grief, as the speaker narrates some event of the Battle of Karbala, which involves and highlights the suffering of the Imam and his followers. It is generally felt that the *masaib* cannot be narrated in English with the same emotional intensity as an Urdu speech can (although the cultural split of English-as-rational and Urdu-as-emotional is ripe for challenge by a new generation of homegrown Shia speakers). In this case, bowing to the prevailing stylistic hegemony, Ali Raza Rizvi seamlessly moves to Urdu after about half an hour. Some, but by no means all, youngsters seize the moment to make another exit to the outdoors. Tonight's *masaib* are especially intense. The community is alive to the realization that the next sunrise brings *Aashoor* and all its collective psychic pain back into their lives. The story of six-month-old Ali Asghar is also a moment of pure grief, a true metaphor for helplessness, fortitude, maternal and paternal anguish, and the loneliness of the Imam-hero at the moment of self-sacrifice. The audience is moved to a crescendo of grief as the *maulvi* concludes his speech. As the speech ends, the lights in the hall are turned off, and in the near darkness, the organizers bring out the replica of a cradle, festooned with flowers and draped in black. In the background, a *nauha* (another form of lament poem) is chanted through the public address system. The members of the congregation gets on their feet, and everyone surges toward the cradle, to touch it, to express their grief, and, in cases like Kazim Bhai and others, to make a supplication to the martyrs of Karbala and plead for intercession in their worldly problems. It is truly a moment of intense collective emotion both raw in its immediacy and recalling a tradition shaped over 1,300 years of the community's history.

The cradle and other replicas are then taken over to the *zanaana* (ladies section), where the women have gathered to be part of the same *majlis.* In an act of hybridization, the women do not passively partake of the mens' *majlis* but supplement it with some independent proceedings. While the women in South Asia have developed their own circuit of *majalis* independent of men (and find in it a way to express their autonomy and enterprise), the women at the Astaana are constrained to join in with the menfolk, for there is not enough separable space to conduct two completely independent functions. A good *maulvi* is difficult to find, and there are not many women in North America who can deliver a complete *majlis*, especially in more than one language. At the same time, the women find ways in which to express their devotion (and their talents) with some level of autonomy. Over the years, a separate circuit of women's *majalis* has emerged, and the new building proposed by the leadership of the Ahle Baith Foundation is expressly aimed at offering women the autonomy to conduct their own program without any need for male input.

The *zanaana* at the Astaana is a separate but flexible physical space, usually consisting of half of the function hall partitioned with movable screens. On a night like *Shab-e-Ashoor*, though, this space is reduced to a mere sliver (the men take most of it), and is mostly occupied by older women and those unencumbered with young children. There is a closed-circuit television in the *zanaana* for the women to virtually join in the proceedings. The women also have the whole basement to themselves, which includes a full-size hall equipped with another television set, and a small annex by the kitchen usually filled with little girls (and boys) and mothers with infants and very young children. There is a television set here as well, but the noise made by the children barely leaves anything audible but shouts such as "rock-paper-scissors."

On *Shab-e-Ashoor* and other such important days, the women start off in the basement with their own *sozkhwani* during which the television set providing a live feed of the men's proceedings is turned off. A *marsiya* is recited (*marsiyas* are mostly performed by first-generation women; the less demanding *nauhas* are sometimes performed by U.S.-born women). Women cry without any inhibition during the *marsiya*, so much that it appears they may well have lost one of their own dear ones. It may well be that they find the emotional space here to let down their guard and cry for whatever might be their life's woes. After the *marsiya*, the television sets are turned on, timed to coincide with the *maulvi* beginning his speech in the men's section. The women turn toward the television set and settle in for the hour-and-a-half-long lecture by Ali Raza Rizvi. Their attitude is participative; they enjoy themselves during the *fazail* and weep piteously during the *masaib*. Understandably, the ability to participate in such a formal process is circumscribed; women with children to mind find the *majlis* quite tedious, since the space is small, and the children tend to get impatient and out of control. Still they are glad to be able to participate in the *majlis* rather than listen to a *majlis* at home over the Internet.[23] The Internet *majlis* has become available only recently because of the increases in data bandwidth available to the community, but it lacks the emotional impact of being in the same space as one's fellow mourners.

Now, however, it is time for *maatam*, where the expression of grief finds a physical outlet. *Maatam* is a typically Shia ritual and involves self-mortification. Tonight, the congregation will primarily raise their hands and strike their chests hard enough for it to sting. Men and women both engage in *maatam*, but for the men, it has arguably become an enactment of their masculinity as well. Not all congregationists engage in the vigorous *maatam*; many stand to the side and listen collectively as the youngsters and some older participants beat their chests in a rhythm that is dictated by a series of *nauhas* recited by a variety of participants. It is interesting to note that the first *nauha* is in Farsi, a language that is the mother tongue of not a single congregant at the Astaana. "Imshab shab-e-maatam-e-Husaina" (Tonight is the night of *maatam* for Husain) chant the congregants, invoking a tradition they brought from Iran to India and Pakistan, and have now transplanted to the sleepy borough where George Washington and Charles Lee had their famous contretemps.

The Wages of Migratory Displacement

> Maanaa ke zamaane ka na hoga yahi aalam
> Tarteeb tamaddun ki ye ho jaayegi barham
> Phir aur kisi rang mein hoga tera maatam
> Duniya ye na hogi, magar Islam rahega
> Shabbir baharhaal tera naam rahega

It is true, that the contours of the world will shift
And the terrain of culture will be turned topsy-turvy
No matter, we will grieve you in different ways
This world is transient, but Islam will remain
Shabbir,[24] under all circumstances, your name will remain. Najam
   Afindi (2000)[25]

The *majlis* at the Astaana provides for us a paradigmatic exemplar of transnationalism within the South Asian Shia community. At one level, some of the practices produce an ineffable sense of anachronism. The modernity of the setting, signified by fluid ethnic identities, metropolitan sensibilities, and live video-casting across spaces, exists alongside much older formations such as gender segregation, the use of incense, and the invocation of 200-year-old poems. The Astaana functions autonomously but finds itself in an informally federated relationship with other such institutions in New Jersey and New York. During the course of a year, around twenty religious leaders may visit the Astaana from different parts of North America, Europe, and South Asia. These speakers become agents of isomorphism as well as heterogeneity, seeding different communities with their ideas, as well as cross-pollinating ideas and information across *imambargahs*. Over time, however, certain *imambargahs* become associated with certain traditions, despite the heterogeneity of their congregatory base. A particular *imambargah* may be seen as being a repository of a South Indian ethos, while another may have a more Punjabi orientation (surprisingly, these do not necessarily reflect the majority ethnic identities displayed in that particular *imambargah*); some might privilege more passionate displays of emotion and longer bouts of *maatam*, while others may prefer workshops and PowerPoint presentations. Institutions that exist outside the space of the *imambargah* also reflect this heterogeneity. Some Shia organizations seek to widen their sphere of concern, such as when the Imamia Medics International[26] organized donations and aid for victims of the January 2010 earthquake in Haiti and took a team of local doctors to Haiti as part of the international medical task force. Others focused on more community-centric efforts, such as providing relief for Shia victims of religious persecution in Pakistan, especially in Parachinar[27] in northwestern Pakistan.

The economic heterogeneities of the U.S. landscape also mediate the spread of the Shia community. Religious centers that exist in urban areas (such as the Al-Khoei Center in Queens, New York, or the Mohammad-iya Center in Paterson, New Jersey) attract larger numbers of working-class members than more suburban centers. Of course the relatively dense population in the New York–New Jersey area makes these divisions less apparent (there are many working-class immigrants in central New Jersey, for instance), but the dynamic does tend to be reinforced at various moments. For instance, the Ahlul Bayt Mosque in Brooklyn has a number of African American converts, as well as members who have been part of the prison-correctional system. This is a relatively unique situation with its own specific history, which can be linked to the perseverance of specific individuals in the mosque community, as well as the disenchantment of several African American Muslim converts with the austere severity being imposed on them by other branches of Islam.[28] At any rate, the specific financial challenges faced by this mosque perhaps makes it deserving of assistance from other centers, whose main financial challenges include augmenting existing buildings and facilities to accommodate growing congregations. That mosque has also taken the lead in creating a soup kitchen, which provides food to local indigents regardless of religious affiliation. The soup kitchen organizers declare the following on their Facebook page: "Without regard to race and religion, we recognize that hunger is a disturbing factor in our community, so we will be creating a soup kitchen in the basement of the mosque…please note that the soup kitchen will be available to EVERYONE regardless of race or religion."[29]

Transnationality also produces a variety of generational and temporal conflicts in the community, which are overlaid further with class heterogeneities. While many "post-1965" Shias have tended to look for ways in which they may find acceptance in the mainstream United States (usually by allying themselves with conservative causes), the younger generation and the later "refugees from neoliberalism" exhibit a far more heterogeneous political approach and tend to be more outspoken against U.S. imperialism and about their experiences with Islamofascism. The specific history of the community perhaps provides a clue to this disconnect. The post-1965 Shias, who were coming into their own in the United States in the 1970s, had flown under the radar of mainstream U.S. consciousness. This changed quite substantially with the 1979 Iranian Revolution and the subsequent U.S. hostage crisis (Farber, 2002). Much of the resentment against Muslims in the United States was focused on the Iranians, and by extension the "Shiites" were presented in the mainstream U.S. press as some sort of a violent and messianic cult. Subsequently, the October 1983 bombing of the U.S. embassy in Beirut, where the primary suspect was Hezbollah, another organization with Shia roots, strengthened the general suspicion of Shias in the mainstream U.S. consciousness. President Reagan's support of the mujahideen fighting the Soviets in Afghanistan, which became an integral part of U.S. policy in the late stages of the Cold War (Mamdani, 2004), was yet another alienating scenario, since many of these fighters were Sunni fundamentalists, whose hatred of Shias was legion. Additionally, the United States had special diplomatic relationships with the Saudi regime, another government that persecuted Shias and denied them civil liberties and religious freedom. Finally, in the Iran-Iraq War that broke out in 1980, the United States supported the regime of Saddam Hussein, who was a known oppressor of Shias. It would be generally accurate to say that the decade of the 1980s was politically difficult for American Shias, as they walked the delicate line between the emerging Islamophobia of the American mainstream and a perception of pro-Sunni diplomatic positions assumed by the U.S. government.[30] While Saddam Hussein fell out of favor with the United States after 1990, the tide did not change substantially. For example, there was hardly any public reaction in the United States when thousands of Hazara Shias were slaughtered in 1998 by the Taliban, the newly emerging rulers of Afghanistan (Rashid, 2001).

The events that followed September 11, 2001, therefore must have presented themselves as an opportunity to those U.S. Shias who had sought to claim a sliver of political space for themselves in the U.S. mainstream, and who saw an opportunity in the fact that the U.S.-Sunni relationship was fracturing on all three fronts (Saudi Arabia, Iraq, and Afghanistan). Some members of the community began to align themselves actively with the U.S. positions, presenting themselves as victims of "Wahhabi" violence all over the world. In our opinion, they were relatively un-thought-out positions, and sometimes Shia leaders even went to the extent of supporting virulent Islamophobes like Daniel Pipes in an attempt to accentuate the Shia-Sunni divide.[31]

However, the later "refugee from neoliberalism" immigrants have a far more direct and immediate understanding of U.S. imperialism, having grown up in political contexts where U.S. foreign policy was seen as dangerous and threatening. They form uneasy and shifting alliances with U.S.-raised Shias, whose experiences while growing up include exposure to naked forms of racism and religious persecution. Counterinitiatives from Shia youth against anti-Sunni movements have led them to link with their Sunni counterparts as well as the broader anti-war movement. Within the Shia community, youth groups have been at the forefront of bridging cultural divides and moving beyond the South Asia–centric paradigms. In June 2006, a Shia-youth-led initiative called Independent Viewpoints[32] conducted a daylong event, which included a dialogue between Sunnis and Shias (moderated by the journalist-activist Amy Goodman) and, in a coup of sorts, managed to have a keynote address by Noam Chomsky. Likewise, the Allied Muslim Youth of North America (AMYNA)[33] is another organization that attempts to help Shia youth engage with the religious and secular spaces in the United States. AMYNA has the following mission: "The AMYNA movement seeks to create a culture of faith-based activism among the young Muslims of North America by connecting and empowering youth initiatives and activists by providing forums, resources and advocacy." Clearly, there are proto-progressive spaces where Shia youth can find acceptance and support, and build bridges with other Muslims and non-Muslims. The intergenerational alliance is uneasy; a common aversion to U.S. imperialism binds the relatively conservative new immigrants to the youth, while an aversion to the Taliban and extremist religious groups such as the Salafis inoculates them against knee-jerk tendencies to view fundamentalist causes as legitimate adversarial responses to Islamophobia.

From an intergenerational standpoint, the religious arena is a space for struggle and incommensurability between generations, but it also carries the potential for harmony and mutual respect. New American Shias struggle with their feelings of having left sanctuary behind but are puzzled when the putative homeland never meets their nostalgic expectations in subsequent meetings. Likewise, the new homeland proves puzzlingly difficult, either to embrace or to scapegoat. Their only hope to understand it is to go to their children, or to their peers born in the Western Hemisphere, and eventually surrender to their wisdom. Likewise,

U.S.-born Shias find that their desire to attain a state of "pure American-ness" is forever interrupted by their brown skin, their curious craving for spicy foods, and their ability to speak in and understand languages that would sound like gibberish to their "regular American" peers. They must look to their parents or to their new-immigrant peers to channel the mythical space that is simultaneously home and not-home. Incommen-surabilities, mutual distastes at each other's habits and attitudes, politics, and aesthetics all have to be managed by both sides of the generational divide, and the South Asian Shia space is another arena where genera-tions kick, scream, and snarl their way toward mutual understanding. The new immigrants manage the initial conditions that make the com-munity possible, the *imambargahs*, the congregations, the templates of *majalis* and other activities. The U.S.-born generation then is tasked with rendering these institutions contemporary, transforming them into idi-oms, metaphors, and cadences that belong to the present. These activi-ties necessarily involve debates and arguments that may not always be harmonious. The transformation of *majalises* from Persian to Urdu in the South Asian spaces a few centuries ago must have been the site of similar struggles. Unfortunately, the community memory is not good enough to channel those experiences. That wheel must be reinvented.

Like many immigrant communities, South Asian Shias in the United States can interest disciplinary social scientists in multiple ways. For instance, an economist might be interested in the dynamics of class and the circuits of labor and capital that are manifested in the com-munity. The story of Kazim Bhai and Batool Aapa is very much a story of circuits of labor and capital, the regimes of dispossession that con-tributed to their migration, and the way in which they earned their living and repatriated some of it to their indigent relatives in India. A psychologist would be interested in how they deployed prayer as a coping mechanism, the stresses they experienced as new immigrants, and specific issues that afflict immigrant groups. A sociologist might wonder how the emerging formal structures such as *imambargahs* in the United States produce legitimacy for themselves, both within the community and in interaction with the broader secular society. These networks of legitimacy are then utilized by immigrants to produce a context for themselves and their place in U.S. society. Anthropologists might see "webs of meaning" in the South Asian Shia experience, while political scientists may analyze the events in light of the broader U.S. experiences with the Shia faith.

But the complexity of the immigrant experience eludes disciplinary boundaries. Neodisciplinary formulations like transnationalism are marginally more helpful, as they allow us to examine how ethnicity, nationality, and religious identity enter into mutual negotiation. For the Shias in the New York area, these discussions are complex. As the cultural minorities within the community develop a critical mass, they are faced with the wrenching decision of how to engage with the broader *ummah* (theological community). Should the Farsi-speaking people of Afghan and Central Asian origins stay at the Mohammadiya Center in Paterson, New Jersey, leaving the Astaana at Englishtown free to imagine itself as a primarily Urdu-centric space? Or should all *imambargahs* attempt to be inclusive of all cultures? How should the Urdu-speaking community of Englishtown reach out to the new African American converts in the Ahlul Bayt Mosque at Brooklyn? Should *imambargahs* continue to focus on providing religious services and rely on the emerging social networks to manage other (economic, gender-oriented, generational) challenges? Will a foray into nonreligious initiatives stretch the community resources too thin? What are the ethical implications of aggressive personal fund-raising in a community where economic heterogeneities may produce alienation among indigent congregants? How do progressive and younger members of the community create a space for their ideas to chip away at what they perceive to be an atmosphere of internalized patriarchy, implicit heteronormativity, and an unexamined classist ethos? Such, then, are the issues that bedevil this spatially dislocated community-in-progress.

Conclusion: A Reimagined Community

South Asian Shias in the United States, over a relatively brief period of less than half a century, have managed to produce an impressive network of institutions that carry the community forward. As is inevitable, the community must grapple with its emerging heterogeneity as it struggles to produce a new identity for itself. In this chapter, we have tried to present a brief set of issues that identify and foreground the dynamics of this American community-under-construction. As members of the community, we see this partly as an act of autoethnography, or of rendering the personal political (Holman Jones, 2005). Our hope is that this analysis of the rhythms of social life of this community finds its way into the sea of American stories, represented sometimes as social science and other times as personal narratives, but ultimately, stories.

As the community sets its roots in the northeastern part of the United States, it confronts two clear challenges: that of the heterogeneity of class positions occupied by its informal membership, and the increasing Islamophobic trends that emerge and get sedimented and legitimized in the mainstream communities they inhabit. In the worsening economy, the travails of marginal community members like Kazim Bhai and Batool Aapa will intensify, and the community may have to reconsider its current spatial dynamics. The relatively wealthy *imambargahs* in the suburbs need to renegotiate their relationship with the urban centers that support a greater portion of the indigent in the congregation. Inability to address this dynamic will produce newer tensions in the community. Likewise, the community needs to renegotiate its approach to U.S. domestic and foreign policy and consider its role in the national discussion on Muslim civil rights. The strategy of distancing the community from Sunnis is shortsighted, as is the community's general quietist attitude in the face of increased discrimination. However, it has been vigorously contested within the community, and that dialogue is likely to get a lot more contentious before resolutions are reached.

Batool Aapa and Kazim Bhai continue to hope that their economic woes will not be exacerbated by deportation. But they take comfort by measuring their pain against the infinite suffering of Imam Husain and by balancing their waiting for communiqués from the Department of Homeland Security with the far more significant wait for the arrival of the Twelfth Imam, the savior of the pious.

NOTES

All websites mentioned in endnotes were last accessed on June 17, 2011.

1. The three identities in this episode are disguised.
2. Jamadussani is the sixth month of the Hijri calendar. It fell in the month of July in 2008.
3. The Astaana-e-Zehra is discussed in greater detail later in the chapter. Also see http://www.astaana.com/.
4. An *imambargah* is a holy place of Shias, not a mosque but a more generally defined place of worship.

5. A ritual of self-mortification conducted by Shias on holy days associated with Imam Husain. For more discussion of the traditions of *maatam* among South Asian Shias, see Pinault (1992, 2000).

6. The tenth day of Mohurrum, which is the first month of the Islamic calendar. For the significance of Ashoora to Shias, see Hyder (2006), Momen (1985). Both books, as well as Nasr (2006), offer brief primers on the Shia faith. For the purposes of this chapter, it is sufficient to note three salient points. First, Shias are a significant (approximately 10 percent) minority among Muslims, who derive much of their identity (and rituals) from a 1,300-plus-year tradition of mourning for Imam Husain, the grandson of the prophet Muhammad, who was martyred in an epic battle on Ashoora and is buried at Karbala in Iraq. Second, Shias self-identify as a persecuted group and have internalized a history of oppression not just of their spiritual leaders but also of their ancestors. Finally, Shias believe that their spiritual leader, the Twelfth Imam, is alive and will emerge to lead the congregation of the pious on the Day of Judgment. Shias, therefore, consider themselves a *muntazar* community, a people in waiting.

7. The Al-Khoei Center in Queens, New York, is the biggest Shia *imambargah* in the New York metropolitan area. It opened in 1989 and houses a school, bookstore, mosque, and library, and is associated directly with the Shia leadership (*marjaiyah*) of Iraq. See http://al-khoei.org/ for some details of its activities.

8. The *majlis* (plural: *majalis*) is the term given by South Asians to a gathering conducted primarily to enact a tradition of mourning. Hyder (2006) provides a meticulous analysis of the *majlis* tradition in South Asia, as do Howarth (2005) and Schubel (1993). Additionally, Walbridge (1997) and Sharif (2005) have written about similar traditions from outside the South Asian diaspora. Walbridge notes that the Lebanese Shias in Dearborn refer to their gatherings as the *majma*, while Sharif refers to the *majlis-al-qiraya* among Iraqi refugee migrants in the Netherlands. Both Sharif and Hegland (1998) comment on the primary role played by women in the *majlis* tradition; indeed, the *majlis* is one place where traditional gender roles can be potentially subverted in a traditionally patriarchal community.

9. The role of religion in producing coping mechanisms among immigrant communities has been well documented (Stepick, 2005). From Fuzhuonese immigrants in Manhattan's Chinatown (Guest, 2003) to Hindus in the suburbs of Pittsburgh (Rayaprol, 1997), and from the churchgoing children of Korean immigrants (Alumakal, 2001) to their Vietnamese American counterparts (Bankston and Zhou, 1995), we have learned of the multiple ways in which immigrants creatively deploy religious institutions to negotiate a cultural space for themselves in the United States. However, for many new-immigrant communities, the mechanisms of coping are mediated by several, often-competing pressures, of which we consider three. First, communities struggle with the promises and perils of *transnationalism* (Levitt, 2001). The broader identities they seek to appropriate are often derived from multiple points of origin, which

are difficult to disentangle. Second, the coming-of-age of children, whose life experiences do not involve dislocation, produces *generational* engagements, as U.S.-born children of immigrants engage with their adults (and their new-immigrant peers) in a dynamic that is fraught with the promise of synthesis as well as the peril of incommensurability (Portes and Rumbaut, 2001). Finally, the community is often challenged by the nuanced task of *political engagement* with the broader society, in terms of both carving a space for religious sovereignty and producing conditions of trust in an atmosphere where they may be viewed with suspicion (Leonard, 2002). In general, Muslims have experienced a great tentativeness in the United States since the attacks of September 11, 2001. However, it can be argued that the greatest social force against the incorporation of many immigrant groups into the mainstream of U.S. life continues to be racism. Ironically, many immigrant communities have internalized and expressed racist (especially anti–African American) assumptions in an effort to gain the acceptance of a putative "mainstream" (Prashad, 2000), a strain that we have unfortunately seen in our research as well.

10. These figures were reported by the Al-Huda Institute of Canada in July 2008. See http://www.islamicinformationcenter.org/interfaith-center/interfaith-center/census-statistics-for-muslims-in-america.html.

11. The Lebanese Shia community has since been augmented in the 1990s by the arrival of several Iraqi refugees. Linda Walbridge's detailed ethnography of the Dearborn Shias suggests that their religious distinctiveness "fosters a sense of well-being—a sort of collective mental health—in the community at large" (1997: 202). That community too grapples with the interplay between religious and secular influences, and, unlike the more recent South Asians, has a third and fourth generation to benchmark the temporal progress and transformation of traditions.

12. This is not to say that Iranian Shias are totally nonobservant. For example, Hegland (2005: 209–213) recounts how a Shia community in Santa Clara, California, mixes religious and political traditions in a Shia *majlis*. Hegland concludes that much of the distancing of Iranian Shias from their religious tradition reflects a class-specific secularization and an antipathy to the perceived excesses of the Iranian Revolution.

13. Quasi-ethnographic accounts of post-1965 immigrants such as those by Kalita (2003) are useful to bring richness to the studies of South Asian immigrants, but very few such accounts have dealt with the Muslim South Asians. One interesting aspect that can be seen when studying Muslim South Asians is the way in which national difference (between Indians, Pakistanis, and Bangladeshis) is juxtaposed against the powerful epistemic category of the *ummah*, a Muslim transnational construct.

14. It is appropriate to note that the presence of substantial immigrants from a certain country in another often reflects an existing imperial or a neo-imperial relationship. Be it Turks in Germany, Jamaicans in the United Kingdom, or

Algerians in France, the circuits of migration are indicators of an extractive relationship between nations (Mir and Mir, 2006). It could be argued that there is a relationship between the influx of "economic refugees" from South Asia into the United States and the structural adjustment policies it spearheaded in the region in the 1980s and beyond by the IMF and the World Bank, and the subsequent influx of U.S. corporate capital in the South Asian economic space. These policies led to the emergence of higher levels of economic disparity in agrarian regions, leading the youth of the lower middle class to attempt migration. Many undocumented South Asians migrate illegally to the United States through the relatively tame modus operandi of entering the country on a visitor's visa and overstaying. For that reason they still tend to be relatively educated and economically privileged (it takes quite a bit of money and cultural capital to secure a visitor's visa). This sharply contrasts with the experience of the Fuzhuonese Chinese (Guest, 2003), who often come by sea in far more perilous circumstances and tend to be of a lower economic class.

15. Of course, the patterns of South Asian migration also include indenture and servitude, leading to the presence of Indian diasporas in places such as Guyana, Fiji, Mauritius, and South Africa. While much of that is beyond the scope of our chapter, it is interesting to see that the mourning for Imam Husain has traveled there as well and exists in highly transformed, albeit recognizable, rituals such as the Hosay Trinidad among Indo-Caribbeans (Korom, 2003).

16. Since the fall of Saddam Hussein, the Iraqi city of Karbala has been host to millions of Shia pilgrims who engage in an unself-conscious enactment of their religious traditions, which had been proscribed for more than three decades under the Baathist regime. An estimated 3 million pilgrims gathered at Karbala on December 28, 2009, to observe Ashoora, greater in size than the congregation that gathered for the hajj performed by the broader Muslim population (see http://news.bbc.co.uk/2/hi/middle_east/7197473.stm).

17. http://www.englishtownnj.com/.

18. See Alden (1951) for an analysis of Charles Lee and the Battle of Monmouth, which is also excerpted in the borough's web page: http://www.englishtownnj.com/history.htm.

19. Around the same time, two other *imambargahs* also came up in central and south New Jersey. Like the Astaana, they were community efforts, which were coordinated by individuals. Dr. Moosa Jaffari coordinated the efforts that led to the opening of the Bait Wali-ul Asr, in Freehold (http://izfna.org/), while Mr. Murad Ali Khan spearheaded the collective effort that helped form the Bait ul Qaimin Delran, a town in southern New Jersey (http://www.shia-nj.org/). Other New Jersey–based Shia centers include the Irvington-based Zainabia (http://zainabia.net/), the Somerset-based Muslim Foundation (http://muslimfoundation.org/), and the aforementioned Englewood-based Mehfil-e-Shah-e-Khorasan. These institutions all have a suburban character and contrast with the more urban *imambargahs* in New York, which have a greater proportion of working-class congregants.

20. As of February 2010, the fund-raising was continuing. The fund-raising drive for the Astaana itself presents a fascinating study of the community and reflected interesting generational shifts. While first-generation immigrants tended to use traditional methods (direct contributions, bank deposits, deployment of social networks), the younger volunteers sold T-shirts, self-produced CDs of *nauhas* recited by community members, and even piggy banks.

21. Hyder (2006: 30–60, 105–136) provides a fascinating analysis of role of the *marsiya* in the South Asian–style *majlis*. Thanks principally to two celebrated poets named Mirza Dabir (1805–1875) and Mir Anis (1801–1874), the *marsiya* has cemented its status over time as one of the legitimate subgenres in Urdu literature in general (Sadiq, 1984; Zaidi, 1993: 159–169).

22. A *maulvi* is an appellation given to a holy man by Shias, who rarely use the term Mullah any more. Anyone who speaks at a *majlis* can be referred to as a *maulvi*. Typically, *imambargahs* in the United States invite learned speakers from South Asia or the United Kingdom for the period of mourning in Mohurrum. The *maulvis* then tour a variety of *imambargahs* across North America, delivering speeches, thereby cementing spatial networks across these geographies and communities, and also acting as agents of isomorphism in practices and norms. Of late, a few U.S.-born men have begun to train themselves to become *maulvis*, including opting for strenuous doctoral-level courses in religious studies from seminaries in Iran and Iraq.

23. The Internet has become a vehicle for the "imagined communities" of the twenty-first century in a way that surpasses Benedict Anderson's notion of print-capitalism (Anderson, 1991), but recalls Marx's prescient 1857 words in *Grundrisse* where he refers to the power of capital, which, while it "must strive to tear down every barrier...to exchange and conquer the whole earth for its markets, it strives on the other side to annihilate this space with time" (Marx, 1973, 538–539). A number of websites allow people to do their version of this annihilation, as they listen live to *majalis* in Karachi, Mumbai, London, and Nairobi. YouTube videos show processions in Hyderabad. There is even a 24/7 webcast of the shrine of Imam Husain in Karbala. Local controversies in India and Pakistan are discussed and debated, and any perceived slander to the Shia ethos is contested using the Internet domain. Indeed, Internet-capitalism contributes to the annihilation of space by time in the same (and sometimes even more accelerated) way as print-capitalism.

24. "Shabbir" is one of the given names of Imam Husain.

25. Najam Afindi was a prominent poet of the Urdu-speaking tradition in South Asian Shias. The poem from which these lines are taken is popular all over India, Pakistan, and among the Shia diaspora in Europe, North America, the Middle East, and Australia.

26. http://www.imamiamedics.org/.

27. For an account of the Shia position on Parachinar, see Ali Jawad's article in Countercurrents: http://www.countercurrents.org/jawad150409.htm.

28. For a specific example of intra-Islamic conflicts within the prison system, see http://www.islamicpluralism.org/documents/943.pdf.
29. http://www.facebook.com/group.php?gid=90305245122.
30. Of course, this perception was inaccurate. As Mahmood Mamdani points out, the U.S. relationship with Islamic extremists throughout the Middle East and South Asia was an extension of their determination to win the Cold War by "all means necessary" (2004: 13). However, it is accurate to say that the United States was willing to tolerate excesses against Shia minorities by the ruling classes of Saudi Arabia and Iraq, and the militias of Afghanistan in favor of anti-communist cooperation.
31. For instance, several Shia leaders endorsed the 2003 nomination of Mr. Pipes to the board of the United States Institute of Peace (see http://www.danielpipes.org/usip/e_13.php).
32. See http://www.independentviewpoints.org/events.html. The board members of this organization include a few non–South Asians as well.
33. See http://amynaonline.org/, where the organization shows a very Western-centric template, with activities such as weekend seminars, conferences, youth meets, retreats, camps, and speaker forums.

REFERENCES

Afindi, Najam. (2000). Shabbir Baharhal Tera Naam Rahega. In Mir Ahmed Ali (Ed.), *Karbala Wale* (12th ed., p. 153). Hyderabad: Salman Book Center.

Alden, John R. (1951). *General Charles Lee: Traitor or Patriot?* Baton Rouge: Louisiana State University Press.

Alumakal, Antony. Being Korean, Being Christian: Particularism and Universalism in a Second-Generation Congregation. In Ho-Youn Kwon, Kwang Chung Kim, and R. Stephen Warner (Eds.), *Korean Americans and Their Religions: Pilgrims and Missionaries from a Different Shore.* University Park: Pennsylvania State University Press, 2001.

Anderson, Benedict. (1991). *Imagined Communities: Reflections on the Origin and Spread of Nationalism.* London: Verso.

Bagby, Ihsan. (2001). *The Mosque in America, a National Portrait: A Report from the Mosque Study Project.* Washington, DC: CAIR Press.

Bankston, Carl, and Min Zhou. (1995). The Ethnic Church, Ethnic Identification, and the Social Adjustment of Vietnamese Adolescents. *Review of Religious Research* 38:18–37.

Bozorgmehr, Mehdi. (1997). Internal Ethnicity: Iranians in Los Angeles. *Sociological Perspectives* 40 (3): 387–408.

Central Intelligence Agency. (2008). *The CIA World Factbook 2009.* New York: Skyhorse.

Diouf, S. (1998). *Servants of Allah: African Muslims Enslaved in the Americas.* New York: NYU Press.

Farber, David (2002). *Taken Hostage: The Iran Hostage Crisis and America's First Encounter with Radical Islam*. Princeton: Princeton University Press.

Guest, Kenneth. (2003). *God in Chinatown: Religion and Survival in New York's Evolving Immigrant Community*. New York: NYU Press.

Haddad, Yvonne, and Adair T. Lummis. (1987). *Islamic Values in the United States: A Comparative Study*. Oxford: Oxford University Press.

Hegland, Mary. (1998). The Power Paradox in Muslim Women's *Majales*: North-West Pakistani Mourning Rituals as Sites of Contestation over Religious Politics, Ethnicity, and Gender. *SIGNS* 23 (2): 391–428.

———. (2005). Women of Karbala Moving to America: Shi'i Rituals Moving to Iran, Pakistan and California. In Kamran Scott Aghaie (Ed.), *The Women of Karbala: Ritual Performances and Symbolic Discourses in Modern Shi'i Islam* (pp. 199–223). Austin: University of Texas Press.

Holman Jones, Stacy. (2005). Autoethnography: Making the Personal Political. In Normal Denzin and Yvonna Lincoln (Eds.), *The Sage Handbook of Qualitative Research* (3rd ed., pp. 763–792). London: Sage.

Howarth, Toby. (2005). *The Twelver Shi'a as a Muslim Minority in India: Pulpit of Tears*. London: Routledge.

Hyder, Syed Akbar. (2006). *Reliving Karbala: Martyrdom in South Asian Memory*. New York: Oxford University Press.

Kalita, Mitra. (2003). *Suburban Sahibs: Three Indian Families and Their Passage from India to America*. New Brunswick, NJ: Rutgers University Press.

Korom, Frank. (2003). *Hosay Trinidad: Muharram Performances in the Indo-Caribbean Diaspora*. Philadelphia: University of Pennsylvania Press.

Leonard, Karen. (2002). American Muslims, before and after September 11, 2001. *Economic and Political Weekly* 37 (24): 2292–2302.

Levitt, Peggy. (2001). *The Transnational Villagers*. Berkeley: University of California Press.

Mamdani, Mahmood. (2004). *Good Muslim, Bad Muslim: America, the Cold War, and the Roots of Terror*. New York: Doubleday.

Marx, Karl. (1973). *Grundrisse* (first published 1857). London: Penguin.

Mathew, Biju. (2008). *Taxi! Cabs and Capitalism in New York City*. New York: New Press.

Mir, Raza, and Ali Mir. (2006). Diversity: The Cultural Logic of Global Capital? In A. Konrad, P. Prasad, and J. Pringle, J. (Eds.), *Handbook of Workplace Diversity* (pp. 167–188). London: Sage.

Momen, Moojan (1985). *An Introduction to Shia Islam*. New Haven: Yale University Press.

Nasr, Syed Wali. (2006). *The Shia Revival: How Conflicts within Islam Will Shape the Future*. New York: Norton.

Pinault, David. (1992). *The Shiites: Ritual and Popular Piety in a Muslim Community*. New York: St. Martin's Press.

———. (2000). *Horse of Karbala: Studies in South Asian Muslim Devotionalism.* New York: Palgrave/St. Martin's Press.

Portes, Alejandro, and Ruben Rumbaut. (2001). *Legacies: The Story of the Immigrant Second Generation.* Berkeley: University of California Press.

Prashad, Vijay. (2000). *The Karma of Brown Folk.* Minneapolis: University of Minnesota Press.

Rashid, Ahmed. (2001). *Taliban: Militant Islam, Oil and Fundamentalism in Central Asia.* New Haven: Yale University Press.

Rayaprol, Aparna. (1997). *Negotiating Identities: Women in the Indian Diaspora.* New Delhi: Oxford University Press.

Sadiq, Muhammad. (1984). *A History of Urdu Literature.* New Delhi: Oxford University Press.

Schubel, Vernon. (1993). *Religious Performance in Contemporary Islam: Shi-I Devotional Rituals in South Asia.* Columbia: University of South Carolina Press.

Sharif, Tahya Hassan Al Khalifa. (2005). Sacred Narratives Linking Iraqi Women across Time and Space. In Miriam Cooke and Bruce Lawrence (Eds.), *Muslim Networks: From Hajj to Hip Hop* (pp. 132–154). Raleigh: University of North Carolina Press.

Stepick, Alex (2005). God Is Apparently Not Dead: The Obvious, the Emergent, and the Unknown in Immigration and Religion. In Leonard, Karen, Alex Stepick, Manuel Vasquez, and Jennifer Holdaway (Eds.), *Immigrant Faiths: Transforming Religious Life in America* (pp. 11–38). Lanham, MD: Alta Mira Press.

Takim, Liyakatali. (2002). Multiple Identities in a Pluralistic World: Shi'ism in America. In Yvonne Haddad (Ed.), *Muslims in the West: From Sojourners to Citizens* (pp. 218–232). New York: Oxford University Press.

Walbridge, Linda. (1997). *Without Forgetting the Imam: Lebanese Shiism in American Community.* Detroit: Wayne State University Press.

Zaidi, Ali Jawad. (1993). *A History of Urdu Literature.* New Delhi: Sahitya Akademi Press.

13

Tracing the Muslim Body

Race, U.S. Deportation, and Pakistani Return Migration

JUNAID RANA

The sovereign, epitomizing the subject, is the one by whom
and for whom the moment, the miraculous *moment*, is the
ocean into which the streams of labor disappear.
—Georges Bataille, *The Accursed Share*, 1991

Introduction: Sovereignty and the Racialized Body

After September 11, 2001, New York City became a different place.
There was tragedy and sorrow in the air, but also fear and intimidation. Spreading with the swiftness of wildfire, a reign of domestic terror
that targeted Muslim Americans and those who appeared Muslim inaugurated a twenty-first-century racial order. Responding to the hyper-
patriotism that followed 9/11 and the immediate dangers confronting
those in the service economy, working-class immigrants prominently
placed American flags in their workplaces. As hate crimes escalated in
the several months after 9/11, racial violence became routinized for a
broad group of South Asians, Arabs, and Muslims.[1] The incorporation
of everyday racism, although not necessarily new, heightened the Muslim body as a visible object of racial containment. With the rise in racial
violence and the threat of deportation facing many Muslim immigrants,

many began to flee the New York area, fearing for their lives and the safety of their families.

Couched within the practices and history of racial violence and terror in the United States, such attacks follow a long lineage of disciplining and retribution used to control communities of color. This particular wave of violence was not limited to those who appeared Muslim but affected a wide range of populations from Southeast Asian Americans to African Americans and Latinos.[2] In this sense, the newness of such racial terror is only remarkable in noting the ever-expanding and flexible potential of racism and the power of the race-concept. As the work of David Roediger and others has shown, race has the uncanny ability to survive amid social movements calling for the eradication of racism,[3] the consequences of which have also generated new responses and repercussions in the twenty-first century.

A few years after the initial wave of attacks subsided, I began talking to people who had returned to Pakistan from the United States. For these migrants, fleeing to other places in the diaspora such as Canada or the Arab Gulf or returning to Pakistan became a necessity. Some of the rationales for leaving the United States included the fear of family separation, the humiliation of detention and deportation, and the danger of racial violence. Their departures were often explained to me, however, in terms that deferred the anguish of these direct responses: the need to return to Pakistan for family reasons, the comfort of return to a home country, or opportunities for better employment in other parts of the diaspora. These accounts revealed a complex set of justifications for the act of return migration in the perceived context of imminent danger. Although not always articulated in a straightforward manner, the accounts were laden with a racialized affect that revealed a system of disciplinary exclusion.[4] For some, this form of affect was clearly a process of racialization, while others internalized these concepts as part of the unpredictable fate of migration.

As the anxiety of the post-9/11 detention and deportation regime circulated via the narratives of return migrants, the global implications of the "War on Terror" exacerbated such fears. For example, returnees in Pakistan interpreted the 2004 Abu Ghraib scandal depicting images of U.S.-perpetrated military torture committed against Iraqi detainees as a warning to migrants of the dangers of the U.S. immigration system and the brutality of the policing powers of the state. As summarized by a returnee:

> What happened in these [Abu Ghraib] pictures is nothing new. We [Pakistanis] know this from the torture done to people in Pakistan. In the U.S., if you are put into deportation [and detention], they used to treat you ok, but after 2001 this is what they do now. You would hear that they would do small things here and there before, but now they want to humiliate people. I have a friend who was deported, and in the prison they would call him bin Laden and terrorist....It's become difficult for Muslims to go to the US.

In this manner many returnees relate the conditions of torture in the detention/deportation regime to the conditions of migration. Such sentiments by Pakistani returnees are common in the everyday analyses of migration systems that organize the possibility of movement and the deportation regimes that regulate migrants as a mechanism of state control. As part of the calculations of risk in post-9/11 labor migration, those considering attempting entry into the United States increasingly assess violence and torture in terms of the possibility of successful migration.

As my fieldwork indicates, in the transnational settings of migrant home countries, these narratives of racialization and calculations of migration pivot on biopolitical notions of life and death, connected to the verbal taunting of racialized Muslims widely reported in the post-9/11 U.S. public sphere[5] and in the detention complex.[6] As the interviewee just quoted later told me, "I still want to go back to the U.S., working and living there is what I know best. I love being in Pakistan, but I don't belong here anymore, and maybe I don't belong in the U.S. either."[7]

Yet such narratives portray only a sample of the affective registers, depicting the exclusion of the Muslim body as a racial object from the U.S. body politic. In this essay, I examine how racial disciplining and boundary making are produced through racial violence and everyday forms of policing to control transnational practices of migration and to ultimately reinforce the logic of the imperial state. Central to my approach are the concepts of racism and sovereign power that are enacted through state and/or extralegal practices.[8] In the post-9/11 global racial system,[9] notions of xenophobic racism, imperialism, and histories of transnational migration are encapsulated in the process of racializing Muslims and migrant bodies. Through an examination of Pakistani migrants in the U.S. deportation/detention regime, I argue that sovereign power is applied to certain racialized bodies to create affective orders of security, authority, and fear that resulted in the massive voluntary and involuntary return migration to Pakistan after 2001. In particular, I refer to the conditions of violence and imposed sovereignty placed upon detainees in custody following 9/11 sweeps and ultimately deported to Pakistan.[10] Such racial disciplining is not merely an exception but rather part of what Engseng Ho identifies as a methodology of the imperial state that includes the concepts of invisibility, dissimulation, and misrepresentation.[11] Through these mechanisms of concealing violence the imperial state is complicit in the sanction of everyday forms of racializing the Muslim body.

Related to the process of racial disciplining in the detention/deportation regime, in the latter part of this essay I discuss fieldwork with return migrants in Pakistan to analyze how technologies of policing are connected to the transnational production of racial affect. In my fieldwork I tracked this forced and voluntary return to Pakistan, where since 2001 Pakistani return migrants from the United States are common.[12] The crisis of 9/11 mobilized an arbitrary system of enforcement and the use of violent force on suspect immigrants to demonstrate the authority of U.S. state power and sovereignty upon Muslim migrant bodies. Yet, this force is not entirely arbitrary; it is part of a longer history of U.S. government warfare on its domestic populations of color and the proliferation of coercive methods of torture across the globe.[13] For example, the measures of policing made permissible through the Patriot Act have had direct consequences in African American and Latino communities and have been used to control and surveil intellectuals and political groups such as environmentalists. As the selective system of deportability deploys the Muslim body as a concrete, objective entity to control and regulate, this logic is central to an expansive racialized terror formation that broadly disciplines migrants into imperial systems of control.

The process of racialization that makes the Muslim body visible for the purposes of containment and, in this case, disappearance through detention, deportation, and return migration is based on a flexible theory of the race-concept that incorporates Islam and Muslims through a combination of social, cultural, religious, and biological difference.[14] Although many of the return migrants who fled the United States after 9/11 did not enter into the detention/deportation regime, voluntary return is the consequence of a related circulation of sovereign power in which the racialization of the Muslim body extends the imperial logic of objectification and domination. The terms of racial conflation are based in visual cues that render sites, objects, and people into a raced and gendered calculus to include terms such as terrorism, fundamentalism, clash of civilizations, fear, danger, panic, peril, patriarchy, oppression of women, burqa-clad, Taliban, violent masculinity, warlike, fanatic, radical, and barbaric. In these everyday practices the Muslim body is racialized according to gendered notions of bodily comportment, dress, social position, and class, reconfiguring notions of racial subjectivity that I refer to as a racial uniform. The idea of terror in the global "War on Terror" is diffuse in these multiple entanglements of sovereignty that, simultaneously, in the everyday life of migrants are also part of an ongoing War on Immigration that seeks to control, exclude, and discipline. In what follows, I first offer a brief history of the detention/deportation regime and the relevant policies of the U.S. government implemented in the aftermath of 9/11. Following this contextual introduction, I provide an ethnographic evaluation of reports documenting the use of racial violence and extralegal force in the detention/deportation regime. In the final section, I examine how returnee narratives describe social disciplining and the production of racial affect in relation to the racial uniform through everyday practices and the reinscription of the imperial state.

9/11 and the Detention/Deportation Regime

In Daniel Kanstroom's history of deportation, he describes how this form of social control is used at the discretion of the security state.[15] Based in English colonial law, the antecedents of contemporary deportation law in the American context find their roots in fugitive slave laws and the forced removal of American Indians exercised in the eighteenth and nineteenth centuries.[16] As Kanstroom argues, deportation law is based on a two-pronged approach of extended border control and postentry social control. Extended border control implements the "basic features of sovereign power: the control of territory by the state and the legal distinction between citizens and noncitizens."[17] Second, and more troubling, are the postentry social controls that derive from what Kanstroom terms the "eternal probation" or "eternal guest" model in which noncitizens are "harbored subject to the whim of the government and may be deported for any reason."[18] In this model, the factor of "eternal" is based on the relationship of surplus labor reserves to the mechanism of deportation. Used as a form of social control, deportation makes immigrants subject to shifting notions of sovereignty that discard them during moments of crisis.

Following 9/11, broadly understood categories of "Muslim-looking" and "terrorist-looking" defined state-sanctioned racial violence in the form of hate crimes against a broad spectrum of immigrants of color.[19] Beginning in January 2002, the U.S. Justice Department identified some 300,000 individuals in the "Absconder Apprehension Initiative" as potential absconders in violation of immigration law and other minor criminal offenses. As part of this initiative, the FBI conducted sweeps of urban Muslim neighborhoods throughout the United States that resulted in some 5,000 immigrants entering into deportation proceedings. In conjunction with these sweeps, in September 2002 the Justice Department launched the National Security Entry-Exit Registration System (NSEERS), also known as "Special Registration," to identify suspect immigrants based on nationality—all from Muslim countries and the purported rogue state North Korea. Approximately 83,310 men considered foreign visitors registered for this program, of which 13,740 were immediately ordered into deportation proceedings. From the demographics of the initial deportees, often called the September 11 detainees, a large portion consisted of Pakistani immigrants overwhelmingly from the New York area.[20] When compared with other Muslim and Arab nationalities, this disparity is due to the greater size of the Pakistani immigrant population and the fact that among these groups they constitute a larger population of recent immigrants to the United States. According to findings by the *Chicago Tribune* in 2003, only 2 percent of unauthorized immigrants are from the twenty-four predominantly Muslim nations, which saw a 31.4 percent increase in deportation orders since 2001. Further, 98 percent of the unauthorized immigrants are from all other countries, which overall saw only a 3.4 percent increase in deportation orders.[21]

However, government statistics of official deportations often obscure the demographic impact on immigrant populations. Many returnees will not appear in deportation statistics because of the process of voluntary return and removal. As a category, providing detainees the option of voluntary return is often used to reduce the demographics of forced removals, an option offered once the detainee is deemed unable to provide any intelligence on criminal, illegal, or terrorist activities. In reality, voluntary removal is a technique of self-deportation that results after plea bargaining by the detainee, or the distress induced by lengthy detention. The goal of such detentions is to force detainees to voluntarily acquiesce to deportation, whether or not they have any criminal violations,[22] and to thus internalize a logic of criminality. Amid the fear of long-term detention through Special Registration and the expanding regime of deportation—and as a strategy to keep immigrant families intact—many Muslim immigrants sought refuge in home countries or tertiary migration destinations such as Canada.[23]

Estimates place the number of return migrants to Pakistan at more than 100,000, a figure that goes well beyond the published statistics of U.S. deportations. As a consequence, the population size of Pakistani communities in U.S. cities decreased dramatically. An example is the largest concentrated enclave of Pakistani immigrants in the United States, in the New York City borough of Brooklyn, which is largely populated by working-class and working poor immigrants.[24] The flight of returnees and forcibly removed deportees halved the size of this population after 9/11. Prior to 2001, the estimated population of the Little Pakistan area along Coney Island Avenue in Brooklyn was reported at 120,000, while after that it fell by an estimated 20,000 to 60,000.[25] From interviews conducted in 2008 with community activists in the Pakistani community of Brooklyn, it is clear that immigrants continue to feel the repercussions of this dramatic shift in the Pakistani population. Legal advocates in Brooklyn's Midwood neighborhood report that although there is a high success rate for claims of legal immigrant status, there remain numerous cases and issues that are beyond the scope of activist intervention that continue to exacerbate out-migration from Brooklyn and the United States.[26] Part of this problem stems from the invisibility of the Pakistani immigrant community and the social position of many of these immigrants as an urban working class disproportionately targeted by the domestic "War on Terror." As a reserve labor force located within the U.S. economy in large part as the working poor, these immigrant workers are often marginalized.[27] For example, in the year 2000, more than a quarter of the Pakistani population living in New York City made less than $20,000 a year, with approximately 28 percent living below the poverty line. Additionally, close to half the population reported limited English proficiency.[28] The disappearance and return migration of these populations to Pakistan, displaced from mostly urban U.S. enclaves, has created entirely new dynamics within the South Asian diaspora. For Pakistani migrants who enter into this global working class, the state system of migration control is an important aspect that continues to construct this labor diaspora.[29]

Carceral Violence and Racial Terror

Since 2001, a number of human rights organizations have reported on the conditions of racial terror for immigrants in the U.S. detention complex. A series of reports published by the American Civil Liberties Union in 2004, as well as interviews, journalist reports, and government documents revealed how immigrant detainees fared after 9/11 through unaccounted-for disappearances, racial profiling, and the separation of families by detention and deportation. The abuses of civil liberties and human rights are based in claims of procedural malfeasance and detainee abuse. In the case of the September 11 detainees, the Office of the Inspector General's (OIG) report on detainees published in April 2003 and December 2003 provided substantiations to firsthand claims and accusations that immediately surfaced from the beginning of the detentions.[30]

The April 2003 OIG report importantly chronicles the incarceration of these detainees as unduly harsh and excessively restrictive, and thus provides evidence that a principle of racial containment was in general use by detention staff. These intentional conditions included inadequate access to counsel, the spread of misinformation to detainee families and lawyers, daily twenty-three-hour lockdown, use of heavy restraints, limited recreation, and inadequate notice to detainees of how to file complaints,[31] thus violating the right to access counsel, families, and support networks—creating a condition of uncertainty and disappearance. The limits and confines of these detention practices parallel those used for prisoners in "solitary confinement," leading a number of organizations to protest these conditions as inhumane.[32] Further, the conditions of detention, based in a psychological approach of "torture lite," made it difficult for detainees to sleep, limited their contact with others, and implemented extreme conditions of confinement, intended to wear down their defenses. The later Supplemental Report of Detainee Abuse released by the OIG in December 2003 documented how intentional violence is systematic and perhaps an informal aspect of training within the U.S. prison system, overstepping the bounds of standard procedures.[33]

As these two reports from the OIG attest, physical violence was compounded by verbal abuse. Taunts of racialized and sexualized epithets included "terrorists," "motherfuckers," "fucking Muslims," and "bin Laden Junior." Samples of the phrases used for detainees include the following:

"Whatever you did at the World Trade Center, we will do to you."

"You're never going to be able to see your family again."

"If you don't obey the rules, I'm going to make your life hell."

"You're never going to leave here."

"You're going to die here just like the people in the World Trade Center died."[34]

Through a combination of physical and verbal abuse that makes carceral violence into racial terror, the body becomes a site of sovereign authority that is forcefully demarcated either through the formal means of detention and deportation or through informal acts of physical/verbal abuse and torture. Subsequently, the body as a material and affective register is taunted through anxiety, humiliation, fear, death, and threats to the physical body, and extended to the families of detainees. As disciplinary forms of self-governance, the detention staff used psychological, physical, and verbal rationales of racial containment that define Muslim detainees as outsiders to the U.S. nation by foregrounding the detainee's body as a foreign body.

Through access provided by deportee information, journalists and human rights activists obtained testimonies regarding the conditions and the circumstances that led to the detention of the September 11 detainees. These interviews importantly add experiential accounts to the reports of violence by the governmental offices represented by the OIG, with specific descriptions of abuse and conditions of detention. Naeem Sheikh, picked up in March 2002 and returned to Lahore, Pakistan, after a month of detention, reported to the ACLU his initial encounter in the detention prison with the FBI and detention staff that constructed his personal racial assignment based on religion and occupation: "He ask me, 'You know Osama bin Laden? You know any terrorist people?'" The agent also asked him if he knew how to pilot a plane—"I said, 'I just know how to drive a taxi'"—and questioned him about his religion. "He said, 'So you are a Muslim?' I said, 'Yes, of course, I'm Muslim.'"[35]

In this exchange, simple explanations that combine terrorism and Islam are part of the cultural repertoire of responsibility and culpability that are then used against detainees. The mobilization of this cultural logic reveals the elements of racialization that imagine connections of fictive kin, occupation, and religious practices. Following the assumptions of imposing religious persecution as psychological torture by the detention staff, Sheikh was initially prohibited from praying and denied halal food, as many other Muslim detainees reported. As the OIG Report states, a detainee who attempted to pray was told to "shut the fuck up! Don't pray. Fucking Muslim. You're praying bullshit."[36] In these circumstances bodily restrictions in detention are based in notions of naturalized culture, including religious ritual and practice, eating habits, but also in terms of biological relations of kinship and assumptions regarding labor stratification.

The immediate power of such imperial control is found in the testimonies of detainees that describe the physical abuse they endured as part of the systematic abuse and humiliation of incarceration. Following his arrest, Anser Mehmood, a forty-four-year-old who operated a trucking company in New Jersey, describes how he was systematically beaten in detention:

> After a night at a holding facility, Mr. Mehmood was taken—in full-body shackles—to the [MDC] in Brooklyn. Upon arrival, he was assaulted by guards while shackled. "They throw me on the wall. My hand was broken at that day. My lip was bleeding. And they terrified me because I was not a criminal. Why they are doing this thing to me? So they repeat the same thing about six or seven times on different walls."[37]

In what Mehmood described as "the grave" of solitary confinement, he said officials "never served me any paper. They never visit me any time—for four months and six days."[38] In his analysis, Mehmood offers the metaphor of death to depict his bodily condition as abused, as much as to describe the legal rights he expected but were denied to him. This circuit of affective violence in the detention and deportation complex disciplines the migrant body into imperial frames of power and dominance with the intention of containing and restricting.

The combination of racial and physical abuse seemed incomprehensible to many detainees, as is much racial terror. The rationale for this by the detention staff is clear: detainees have violated some law, and by extension U.S. sovereignty, that requires a disciplinary apparatus to literally impose the authority of sovereign power through physical, verbal, and psychological abuse. As undocumented immigrants who have overstayed their visas, they violate territorial sovereignty, and in some cases have committed small criminal offenses that violate social conventions of sovereignty that maintain the rule of law. Both of these circumstances combine a rationale of traditional sovereignty into the imagination of informal networks within the detention and deportation system that permits prison guards to perform extralegal violence and terror as exercises of sovereign power and the disciplinary indoctrination of the simulated judicial hand of state dominance. Sovereignty, thus, is not only about the authority of the state but also about the excess of violent policing that purportedly delineates the rule of law and the reinscription of state power.

Racializing the Diasporic Muslim Body

The racialized Muslim body, as much as it is an object, is also located spatially in a geography that designates spaces of suspicion across the U.S. landscape such as places of work and worship and particular neighborhoods.[39] Following patterns of surveillance and infiltration of communities of color historically used by the U.S. government, the domestic "War on Terror" has targeted immigrant communities with renewed vigor. The relevance of these racial geographies to the Muslim body is based in a set of profiles that determine identity and the mapping of spatial boundaries. As the cases of the early post–September 11 detainees make evident, the suspicion of Muslim immigrants followed assumptions based in racial profiling that classified certain immigrants according to class and social status as more susceptible to detention and deportation. For example, small-scale entrepreneurs, independently employed individuals, and workers in service industries are disproportionately targeted for immigration policing based on visa status or petty criminal violations.[40] Further, the Special Registration program of the U.S. government used nationality, age, and gender as specific determinants of suspicion. Based in a racial logic that predates 2001, the Muslim body has come to represent a site of twenty-first-century disciplining of sovereign power. It is in this sense that Ruth Gilmore argues for a definition of racism as "state-sanctioned and/or extralegal production and exploitation of group vulnerability to premature death."[41] If racism in its most basic form is the enforcement of boundaries and everyday forms of restriction from which life is circumscribed toward death, then this process is of particular hazard for labor migrants as they pursue social and economic resources with the known risks of violence, harassment, social death, incarceration, deportation, and, at its extreme, extermination.

For return migrants to Pakistan fleeing deportation and detention, the danger of remaining in the United States is often articulated through associations that combine Islam with nationality and appearance. Such an articulation, I suggest, is formulated in response to forms of racial objectification of the Muslim body that equate phenotypic difference with cultural and social difference to incorporate everything from comportment, dress, and clothing to language and religious belief. Following the work of Sara Ahmed and Linda Alcoff, I argue that in post-9/11 processes of racialization, bodily comportment and adornment are increasingly used as instruments of visual racial difference.[42] These assessments are used to classify the body of the racialized Muslim, and to discern this difference through naturalized conceptions that connect culture and political identity to the idea of phenotypic difference. Second, this idea of the racialized Muslim body is enforced through the production of racial affect to exclude, intimidate, and imperil. Discussing racialization, then, in terms of ethnographic research raises the issue of how to contextualize the race-concept—particularly when race itself is not necessarily part of everyday discussions—and whether it needs to be in order for racism to exist. Certainly, discrimination based on clothing such as the hijab and other gender-specific headgear is extensive.[43] But how does clothing in specific become identified with elements of racism generally based in phenotype? And how are these assumptions used in practices of cultural and social dominance that produce racial affect?

To address these issues, I offer two ethnographic vignettes that illustrate the complex issues of race, the Muslim body after 9/11, and the contradictions of return migration. In particular, these examples examine how boundary making through gendered frameworks is enacted through notions of racialized masculinity/patriarchy and the concept of the racialized Muslim. In both accounts, it is women who are made vulnerable in the active practices of racializing Muslims through assumptions of Islamic patriarchy and narratives of the victimization of the imperiled Muslim woman by the dangerous Muslim man.[44] These quotidian encounters are emblematic of the contradictions of everyday scripts through which immigrants are imagined as problematic figures.

The first account is that of a Pakistani return migrant Altaf and his wife, a Haitian immigrant. Working in a bank in the New York area, Mary—who also went by her Muslim name, Mariam—met Altaf through mutual friends and immediately hit it off. The two soon decided to marry and move in together. Altaf worked odd jobs, including working at a grocery store, and was at times a computer-networking consultant. After they married, Mary converted to Islam and asked to be called Mariam, and she slowly began adopting religious dress and donned the hijab at work. She recalled how this only made her position in her workplace more noticeable, specifically after the attack on the World Trade Center. Previously, she was treated with indifference and mild disregard, but immediately after 9/11 she faced direct comments and rude behavior. Female coworkers surmised that she began covering because her "husband made her do it," or that "she was becoming a terrorist too." At first treating such comments as jokes in the workplace, Mariam explained that she would try to clarify to her coworkers that her husband never forced Islam on her and that she was the more religious of the two. Ultimately her decision to veil was based on visits to the local mosque and her interactions with other Muslim women. Nonetheless, her workplace racial position as black and a Haitian immigrant began to take shape in relation to her husband's religious/national background as a Muslim and a Pakistani, rather than just on her own religious beliefs. As Altaf explained, the treatment his wife experienced coupled with the threat of deportation after 9/11 forced them to consider moving to Pakistan:

> Americans see that my wife is black and they treat her badly even though she has a good job. It doesn't matter that she is in a bank. People are always saying things indirectly, but you feel it. They would say things because she was an immigrant and dark. They would joke and she would listen to them at first, and later it was tough. I knew I might be in trouble because my visa ran out so I left for Pakistan. I knew they wouldn't just let me go, and so I told my wife I would go back to Pakistan for a while until things settled and I can come back. But she was afraid of being alone, so she came with me.

The generation of indirect comments and the creation of racial affect, although only alluded to, created an atmosphere of discomfort for both of them. What happened in Mariam's workplace than translated into interactions with Altaf, as he was clearly informed of her situation. After Special Registration (NSEERS) began in 2002 Altaf knew that his visa status might get him into trouble, so rather then registering with the U.S. government, he decided to return to Pakistan. Through this combination of state enforcement of immigration policy and the practices of everyday forms of racialization, Altaf and Mariam came to understand their place within U.S. racial hierarchies through a feeling of not belonging.

Although this is a common story of return migration, several aspects make it notable in post-9/11 racial thinking and the processes of suspicion, racial translation, and gendered comportment. In the first case, the suspicion ascribed to Mariam by her coworkers was constructed in relation to Islam and her marriage to Altaf. As a marker of further racial difference, her donning of the hijab articulated a social and religious transformation and a social construction of learnable religious beliefs that amplified the sense of distrust she faced in the workplace. For Mariam's coworkers, Islamic garb and practice are translated into violence and danger, code words for terrorism, that they condemned through verbal taunting and social boundary making. Second, the presence of a phenotypic racism based on a passive antiblack and anti-immigrant sentiment intensified through an association with Islam and the shift in dress that then marked Mariam as a racialized black immigrant *and* a Muslim. Finally, conversion and the donning of Islamic garb represented gendered notions of self-oppression to her coworkers, who interpreted her transformation as a social threat, thus eliciting direct engagement and verbal responses, the intent of which was to circumscribe Mariam's social position within the workplace to an inferior and subordinate status. The continued restriction of Mariam's social space within the workplace is a kind of calculated anxiety of racial affect that seeks to instill fear into the daily lives of immigrants by imposing racialized scripts of domination and ultimately the metonymic fallacy of Islam-as-terror.

The return of Altaf and Mariam to Pakistan was further fraught with problems of adjustment to family and friends. Although they initially thought they might settle in Lahore, the disruptions their marriage caused in Altaf's extended family caused them to separate. As other family members explained along with Altaf, the inability of his family to accept cultural differences, language barriers, and lack of future opportunities led Mariam eventually to return to the United States. Altaf continued to travel to the Gulf for work. He insisted that he would return to the United States eventually, but not until the situation improved. Even with the distance of having returned to Pakistan, he remained fearful of the threat of the detention and deportation regime. Having never been apprehended for a visa violation, Altaf wanted to wait until he could reconcile with his wife or until another opportunity presented itself. His familiarity with the everyday forms of racial restriction that followed 9/11 increased his vigilance of forms of abjection used to differentiate social groups. As he explained, this was not going to change any time soon, and to succeed in the United States, one had to learn to deal with these things in everyday life.[45]

In the second example, Amina, a veiled woman in her late twenties born and raised in the United States and married to a man from Pakistan, told me of the encounters she had with personnel she described as mostly white male Americans at the U.S. consulate in Islamabad to obtain the proper papers for her husband:

They looked at me like I was uneducated and didn't know what I was talking about, even though I speak perfect English. But it was also clearly because I wear the veil and my husband was dressed in *salwar kameez* [traditional dress] and wears an *amama* [Islamic headgear]. They would look at him and think we had a forced marriage. Just because we are doing things the Islamic way, we are discriminated against.

In this story a number of commonplace themes that deal with gender, class, and ultimately racialized interactions emerge within a narrative that breaks normative patterns. Because her husband, Waqas, did not speak English, and the language of communication between the two of them was mainly Punjabi, language proficiency created a number of difficulties for them. Married in 2000, they encountered increased attention after 9/11 from immigration officials and difficulties traveling back and forth between the United States and Pakistan. Although they did not have an arranged marriage in the strict sense according to Amina, their union was organized through her family and the mosque they attended in the States. As was clear to her, much of the skepticism they faced was based on the assumption of "marrying for papers" and the disapproval of arranged marriages by what she referred to as Americans. As she exclaimed in response to this, "I might be American, but I'm Muslim American," distinguishing herself from the consular officials who were white Americans.

This interaction exemplifies a number of points in terms of dress, racialization, and the attributes of particular ideas that assume gender oppression is interpretable through Islamic dress and cultural practices such as marriage. Consular officials constructed Amina as the imperiled woman, even though she was defiantly a feminist in her own right, as she argued to me. Amina and Waqas were nonetheless read as uncivilized because she dressed in the full veil, including niqab and burqa, thus exposing only her eyes, and he wore traditional Pakistani clothing and had a full beard. Assumptions based on phenotypic appearance were not the only modes of racial difference; dress, bodily comportment, and mannerisms additionally presented Amina as a particular kind of racialized and gendered figure constructed through the stereotype of the domination of uneducated Muslim women under Islamic patriarchy. Waqas was not only seen as a conservative Muslim man; elements of class status, literacy, and education also entered into interpretations of him because he did not speak English. The inference of a lack of education translated to Amina as well, even though she had completed a bachelor's degree in accounting in the United States and was the primary wage earner while her husband planned on matriculating in college. To add to her ongoing disruption of stereotypes of the oppressed, veiled Muslim woman, Amina often functioned as a translator for her husband. Uncertain of this behavior, consular officials forced Amina into ready-made categories such as Razack's notions of the "imperiled woman" and the "dangerous Muslim man" as much as she defied them.[46] Further, Amina's clear frustration and anger over this treatment continued to magnify feelings of social difference and ostracism that simultaneously invigorated her religious faith. The logic of this encounter did not escape her or her husband but instead left them confounded at the moral authority of those who judged them. In the terms of this racial encounter, their feelings of injustice solidified their Islamic practices of renewal and piety. As they explained, their religious belief remained their source of refuge when confronting racism. This response to the production of racial affect for them, although not entirely liberating, allowed them to cope with the seemingly vexing assumptions of religious and social comportment that they inhabit. In the end, Amina and Waqas, feeling disillusioned, gave up on returning to the United States and instead settled in the United Arab Emirates.[47]

In the context of Amina's marriage to a Pakistani citizen, donning traditional and Islamic garb created a state of racialized subjectivity that related to her and her husband's clothing. As a form of comportment that evokes the concept of the racial uniform,[48] in the Du Boisian sense of a racialized subjectivity,[49] Amina contradicted constructed notions of what it means to be a proper American. Although Amina is a U.S. citizen, and Mariam was a green card holder, Islamic dress as a racial uniform translates these women into external threats because of their nonnormative gender comportment in relation to notions of American ideals of femininity and their construction as immigrants in relation to racial whiteness. In this sense, the racial uniform materializes the racialized Muslim body into a post-9/11 framework of racial formation through a complex assortment of visual cues. Through the racial conflation of cultural practices associated with Muslims and

Islam, and ultimately a reified notion of terror, these bodies are rendered as racialized Muslims according to the ideological underpinnings of a U.S. nationalism predicated on whiteness and particular notions of gender normativity. It is this combination of the Muslim body and the racial uniform that is part of the grammar of post-9/11 racialization that makes Muslim a racial category. Clothing and comportment become objects of racialization to designate important visible cues of racial assignment and categorization. Donning a racial uniform is to claim a part as, and be claimed as part of, the figure of the racialized Muslim, and thus a broad constituency of Muslims who differ by race, ethnicity, nationality, and social and cultural background.

Conclusion: Sovereign Terror and the Necropolitics of Migration

In November 2009, the landmark case of *Turkmen v. Ashcroft* settled a class action civil rights lawsuit against the U.S. government for $1.26 million, headed by the lawyers of the Center for Constitutional Rights on behalf of plaintiffs, including Muslims from Egypt, Pakistan, and Turkey, and a Hindu man born in India rounded up in raids after 9/11, who claimed abuse while in the Metropolitan Detention Center in Brooklyn, New York.[50] Although this case signaled an important shift in the judicial response to the use of state-sanctioned force after 9/11, such abuse is indicative of a much broader racism that is complexly interwoven with state interests and local actors. Alongside the legal reform of state practices, everyday racism continues in the form of racial containment and disciplining from which immigrants are excluded, controlled, and disappeared, thus continuing the hidden work of sovereign power and the imperial state.

The necropolitics of migration that propels migrants toward death dictates that certain workers must disregard their bodies with the gamble of greater life chances.[51] Labor migrants live an extreme form of this tenuous existence in the current global economy while unprotected by the stakes of global capitalism. The place of the Pakistani immigrant within the complex political economies of migration to the United States takes on a greater complexity in the face of state-endorsed racism after September 11 that attributes negative moral values to them such that their removal remains unremarkable. The consolidation of a state-sanctioned racism against Muslim immigrants is part of a history of racial terror and imperial technologies of violence prevalent in the subordination of racialized groups developed in the United States and expanded across the globe.

Such a terror formation is the culmination of a steady history of state control that implements policing, surveillance, immigration control, detention, deportation, and incarceration onto the bodies of immigrants. The effect of this state terror formation is to instill a sense of security in the nation while identifying potential threats and dangers to state sovereignty. Such threats are part of a process of making racism everyday. It is thus that through multiple registers of sovereign power, the violence of racism is the means to make unwanted labor disappear.

NOTES

This essay is a revised version of chapter 6, "The Muslim Body," in *Terrifying Muslims: Race and Labor in the South Asian Diaspora* (Durham, NC: Duke University Press, 2011). My thanks to Miabi Chatterji, Manu Vimalassery, and Vivek Bald for their hard work and persistence.

1. Ahmad (2002, 2004).

2. For example, see the work of Bill Ong Hing (2006) and the special issue of *Amerasia* Hing edited on the topic (2005). For an assessment of post-9/11 governmental policies on immigrant communities in the United States, see Nguyen (2005) and De Genova and Peutz (2010).

3. Roediger (2008) makes this cogent argument by examining U.S. history. See also Goldberg (2009), Silva (2007), and Winant (2001) on the persistence of race as a concept to mobilize violence and systematic oppression.

4. In this sense, I follow the work of Sara Ahmed (2004, 2006) on racial affect as intensified emotions that mediate social relations of exclusion and the circulation of an embodied sense of disciplinary power.

5. Cainkar (2009); Naber (2006).

6. Shiekh (2004, 2008).

7. Interview, Lahore, Pakistan, male, forty years old, February 2006.

8. For this theory of racism, see Mullings (2005) and Gilmore (2007). Following the theorizations of Michel Foucault (1979, 1991, 2003, 2007, 2008), Georges Bataille (1991), Carl Schmitt (1996, 2005), and more recently Giorgio Agamben (1998, 2005), anthropologists have productively examined sovereignty in everyday life (Hansen and Stepputat 2005, 2006; Ong 1999, 2006). As I am using it, sovereignty is a form of power that seeks to control everyday life through the state, statelike actors, and extralegal means through technologies of discipline and biopower.

9. For an elaboration of the global racial system, see Mullings (2005) and Winant (2001).

10. Mark Dow (2004) argues that the use of secrecy and excessive force in the detentions after September 11, 2001, is an extension of long-standing biases and mistreatment of immigrant detainees that in many ways normalized the abuse of Arab, South Asian, and Muslim immigrants.

11. Engseng Ho (2004) argues the lineage of the current global "War on Terror" is connected to a history of European imperial expansion through violent military might and direct colonial authority. The consequences of these imperial models in Africa, Asia, and the Americas created massive social upheaval and oppositional formations of transnational and diasporic populations. In the present imperial moment, the model of U.S. empire operates without colonial occupation, a task that under the approach of neoliberal capitalism delegates "security, military, and colonial functions…to private companies, removing them from political oversight" (Ho 2004, 239). Although the means of this imperial formation remain military might and excessive force, it is through the expansion of free-market principles and the relinquishing of formal colonization that the authority of U.S. empire continues to flourish. Through methods of invisibility, dissimulation, and misrepresentation, the U.S. imperial model without colonies is now the custodian of a hidden empire in which sovereign power exerts itself in autonomous zones of economic and social activity through the language of extraterritoriality. Ho is also careful to acknowledge the U.S. colonialism of overseas occupations, the conquest of the Southwest, and the genocide of Native Americans (2004, 230), that while colonial relations are admonished, coercive actions from military strikes and espionage to the select dispersion of information maintains U.S. authority around the globe.

12. From 2003 to 2008, I interviewed Pakistanis in Brooklyn, New York, and recent return migrants in Pakistan to gather information of the conditions and reasons for fleeing the United States. All names have been changed to maintain anonymity.

13. On the war against communities of color, see James (2007); on the development of techniques of torture by the U.S. government and other democratic countries, see McCoy (2006) and Rejali (2007).

14. On a theory of the race-concept in relation to the history of Islamophobia and anti-Muslim racism, see Rana (2007). Also see Bayoumi (2006).

15. Kanstroom (2007).

16. In the wake of 9/11, what appeared in the guise of a new state security system—the revitalization of immigration controls through legal, social, and state-sanctioned forms of policing—was in fact a magnified and expanded version of practices of legal sovereignty already in place (e.g., Chang 2002; Cole 2003; Cole and Dempsey 2002). The Patriot Act of 2001 enacted a wide range of law enforcement powers by expanding the use and domains of surveillance in intelligence investigations. Drawing from the McCarran-Walter Act

of 1952, the Patriot Act also restricts foreign speakers from entering the United States based on the threat of ideologically dangerous ideas. Most immediately preceded by the 1996 Illegal Immigration Reform and Immigrant Responsibility Act, the Patriot Act is based on a historical genealogy of legal regulation. As legal scholar David Cole argues, the legal basis of such controls was long in the making, as evidenced by the construction of the category of the "enemy alien" (2003). As a legal classification, the enemy alien category allows for perceived threats from suspect populations, whether through ideology, identity, or a predisposed opposition to U.S. interests, to be isolated and removed from the U.S. populace through the force of deportation. The legal history of this category can be traced to a number of laws and events, including the Alien and Sedition Acts of 1798 that included that Alien Enemies Act; the Chinese Exclusion Acts of 1882; the Palmer Raids that targeted suspected anarchists, largely immigrants, at the beginning of the twentieth century; the internment of Japanese immigrants and Americans during World War II; and the infamous Cold War–era Red Scare led by Senator Joseph McCarthy (Cole 2003, 7–8).

17. Kanstroom (2007), 5.
18. Ibid., 6.
19. Ahmad (2002, 2004).
20. See "The September 11 Detainees: A Review of the Treatment of Aliens Held on Immigration Charges in Connection with the Investigation of the September 11 Attacks," U.S. Department of Justice. Office of the Inspector General, April 2003, www.justice.gov/oig/special/0306/press.pdf. Also Cam Simpson et al., "Immigration Crackdown Shatters Muslims' Lives," Tossed Out of America Series, pt. 1, *Chicago Tribune*, Nov. 16, 2003. Although these are the specific numbers released from these particular programs, the total number of those detained and deported under a similar logic is uncertain.
21. Ibid.
22. Welch (2002).
23. Nguyen (2005).
24. "Census Profile: New York City's Pakistani American Population," Asian American Federation of New York, December 2004, http://www.aafny.org/cic/briefs/Pakistani.pdf.
25. The large disparity reflects the different sources of reporting. The lower figure comes from U.S. government officials and the Pakistan consul in New York. These numbers are a combination of those deported and those estimated to have returned to Pakistan. See Daniela Gerson, "For Some, Harder Times since 9/11," *New York Sun*, Oct. 1, 2003; and Tatsha Robertson, "Deportation Surge Leaves Void in Brooklyn's Little Pakistan," *Boston Globe*, Aug. 14, 2005. The higher number comes from community activists working in the Pakistani immigrant community; see Andrea Elliot, "In Brooklyn, 9/11 Damage Continues," *New York Times*, June 7, 2003.
26. Interview, May 14, 2008.

27. On the class demographics of immigrants in the NSEERS process, see AALDEF, *Special Registration: Discrimination and Xenophobia as Government Policy*, report from the Asian American Legal Defense and Education Fund, January 2004, http://www.aaldef.org/article.php?article_id=133.
28. Census Profile: New York City's Pakistani American Population."
29. Rana (2009).
30. As the report on detainee abuse states: "The evidence indicates a pattern of abuse by some correctional officers against some September 11 detainees, particularly during the first months after the attacks. Most detainees we interviewed at the [Metropolitan Detention Center] alleged that MDC staff physically abused them. Many also told us that MDC staff verbally abused them with such taunts as 'Bin Laden Junior' or with threats such as 'you will be here for the next 20–25 years like the Cuban people.' Although most correctional officers denied such physical or verbal abuse, the OIG's ongoing investigation of complaints of physical abuse developed significant evidence that it has occurred, particularly during intake and movement of prisoners" (OIG Report April 2003, 162).
31. OIG Report April 2003, 157–161.
32. Meeropol (2005).
33. See "Supplemental Report on September 11 Detainees' Allegations of Abuse at the Metropolitan Detention Center in Brooklyn, New York," U.S. Department of Justice, Office of the Inspector General, December 2003, www.justice.gov/oig/special/0312/final.pdf. The OIG report concluded: "Based on videotape evidence, detainees' statements, witnesses' observations, and staff members who corroborated some allegations of abuse, that some MDC staff members slammed and bounced detainees into the walls at the MDC and inappropriately pressed detainees' heads against walls. We also found that some officers inappropriately twisted and bent detainees' arms, hands, wrists, fingers, and caused them unnecessary physical pain; inappropriately carried or lifted detainees; and raised or pulled detainees' arms in painful ways. In addition, we believe some officers improperly used handcuffs, occasionally stepped on compliant detainees' leg restraint chains, and were needlessly forceful and rough with the detainees—all conduct that violates [Bureau of Prison] policy" (OIG Report Dec. 2003, 28).
34. OIG Report Dec. 2003, 28.
35. See "America's Disappeared: Seeking International Justice for Immigrants Detained after September 11," American Civil Liberties Union, Jan. 2004, 7, www.aclu.org/FilesPDFs/un%20report.pdf.
36. OIG Report Dec. 2003, 29.
37. ACLU Jan. 2004, 18.
38. ACLU Jan. 2004, 19.
39. Bayoumi (2008).
40. Cf. Maira (2009); Nguyen (2005); Shiekh (2004, 2007, 2011).
41. Gilmore (2007, 247).

42. Ahmed (2000, 2004); Alcoff (2001, 2006).
43. For example, Louise Cainker (2009) reports that after 9/11 in metropolitan Chicago, women who wore hijab were more vulnerable to attack than Arab and Muslim men. She usefully calls this cultural sniping to examine how women's bodies become specific targets over ideological issues.
44. Razack (2008).
45. Interviews, Lahore, Pakistan, January 2006.
46. Razack (2008).
47. Interviews, Lahore, Pakistan, January–February 2006.
48. See Yu (2001) on the concept of racial uniform by Robert Park and his colleagues of the Chicago school of sociology as part of a racialized body in relation to social distance, assimilation, and accommodation. Rather than strictly dismissing this approach as victimizing, I wish to invert these terms to understand the racial uniform as imposed in relation to racialized notions of Islam and the Muslim body.
49. See Du Bois (1993). For a dialectical argument of Du Bois's racial veil see Winant (2004, 25–38).
50. See http://ccrjustice.org/ourcases/current-cases/turkmen-v.-ashcroft.
51. Mbembe (2003).

BIBLIOGRAPHY

Agamben, Giorgio. 1998. *Homo Sacer: Sovereign Power and Bare Life*. Stanford, CA: Stanford University Press.
———. 2005. *State of Exception*. Chicago: University of Chicago Press.
Ahmad, Muneer I. 2002. Homeland Insecurities: Racial Violence the Day after September 11. *Social Text* 20 (3): 101–115.
———. 2004. A Rage Shared By Law: Post-September 11 Racial Violence as Crimes of Passion. *California Law Review* 92 (5): 1259–1330.
Ahmed, Sara. 2000. *Strange Encounters: Embodied Others in Post-coloniality*. New York: Routledge.
———. 2004. *The Cultural Politics of Emotion*. New York: Routledge.
———. 2006. *Queer Phenomenology: Orientations, Objects, Others*. Durham, NC: Duke University Press.
Alcoff, Linda. 2001. Toward a Phenomenology of Racial Embodiment. In *Race*, edited by R. Bernasconi. Malden, MA: Blackwell.
———. 2006. *Visible Identities: Race, Gender, and the Self*. New York: Oxford University Press.
Bataille, Georges. 1991. *The Accursed Share: An Essay on General Economy*. Vols. 2 and 3. New York: Zone Books.
Bayoumi, Moustafa. 2006. Racing Religion. *New Centennial Review* 6 (2): 267–293.
———. 2008. *How Does It Feel to Be a Problem? Being Young and Arab in America*. New York: Penguin.

Cainkar, Louise. 2009. *Homeland Insecurity: The Arab American and Muslim American Experience after 9/11*. New York: Russell Sage Foundation.

Chang, Nancy. 2002. *Silencing Political Dissent*. New York: Seven Stories Press.

Cole, David. 2003. *Enemy Aliens: Double Standards and Constitutional Freedoms in the War on Terrorism*. New York: New Press.

Cole, David, and James X. Dempsey. 2002. *Terrorism and the Constitution: Sacrificing Civil Liberties in the Name of National Security*. 2nd ed. New York: New Press.

De Genova, Nicholas, and Nathalie Peutz, eds. 2010. *The Deportation Regime: Sovereignty, Space and the Freedom of Movement*. Durham, NC: Duke University Press.

Dow, Mark. 2004. *American Gulag: Inside U.S. Immigration Prisons*. Berkeley: University of California Press.

Du Bois, W. E. B. 1993 [1903]. *The Souls of Black Folk*. New York: Knopf.

Foucault, Michel. 1979. *Discipline and Punish*. New York: Vintage.

———. 1991. *The Foucault Effect: Studies in Governmentality: With Two Lectures by and an Interview with Michel Foucault*. Chicago: University of Chicago Press.

———. 2003. *Society Must Be Defended: Lectures at the College de France, 1975–76*. New York: Palgrave Macmillan.

———. 2007. *Security, Territory, Population: Lectures at the College de France, 1977–1978*. New York: Palgrave Macmillan.

———. 2008. *The Birth of Biopolitics: Lectures at the College de France, 1978–79*. New York: Palgrave Macmillan.

Gilmore, Ruth Wilson. 2007. *Golden Gulag: Prisons, Surplus, Crisis, and Opposition in Globalizing California*. Berkeley: University of California Press.

Goldberg, David Theo. 2009. *The Threat of Race: Reflections on Racial Neoliberalism*. Malden, MA: Wiley-Blackwell.

Hansen, Thomas Blom, and Finn Stepputat. 2005. *Sovereign Bodies: Citizens, Migrants, and States in the Postcolonial World*. Princeton: Princeton University Press.

———. 2006. Sovereignty revisted. *Annual Review of Anthropology* 35:295–315.

Hing, Bill Ong, ed. 2005. Deporting Our Souls and Defending Our Immigrants. *Amerasia* 31 (3).

———. 2006. *Deporting Our souls: Values, Morality, and Immigration Policy*. New York: Cambridge University Press.

Ho, Engseng. 2004. Empire through Diasporic Eyes: The View from the Other Boat. *Society for Comparative Study of Society and History* 46 (2): 210–246.

James, Joy, ed. 2007. *Warfare in the American Homeland: Policing and Prison in a Penal Democracy*. Durham, NC: Duke University Press.

Kanstroom, Dan. 2007. *Deportation Nation: Outsiders in American History*. Cambridge: Harvard University Press.

Maira, Sunaina. 2009. *Missing: Youth, Citizenship, and Empire after 9/11*. Durham, NC: Duke University Press.

Mbembe, Achille. 2003. Necropolitics. *Public Culture* 15:11–40.

McCoy, Alfred W. 2006. *A Question of Torture: CIA Interrogation, from the Cold War to the War on Terror*. New York: Holt.

Meeropol, Rachel, ed. 2005. *America's Disappeared: Detainees, Secret Imprisonment, and the "War on Terror."* New York: Seven Stories Press.

Mullings, Leith. 2005. Interrogating Racism: Toward an Antiracist Anthropology. *Annual Review of Anthropology* 34:667–93.

Naber, Nadine C. 2006. The Rules of Forced Engagement: Race, Gender, and the Culture of Fear among Arab Immigrants in San Francisco Post-9/11. *Cultural Dynamics* 18 (3): 269–292.

Nguyen, Tram. 2005. *We Are All Suspects Now: Untold Stories from Immigrant Communities after 9/11.* Boston: Beacon Press.

Ong, Aihwa. 1999. *Flexible Citizenship: the Cultural Logics of Transnationality.* Durham, NC: Duke University Press.

———. 2006. *Neoliberalism as Exception: Mutations in Citizenship and Sovereignty.* Durham, NC: Duke University Press.

Rana, Junaid. 2007. The Story of Islamophobia. *Souls: A Critical Journal of Black Politics, Culture, and Society* 9 (2): 148–161.

———. 2009. Controlling Diaspora: Illegality, 9/11, and Pakistani Labour Migration. In *Pakistani Diasporas: Culture, Conflict, and Change,* edited by V. Kalra. New York: Oxford University Press.

Razack, Sherene. 2008. *Casting Out: The Eviction of Muslims from Western Law and Politics.* Toronto: University of Toronto Press.

Rejali, Darius M. 2007. *Torture and Democracy.* Princeton: Princeton University Press.

Roediger, David R. 2008. *How Race Survived US History: From Settlement and Slavery to the Obama Phenomenon.* New York: Verso.

Schmitt, Carl. 1996. *The Concept of the Political.* Chicago: University of Chicago Press.

———. 2005. *Political Theology: Four Chapters on the Concept of Sovereignty.* Chicago: University of Chicago Press.

Shiekh, Irum. 2004. Abuse in American Prisons. *Muslim World Journal of Human Rights* 1 (1): 1–13.

———. 2007. Government Spy or a Terrorist: Dilemmas of a Post-9/11 Academic Researcher. *Amerasia* 33 (3): 26–40.

———. 2008. Racialising, Criminalizing, and Silencing 9/11 Deportees. In *Keeping Out the Other: A Critical Introduction to Immigration Enforcement Today,* edited by D. Brotherton and P. Kretsedemas. New York: Columbia University Press.

———. 2011. *Detained without Cause: Muslims' Stories of Detention and Deportation in America after 9/11.* New York: Palgrave Macmillan.

Silva, Denise Ferreira da. 2007. *Toward a Global Idea of Race.* Minneapolis: University of Minnesota Press.

Welch, Michael. 2002. *Detained: Immigration Laws and the Expanding I.N.S. Jail Complex.* Philadelphia: Temple University Press.

Winant, Howard. 2001. *The World Is a Ghetto: Race and Democracy since World War II.* New York: Basic Books.

Yu, Henry. 2001. *Thinking Orientals: Migration, Contact, and Exoticism in Modern America.* New York: Oxford University Press.

14

Antecedents of Imperial Incarceration

Fort Marion to Guantánamo

MANU VIMALASSERY

Three months after invading Afghanistan, the United States opened a prison camp at Guantánamo Bay, Cuba, where it would eventually imprison about 550 men arrested in Afghanistan and Pakistan under pretext of association with Al Qaeda or the Taliban.[1] Too often, the architecture of the "War on Terror" has been described as "unprecedented," effacing continuities in U.S. imperialism, and foreclosing visions of a broad program of decolonization and liberation. Working against this mold, this essay looks to a history of imperial prisons to find precedents for the U.S. "War on Terror." Drawing on Anne McClintock's evocation of imperial déjà vu, I mention these links to raise questions and explore imperial continuities: to chart possible grounds for anticolonial alliances. We might glimpse the dissolution of imperial control in contradictions of the imperial project that course through these continuities.[2]

Some scholars and advocates working against imprisonment and detention in the "War on Terror" have looked to earlier moments in U.S. national history as precedents for state strategies, and for critical responses. Some have drawn connections to Japanese American internment during World War II, and political and legal movements to contest that policy; others, to the Palmer Raids against radicals in the United States in the years after World War I. However edifying these links are, resting our historical perspective in such cases limits our political vision to a nation-state framework, taking the U.S. nation-state for granted as a geographic entity, and as the sphere of politics. This averts attention from historical precedents and ongoing processes of settler colonialism, which ground and shape these United States that are fighting a "War on Terror," limiting the scope of our political vision away from engaging thought and politics of indigenous sovereignty, so vital to any thoroughgoing critique of U.S. imperialism.[3]

In his memoir, Moazzam Begg, a British Asian formerly imprisoned at Guantánamo, described his childhood in England, marked by the rise of the British National Party, and a growing awareness of the importance of Islam in his life as he found his place in the world, a process marked, in part, by a sense of sympathy with Native Americans. Begg later recalled his interactions with two particular guards during his imprisonment: Cody, who sometimes identified with North Carolina Cherokees whose community he grew up in, and Warnick, a Pacific Islander, describing the openings of conversations that offered mutual recognition but were swiftly closed under the mechanics of prison brutality and covered by the banalities of U.S. national rhetoric.[4] These glimpses of sympathy and recognition across embodied imperial histories provide fleeting reminders of the importance of the search for precedents, grounded not in the rule of law or the pious condescension of liberal pity but in the survival of long-standing and ongoing colonial domination.

Sohail Daulatzai traced torture experiments on Black Muslim prisoners in the early 1960s as precedents for contemporary torture policies in U.S. domestic and international prisons. Drawing out the centrality of African American Muslims as domestic, internal threats in the "War on Terror," Daulatzai connected these policies with the production of the nation as prison, whether in Israel and Palestine, the United States and Mexico, or Afghanistan and Pakistan.[5] There is a connection to draw out here, with the indigenous sovereign subject as the limit of U.S. imperialism, of settler colonialism as a process of incarceration overlaying indigenous sovereign space. This is especially vital and necessary, as it denaturalizes any claims of stability for the settler nation-state and underscores imperial imprisonment as a founding and ongoing impulse fueling U.S. sovereignty.

That sovereignty, itself, becomes most gruesomely visible in imperial prisons. According to Amy Kaplan, to ask "Where is Guantánamo?" poses the prior question, "Where is the U.S.?"[6] This is fundamentally a question of sovereignty, where national jurisdiction is manifest in an act of veiling imperial historical geographies. In a December 2001 memo, John Yoo and Patrick Philbin, of the White House Office of Legal Counsel, argued that while the United States enjoyed "complete jurisdiction and control" over the base, Cuba retained "ultimate sovereignty," and hence, the prison operations there were not subject to U.S. criminal law.[7] These lawyers invoked sovereignty in broad terms for their argument, papering over decades of willful reticence from the United States toward calls from the Cuban government to renegotiate the terms of base operations at Guantánamo. The tangle of sovereignties in a space like Guantánamo, rooted in a lease that U.S. occupiers imposed on the Cuban government as part of the 1899 Platt Amendment, has been productive for policies of imprisonment and torture, echoing earlier entanglements that marked military prisons masquerading as schools and tourist spectacles.[8]

This imperial continuum unmasks a lingering anxiety over the threat of contamination, where the fragile thread of settler sovereignty could unravel into incoherence, or worse yet, settler sovereignty turns inward to cannibalize itself, underscoring a dual process of incorporation and quarantining that Jasbir Puar explored in her analysis of the production of the terrorist queer. At the outset of the "War on Terror," Puar argued, national consolidation of a normative patriotism emerged through a discursive and physical quarantine of perversely racialized Others, in part, to manage and control anxieties of threats from within, of terrorists masquerading as upright neighbors and patriots.[9] This process of incorporation and quarantining, I would suggest, raises imperial déjà vu, of the forced assimilation of indigenous people into an expanding U.S. nation-state that emerged through an ambiguous logic: the imposition of settler control and the enactment of settler sovereignty, containing within itself the danger of contamination, the threat of contagion. U.S. imperial sovereignty has not yet discovered a vaccine to inoculate itself from this threat.

This essay leaps nation-state confines to examine regional connections and precedents for the U.S. prison at Guantánamo, in Fort Marion, near St. Augustine, Florida, which was used as a prison during an earlier period. Both of these prisons were established over indigenous lands. Rooted in histories of indigenous habitation in Cuba and Florida, these connections developed during the conquest of the region, which became a staging ground of interimperial rivalry. The geographic footprint of Fort Marion expanded over the nineteenth century, when it was used to imprison native peoples from the southern Plains and the Sonoran Desert.

Rather than a history of Indian wars, this essay focuses on precedents for "War on Terror" incarceration in techniques of settler colonial imprisonment, and in the prison sites themselves, which, in their specificity, stand in for the settler colonial nation-state as a whole. It is a key contention of this essay that to locate historical precedents for U.S. imperial prisons, it is necessary to think through a history of the invasion and occupation of indigenous life and land. This essay proceeds from a focus on indigenous presence and indigenous sovereignty as historical, but also as contemporary, against fantasies of native disappearance, a contemporaneity that poses challenges and offers possibilities for the establishment of alliances to combat U.S. imperialism in South Asia, no less than in North America. Much more than a search for precedents to understand recent U.S. imperial policies, this history is directly relevant to contemporary anti-imperial possibility. The mutual recognitions and alliances that could emerge out of a deeper understanding of indigenous history facilitate understanding simultaneous experiences of colonialism animating the heart of the self-proclaimed liberal nation-state, and those beyond its self-proclaimed borders. Any thorough anti-imperialist opposition to "War on the Terror" should proceed from this ground.

* * *

Cuba is in the Greater Antilles, ground zero of the European invasion of the Americas. By the time the three Spanish-chartered ships landed on the shores they christened Española and inaugurated a period of terror, pandemic disease, and mass murder that continues unabated, indigenous peoples had inhabited these islands for countless generations. In the course of their research, archaeologists estimate that the distinct cultures Europeans first encountered on the islands began to coalesce at least 4,000 years earlier.[10]

Taíno communities were centered in the Greater Antilles and developed their culture on the islands, although groups may have repeatedly set forth to the islands from what are now Yucatán, Guiana, and Venezuela. Despite a shared culture, Taínos spoke different languages and organized their communities in a range of ways, from confederations of large villages under the highly centralized authority of a cacique, to smaller communities. In contrast to continent-based perspectives that presume isolation of island cultures, they moved frequently between islands, with large canoes capable of carrying more than a hundred passengers, and technology that allowed them to navigate the region. Boriqúen, renamed as Puerto Rico, seems to have been home to the largest Taíno communities, the center of regional trade, and Española, where the Europeans first landed, was home to large and influential communities. Compared with these, the communities on Cuba may have been provincial upstarts, concentrated on the eastern end of the island, near contemporary Guantánamo.[11]

Cuban Taínos suffered almost immediately from devastating epidemics after the Europeans' arrival, and those Europeans who claimed Cuban lands as their own fiefs tortured native people into forced labor. The survivors organized to defend their lands and cultures, most substantially in a revolt led by the cacique Hatuey in 1511, who had fled from what is today Haiti to mobilize Taíno communities in Cuba, a revolt ultimately suppressed with massacre. Following this defeat, surviving Taínos relocated to the mountains, outside direct imperial control, where they have survived to the present.[12] It was from these mountains that the 26th of July Movement waged a victorious campaign of guerrilla warfare against the Batista regime, launching the Cuban Revolution.

Scholars have researched links between native communities in the Antilles and southeastern North America, and argued against them, despite suggestive possibilities. Conjecture aside, by the early 1600s, after Cuba was elevated to the administrative seat of Spanish imperial power in the Americas, native peoples were mobile in new ways; groups of indigenous captives from South America were shipped to Cuba as servants or slaves; native allies of Spanish missions, in La Florida, for example, also traveled to Cuba. Here was the dialectic of colonialism played out in its earliest phases: emphatically answered by, and adapting to, the fact of indigenous survival.[13]

* * *

Across the Florida Straits, construction of the Castillo de San Marcos, a focal point of Spanish authority in La Florida, began in 1672, by conscripted laborers from Guale, Apalachee, and Timucua communities, mostly young men, paid wages below those of convicts, joined by small complements of enslaved Africans, convicts, and skilled craftsmen from Cuba.[14] As the local seat of Spanish imperial power, the Castillo was a site of European competition.

The British Carolina colony organized a force, almost a fourth of which was made up of Indian allies, to attack the Spanish missions in 1702. This group overran the Spanish missions, moving on to lay a siege on the Castillo that was only broken when Spanish naval reinforcements arrived from Cuba. In 1739, conflict between the Europeans flared again, and the governor of British Georgia raised an outfit of British and colonial regulars, and Muscogee and Chickasaw warriors to invade Spanish settlements near St. Augustine. By June 1740, they reached St. Augustine, driving Spanish families in the area to seek protection in the Castillo, until the Spanish navy again broke the siege. The onset of hurricane season forestalled further attacks, and the British and their Indian allies withdrew once again, having wrought havoc on Spanish colonial communities, and on neighboring Native communities.[15]

These were local flash points of global competition between the major European powers. The empires continued to contest authority over La Florida into the nineteenth century, only to settle these claims in the 1819 Adams-Onís Treaty, when Spain ceded control over La Florida to the United States in exchange for U.S. renunciation of any claims to Texas resulting from the Louisiana Purchase.[16] The Castillo de San Marcos, renamed Fort Marion when the United States took control of it in 1819, was a central location of these colonial era conflicts.

* * *

Two centuries of disease, interimperial violence, and coerced labor took their toll on indigenous communities increasingly drawn into the orbit of Spanish power in La Florida, and by the early nineteenth century they were decimated, surviving only beyond the reaches of colonial knowledge. The violence took a toll on colonists as well. In 1763, when the Spanish formally ceded Florida to British control, Spanish authorities and settlers embarked for Cuba from St. Augustine, perhaps gazing at the walls of the Castillo, which had been their refuge, as they set sail.[17]

To the north, in British Georgia, communities in the Muscogee Confederacy that the British would come to refer to as "Creeks" also felt the impacts of imperial incursion. Drawn increasingly into trade with the British, some began to move into Florida, where they came into contact with surviving indigenous communities. With no immediate British presence in these areas, they built towns and farms and participated in the deerskin trade. After the Spanish resumed control of La Florida in 1783, these communities extended their trade southward, trading with Cuban fishermen. Since the 1760s, some of them built cypress canoes, voyaging to the Florida Keys, the Bahamas, and Cuba to trade deerskins, furs, dried fish, honey, and bear oil for cigars, coffee, rum, and sugar.[18]

When Andrew Jackson invaded Pensacola in 1814, the imperial history of Florida fundamentally shifted. Few U.S. citizens were interested in trade with indigenous communities; rather, the promise of land for speculators or homesteaders animated their gaze southward. Native communities in northern Florida continued to farm, hunt, and trade, occasionally moving their villages to take advantage of fertile soil, on lands that U.S. speculators and homesteaders coveted. Jackson's Indian policies removed Muscogees and other southeastern Indian nations from their lands, auguring a new round of struggle, and some moved into Florida after the Red Stick War, bringing direct experience of settler colonialism and the violence it wrought, with a spirit of resistance, exemplified in the teachings of Red Stick prophets like Otulke Thlacco, who moved to Florida and played an important role during the Second Seminole War.[19]

Federal authorities settled on a policy of removing Florida native communities, whom they had come to call "Seminoles," a bowdlerization of the Spanish "cimarrones." In September 1823, federal commissioners called Seminole leaders to Moultrie Creek, a few miles south of St. Augustine, to negotiate a treaty ending the First Seminole War, which stipulated the creation of a reservation in central Florida with boundaries drawn to prevent Seminole interactions with Cuban and other Caribbean traders.[20]

Following the break of an unstable truce that ended the first war, the U.S. Army attacked Seminole villages deep in the Everglades in the Second Seminole War, the longest and costliest of the U.S.-Indian wars. During this war, the army imported a group of bloodhounds and their Cuban handlers, inspired by the use of dogs to suppress slave revolts in Jamaica. Facing high casualties and unable to deal a decisive blow, the army sifted through commanders until General Thomas Jesup was finally able to strike publicity coups by capturing Seminole leaders who came into his camp under a flag of truce. Jesup imprisoned these leaders in Fort Marion, where other prisoners were sent to join them. A small contingent, led by Coacoochee, escaped Fort Marion, leaving behind their sick and elders.[21]

The capture of community leaders and declining ability of Seminole communities to continue fighting shaped the context for an end to the Second Seminole War. Ending the war, some Seminoles won the right to remain on their land, a singular achievement in the Indian wars, accomplished at a staggering price: by the war's end in 1842, fewer than 300 Seminoles remained in Florida; 4,420 were captured and deported to Indian Territory; several hundred were killed in the conflict; 1,500 U.S. soldiers lost their lives.[22]

Enduring more than forty years of war, previously independent Seminole communities developed a sense of cultural and political unity in camps isolated from whites, under the guidance of elders. In addition to the cultural resources they drew upon, they continued trading with allies and contacts; a persistent rumor had it that Cuban fishermen supplied ammunition to Seminole camps along the southern Atlantic and Gulf coasts throughout the war years. With the end of the Third Seminole War, the remaining independent Seminoles willing to treat with the United States were removed to the Creek Reservation in Arkansas. They were not the last, though. At least 200 Seminoles continued to live in southern Florida. In these years, whites in Florida knew real terror, fearing a threat out of proportion with the small and struggling Seminole war groups, a terror that organized the settling of Florida.[23] Leading politicians and advocates in the United States justified the Seminole wars as wars against terror, barely concealing the underlying motivations of territorial covetousness and a desire to establish the stability of private property, including land and enslaved people, on their own terms.

* * *

A few decades later, Fort Marion reprised its function as a prison in U.S. wars against Indian communities. In April 1875, the U.S. Army moved seventy-four Kiowa, Caddo, Comanche, Arapaho, and Cheyenne men from Fort Sill, Indian Territory (now Oklahoma), to Fort Marion, ending the so-called Red River War, which the army fought to forcibly relocate indigenous communities from the southern Plains to reservations in Indian Territory, a war stoked by sensationalist coverage in national newspapers of a raid on the Germans, a Kansas settler family.[24]

Earlier in March, at the Southern Cheyenne Agency, the commanding officer had ordered Cheyennes to stand in line for identification. The process dragged on through the day, and as the sun began to set, he impatiently ordered eighteen men standing at the back of the line to be sent to Fort Sill and held indefinitely as prisoners.[25] Among them, one group was charged with involvement in raids and murders, some of which preceded the Red River War and were already resolved, another with involvement in kidnapping the German girls, a third with stealing stock from settlers, and a fourth as being "ringleaders." The majority of them were held without charges.[26] None of these prisoners was allowed to answer their charges in trial.

Federal authorities debated what to do with the prisoners, eventually agreeing on Fort Marion as a site for imprisonment, exiling them from their homes and from contact with their communities.[27] Lieutenant Richard Henry Pratt was given command of the transfer and oversight of the prisoners. Pratt, an officer in the Tenth U.S. Cavalry, served in the Indiana volunteers during the Civil War, later commanded regiments of freedmen, called Buffalo Soldiers, and fought in the Red River War.

The prisoners were moved to Fort Leavenworth, Kansas, where Grey Beard, a Cheyenne elder, attempted to hang himself while they awaited a train to Florida. Pratt ordered his hands tied and fastened to a train bench, but during the journey, Grey Beard freed himself and jumped from the moving train. Pratt stopped the train and sent groups to search for him, to no avail. Informed by the engineer that the train could be delayed no longer without disrupting traffic, Pratt detailed a group to remain and search for the escaped prisoner, but as the train slowly began to move, a sergeant spotted Grey Beard and shot him dead, in self-defense, he said, from a man who had jumped from a moving train while wearing shackles.[28] Lean Bear, another Cheyenne, stabbed himself twice, and then two soldiers, as the train approached Nashville. Pratt left him behind to die in Nashville, but he recovered and was sent on to Florida, where he was held in solitary confinement in a damp cell, under the rationale that he was mentally ill, a diagnosis and "treatment" advocated by the post surgeon. Pratt assured his superiors that Lean Bear was a leader of Cheyenne resistance.[29] Lean Bear died on July 24. He was not the last to die in this prison.[30]

In Fort Marion, the prisoners' travails continued. Taken from the southern Plains to coastal Florida, many of them suffered health problems, compounded by the poor condition of the fort.[31] Some officers recognized the problem and gained permission to take the prisoners on short trips to nearby Anacosta Island for fresh air and open skies.[32] Security, not health, governed the army's approach. In his initial orders to ready the fort for the prisoners, the army chief of engineers was instructed, "You will cause such repairs to be put on the Fort as will make it secure enough to keep them. They will occupy the area of the Fort and there will be no need of putting the rooms in repair except so far as may be necessary to prevent an escape."[33] Officers repeatedly and unsuccessfully requested army funding to repair the fort's deteriorating sewage system, to reconstruct the casements, where walls dripped with dampness, and to reinforce roofing over the grounds.[34]

Disease, death, and exile all reinforced the toll of imprisonment in Fort Marion, but some prisoners attempted to escape. A carefully laid plan among the Kiowa prisoners to escape through the woods was exposed to Pratt by Ahkeha, apparently under duress.[35] Pratt did not forget the favor, requesting Ahkeha's release a year later.[36] Soon after their arrival in June 1875, Pratt requested to have the prisoners' wives and children brought to Fort Marion, seeing this as a way to establish a sense of stability.[37] These proposals circulated between the army and the Interior

Department, stalled by lack of support from commanding generals on the Plains, and Indian agents who reported that the women named by the prisoners as their wives refused to go to Florida; some had remarried, while others were perhaps unwilling to undertake their own exile.[38]

The record shows how imprisonment led the federal government into greater intrusions into Plains Indian community life, as federal agents spent the summer of 1875, the first months of Plains Indian imprisonment at Fort Marion, wading the morass of defining "legitimate" marriages between prisoners and women living near agencies.[39] The secretary of the interior urged the secretary of war to "send the actual wives, not exceeding one wife to one Indian, and send the children under twelve years of age."[40] Moreover, these records give an important reminder that the impact of incarceration reverberated onto the communities from which prisoners were removed. Some messages between the families of prisoners, and the prisoners themselves, passed through correspondence between Pratt and the Indian agents, and prisoners' families sent items for their relatives' needs and comfort.[41] In June 1876, leading Kiowas prepared a petition addressed to the president, asking for clarity in how long their relatives would be imprisoned, drawing special attention to cases of imprisonment without charge.[42] The following February, the prisoners prepared their own petition to be sent to Washington, asking for clemency.[43]

There were others, however, who projected personal benefit in the imprisonment. St. Augustine boosters incorporated visits to Fort Marion into their tours, taking tourists into the fort to meet prisoners, which afforded opportunities for prisoners to strike connections for their own benefit.[44] Tourism contributed to the spectacle of imprisonment, a vicarious way to celebrate wars of conquest on the Plains, and the further development of settler national identities. For example, the Great Atlantic Coast Line unsuccessfully requested permission to photograph some of the prisoners to use in advertisements.[45] Mixed with these impulses, tourist visits exposed the conditions of imprisonment to a broader public; some of the earliest visitors were abolitionists who, in later decades, animated the core of the self-proclaimed "Friends of the Indian," who drove Indian policy at the close of the nineteenth century.[46]

A key item of trade with tourists were ledger books, which contained prisoners' drawings of their personal and community histories, and their experiences of imprisonment, which were traded among tourists and army officials.[47] Drawn in color, rich in symbolism, these books formed a sort of currency as they circulated among officials oversee-ing the imprisonment, and later, among collectors and libraries, and they now provide records of individual southern Plains Indian voices from the mid-nineteenth century. In a more prosaic sort of work, a St. Augustine businessman who produced curios for the tourist trade paid the prisoners about $300 for polishing sea beans and alligators' teeth.[48] As Pratt wrote to his superiors, "They say they have never had anyone to show them how to work like the white men, and they say truly." Prison labor, then, was incorporated into assimilation policies.[49]

Pratt began to organize the prisoners along military lines as a guard detail, dressed in army uniforms, and practicing drills.[50] Requesting the funds and authorities to do so, Pratt wrote to his superiors, "This is per-fectly feasible, and will add in every way to the success of their man-agement. They are trustworthy, and will act against each other under orders as well as soldiers," a policy that echoed the establishment of police forces on reservations that were independent of community con-trol and authority.[51]

From military drills, Pratt began to develop a system of education for his prisoners. Federal treaties with Plains Indian communities had detailed the construction, maintenance, and staffing of schools on res-ervations since midcentury, with an overriding impulse of assimila-tion into market agriculture. Pratt made a key innovation, organizing a school among a captive population isolated from their communities and families. Constrained by prison life, these courses emphasized lit-eracy and Christianity, rather than market agriculture.[52] Local women volunteered to teach the classes, and in time their effects on the pris-oners impressed humanitarian visitors to Fort Marion.[53] Pratt intended these students to act as a "civilizing element" in their communities, at one point requesting prolonged imprisonment for his best students in order to continue their education.[54] Pratt's experiences as a prison war-den and educational pioneer at Fort Marion shaped the remainder of his life's work, after he established the Carlisle Indian School in Penn-sylvania, and a whole generation of Indian children came of age in enforced isolation from their families and forced assimilation into the settler culture.[55]

By April 1877, Generals Sheridan and Sherman agreed to release the prisoners after two years of exile, and in June, the Indian agents added their assent.[56] Still, release was delayed by brutal accounting logic, when the secretary of war instructed:

> The release of a part of the Kiowa and Comanche prisoners at Fort Marion, Fla. would be inconvenient, as a part would remain, necessitating a guard and nearly as much expense, as the whole. There are good reasons for delay till the autumn, say October, when I recommend that the whole be transported to Fort Sill, delivered over to the Indian Agent there, and a few of the worst might be put in the guard house there.[57]

* * *

Fort Marion did not remain empty for a decade after the Plains Indian prisoners were released. From spring 1886 to spring 1887, between 450 and 490 Chiricahua Apaches were sent there and held as prisoners in three groups. Their road to Fort Marion began in March 1886, when Chihuahua, a Chiricahua leader, was in the midst of negotiating with General George Crook an end to a long war against the United States in Cañon de los Embudos, near the Mexican border in New Mexico Territory. Before their surrender was accepted, the U.S. attorney general instructed an Arizona attorney: "Do not let civil authorities interfere in any way with any Indians that General Crook may have as prisoners 'till further directions from this Department. This is to be kept to yourself."[58] The president had decided to hold them "as prisoners until they can be tried or otherwise disposed of," according to the secretary of war.[59] A group of Chiricahuas including Geronimo left the treaty proceedings, to continue fighting for another six months, and in the following September, they negotiated peace with General Nelson Miles in Skeleton Canyon, Arizona Territory.[60] By this time, army leadership had also decided to treat their relatives living in the San Carlos and White Mountain Reservations as prisoners of war.[61]

The decision to imprison the Chiricahuas in Fort Marion contradicted the peace terms that Crook had offered, and Crook reported to his superiors that he would not inform the Chiricahuas of the president's disapproval of their peace terms.[62] The day after Crook wrote these words, April 5, 1886, seventy-seven were dispatched to Florida from Fort Bowie, in Arizona Territory.[63] While the last Chiricahuas agreed to lay down their arms, their families had been hastily transferred from Fort Wise, in Colorado Territory, to Fort Marion. Romeyn Ayres, who headed the regional command in Florida, was instructed to ready the fort for the prisoners' arrival; the casements were aired out and funds requested to dig a well within the fort.[64]

When the Chiricahuas arrived, they were issued food and cloth, but tents did not arrive for two weeks, while officers requested money to construct a sewer system leading from one of the casements to the sea.[65] The post surgeon reported that it would be necessary to construct flushing sewers and increase the water supply for the fort. He also recommended the construction of a bathhouse near the sea, stating that the prisoners should be kept from contact with St. Augustine residents, noting the prevalence of "contagious eruptive diseases" in town.[66] These requests did not receive swift replies. The following month, post officers continued to request authority to move the prisoners to Ocean Beach for fresh air, and for authority to build latrines.[67]

In Arizona, General Miles saw collective imprisonment in Florida as only a temporary solution to U.S. wars against Chiricahuas.[68] Miles and his fellow officers understood imprisonment as part of a military effort against the entire Chiricahua community. Later that month, Philip Sheridan, general-in-chief of the U.S. Army, relayed to Miles the president's order to arrest all of the Warm Springs Apaches living at San Carlos, to be held as prisoners of war at Fort Marion, despite reports that the fort could hold no more than seventy-five more prisoners.[69] A month later, 434 men, women, and children were sent to Fort Marion.[70] In October, fifteen men who had surrendered in the past March to General Crook were sent to Fort Pickens, in Pensacola, and the eleven women, six children, and two enlisted scouts who constituted the rest of their group were sent to Fort Marion.[71]

While the Plains Indians were held under a pretense of criminality, even though most of them were not charged with a crime, the Chiricahuas were held at Fort Marion as hostages, a policy of collective banishment.[72] According to a report prepared by Ayres, of the eighty-two adult men imprisoned at Fort Marion, sixty-five had served in the army as scouts, and of the remaining men, four played leading roles in diplomacy with the United States. Of the women and children imprisoned at the fort, 284, according to this report, made up the relatives of the scouts and these four elders. "Care has been taken," Ayres assured his superiors, "to prevent this information from going public."[73] The imprisonment of scouts and their relatives became a key point of criticism, from members of the U.S. public, of Chiricahua imprisonment.[74]

Another major point of the concerned citizens' critique was overcrowding. Fort Pickens, where the Chiricahua war leaders were being held, was much larger and more spacious, opening a debate among local residents about their willingness to house prisoners who had been so vilified in the national press. In this instance, Pensacola citizens approached the secretary of the interior, requesting the government to imprison Geronimo at nearby Fort Pickens, sensing a way to raise the visibility of their community.[75]

The structural dilapidation of Fort Marion persisted from the earlier era of Plains Indian imprisonment, and officers regularly requested funds to repair the walls of the casements and the roof, only addressing the sewage crisis at the fort through a series of repairs in the winter of 1887.[76] To avoid the effects of rain and dampness, the prisoners camped along the terreplein, where cannons were formerly mounted, in crowded conditions that threatened the outbreak of an epidemic.[77] The families lived throughout the seasons in army-issue summer tents.[78] Imprisonment at Fort Marion took its toll, especially on infants and elders among the Chiricahuas, and by April 1887, twenty-four had died. Tuberculosis claimed adults, and infants born in the prison were often unable to survive their first month.[79]

Earlier educational experiments shaped this era of imprisonment at Fort Marion. In an echo of Spanish imperialism that linked Apache homelands with Florida, nuns from the nearby convent of Saint Joseph's taught classes to Chiricahua children.[80] A St. Augustine resident, with the ironic name of Warden, furnished tools, lumber, and a mechanic to instruct men in carpentry.[81] In June 1886, an officer requested that a Chiricahua student named Bonito be sent from Carlisle to Fort Marion, to convince the prisoners of the benefits of a Carlisle education, and in August, another officer urged that all the prisoners be sent there.[82] The secretary of the interior eventually asked Pratt to accept Chiricahua prisoners between twelve and twenty years old as students at Carlisle, and forty-four of them were sent in November and December.[83] While Ayres wanted to send all the Chiricahua children to Carlisle, Pratt would take only those of school age.[84] Pratt insisted on meeting the children before accepting them at Carlisle, and he returned to Fort Marion in April 1887 to inspect the legacy of his work as educator and captor.[85]

By March 1887, criticism of the communal incarceration, mixed with mounting costs of repairs and provisions, augured a shift in policy.[86] The army sold 140 ponies, horses, and mules, taken from the Chiricahuas upon their surrender, and used the $2,599 in proceeds to cover costs of imprisonment.[87] A gradual process now began to move those held at Fort Marion to other locations. The majority of the Fort Marion prisoners—69 men, 167 women, and 118 children—were sent to Mount Vernon Barracks in Alabama, on former Muscogee lands; of the rest, 20 women and children were sent to rejoin family members in Fort Pickens; finally, 13 men, 17 women, and 32 children were sent to Carlisle.[88] Not all were happy with this. C. Meyer Zulick, governor of Arizona Territory, cautioned the secretary of the interior against allowing the Chiricahuas to return to Arizona, writing, "Mercy to them now is cruelty to us. Arizona has rendered her holocaust to this humanization sentiment."[89] Eventually, the Chiricahuas were sent to Fort Sill, in what was now Oklahoma Territory, where the Plains Indian prisoners were initially held. Fort Sill functioned as a hybrid Chiricahua agency and prison, with land allotted to individuals, followed by the establishment of a reservation.[90]

* * *

Twelve years after the Chiricahuas were released from Fort Marion, the United States jumped its continental boundaries, inaugurating its era of overseas imperialism. A major touchstone in this was the first combat landing by U.S. Marines, when they invaded and took control of Guantánamo Bay. The United States built its first overseas military base in Guantánamo, initially as a coaling station, then as the forward naval base for the region, when it became a symbol of enforced Cuban dependency on the United States, which eventually built detention camps there to hold Haitians and Cubans seeking refugee status.

These detention camps provided the infrastructure for the current prison, housing long-term detainees in the "War on Terror" inaugurated in October 2001.[91] The question, "Where is Guantánamo?" can be answered, quite thoroughly, with a history of Cuban labor on the U.S. military base, as Jana Lipman has done.[92] For, just as torture techniques, such as waterboarding, bear forgotten imperial histories, so are imperial prisons erected upon forgotten foundations.[93]

The imprisonment of indigenous people at Fort Marion is a precedent for the current prison at Guantánamo in more than an abstract and general sense. The space between these places is a space of imperial déjà vu, of uncannily specific recurrences and repetitions in a centuries-long project of imperial violence. These include the imprisonment of elders and children, and parents and their children together; the use of solitary confinement as a long-term method of control and punishment; the complicity of medical staff in prisoner abuse; gendered logics of imprisonment, and the impacts on the prisoners' own communities, through such means as development and aid policies; a sense of "terror" out of proportion with any actual threat, as a spur for imperial violence; and speculative capitalists' demands spurring imperial policies. Critical responses to these policies, from within U.S. society, also bear precedents, both in effectiveness and in limitations. Nineteenth-century humanitarians pushed an end to particular indigenous incarcerations, even as they did not end the use of imprisonment as a method of colonialism. Their critiques centered on incarceration in isolation from the larger processes of expansion and settler colonialism. The impacts of these critiques, and the ways they were limited by or even resonant with investments in settler colonialism, should provide vital perspective for our contemporary moment: to articulate and act on a program that is not just for human rights and rule of law within a national framework, but to work through anti-imperialist perspectives, proceeding from engagement and alliance with politics of indigenous sovereignty. For, as Jodi Byrd has reminded us, "Anti-immigration legislations, internments, and incarcerations are not exceptions but the rule of U.S. liberalism born through colonialism."[94]

What is to be done about Guantánamo? A rights-based perspective focuses on the restoration of habeas corpus rights to prisoners and their charge and trial based on international and national law, a perspective that has shed light on what has happened behind barbed wire and inside cages at the prison camp, and has helped at least some prisoners free themselves.[95] Stopping there, however, would do nothing to address the imperial foundations of the prison. Attention to the spectacular sites of U.S. imperialism compels us to notice the shadow sites of U.S. empire: secret prisons and detention centers, or local conflicts that a U.S. imperial presence fuels and exacerbates.

Attention to these sites should also turn our vision to precedents of U.S. imperial power. Before the United States was a global power, it was a settler-colonial power. Historically, and in the present moment, settler colonialism is the political, economic, and cultural foundation of the presence of the United States in the world. Much more than in the maps and borders it claims over indigenous peoples' territories, the United States is manifest in those places and institutions where it acts as a settler colonial power—prisons, for example. As a site of U.S. imperial incarceration, Fort Marion makes visible the ways that a national version of history cuts out broader regional connections. If Fort Marion was a key site for the subjugation of indigenous resistance to settlement in Florida, the southern Plains, and the Sonoran Desert, it was also located within a Caribbean world. A regional perspective is especially relevant today, when the United States deepens its occupation of Afghanistan against the possibility of a regional approach to ending that war.[96]

Sundering these regional links in the Caribbean and in South Asia, U.S. sovereign legitimacy, however, is only based on a prior (in a historical and logical sense) relationship with indigenous communities. From this perspective, we can understand the prison at Guantánamo as the rule, and not the exception, of U.S. sovereign enactment.[97] The stark visibility of U.S. global power in the early twenty-first century should prompt us to examine settler-colonial power as it continues to animate and structure U.S. claims to legitimate sovereignty, over and against the autonomy and self-determination of indigenous communities within its self-proclaimed borders. Contrary to so many criticisms of U.S. antiterrorism policies, there is little about the "War on Terror" that is "unprecedented." Against the spectacular violence of U.S. imperial power at its seemingly disparate sites, we are called to draw connections, and to forge a broad platform of decolonization that dismantles U.S. pretensions to sovereign legitimacy, in their various and sundry guises.

NOTES

An early version of this essay was presented at the 2009 meeting of the Native American and Indigenous Studies Association. Its subsequent development was shaped by the critical reponse of audience members, and especially the critically engaged feedback of Vicente Diaz. Vivek Bald, Jodi Byrd, Sujani Reddy, and Robert Warrior provided valuable feedback on later drafts.

1. Michael Ratner, "The Guantánamo Prisoners," in Rachel Meeropol, ed., *America's Disappeared: Secret Imprisonment, Detainees, and the "War on Terror,"* New York: Seven Stories Press, 2005, pp. 31–43. Murat Kurnaz, *Five Years of My Life: An Innocent Man in Guantánamo*, New York: Palgrave Macmillan, 2007.

2. Anne McClintock, "Paranoid Empire: Specters from Guantánamo and Abu Ghraib," *small axe* 28(13), March 2009, p. 51.

3. For a critique of post-9/11 military commissions, which touches on some of the history in this essay, see Jace Weaver, *Notes from a Miner's Canary: Essays on the State of Native America*, Albuquerque: University of New Mexico Press, 2010, chap. 6, "Turtle Goes to War."

4. Moazzam Begg, *Enemy Combatant: My Imprisonment at Guantánamo, Bagram, and Kandahar*, New York: New Press, 2006, pp. 45, 124–128.

5. Sohail Daulatzai, "Protect Ya Neck: Muslims and the Carceral Imagination in the Age of Guantánamo," *Souls* 9(2), 2007, pp. 133, 137

6. Amy Kaplan, "Where Is Guantánamo?," *American Quarterly* 57(3), 2005, p. 832.

7. John Yoo and Patrick Philbin, "Memorandum for William J. Haynes, II," December 28, 2001, p. 3, http://www.torturingdemocracy.org/documents/20011228.pdf.

8. See Louis, Perez Jr., *Cuba and the United States: Ties of Singular Intimacy*, Athens: University of Georgia Press, 2003.

9. Jasbir Puar, *Terrorist Assemblages: Homonationalism in Queer Times*, Durham, NC: Duke University Press, 2007, p. 47.

10. Samuel Wilson, *Hispaniola: Caribbean Chiefdoms in the Age of Columbus*, Tuscaloosa: University of Alabama Press, 1990, p. 2.

11. Basil Reid, *Myths and Realities of Caribbean History*, Tuscaloosa: University of Alabama Press, 2009, pp. 11–48, 58, 74, 104–107, 123–128. José Oliver, *Caciques and Cemí Idols: The Web Spun by Taíno Rulers between Hispaniola and Puerto Rico*, Tuscaloosa: University of Alabama Press, 2009, pp. 7, 17, 28. Samuel Wilson, *The Archaeology of the Caribbean*, New York: Cambridge University Press, 2007, pp. 3–6, 56, 102–110, 151. Wilson, 1990, pp. 4, 26, 28, 53, 59, 132. Louis Pérez Jr., *Cuba: Between Reform and Revolution*, New York: Oxford University Press, 2006, p. 12.

12. Wilson, 2007, p. 160. Oliver, pp. 222, 227–228. Mary Berman, Jorge Febles, and Perry Gnivecki, "The Organization of Cuban Archaeology: Context and Brief History," in L. Antonio, Shannon Dawdy, and Gabino La Rosa Corzo, eds., *Dialogues in Cuban Archaeology*, Tuscaloosa: University of Alabama Press, 2005, pp. 42–43. Pérez, 1988, p. 8.

13. William Sturtevant, "The Significance of Ethnological Similarities between Southeastern North America and the Antilles," in *Yale University Publications in Anthropology*, no. 64, New Haven: Yale University Department of Anthropology, 1960. Oliver, p. 237. Wilson, 2007, pp. 54–55, 160. Déborah Berman Santana, "Indigenous Identity and the Struggle for Independence in Puerto Rico," in Joanne Barker, ed., *Sovereignty Matters: Locations of Contestation and Possibility in Indigenous Struggles for Self-Determination*, Lincoln: University of Nebraska Press, 2005.

14. See Jerald Milanich, "The Timucua Indians of Northern Florida and Southern Georgia," Rebecca Saunders, "The Guale Indians of the Lower Atlantic Coast: Change and Continuity," and Bonnie McEwan, "The Apalachee Indians of Northwest Florida," all in Bonnie McEwan, ed., *Indians of the Greater Southeast: Historical Archaeology and Ethnohistory*, Gainesville: University Press of Florida, 2000. *Castillo de San Marcos: A Guide to Castillo de San Marcos National Monument, Florida*, produced by the Division of Publications, National Park Service, Washington, DC: U.S. Department of the Interior, n.d., pp. 14–19. Milanich, pp. 20–21. See also Donald Merrit, "Beyond Town Walls: The Indian Element in St. Augustine," in Kathleen Deagan, ed., *Spanish St. Augustine*, New York: Academic Press, pp. 125–147, 1983.

15. See Rochelle Marrinan, "The Archaeology of the Spanish Missions of Florida: 1565–1704," in Kenneth Johnson, Jonathan Leader, and Robert Wilson, eds., *Indians, Colonists, and Slaves: Essays in Memory of Charles H. Fairbanks*, Florida Journal of Anthropology, Special Publication no. 4, Gainesville, Florida Anthropology Student Association of the University of Florida, 1985. John Hann and Bonnie McEwan, *The Apalachee Indians and Mission San Luis*, Gainesville: University Press of Florida, 1998. Bonnie McEwan, ed., *The Spanish Missions of La Florida*, Gainesville: University Press of Florida, 1993. Jerald Milanich, *Florida Indians and the Invasion from Europe*, Gainesville: University Press of Florida, 1995.

16. William Weeks, *John Quincy Adams and American Global Empire*, Lexington: University Press of Kentucky, 1992.

17. John Missall and Mary Missall, *The Seminole Wars: America's Longest Indian Conflict*, Gainesville, University Press of Florida, 2004, pp. 4–5, 11. Brent Weisman, *Unconquered Peoples: Florida's Seminole and Miccosukee Indians*, Gainesville: University Press of Florida, 1999, pp. 80–82. Milanich, p. 22. James Covington, *The Seminoles of Florida*, Gainesville: University Press of Florida, 1993, p. 5.

18. Missall and Missall, pp. 3, 8, 22. Weisman, pp. 5–16. Brent Weisman, "Archaeological Perspectives on Florida Seminole Ethnogenesis," in McEwan, pp. 302–303. Covington, pp. 5–14, 26–27. William Sturtevant, "Creek into Seminole," in Eleanor Leacock and Nancy Lurie, eds., *North American Indians in Historical Perspective*, New York: Random House, 1971, pp. 98–103.

19. Susan Miller, *Coacoochee's Bones: A Seminole Saga*, Lawrence: University Press of Kansas, 2003, pp. 8–10, 118. Weisman, pp. 19, 22–27, 48–49.

20. Sturtevant, p. 105. Charles Fairbanks, "The Ethno-Archaeology of the Florida Seminole," in Jerald Milanich and Samuel Proctor, eds., *Tachachale: Essays on the Indians of Florida and Southeastern Georgia during the Historic Period*, Gainesville, University Press of Florida, 1978, p. 171. Missall and Missall, pp. 63–67. Weisman, pp. 45–46. Covington, pp. 52–54.

21. Miller, p. 24. Missall and Missall, pp. xii, 134, 140–141, 169–173. Weisman, pp. 56, 58. Covington, pp. 93, 98.

22. Weisman, pp. 50, 57. Covington, p. 109.

23. Weisman, pp. 1, 38, 59–60, 72–73. Missall and Missall, pp. 94, 100, 125–126, 212, 221–222. Covington, p. 83.

24. E. D. Townsend to W. T. Sherman, March 13, 1875, Letters Sent (hereafter LS), Office of the Adjutant General (hereafter OAG), National Archives and Research Service (hereafter NARS). List of Indian Prisoners sent to Florida in accordance with orders from the Headquarters of the Army, War Department Adjutant General's Office, May 19, 1875, Letters Received (hereafter LR), OAG, NARS. J. W. Darlington to Office of U.S. Indian Agency, Cheyenne and Arapaho Agency, Jan. 21, 1875 Brad Lookingbill, *War Dance at Fort Marion: Plains Indian War Prisoners*, Norman: University of Oklahoma Press, 1969, pp. 22–23, 58. Henrietta Mann, *Cheyenne-Arapaho Education, 1871–1982*, Niwot: University Press of Colorado, 1997, pp. 40– 43.

25. E. A. Hayt to Secretary of Interior, Nov. 10, 1877, LR, OAG.

26. Fort Leavenworth, Kansas, May 17, 1875. Richard Henry Pratt Papers, Beinecke Library. July 1875, LR, OAG.

27. In the same message detailing the transfer of prisoners to Florida, Sherman described a party, to be escorted by G. A. Custer, in a mission of exploration to the Black Hills. Sherman to W. W. Belknap, April 9, 1875, LR, OAG.

28. Pratt to Adjutant General, May 23, 1875, Pratt Papers, Beinecke Library, Yale University.

29. J. O. Skinner to Post Adjutant, St. Augustine, July 1, 1875. Pratt to Post Adjutant, St. Augustine, June 30, 1875. Letters Received, Office of Indian Affairs, Cheyenne and Arapaho Agency, NARS.

30. Pratt later claimed that Lean Bear starved himself to death. "The Florida Indian Prisoners of 1875 to 1878," Pratt Papers. Pratt to R. C. Drum, July 31, 1875. Mahmante, a Kiowa leader, died of dysentery that month. Pratt to Adjutant General, July 24, 1875, LR, OAG. Pratt, July 27, 1875, LR, OAG. Two more prisoners, Ihpaya and Big Moccasin, died of disease in October and November 1875. Pratt, October 5, November 5, 1875, LR, OAG. Spotted Elk died of consumption in January 1877, and Ahkeha suffered from the same disease, and was released to die at home. Pratt, April 8, 1877, LR, OAG. Heap of Birds died of heart disease, the third of four Cheyenne leaders to die in prison. Pratt to Sheridan, October 16, 1877, LR, OAG.

31. Pratt, April 1877 report on prisoners, Pratt to Sherman, April 8, 1877, Pratt Papers.

32. J. Hamilton, September 7, 1875, LR, OAG.
33. E. D. Townsend to Chief of Engineers, March 31, 1875. Townsend to Sherman, April 20, 1875, LS, OAG. D. A. Gilmore to J. C. Post, April 3, 1875, LR, OAG.
34. Thomas Vincent, July 8, 1875, LS, OAG. Gilmore to A. A. Humphreys, June 22, 1875, LR, OAG. Jasper Post to Gilmore, April 20, 1875, LR, OAG.
35. George Fox, interpreter, to Pratt, April 4, 1876, Pratt Papers. Pratt to Adjutant General, July 17, 1875, LR, OAG.
36. Pratt to F. L. Dent, April 7, 1877, Pratt Papers. Adjutant General to Dent, April 13, 1877, LR, OAG.
37. Pratt to Adjutant General, June 11, 1875, LR, OAG.
38. Charles Forsyth to Pratt, January 25, 1876, Pratt Papers. R. C. Drum to Pratt, August 3, 1875, Pratt Papers. J. M. Haworth to Edmund Smith, August 5, 1875, LR, OAG.
39. C. Delano to Secretary of War, July 22, 1875, LR, OAG. Pratt to Adjutant General, July 19, 1875, LR, OAG. Edmund Smith, to John Miles, July 23, 1875, LR, OAG. P. H. Sheridan to Adjutant General, July 31, 1875, LR, OAG.
40. A. H. Merrill to Pratt August 6, 1875, Pratt Papers.
41. For example, see J. A. Covington to Pratt, Sept. 4, 1875, Pratt Papers.
42. June 23, 1876, LR, OAG.
43. February 20, 1877, LR, OAG.
44. Lookingbill, pp. 83–85, 90.
45. J. W. Walker to Commissioner of Indian Affairs, June 29, 1873, LR, OAG. Thomas Vincent to Walker, July 2, 1875, LS, OAG.
46. Harriet Beecher Stowe visited Fort Marion during a vacation in Fort Augustine and tried to gain access for some of the younger prisoners to Amherst Agricultural School. Pratt, April 7, 1877, Pratt Papers. Pratt to OAG, April 8, 1877, LR, OAG.
47. "The Florida Indian Prisoners of 1875 to 1878," Pratt Papers. Sherman to Pratt, January 10, 1876, Pratt Papers.
48. "The Florida Indian Prisoners of 1875 to 1878," Pratt Papers.
49. Pratt to Adjutant General, July 17, 1875, Pratt Papers.
50. "The Florida Indian Prisoners of 1875 to 1878," Pratt Papers.
51. Pratt to Adjutant General, July 17, 1875, Pratt Papers.
52. Pratt to Sheridan, March 17, 1876, LR, OAG.
53. Pratt to Adjutant General, September 6, 1875, LR, OAG. Pratt's experiments inspired some Floridians to advocate the expansion of schools for Seminoles. Covington, pp. 155–156.
54. Pratt to Sherman, April 17, 1876, LR, OAG.
55. David Adams, *Education for Extinction: American Indians and the Boarding School Experience, 1875–1928*, Lawrence: University Press of Kansas, 1995.
56. Sheridan to James Forsyth, April 18, 1877. Sherman to Pratt, April 27, 1877, Pratt Papers. A. Bell to Secretary of Interior, Washington, June 14, 1877, LR, OAG. J. M Haworth to William Nicholson, March 26, 1877, LR, OAG. John Miles to William Nicholson, May 12, 1877, LR, OAG.

57. Chief clerk of the Secretary of War to the Secretary of the Interior, June 26, 1877, Pratt Papers.

58. A. H. Garland to O. T. Rouse, February 1, 1886, LR, OAG.

59. W. C. Endicott to R. C. Drum, September 8, 1886, LR, OAG.

60. O. O. Howard to Adjutant General, telegram, Sept. 7, 1886. H. Henrietta Stockel, *Shame and Endurance: The Untold Story of the Chiricahua Apache Prisoners of War*, Tucson: University of Arizona Press, 2004.

61. Sheridan to Secretary of War, September 30, 1885, LR, OAG. Sheridan, October 7, 1885, LR, OAG.

62. George Crook to Sheridan, April 4, 1886, LR, OAG.

63. J. C. Kelton to W. D. Whipple, April 6, 1886, LR, OAG. J. M. Schofield to Adjutant General, April 14, LR, OAG. R. B. Ayres to Assistant Adjutant General, Headquarters of the East, April 16, 1886, LR, OAG.

64. Ayres to AAG, April 16, 1886, LR, OAG.

65. Ayres to AAG, April 30, 1886, LR, OAG.

66. J. R. Gibson to Post Adjutant, April 30, 1886, LR, OAG.

67. W. D. Whipple to Adjutant General, May 21, 1886, LR, OAG.

68. Nelson Miles to AAG, Division of the Pacific, July 7, 1886, LR, OAG.

69. Sheridan to Miles, July 31, 1886, LR, OAG. L. Lamar to Secretary of War, August 10, 1886, LR, OAG. Loomis Langdon to Drum, August 21, 1886, LR, OAG. Langdon to Drum, August 24, 1886, LR, OAG.

70. J. C. Kelton to Commanding Officer, Fort Marion, September 7, 1886, LR, OAG.

71. Endicott to Sheridan, October 19, 1886, LR, OAG.

72. General Field Orders No. 12, A. T. Willcox, October 7, 1886, LR, OAG.

73. Ayres to Sheridan, March 25, 1887, LR, OAG.

74. See Herbert Welsh, *The Apache Prisoners in Fort Marion, St. Augustine, Florida*, Philadelphia: Office of the Indian Rights Association, 1887.

75. Letters to Secretary of the Interior, September 14, 1886, LR, OAG.

76. Ayres to AAG, March 1, 1887, LR, OAG.

77. J. M. Schofield, March 28, 1887, LR, OAG.

78. S. B. Hollbrid to Secretary of War, September 7, 1886, LR ,OAG. J. C. Kelton, September 9, 1886, LR, OAG.

79. Ayres, April 1, 1887, LR, OAG. R. B. Ayres to AAG, April 27, 1887, LR, OAG. Ayres, December 31, 1886, LR, OAG. Ayres to AAG, March 1, 1887, LR, OAG.

80. Landgon to AAG, August 20, 1886, LR, OAG. Ayres to AAG, March 1, 1887, LR, OAG. Stephen Mills to Post Adjutant, November 11, 1886, LR, OAG.

81. Ayres, April 1, 1887, LR, OAG.

82. Stephen C. Mills to Adjutant General, June 20, 1886, LR, OAG. Langdon to AAG, August 23, 1886, LR, OAG.

83. L. Lamar to Secretary of War, October 15, 1886, LR, OAG. L. Lamar to Secretary of War, October 23, 1886, LR, OAG. J. M. Schofield to Adjutant General, November 2, 1886, LR, OAG.

84. Ayres, December 31, 1886, LR, OAG.

85. Adjutant General to Commanding Officer, St. Francis barracks, April 18, 1887, LR, OAG.

86. For example, see Helen Rosalie Foote to William Endicott, Secretary of War, March 19, 1887, LR, OAG. H. M. Teller to Endicott, March 21, 1887, LR, OAG. Endicott to Foote, March 28, 1887, LR OAG. See also petitions from citizens of New Haven, Connecticut, to the President, April 5, 1877, LR, OAG; and from citizens of Pittsfield, Massachusetts, to the President, April 4, 1887, LR, OAG.

87. Miles to Adjutant General, March 1, 1887, LR, OAG.

88. J. C. Skelton to Quartermaster General, April 18, 1877, LR, OAG. Drum to Ayres, LR, OAG. Ayres to Drum, April 26, 1887, LR, OAG.

89. C. Meyer Zulick to L. Lamar, April 8, 1887, LR, OAG.

90. W. A. Jones, Commissioner of Indian Affairs, to Secretary of the Interior, January 4, 1902, LR, OAG.

91. Stephen Schwab, *Guantánamo, USA: The Untold History of America's Cuban Outpost*, Lawrence: University Press of Kansas, 2009, pp. 8–9, 59, 94, 226–229.

92. Jana Lipman, *Guantánamo: A Working-Class History between Empire and Revolution*, Berkeley: University of California Press, 2009.

93. On the use of waterboarding during the U.S.-Philippines War, see Paul Kramer, *The Blood of Government: Race, Empire, the United States, and the Philippines*, Chapel Hill: University of North Carolina Press, 2006.

94. Jodi Byrd, *Transit of Empire*, Minneapolis: University of Minnesota Press, 2011, p. 365.

95. See Joseph Margulies, *Guantánamo and the Abuse of Presidential Power*, New York: Simon and Schuster, 2006; Clive Stafford Smith, *Eight o'Clock Ferry to the Windward Side: Seeking Justice at Guantánamo Bay*, New York: Nation Books, 2007; Mark Denbeaux and Jonathan Hafetz, eds., *The Guantánamo Lawyers: Inside a Prison Outside the Law*, New York: NYU Press, 2009.

96. Tariq Ali, *The Duel: Pakistan on the Flight Path of American Power*, New York: Scribner, 2008, p. 247.

97. Patrick Wolfe, "*Corpus nullius*: The Exception of Indians and Other Aliens in US Constitutional Discourse," *Postcolonial Studies* 10(2), 2007, pp. 127–151.

Afterword

VIJAY PRASHAD

On a snowy evening in December 1994, I got some good news. My PhD done, I was working as a community organizer at Direct Action for Rights and Equality (DARE) in Providence, Rhode Island. It was fantastic work, giving me an opportunity to join the contingent classes of late twentieth-century America in some of our fiercest fights. Police brutality was high on the agenda, but so too was the attempt by home day care providers for union cover. But it was also tiring work, with little time left in the day for reading. I missed the solitary timelessness of reading—something that I enjoyed when I just got to graduate school, and that I really cherished when I was doing my field research in India.

The phone call came from Professor Susanne Rudolph of the University of Chicago, where I had taken my degree. Susanne had an unusual request. Cornell and Syracuse had won a National Endowment for the Humanities grant to offer Indian history. They had hired a person who quit at the last minute, and the term was to begin in a few weeks. They needed a replacement. But the real question was this: Could I drive, and did I have a car? I would have to teach one class each at both schools. Compared with my salary in Providence, Cornell-Syracuse would pay a king's ransom. DARE let me off the hook for four months, and I arrived in Ithaca for my onetime gig.

As I got settled into McGraw Hall, I met one of my neighbors. In the thick of winter he wore a Hawaiian shirt and a friendly smile. It turned out that Gary Okihiro was the head of the Asian American Studies Program, and casually he asked me if I would like to teach a class on the South Asian diaspora. Apparently there had been requests for such a class from the undergraduates, but there was no one able to do such a course. I trained as a historian and anthropologist of India, so I had no expertise. However, I had lived in the United States since my late teens, had written about life and politics in our community, and actively participated in the various conferences and celebrations organized to think about and dance through our lives (such as the South Asian Students Association meetings across the United States and Desh Pardesh in Toronto, Canada). If the Indian history class could fall into my lap, why couldn't the South Asian diaspora?

The problem came with the syllabus. There was no obvious candidate for the reading list, and no set narrative. I remember walking along the bookshelves in the library with a notebook, jotting down names of books and making imaginary maps of the syllabus. Where does one begin? In the boats that left the Indus Valley port of Lothal for Ur in Sumeria, or in the boats that left Calcutta for Caroni? I decided on the modern period, starting from the indentured labor moving to the Caribbean, to Southeast Asia, and to the French colonies off the African coast. We then moved quite rapidly to the story of the migration to Europe in the nineteenth and twentieth centuries, to the Gulf States after the oil boom, and then to the United States—where my students' interest peaked. The last section was a mess largely because the work on South Asian lives in the United States was very limited. A book by Karen Leonard on Punjabis in California (*Making Ethnic Choices*, 1992) was the only good thing that crossed my palm. I had a collection of poems, essays, and stories by South Asian Americans (*Our Feet Walk the Sky*, 1993) that had been produced out of a class on South Asian American writing at UC Berkeley in 1991. And then I had issues of the *South Asian Magazine for Action and Reflection* (*SAMAR*; 1992 onward) and of the *Committee on South Asian Women Bulletin* (*COSAW Bulletin*; 1982 onward). These were a lifeline.

A hundred students signed up for the class (ninety-eight of them South Asian Americans; one East Asian American; one African American). I think it was the most meaningful class I have ever taught, or am likely to teach. The lecture notes for that course were the basis for my book *The Karma of Brown Folk*, written over a summer after my dissertation book had been refused by too many presses (it was eventually published because of the intercession of my friend the brilliant editor Bela Malik, whose life was cut short in 2007). Not only did the students devour the rather tattered syllabus, but their own conversations and interventions ended up being the course's textbook. It was not narcissism, but hunger. They sought a framework to understand their lives in a land that had not yet made sense of them (which means that it had not yet fully figured out how to dismiss them).

In 1995 and 1996, a group of us organized panels at the South Asian studies conference in Madison on themes of diaspora, but with an emphasis on the political orientation of Indian Americans. The issue at hand was the rise of the Hindu Right within the United States, and its funding connection to the Hindu Right in India. These were perilous times. Little original research on history took place there, largely because most of us were impacted by the violence in India in 1992–1993, after the destruction of a sixteenth-century mosque at Ayodhya. In May 1996, Biju Mathew and I organized a roundtable discussion at the Association of Asian American Studies conference titled "South Asian American Identity." A group began to form: people like Sunaina Maira, Rajini Srikanth, S. Shankar, Kamala Visveswaran, Ali Mir, Raza Mir, and others. Most of us were born and raised in South Asia, having come to the United States for college or in the late years of our high school education. We had no numerical generation to count as our own (neither properly first generation, in other words, the highly skilled scientists of the post-1965 era, nor second generation, in other words, the children of those skilled professionals). Mutterings of marginality at these conferences always irritated me. No sense in being annoyed if you don't try to seize the space, and in particular, if the space is not being actively reserved against you. So, we took the space and created room for South Asian American thinking within the institutions of South Asian studies and Asian American studies. Sunaina was doing her doctoral work at Harvard's School of Education on South Asian youth in New York City. She was the only one in our group with proper credentials. The rest of us were amateurs. Three volumes came out of our early experimentation: a special issue of *Amerasia Journal* entitled "Satyagraha in America: The Political Culture of South Asian Americans" (1999–2000), an academic collection on the place of South Asians in Asian America (*A Part, Yet Apart*, 1998) and the award-winning anthology *Contours of the Heart* (1998).

Those days seem so remote now. Reading the essays in this book reminds me of the distance traveled in so short a time. Imagine if my students then could have this book to hold as one of their central texts. It would have made my life so much easier. But of course it might not have been sufficient to quell their hunger. What they needed as much as anything was to clear the field, plant the seeds, and tend them as they grew. That is how they went at their research papers—taking time off to interview gas station attendants, taxi drivers, nurses, engineers, doctors, professors, librarians, priests, parents, sisters, neighbors—their papers were a treasure trove for me, and an engagement with their present for them. In a box hidden in my office, I still hold on to those papers, and occasionally, just for fun, I go back and read them. But to have my students read these histories, now unearthed with such finesse, would have been a complement to the stories they heard and to the futures they wanted to live.

* * *

Part of the work of these essays has been the excavation of the international lives of the migrants from South Asia to the United States. These journeys, across the Pacific Rim, from Singapore to Mexico, and into California, or across the Indian and Atlantic Oceans into New York and New Orleans, formed global actors whose visions of life and liberty expanded along with their travels. Forms of cosmopolitanism such as produced by these early migrants give us some hope against the forms of parochialism that today's migrations can surprisingly produce. The histories entertain presents that seem impossible but are already imminent in our bodies and dreams. This is the power of the histories—they do more than document, settle the affairs of the past; they are a testament to what is possible in our lives, in the world we bequeath to those that follow us.

Even more so, these essays allow us to seek other contexts of the lives of the migrants. The typical story is of the migrant coming into the United States to seek freedom. It is the celebratory tale that forgives everything else about the United States. Slavery is of the past, police brutality is of the margins; if these things were truly representative, why would people clamor to come across the borders, with or without papers? Those who are critical of the United States are often provided with this cautionary question. But, as these essays show, if the context is widened, we learn to read migrant lives in a different way. There are 700 U.S. military bases in 130 countries across the planet. These bases are the manifest tips of the tentacles of American power. Other kinds of images of power appear, but with not as much concrete solidity: U.S. finance is invisible, and U.S. corporate power is shrouded in the new geography of production through the veil of subcontracting. The heat of these essays brings the invisible inklings of power to light. Once on the surface, it becomes easier to see how this power detaches people from their moorings, throws them in dire need of migration, and draws them to stand, like penitents, at the doors of the U.S. embassy, or cross, like thieves, over the Walls of Un-Freedom. Without imperialism as context, the story of migration is bewildering: one can make no sense of the Mexican farmer's distressing need to abandon life for the trials of El Norte, or the Malayali nurse's need to ferret out an existence apart from her social milieu through the mixed offices of the Rockefeller Foundation.

The work in this anthology follows the tracks laid out by the characters in the essays, people like Julio Jubala and Kumari Lakshmi Devi. They enable the new narratives. But so too do the earlier intellectuals whose work has been erased, people like the radical journalist (and onetime actor) Kumar Goshal (1899–1971). Writing in the *Pittsburgh Courier* and in the *National Guardian*, Goshal laid out an impress for an anti-imperialist account of India's struggle for freedom and of America's self-imposed obligations for empire. From his first article ("India— A Key to Victory" [1942]) to his last ("Books as Anti-war Weapons" [1966]), Goshal wrote to "give more people the courage to protest." This volume is heir to Goshal, carefully tracking the histories and the lives that straddle South Asia and the United States, and giving us intellectuals the courage to stand for different histories, for submerged realities.

Index

About the Contributors

Vivek Bald is an associate professor of writing and digital media in the program in Comparative Media Studies at the Massachusetts Institute of Technology. He is the author of *Bengali Harlem and the Lost Histories of South Asian America* (Harvard University Press, 2013) and the director of three documentary films: *Taxi-vala/Auto-biography* (1994), *Mutiny: Asians Storm British Music* (2003), and *In Search of Bengali Harlem* (forthcoming).

Miabi Chatterji received her PhD in American Studies from New York University. She is preparing a manuscript that examines the workings of race, gender, documentation status, and class in the low-wage urban service economy, focusing on the experiences of recent immigrants from South Asia in New York City. She is the president of the board of directors of the RESIST Foundation, based in Somerville, Massachusetts.

Amanda Ciafone is an assistant professor of media and cinema studies at The College of Media at the University of Illinois-Champaign. She is currently working on a manuscript tentatively entitled *Counter-Cola: A Multinational History of the Global Corporation*.

Gayatri Gopinath is an associate professor and director of the Asian/Pacific/American Studies Program in the Department of Social and Cultural Analysis at New York University. She is the author of *Impossible Desires: Queer Diasporas and South Asian Public Cultures* (Duke University Press, 2005).

Farah Hasan is a software professional who works in New Jersey. She graduated from Temple University with a master's degree in computer science and has been associated with International South Asia Forum (INSAF) in New York City.

Raza Mir is the Seymour Hyman Professor of Management at William Paterson University. He is the coauthor of *Anthems of Resistance: A Celebration of Progressive Urdu Poetry* (Roli Books, 2006) and the coeditor of *Organizations, Markets and Imperial Formations: Towards an Anthropology of Globalization* (Lon Edward Elgar Press, 2009). He is an associate editor of the journal *Organization*.

Naeem Mohaiemen is a visual artist and a PhD student in anthropology at Columbia University. His projects (www.shobak.org) look at the revolutionary Left and failed utopias and have shown at, among others, the Bangladesh Shilpakala Academy, Kolkata Experimenter, and Whitney Museum. Project themes have been described as "not yet disillusioned fully with the capacity of human society" (Vijay Prashad, *Take on Art*) and "more illuminating than Jacques Rancière's microscopic examinations" (Ben Davis, *ArtNet*). Naeem is editor of *Between Ashes and Hopes: Chittagong Hill Tracts in the Blind Spot of Bangladesh Nationalism* (Drishtipat, 2008). His essays include "Islamic Roots of Hip-Hop" (*Sound Unbound*, MIT Press), "Waiting for a Real Reckoning on 1971" (*Lines of Control*, Johnson Museum), and "These Guys Are Artists and Who Gives a Shit" (*System Error*, Silvana).

Soniya Munshi completed her doctorate in sociology and women's/gender studies at the City University of New York Graduate Center. Her current research examines relationships between institutional interventions and community-based work that address intimate violence in South Asian immigrant communities in New York City.

Immanuel Ness, PhD, is a professor of political science at Brooklyn College of the City University of New York. He is general editor of the *Encyclopedia of Global Human Migration* (2013); author of *Guest Workers and U.S. Corporate Despotism* (University of Illinois Press, 2011) and *Immigrants, Unions, and the New U.S. Labor Market* (Temple University Press 2005); editor of the *International Encyclopedia of Revolution and Protest: 1500 to the Present* (Wiley-Blackwell, 2009); and coeditor of *Ours to Master and Own: Worker Control from the Commune to the Present* (Haymarket Books 2012. Since 1999, Ness has been editor of *Working USA: The Journal of Labor and Society*, an international peer-review quarterly social science journal examining labor and social class in an international context.

Vijay Prashad is the George and Martha Kellner Chair in South Asian History and professor of international Studies at Trinity College in Hartford, Connecticut. He is the author of several books, including *Uncle Swami: South Asians in America Today* (New Press, 2012); *Arab Spring, Libyan Winter* (AK Press, 2012); *The Darker Nations: A People's History of the Third World* (New Press, 2007); *Everybody Was Kung Fu Fighting: Afro-Asian Connections and the Myth of Cultural Purity* (Beacon Press, 2002); and *The Karma of Brown Folk* (University of Minnesota Press, 2000).

Junaid Rana is an associate professor of Asian American studies at the University of Illinois at Urbana-Champaign. He is the author of *Terrifying Muslims: Race and Labor in the South Asian Diaspora* (Duke University Press, 2011).

Sujani Reddy is Five College Assistant Professor of Asian/Pacific/American Studies in the Department of American Studies at Amherst College. She is currently working on the manuscript for *Nursing Globalization: Indian Nurses Immigrate to the United States*.

Nayan Shah is a professor and chair of American Studies and Ethnicity at the University of Southern California. He is the author of *Stranger Intimacy: Contesting Race, Sexuality and the Law in the North American West* (University of California Press, 2011); *Contagious Divides: Epidemics and Race in San Francisco's Chinatown* (University of California Press, 2001); and "Sexuality, Identity and the Uses of History" (Routledge, 1998).

Seema Sohi is an assistant professor in the Department of Ethnic Studies at the University of Colorado, Boulder. She is currently completing the book *Echoes of Mutiny: Race, Empire, and Indian Radicalism on the Pacific Coast*.

Linta Varghese teaches in the Asian American Studies Program at Hunter College, City University of New York. She is currently working on a manuscript examining the moral economies produced in the interactions between the Indian state and Indian diasporic entrepreneurs.

Manu Vimalassery is an assistant professor of history at Texas Tech University. His manuscript *Skew Tracks: Imperialism, Racial Capitalism, and the Transcontinental Railroad* rethinks capitalism through Plains Indian and Chinese migrant histories.

www.ingramcontent.com/pod-product-compliance
Lightning Source LLC
Chambersburg PA
CBHW022131020426
42334CB00015B/849